Extended Families in Africa and the African Diaspora

EXTENDED FAMILIES
IN AFRICA AND
THE AFRICAN DIASPORA

Edited by

Osei-Mensah Aborampah
and
Niara Sudarkasa

AFRICA WORLD PRESS

TRENTON | LONDON | CAPE TOWN | NAIROBI | ADDIS ABABA | ASMARA | IBADAN | NEW DELHI

AFRICA WORLD PRESS
541 West Ingham Avenue | Suite B
Trenton, New Jersey 08638

Book and cover design: Saverance Publishing Services

Library of Congress Cataloging-in-Publication Data

Extended families in Africa and the African diaspora / edited by Osei-Mensah Aborampah and Niara Sudarkasa.
    p. cm.
Includes bibliographical references and index.
ISBN 1-59221-811-3 (cloth) -- ISBN 1-59221-812-1 (pbk.)
1. Families--Africa. 2. Africa--Social life and customs. 3. African diaspora. 4. African American families--History. I. Aborampah, Osei-Mensah. II. Sudarkasa, Niara.
HQ691.E98 2011
306.87089'96--dc22
                        2010054242

CONTENTS

INTRODUCTION

EXTENDED FAMILIES IN AFRICA AND THE AFRICAN DIASPORA

Osei-Mensah Aborampah and Niara Sudarkasa

The study of extended families has been integrated into a number of disciplines, including anthropology, demography, history, and sociology. Leading sociological and anthropological theorists such as Louis Wirth, Ralph Linton and Talcott Parsons, for example, made the case that the processes of industrialization and urbanization were incompatible with the extended family structure and thus had to give way to the nuclear family structure believed to be more compatible with the said processes, especially with their attendant rapid mobility of human capital. In fact, these theorists regarded the isolated nuclear family as an ideal form for western industrial societies.

In recent times, however, other sociologists and historians have attempted to debunk the theory of socio-cultural transition from extended to nuclear family structure. These scholars have argued consistently that family structure has remained unchanged and overwhelmingly nuclear in western Europe and North America (Marsh and Aber, 1992). The attack on the extended to nuclear family model began in earnest in the 1950s and this revision also is generally accepted as empirical fact. Stem and joint families have been identified as variants of one or the other model. However, regardless of the contending theses of extended to nuclear family or of stable nuclear family and their variants, the prevailing view is that the nuclear family remains the predominant family structure in western industrial society. Smith (1986, p. 88), for example, maintains that families in western industrial societies have been characterized by "essential and perdurable nuclearity."

The fact that Japan's experience is quite the contrary cannot be over-emphasized. The extended family still remains an important family type in contemporary industrialized and urbanized Japan, which presents a challenge to the widely accepted theory in the comparative and historical family research just summarized. The implication is that economic development and urbanization are not grossly inconsistent with extended residence, and that the extended residence can be an adaptive strategy within the modern context. Numerous studies report about the resiliency of the extended family (Stokes, LeClere and Yeu, 1987, for Taiwan; Morgan and Hirosima, 1983, for Japan; and Ram and Wong, 1994, for India). In Africa, researchers have stressed the persistence of extended family networks as cultural bridges in modernization rather than impediments to development (Silverstein, 1984).

Extended family ties are of crucial importance in African world societies. They are socially and economically significant in the context of shared labor, socialization of children, education and placement of relatives, and support for the elderly, just to mention a few. In that regard, this volume provides a comprehensive analysis of the structure, processes, and functioning of extended families in Africa and the African Diaspora. In spite of huge spatial and temporal diversity within the continent of Africa and the Americas, shared historical experiences, globalization, elevated state of consciousness, among others, have all conjoined to spawn striking similarities across various regions in relation to ethnic composition, familial institutions, and other forms of social organization. Particularly, extended families in the African world have been pervasive and pivotal in ensuring the economic stability and psychological well-being of their members. As highlighted in the preceding paragraphs, much has been written about the disappearance of this familial institution, the argument being that as various developing countries become more industrialized and /or urbanized, families in these countries become more nucleated. That is, the nuclear family becomes a more efficient, independent unit. Moreover, whenever their economic systems expand, it is expected that kinship ties will dissolve. As pointed out earlier, these arguments derive from western notions about reproduction and nurturing which postulate the nuclear family as universal and necessary (See, for example, Murdock, 1949). The literature on this issue has been reviewed extensively in such sources as Miller (1984), Barrow (1996), and Sudarkasa (1996).

Overall, the extent to which industrialization or urbanization affects families of developing societies appears to be greatly exaggerated. The cross-cultural studies reviewed by Miller, for example, showed that different aspects of industrialization exerted influence on different dimensions of the extended family. Upon reflection, the editors have come to appreciate how family members recognized kin relations, how members pooled and shared resources. Collective socialization was one of the processes through which we learned about our kinship relations, and incorporated attitudes and behaviors considered appropriate by our respective groups. Indeed, members recognized common responsibility.

In the case of the lead Editor, who was born and reared in Ghana, the economic processes of production, distribution and consumption occurred within the extended family context. Labor and skills necessary for these processes were funneled through the extended family. As a young man, the lead Editor had to assist not only in the farming and trading activities of his parents, but also in those of his grandmothers, uncles and distant brothers living in different communities. In addition, there was a recognition of the duty of every one to work to promote community welfare and prosperity. His formal western education, for example, was sponsored by a number of members in his matrilineage. As a growing child and in the course of his education, he was shifted around among his extended family members. In his hometown alone, he lived with no less than three extended family members, including the current Queenmother. In this regard, lineage, as well as extended family, membership was critical to having access to resources.

Coincidentally, the co-Editor also grew up in the context of her extended family. She was born and reared in south Florida, where she and her brothers were brought up in the household of her maternal grandparents. Her grandmother and grandfather, who had both immigrated to Florida from Andros Island in the Bahamas, were responsible for the day to day care of the children even though their mother lived and worked in the same town. Financial responsibility for the children as well as all decision-making regarding their upbringing was shared between their mother and her parents. The fathers of the children contributed some to the cost of their care, but otherwise they were not involved in their children's upbringing. After their mother moved to New York, the grandparents had sole responsibility for one of the boys who did not want to move to New York; the other two boys moved with their mother. By this time, our co-Editor was in college as an early entrant, and she spent her holidays between the two residences in Florida and New York. Her upbringing involved considerable interaction with members of her extended family from the Bahamas as well as those who lived in Florida and New York.

The point is that in spite of our formal education, in spite of our social mobility, in spite of being cosmopolitan in outlook, reciprocal assistance patterns exist among our extended family members. We have provided these personal anecdotes to underscore the tenacity of kinship networks even in the midst of industrialization and urbanization in developing societies, and in the highly developed United States of America.

In fact, a review of the literature pertaining to families in Africa and wherever the African Diaspora is found, indicates that extended families continue to exist as culturally meaningful units. Industrialization or urbanization does not necessarily lead to the emergence of a single type of family. Rather, multiple familial forms may emerge. The extended family may not be the dominant type of family in most developed societies, nor in several developing societies, but they are prevalent among lower and even middle classes in some of these societies. Among various populations, extensive patterns of extended family help and assistance, as well as an interdependence of affection and emotional ties have been reported to prevail.

Historically, a helping tradition has evolved and has become part of the African world cultural heritage. While contemporary forms of reciprocal assistance and mutual aid among the lower classes may be based in survival strategies, those of the higher classes may be based on the need to maintain, sustain, and/or promote family wealth, power, and prestige. Psychological and social linkage may prevail regardless of geographical or social mobility. It is the severance of emotional attachment to the kin group that may signal the demise of the extended family, not industrialization or urbanization per se. Moreover, the extended family may be adaptable to changing conditions. A recent headline in the New York Times (March 19, 2010) read: "Extended Households Are on [the] Rise." The article was written by Sam Roberts and pertains to families in the United States. Factors alleged to account for the rise include delayed marriage, longevity, more grown children with whom the elderly can share a household, Medicare cuts enacted in 1997, and the growing number of immigrants, who are more likely than native-born Americans to live in extended families. With the emergence of the information super highway (internet, phones, faxes, etc.), maintenance of social-psychological contacts may be possible, even as the frequency of physical contacts diminishes.

In this regard, the present volume seeks to articulate the principles underlying African traditional extended family organization and their manifestations in the Americas. Additionally, the volume reviews sociohistorical data and important trends to assess the current processes of family functioning in the relevant regions. It is reasonable to assume that African principles and the values underlying them helped to shape the development and institutional transformations within African families in the Americas. In this volume, we proceed from the position that the extended family is a meaningful social entity for the African world although the nature and content of extended family networks may vary from one society to another. To this end, several fundamental differences in the structures and functioning of the extended family and the nuclear family are emphasized throughout the volume. Traditionally, in African families, the Extended family was the basic unit in which production and consumption of material goods and services took place. The consanguineal core (usually in the form of part of a lineage) was the nucleus of the extended family. In contrast, the conjugal pair has historically served as the nucleus for nuclear family organization. Another fundamental difference occurs in family formation. In African families, couples normally joined existing compounds, instead of starting new ones.

The nuclear family structure is a predominant ideal in western and Euro-American societies, but even then the extended family plays a vital role in the African and African American communities based in Europe and the Americas. There could be no better example to illustrate the latter case than to draw attention to the current extended family structure that prevails in the White House. Upon election as the 44th president of the United States, President Barack Obama and Ms. Michelle Obama invited the latter's mother to join the household to assist in the rearing of the couple's two children. However temporary this arrangement might turn out to be, it goes to underscore an African American cultural practice that is well understood within the community.

Grandparents serve as important agents of socialization. They help grandchildren to develop inner strength necessary to make personal sacrifices for the protection and well-being of future generations of their own children. Grandchildren's educational achievement can be inspired by the example and encouragement provided by grandparents and such issues may well have factored into the decision of the Obamas to ask their children's grandmother to join their household.

Among blacks in the Caribbean, alternative family forms have developed that do not fit the nuclear family model. Because of limitations imposed by conditions of slavery and other factors, non-legal unions and common-law family structures became common features. For many, emotional support, affirmation from kin, and role modeling were essential motivating factors when parental economic support was lacking. Today, the greatest contribution of kin is their support in the upward mobility and self-esteem of family members, especially children.

For large numbers of rural families in the Caribbean, as in Africa, upward mobility is exceedingly difficult to achieve, and for most, the passing of wealth is inconceivable. It requires intensive efforts and perseverance in order for family members to survive. Older members who are able to provide help are not easily forgotten. Many of those who receive assistance return the favor to both the older and younger members of their extended families. As in Africa and the United States, people's sense of obligation is not limited to their parents only. Older children try to help out financially in meeting the needs of their younger siblings and other relatives. Thus, in this volume, contributors demonstrate and argue forcefully that family organization in Africa and the African Diaspora are not distorted versions of the nuclear family, but instead are vital and productive forms of the family that have developed in their respective cultures in response to socio-economic conditions with which they are confronted.

Structurally, the chapters are divided into three parts to cover the geographical regions of Africa, African America, and the Caribbean. Regarding Africa, Chapter One begins with Mario Azevedo's examination of the impact of modernity, economic constraints and the emerging chronic and infectious diseases on Africa's oldest and most celebrated institution, the extended family, and assesses the strength of its support system in light of its integration into a globalized cultural system. Specifically, the chapter discusses the following issues: the role of conjugality and consanguinity, the status and future power relations both in traditional and western-influenced family settings, the evolution of dyadic relationships and modalities of child development, the constraints and exigencies of family size and divorce, and the ominous consequences of the HIV/AIDS pandemic. Rather than predict the demise of the African family, the author acknowledges the tremendous strains to which it is subjected, but stresses, nonetheless, that it will continue to endure. In this regard, the author presents a view that neither minimizes the crisis of the African family nor downplays the need for the institution's fundamental adjustment if it is to maintain its sustainability beyond the twenty-first century and survive the cultural onslaught of the age of globalization. The implication here is one that holds the possibility of an institution capable of adapting to a changing environment.

In chapter two, Niara Sudarkasa employs 'motherhood' as a form of culturally defined kinship to examine the impact of family structure on the behaviors and ideologies associated with motherhood in the United States and Africa. The focus is on motherhood as it has evolved in nuclear versus extended family structures in the West and in Africa, respectively and its African transformations in the Americas. It provides conceptual clarifications of 'nuclear' and 'extended' families, as well as the latter's constituent components—conjugal family and consanguineal family as proposed by Ralph Linton. Additionally, it discusses the dimensions of women's roles as wives and mothers in nuclear versus extended family settings. The author notes the different meanings and implications attached to notions of 'half-sibling,' 'marital stability,' and 'family stability.' The author concludes with a presentation of the impact of the diffusion of nuclear family ideologies from western to African societies and speculates on the possible family ramifications of the spread of HIV/AIDS.

Contemporary extended family networks in Ghana are examined by Osei-Mensah Aborampah in chapter three. Employing ethnographic data of his own matrilineage, the author provides an overview of Akan matrilineage, describes the day-to-day functioning of a segment of this lineage, and discusses the changes that are taking place across space and time. The author questions the view that the extended family will disappear in the face of urbanization in the information age. Great numbers of Ghanaians continue to participate in their extended family networks despite the trend toward urbanization, in a large measure because economic activities and childbearing practices continue to be governed by what Caldwell (1982) calls "family morality and theology." Those driven by a sense of obligation and sincere concern for the welfare of extended family members continue to support needy members in any way they can.

Africa has been much cited as a continent where the extended family structure remains strong, acting as a major social institution uniting the society together. Kinship ties have done much to unite families and still do. Yet, using Cameroon as a case study, Nchinda also explores, in chapter four, the gradual transformations occurring within the extended family structure, particularly from marriage arrangements and birth to divorce and death ceremonies. He explains that the cohesive family structures of the past are gradually cracking under the weight of modern changes. The poverty generated by the external pressures of the IMF/World Bank policies, western dominated globalization, and the internal failures of the Biya regime have all produced much strain on Cameroonian families and led to unintended consequences. They have caused a fracture in the extended family safety net and transformed family responses and reactions to emerging problems such as street children, orphanages, parenthood, abortion, and internet dating. Children and family ties that used to be the bedrock of the society are gradually being transformed and nowhere is this more visible than in the nation's two larger urban centers of Yaoundé and Douala.

In chapter five, Alfred Kisubi takes another look at African extended family networks by examining marriage and procreation among the Abagusii of Kenya, emphasizing extended family involvement in the marriage process. Using the Kisii sub-group as a case study, Kisubi describes the intricacies of Gusii traditional marriage customs and ceremonies including courtship, bridewealth payment, and traditional wedding. He lays out the role played by the adult members of the extended family to underscore the collective dimension of the marital process. Finally, the author evaluates the challenges of modernization on Abagusii extended families in particular, and Kenyan families in general, stressing the adaptability of both institutions to the changing environment.

In chapter six, Mario Azevedo offers an expansive review of diseases/ infections and their impact on extended families in Africa. Included in the discussion of various types of diseases that afflict families in Africa are malaria, tuberculosis, water borne diseases, HIV/AIDS, and other sexually transmitted diseases and infections. Colonial penetration of Africa brought in its wake new diseases and exacerbated endemic ones that continue to kill many Africans. Members of the extended family are dying prematurely and at a faster rate than ever before due to the scourge of HIV/AIDS. More breadwinners are succumbing to AIDS and an unprecedented number of children are being orphaned. In spite of the ravages of disease, the extended family has served as a durable support system to members. However, a critical question is whether the traditional family values of solidarity, compassion, and hospitality can survive the changes sweeping across the continent. The author suggests that the extended family will weather the storm by adapting itself to survive and thrive in the decades to come.

Responses to the threat of the HIV/AIDS pandemic on African families are considered in chapter seven by Florence Kyomugisha and John Rutayuga. The authors focus on Tanzania and Uganda, where communities are showing resilience in their responses to the impact of AIDS. In the absence of government and other agencies' intervention for orphans, and despite the fact that many households that take in orphans often are locked in a vicious circle of deprivation and increased vulnerability to poverty, there is a strong resilience of the traditional African extended family system of fosterage. Analysis of a grassroots organization in Ukimwi orphans assistance in the Kagera region of Tanzania indicates that extended family linkages provide the vast majority of orphans with the care, love, stability, a sense of identity, practical knowledge, and skills that are necessary for adult life.

Part two of the volume focuses on African-American extended families. A reading of the extant literature on African-American families suggests that the African forebears brought a large store of what Herbert Gutman (1976) calls social memory and handed this system of orientations to the generations of the enslaved who were African born and American born. Of course, the African social and moral system of expectations and taboos was severely tampered and modified as a result of slavery. Whereas Africans placed more emphasis on rituals, sexual and other codes, the African-American forebears infused some of them with Christian religious ethics, over time, to influence the behavior of slave community members. Gutman's (1976) study of Good Hope slave community in South Carolina offers a number lessons regarding the pace, nature and degree of family functioning and institutional development. First, it illustrates how generalized African kinship traditions, beliefs and practices were passed on from one generation to another. Second, it shows European influences, especially in the course of the transition to protestant evangelical Christianity as their new faith. Third, it demonstrates the adaptive capacities of the enslaved Africans and those born to them and their children. Lastly, and as Gutman argues, the story of Good Hope bears no visible relationship to the tangle of pathology alleged by Moynihan (1965) and the widespread family disorganization imputed by Frazier (1939) before him.

Good Hope birth registers contained more than 200 slave men, women and children. Interestingly, the first recorded birth is said to have occurred in Africa in 1760. According to Gutman, the register contained nearly the entire formative African American experience, ranging from births in Africa, enslavement, South Carolina slavery, the development of an adaptive slave culture, to emancipation and legally free men and women. A reading of the genealogies shows that kin networks linked slaves born in different generations. Good Hope children grew up in large families and by 1857, a number of grandparents were residing with their children or other relatives. According to Gutman, the development of intra- and inter-generational ties can be ascertained from the fact that about 2 in 5 children born between 1800 and 1857 had blood ties with three elderly blacks living on the plantation. Such ties helped children to absorb values from parents, grandparents, other adult kin, and adult non-kin.

As Gutman argues, such ties demonstrate how it became possible for the slaves of one generation to absorb changing socio-cultural experiences and pass their meaning on to the next so that cumulative transgenerational memory would become the primary source for the development of African American culture. Gutman says slave children born in the 1840s or 1850s grew up in a slave community made up of interrelated but well defined immediate families. Although affinal and consanguineal ties bound together this slave community, involving several generations, it is clear that the African patrilineal or matrilineal groupings could not be replicated on this plantation and elsewhere in the south. What one sees is a process of nucleation due to European influences. Monogamous marriages became the norm. This process was facilitated by the infusion of Christian beliefs, after the Great Awakenings of the 1730s through the 1760s. Weddings, for example, became a significant feature from about the 1800s. Fidelity was expected from slave men and women after marriage. Church pressures often enforced dominant marital norms

Children growing up in the slave community were collectively reared by adult members, although primary responsibility lay with the immediate parent(s). Clearly, the helping tradition of African extended families continued. Fathers, mothers, aunts, uncles, brothers, sisters, cousins, all supported one another in diverse ways. Informal adoption and absorption of children into African American extended families were common practices during the post-civil war era. In addition, respect for elders and the reciprocal assistance patterns endured long after the civil war. As we have attempted to demonstrate, the slave community in Good Hope might have formed groupings similar to West African compounds with many of the features of African extended families.

For Sudarkasa (1996), one of the institutions already suited or pre-adapted for survival in the New World was the extended family. She observes that the African extended family has served, in various environments and in different political contexts, as a unit of production and distribution, as an agent of socialization, education, training and social control, and as a unit of emotional and marital support. Sudarkasa elaborates further that the extended family networks formed in slavery were based on the African institutional heritage but the specific forms they took reflected European and other New World influences. In other words, enslaved Africans utilized their social memory, along with other socio-cultural capital at their disposal, to create their family and other social institutions. The presence of some of the African extended family patterns among contemporary African American families has been well documented for African Americans by a number of scholars, including Carol Stack (1974), Joyce Ladner (1971), Niara Sudarkasa (1981), Joyce Aschenbrenner (1975), Ann Creighton Zollar (1985), and Elmer and Joanne Martin (1978). These historical and contemporary themes are taken up in the next four chapters.

In chapter eight, Gwendolyn Prater examines the current state of the black family in the United States, probing into such issues as the merits of the prevailing theoretical frameworks, the sources of strengths and constraints embedded in the African American family, the changing roles and behaviors of family members, the requirements of modern life, and the impact of the seemingly dwindling population of marriageable African-American men, and attempts to project what this basic social unit's trajectory might be in the decades to come.

Rhunette Diggs examines two particular contexts for the creation of African American extended families in chapter nine. Utilizing the analytical perspective of autoethnography, the author's African-American extended family heritage and immersion in an Ethiopian culture are explored to provide insights into the characteristics and meanings of extended family in black societies. A review of relevant literature provides background information about the societal and organizational factors that generate and influence the concept of extended families. Additionally, the family communication model is utilized to delineate the systemic features of extended families. This communication focus acknowledges that extended families are formed and maintained by societal and family values, family identity, and the nature of the communication exchanges that occur among interactants in close proximity, physically and/or psychologically.

Chapter ten, by Bamidele Demerson, examines the social organization of the Gullah people who live in rural communities on the chain of low-lying Sea Islands that fringe the coastal plain of South Carolina, Georgia, and northeast Florida. The Gullah are African Americans and, like societies throughout Africa, the normative family is often a contiguous multi-household unit with intergenerational depth. This ethnographic portrait of Sea Island social organization focuses on the social, economic, and spiritual contributions of women to the well being of both their affinal and natal compounds. When men and women marry, couples are expected to establish households in the compounds of the husbands. This virilocal pattern of post-marital residence signals that over the course of their adult lives, women have rights and responsibilities in two family compounds. Their rights and responsibilities in the affinal setting accrue through their roles as wives and mothers. But in the natal context, rights and responsibilities conferred at birth are primarily based on their roles as daughters and sisters. To this end, the topics examined explore women in relation to: marriage, widowhood, and divorce; rights to land use, ownership, and inheritance; childcare and fosterage; and employment. Finally, the author discusses the implications of the ethnographic data for explaining the resilient African heritage that may be operative in the structure, functioning, and values of Gullah families.

In chapter eleven, Erin Winkler posits that the racial socialization of children is one component of "kin-work" that is shared collectively amongst extended African-American family networks. Racial socialization is the process through which children come to understand the meaning of race in various contexts, and how race will function in their lives. Through racial socialization, families both teach their children about the value of African and African-American heritage (*procultural* racial socialization), and also respond to negative messages about blackness communicated to children through sources outside of the family (*responsive* racial socialization)

(Winkler, 2008). In this chapter, the author uses data collected through 47 open-ended, qualitative interviews conducted with 19 African American mothers and their 28 middle school-aged children in Detroit, Michigan to illustrate the role of extended family in this particular area of "kin-work." Among other findings, the data reveal that extended family members are critical in sending children both procultural and responsive racial socialization messages, particularly regarding the historical struggle of African Americans in the face of oppression.

Concerning the Caribbean, which is the focus of part three, it has been suggested that captives, planters, workers, colonists, and others who arrived from Africa, Europe, and Asia contributed to the structuring of distinctly local forms of kinship in the Caribbean (Douglass, 1992, p. 15). The development of Caribbean kinship and family structures has been influenced by historical and cultural events, not the least among them are the impacts of slavery, color, class, and gender. According to Barbara Bush (1990, p. 105), the extended kinship group was the integrating force behind the well-being of enslaved Africans in the Caribbean, very much like the patterns in West Africa. She says that slaves recreated kinship links and adapted them to their situation. For example, fictive kinship relations were developed in place of real kin relations. Bush (1990, p. 105) quotes Bryan Edwards as observing that "old established negroes of both sexes 'adopted' young Africans, perhaps to replace children lost by death." Interestingly, Bush reports that new arrivals considered themselves as adopted children and referred to the slaves who cared for them as parents. Bush adds that the respect for parents and veneration for the aged is strong evidence for the importance of kinship links in slave society. She goes on to reiterate the point that, as in Africa, grandparents played a highly important role in socializing slave children.

Concerning household organization, the grandmother figure was a well defined, as well as a respected elderly person. Among Jamaican blacks, the grandmother figure offered a strong sense of family and kin relationships. She offered advice, guidance, moral support and closeness of love. She acted as a dominant family figure depending on circumstances. The dominant figure was selected based on age relationship rather than on a "blood" one (Beckwith, 1969, p. 52). As among African Americans, this person had to provide for their family in many ways. He/she made sure the family was fed, clothed, and was raised with a "good education," if possible. The dominant family figure also served as the disciplinarian and mediator. This figure was the one who saw that family values were enforced, in other words, she/he was the one who taught right from wrong. In short, and in the words of Henriques (1968, p. 103), the dominant figure helped the family to serve two basic functions. The first is leadership which gave the family a sense of security and wholeness from within, and second helped to promote welfare for those family members in need of assistance. One might add that these patterns of mutual aid prevail within the confines of African Caribbean family households today.

On parental responsibility, Bush (1990, p. 103) insists that slaves did care for and love their children. She argues that enslaved Africans' behavior towards their children was determined to a significant degree by their African cultural heritage, and cautions observers to examine the attitudes of slaves to their children within this context. Another feature discussed by Bush and worth mentioning here is that enslaved Africans were generally affectionate towards their friends, kindred, and offspring. "The fact that parents and grandparents of both sexes had an important role in family and community life constitutes additional evidence against the oversimplified model of the slave family as an isolated unit consisting solely of mother and children" (Bush, 1990, p. 106).

After the end of slavery, the two factors of class and gender continued to interact with other forces, such as processes of development and urbanization, to create great divisions within Caribbean societies, most notably divisions along race, color, gender, and class lines. All classes, including the middle and upper classes, tended to display a pattern of kin networks at one level or another based on the local meanings attached to those social constructions (Douglass, 1992). In recent times, the study of household composition has shown that a variety of kinship ties may be activated to bring people together into the same dwelling unit. Additionally, attention has been given to charting the shape and strength of the various relationships within them. Thus, Smith (1988) and others have attributed the development of 'matrifocality' as a domestic and family organization to socio-economic forces that historically marginalized lower-class husbands/fathers in their roles as household heads.

According to Barrow (1996, p. 461), however, "middle class men are also 'marginal' to the family, perhaps even more so than their lower class counterparts for whom marginality is not a constant preoccupation." Barrow cautions that this observation should not be interpreted to reflect a Creole family uniformity, especially when it comes to the meanings of specific family practices, such as common-law unions and outside children. Although legal monogamous marriage is accepted as the ideal, in practice most children are conceived and born outside of marital relationships, resulting in the patterns called out by Smith and Barrow. Nonetheless, kinship bonds among Caribbean people of African descent have remained strong and resilient over the years.

Today, individuals subjectively select a circle of intimate kin for daily interaction. In other words, the boundaries of their extended family structures may be more or less permanent. As earlier research has shown (Smith, 1988; Douglass, 1992), the boundaries may be delimited by a genealogical connection to a universe of kin from which a circle of intimate kin may be drawn upon for daily or regular interaction. Like the African-American experience, African Caribbean family functioning takes on characteristics of the African extended kinship network which is hypothesized to have been pre-adapted for conditions in the New World. The slave regime did leave some room for adaptations based on African and other familial principles. A strong sense of collective responsibility and the cultivation of a sustaining core of reciprocal assistance patterns have evolved into extended family helping traditions in various diasporan societies. Even though kin groups may be widely dispersed, the sense of obligation toward one another remains strong.

Within the context of these historical realities, Michele Sogren provides insights into the Caribbean family in chapter twelve. The chapter attempts to provide a socio-historical analysis of the Caribbean family and ultimately to create a new debate about Caribbean family life, a life that is neither pathological, nor deviant, nor defensive. The review of the literature and the insights of contemporary scholars are complemented by a qualitative study in a specific Caribbean country, Trinidad and Tobago. The chapter advances the argument that understanding the significance and applicability of legacy, tradition, and experiences on the current portrait of family life of the Caribbean people is critical to policy, program planning, and service development and delivery.

In chapter thirteen by Christine Barrow, Caribbean literature is reviewed to assess the role of kin and other institutions in the care and support of children. After a brief historical and cultural overview and a discussion of social policy for children in Barbados, the author reviews the findings of research that focuses on child care patterns among extended family members. The findings neither support the sweeping generalizations of family breakdown nor the comforting image of extensive supportive networks of kin. Nonetheless, the adoption of children and their care as a female activity within extended families remains a norm of Caribbean childhood. The author calls for more research that privileges children's voices, as well as the daily realities of Caribbean families in order to deepen the knowledge base about Caribbean family dynamics. Additionally, the author advocates a design of supportive social policy for children and their families.

Chapter fourteen by Stacey Brodie Walker and Kai Morgan explores the historical antecedents of family structure in Jamaica and its current impact on child developmental issues, such as identity, attachment, sexuality, aggression, and delinquency. The authors discuss also the role of the family in therapy, and highlight challenges as well as treatment recommendations for therapists working with Jamaican families. Anecdotal information and empirical findings are employed to explain these identified relationships within extended, blended, and single-parent families.

In order to appreciate the present dynamics of extended families in Africa and the Diaspora, it is important to understand past family traditions that continue to show their influence today. Features associated with African world families include consensual unions or common-law unions, separation of spouses and/or resources, children fostered to own or other relatives, and continued provisioning of households by mothers. In addition, there seems to be a marked segregation of conjugal roles in the marital unions of the rural folk and lower classes. On the other hand, middle-class households now tend to emphasize joint husband and wife activities. In spite of class variations in marital and household arrangements, a continuing distinctive feature of African societies is the strong sense of kin. This collection of essays clearly emphasizes these features. It is equally important to indicate that the pattern of primary association and/or relationship is fundamentally different from that of the western and Euro-American societies. The differences can be separable analytically if clear conceptual distinctions are made between families (both nuclear and extended) and households. Because individuals may belong to both a family and to a household, we need to examine separately the structure and functioning of both types of units. A number of the chapters in this volume make such a contribution by reassessing and reinterpreting the principles, traditions, and practices that marked the development of extended families by peoples of African descent in the Diaspora.

In this volume, close attention is paid to the "functioning" of the variety of identifiable structures, including not only blood relatives, but also community groups. It may be argued that it is the extensions of the functions that are critical to the survival of members today. Solidarity may be built with a wide or narrow range of kin depending on one's age, gender, class, race, ethnicity, etc. "Kinship ties" also can be created out of co-residence so that community or neighborhood members can act toward one another as kin based on the enduring solidarity and reciprocal assistance established among them. The task then is to offer a more meaningful assessment of the concepts appropriate for a cross-national comparison of the functioning of extended families in black societies.

Contributions provided in this volume clearly help correct the erroneous characterization of diasporan families as being all too often pathological. The debate about the historical and contemporary functioning of African and diasporan extended families rages on. Aside from detailing the instrumental and expressive functions of the extended family, a number of the chapters clarify the tendency for conjugal units in African and diasporan societies to be weak in regard to an array of structural and psychological issues, including marriage, child care, sleeping arrangements, and sex roles. In many African and diasporan societies, consensual, common-law and visiting unions tend to be the most common marital arrangements even though legal marriage appears to be the ideal form. Adults tend to exhibit strong negative sanctions against having children outside of marriage and yet, they ultimately come around to welcome the new additions to their extended families. Also, it is made abundantly clear that the stability of extended families in black societies does not depend on the stability of conjugal unions. Factors that shape the self-esteem and the overall (racial) development of black children across various diasporan societies are analyzed. In the face of the threat posed by the dreadful disease of HIV/AIDS, what are the changing sexual and overall behavioral adaptations observed in African world societies?

As summarized in the preceding paragraphs, a number of models are reviewed with the goal of articulating the simultaneous and interactive effects of a combination of social constructions and health factors, including race, class, gender, age, ethnicity, colonialism, imperialism, 'tribalism,' and HIV/AIDS. For many of the continental African societies covered in the volume, race is far less salient a social construction than colonialism, 'tribalism,' class, gender, age, and ethnicity as far as trends affecting families are concerned. On the other hand, race, class, and gender are far more salient social divisions than anything else in the analyses of African-American and African Caribbean family and kinship. Because the factors are mutable social, cultural, and ideological constructions, they are subject to change as the authors observe. Overall, then, the intersection of a combination of factors have produced and will continue to produce distinct kinship outcomes and each of the authors discusses on-going societal changes and their impact on extended families in the African and diasporan societies under study.

References

Alleyne, M. (1988) *Roots of Jamaican Culture. London*: Pluto Press.

Aschenbrenner, J. (1975). *Lifelines: Black Families in Chicago. New York*: Holt, Rinehart and Winston.

Beckwith, M. (1969) *Black Roadways: A Study of Jamaican Folk Life.* New York: Negro University Press.

Berry, M. F. & J. W. Blassingame. (1980). *Long Memory.* New York: Oxford University Press.

Burton, R. (1997). *Afro-Creole: Power, Opposition and Play in the Caribbean.* Ithaca: Cornell University Press.

Bush, B. (1990). *Slave Women in Caribbean Society* 1650-1838. Bloomington: Indiana University Press.

Douglass, L. (1992). *The Power of Sentiment: Love, Hierarchy and the Jamaican Family Elite.* Boulder, *CO*: Westview Press.

Frazier, F. E. (1939). *The Negro Family in the United States.* Chicago: University of Chicago Press.

Gutman, H. (1976). *The Black Family in Slavery and Freedom*, 1750-1925 New York: Random House.

Henriques, F. (1968). *Family and Colour in Jamaica.* London: MacGibbon and Kee.

Ladner, J. (1971) *Tomorrow's Tomorrow: The Black Woman.* Garden City, NJ: Doubleday.

Linton, R. (1959). The Natural History of the Family. In R. N. Anshen (Ed.) *The Family: Its Function and Destiny.* New York: Harper.

Marsh, C. & S. Aber (Eds.) (1992). *Families and Households: Divisions and Change.* New York: Macmillan.

Martin, E. P. and J. M. Martin. (1978). *The Black Extended Family.* Chicago: University of Chicago Press.

Miller, K. R. (1984). The Effects of Industrialization on Men's Attitudes Toward the Extended Family and Women's Rights: A Cross-National Study. *Journal of Marriage and the Family*, 46(1), 153-160.

Mintz, S. & R. Price. (1992). *The Birth of African American Culture: An Anthropological Perspective.* Boston, Mass: Beacon Press.

Morgan, S. P. & K. Hirosima. (1983). The Persistence of Extended Family Residence in Japan: Anachronism or Alternative Strategy? *American Sociological Review*, 48, 269-281.

Moynihan, D. P. (1965). *The Negro Family: The Case for National Action.* Washington, DC: US Department of Labor, Office of Policy Planning and Research.

Murdock, G. P. (1949). *Social Structure.* New York: The Macmillan Co.

Parsons, T. (1943). The Kinship System of the Contemporary United States. *American Anthropologist*, 45, 22-38.

Parsons, T. & R. F. Bales. (1955). *Family, Socialization, and the Interaction Process.* Glencoe, IL: Free Press.

Parsons, T. (1959). The Social Structure of the Family. In R. N. Anshen (Ed.) *The Family: Its Function and Destiny.* New York: Harper.

Ram, M. & R. Wong. (1994). Covariates of Household Extension in India: Change Over Time. *Journal of Marriage and the Family*, 56, 853-864.

Roberts, S. (2010). Extended Family Households Are on [the] Rise. *The New York Times National* (Friday, March 19), p. A12.

Silverstein, S. B. (1984). Igbo Kinship and Modern Entrepreneurial Organization: Transportation and Spare Parts Business. *Studies in Third World Societies*, 28, 191-209.

Smith, D. S. (1986). Accounting for Change in the Families and the Elderly in the United States. In D. V. Tassel & P. N. Stearns (Eds.) *Old Age in a Bureaucratic Society: The Elderly, the Experts, and the State in American History.* Westport, CT: Greenwood Press.

Smith R. T. (1988). *Kinship and Class in the Study of Jamaica and Guyana.* Cambridge: Cambridge University Press.

Stack, C. B. (1974). *All Our Kin.* New York: Harper and Row.

Stokes, C. S., F. B. LeClere, & S. H. Yeu. (1987). Household Extension and Reproductive Behavior in Taiwan. *Journal of Biological Science*, 19, 273-282.

Sudarkasa, N. (1996). *The Strengths of Our Mothers, African & African American Women and Families: Essays and Speeches.* Trenton, NJ: Africa World Press.

Winkler, E. N. (2008). "It's Like Arming Them": African Amerian Mothers' Views on Racial Socialization. In F. Rudd & L. Descartes (Eds.) *The Changing Landscape of Work and Family in the American Middle Class: Reports from the Field.* Lanham, MD: Lexington Books (Rowan & Littlefield).

Wirth, L. (1938). Urbanism as a Way of Life. *American Journal of Sociology*, 44, 1-24.

Zollar, A. C. (1985). *A Member of the Family: Strategies for Black family Continuity.* Chicago: Nelson-Hall Publishers.

Part I
AFRICA

CHAPTER 1

THE AFRICAN FAMILY AND THE CHALLENGES OF THE 21ST CENTURY

Mario J. Azevedo

INTRODUCTION

Under siege from Christianity, Islam, changing laws, and Western practices adopted by independent African governments, which have tended to view a family from the prism of the union of one man and one woman with the minimum number of offspring, thus frowning upon the centuries-old concept of polygyny in the form of polygamy, Africa's family structure and function are at a crossroads, with its very survival at stake. Respected sociologists, anthropologists, historians, and the gloomy pathologists of the black family, fear that the institution, as we have known it, might eventually become dysfunctional and collapse altogether. Some twenty-eight years ago, David Popenoe wrote that "Family groups [including the African family] are becoming internally deinstitutionalized, carrying out fewer traditional functions, losing power relative to the state, and becoming smaller and more unstable, and that the cultural value of families is weakening in favor of self-fulfillment and egalitarianism" (Weisner & Bradly, 1997, p. 8-9). Indeed, as these two authors write, "there is a broad-based and realistic perception that the African family has changed dramatically and not necessarily for the better" (1997, p. xxii). The arguments advanced to doubt the survivability of the African family has been made the more ominous by the prevailing modern life exigencies of providing schooling, employment, and health care to all children in a social context of meager resources, while experiencing simultaneously the catastrophic impact of worldwide conditions favoring the nuclear rather than the extended family pattern.

Using the current sources and views of Africans and Africanists on the continent and the Diaspora, this chapter purports to answer questions posed by modernity, religious dogmatism, and a diseased environment, as they impact the survival prospects of Africa's oldest and most celebrated institution, and assess the strength of its support system and the fate of its integration into a globalized cultural system. Specifically, the following work addresses such views as those advanced by African scholars and the contribution of non-scholars who have focused their work on the role of conjugality and consanguinity, the status and future relations both in the traditional and Western-influenced family settings, the evolution of didactic relationships and modalities of child development, the constraints or exigencies of family size and divorce, and the ominous consequences of HIV/AIDS, even though the impact of disease is the subject of another chapter in this book. However, when all is said and done, rather than predicting the demise of the African family, this chapter holds a different view point, one that neither minimizes the crisis of the institution nor downplays the need for its fundamental adjustment if it is to maintain its sustainability beyond the 21st century and survive the cultural onslaught of the age of globalization.

PERSPECTIVES ON THE FAMILY

There is a tendency in the hegemonic Western culture and among some of its social scientists and politicians to claim that there is only one type of family, the model family that deserves that name, namely, the nuclear family, hurriedly and forcibly imposed on Africa by the West during the colonial period and thereafter. Yet, Africans did not easily cave in to the newly-imposed family model. As Plon et al. put it, "through covert and overt means, the traditional social system organized true resistance against the emergence of the nuclear family" (Plon et al., 1997, p. x). Sara Mvududu and Patricia McFadden argue that the major problem found in the debate over the African family lies in the fact that scholars attempt to "homogenize" and "universalize" the family, neglecting the impact of culture, while forgetting the issue and meaning of diversity and plurality of the institution we call family. The two authors write: "The search for universal categories leads us to a situation where we can see how culture constructs family in different ways at different times in different places" (Mvududu & McFadden, 2001, p. 1).

The two also note that ethnocentrists and patriarchal men would like to see the family mean the same thing to everybody, with the concept and practice of heterosexuality of a nuclear family (already imposed on the world), backed by religion and "marriage rituals," becoming the most important element. In the study of African American family, this type of thinking, which declared the pathology of the black family, is known as the cultural ethnocentric school (See Dodson, 2007, p. 52). Mvududu & McFadden also criticize those, especially politicians, who tend to see the family as an institution where the paramount responsibility of a man and a woman is to raise children, or view the "mother-child nexus" as the most important element of the family and do not consider the impact of history, culture, and the particular environment in which different human beings live and adapt. In the African American family discourse, this thinking, which ultimately defends the adaptability and survival of the black family, is sometimes called "cultural relativity" (McAdoo, 2007, p. 60). In other words, the consensus among these experts on the family asks us to look at the ways culture impacts and constructs the meaning of family differently. In a similar vein, Mvududu & McFadden warn us to look at how women, who often find themselves "at the intersection" of the different spectra of meanings of family advanced by the differing classes in society, especially the middle and lower classes, respond to the demands and pressures imposed on them (Mvududu and McFadden, 2001, p. 18). Another important point of contention regarding the family comes from the relation and attitude groups develop about their environment, the type of relations amongst themselves, and the means used to forge what we call the family.

Along these lines, African pioneering female sociologists Diane Kayongo-Male and Philista Onyango have distinguished three schools of thought that have emerged over the past decades. They call the first the "structure or organization school," the second the "conflict perspective," and the third the "symbolic interaction school." The structural school originated with Winch's writings in 1961 and 1979 (Winch, 1961; 1979, p. 352-355). Winch proposed that the organization of the family has been determined by the physical milieu and population pressures, forcing members to adapt to a life of farmers, fishermen, or hunters. For this school, "...the mode of production is the most basic though not the only factor contributing to the nature of the family organization, which "... regulates social inequality, settlement type, inheritance, and residence patterns" (Kayongo-Male and Onyango, 1984, p. 96). As one can deduct from this theory, the family does not seem to be an agent but one that follows and adapts to the ecology in order to survive. Yet, experience teaches us that families or people do make genuine decisions that may be contrary to the whims of the environment and demographic pressures. It is true, for example, that even during the time of famine caused by the loss of cattle, Ethiopian pastoralists have refused to adapt to the life of farmers and, vice-versa, when farmers are struck by famine from drought, flooding, or other natural phenomena, they do not abandon their agricultural lifestyle to become pastoralists. The second theoretical framework on the family--the conflict theory--views society, groups, including the family, and individuals primarily as competitors, even to each other. Competition always results in conflict which is resolved or reasonably managed with the purposeful aim of creating a peaceful environment through negotiation, threats, aggression, and power. This theoretical framework tends to emulate the theory of the social contract propounded centuries ago by Thomas Hobbes (1651), John Locke (1689), and Jean-Jacques Rousseau (1762). The social contract transcended the disorganized nature of "primitive" bands of humans and eventually gave us the family and civilized society.

The third school or tool of analysis, noted above, uses the concepts of symbolic interaction to explain how families emerged and continue to survive as units. The proponents of the theory reject the idea that the environment or conflict from competition is the sole factor responsible for family formation. They concede that the two previous theories have their merit, but that intra-group planning and action, effective use of words, symbols, rituals, and self-reference, perhaps reinforced, as in Africa, with warnings attributed to the power of the ancestors, witchcraft, sorcery, magic, and organizational patterns, are all important as they influence behavior and create a community where people work together and share resources. The effort results in the successful taming of or adaptation to the environment, role assignment, and community responsibility. Symbolic interaction is a dynamic process where the members of the family and future generations and their households are the primary actors and not the environment or intra-group competition, conflict, and conflict management.

In their effort to define family, some scholars have found that there is no one family that has all elements that fit what societies and groups of people expect of a family. The only way to arrive at such a definition is perhaps to concoct one that examines family functions. Once that becomes the tool of analysis, it levels all types of families to the same denominator, and, as a result, any familial patterns that do not conform to it are dismissed. Harriett Pipes McAdoo, in her defense of the African American family against such pathologist scholars and politicians as E. Franklin Frazier, Daniel Patrick Moynihan, and Lee Rainwater, who claimed that the black family institution in the United States was dysfunctional and needed quick repair, says that "It is a myth to believe that a statistical model of the American family can be identified for use in measuring all families in the multitude of cultural groups in the matter" (McAdoo, 2007, p. 57). The same thing can be said of the African family, about which most of the conclusions are based on inaccurate and meager statistics and the personal observations of strangers who spend a few days in an African village and come up with grandiose scientific-sounding conclusions about African family life. Thus, the best way is either to define types of families separately and forget the "model family" or to incorporate into the definition family structure or organization, function or purpose, the cultural environment in which it functions, its historical origins, and examine how the members in general view and behave towards each other. It appears that the latter option, even though more encompassing and complex, makes much more sense, and will therefore guide the following discussion of the family in Africa, as the continent enters in earnest the twenty-first century.

Some scholars also point out that the concepts of family and household should not be confused and used synonymously, as was commonly done up until the 1950s. Thereafter, the "concept of 'family' was no longer identifiable as a group of people living together in a house" or guided by "the perception that the nuclear family was the most modern or advanced family form" (Weisner & Bradley, 1997, p. xxv). The other caveat coming from the two authors is that, in much of the research on the family, as a "tool of analysis, household always implies economic and political variables." In the following discussion, the author uses both words of family and household, taking into account the preceding warning.

Whatever the disagreement among the experts, it is usually agreed that a family is one of the basic social units that contributes to the survival of the species through procreation and inculcation of survival strategies in the offspring, normally done by mother and father and, in some societies, by others who feel united by historical or recent roots who see their survival as inexorably linked to that of the bonded group. As most scholars also generally agree, the family has had four survival and adaptive needs, namely, reproductive, subsistence, communication, and social regulation (Weisner & Bradley, 1997, p. xxviii). Other scholars express these functions as reproduction, affection, socialization, economic cooperation, and religious upbringing (Kayongo-Male & Onyango: 1984, p. 12). In so far as Africa is concerned, the concepts that all scholars deal with are kinship, the extended family, conjugal units, consanguineal unions, the act of marriage, households, matrilinearity and patrilinearity, patriarchy and matriarchy, matrilocality and patrilocality, levirate, concubinage, courtship, bridewealth or *lobola*, divorce, separation, triangular unions, polygamy, especially polygyny, inheritance, and woman-to-woman marriages. The latter rarely occur on the continent. The question that those who predict the demise or the weakening of the African family today must answer is, which element, among those enumerated above, is so essential that, when it is lost, one can say that the family has altered unrecognizably, is unable to fulfill its function, or has lost the organizational or structural coherence that guarantees the proper functioning and a bonded group's continued survival.

The conjugal or nuclear family, which is prevalent in the West and was unsuccessfully imposed on the middle class and the religious-prone individuals within the African population during the colonial period, is predicated upon the union and the permanency of a life spent together by a woman and a man, who not only promise to endure any adversity until death "do them part," but who are also expected to "produce" offspring, normally no more than three children. As they grow up, the children are then expected to move out of the family dwelling and begin their own families, maintaining strong ties only with their parents, grandparents, and siblings or perhaps first degree cousins. Comparing the nuclear with the extended (African) family, Stephen McCarthy stresses the major difference between the two by noting that: "Whereas Westerners generally have little family awareness beyond, say, first cousins, to the African such a mental map of family is the focus and center of his identity" (McCarthy, 2004, p. 14). In the context of the African extended family, one's occupation or profession is not as important to the sense of "belonging" and "acceptance" as the bond nurtured with one's parents, relatives, and extended kin.

Therefore, the traditional extended African family encompasses the parents, the offspring, the uncle, who often is called father, aunts, also labeled as mothers, all cousins, grandparents, distant relatives, all those who are related by blood or are consanguineal, and all others who might not be blood-related but have been accepted as kin. The family is linked to the lineage (families descending from the same founder) and to the clan (or a group of families claiming to have the same founder and ancestor, even though this cannot always be proven), and, ultimately, to the ethnic group. Kinship based on the clan is still extremely important in Africa. Indeed, even though people cannot prove that they are related to a common ancestor, any kinsman may share moral responsibility: "A man may be held accountable for the crimes committed by his kinsmen. Similarly, if one man 'sins,' divine [or ancestral] punishment may strike anyone in his group. It follows that, not only kinsmen are supposed to help each other, but also to govern each other's behavior" (Azevedo, 2005, p. 374). The ethnic group involves the claim of a distant common ancestor(s). In most cases, even though exceptions exist, as when a group adopts and speaks another ethnic group's language (a case in point is Chad among some historically enslaved populations), the ethnic group identifies itself through its distinct language, unique cultural traditions, and specific territory of origin. At times, ethnic loyalties may transcend the loyalty to the community and the family. The recent rivalry between the Kikuyu and the Luo stemming from Kenya's highly contested results of the presidential elections in December 2007, which caused over 1,000 deaths, illustrate the degree of allegiance to the ethnic group, despite Kenya's more than forty years of independence. The fundamental reason of the occurrence in Kenya is the thought that, if the ethnic group disappears or has no control over its resources because of the loss of power, family and community identity is gravely threatened.

The distinction between patrilineal families, which constitute about 85 percent of the ethnic groups in Sub-Saharan Africa, and matrilineal families is important in the pluralistic African cultural context. Patrilineal families trace their ancestry through the male or father's line, which does not imply that the mother's line is not important, but shows that the father's male relatives must have historically played a greater role in the survival of the unit and therefore have a free hand on such issues as disciplining the children and determining inheritance rights, which usually favor the male line. In matrilineal families, which function among the estimated 12 percent of the African ethnic groups, the tracing of ancestry is done through the mother's line. Matrilienal societies are found in the so-called matrilineal belt, extending from parts of West Africa through Central and a few pockets of East Africa.

In the matrilineal setting, women and their kinsmen tend to have a higher degree of participation in decision-making, especially if they are from wealthy families. Here, the children's uncle has the right to discipline them and plays a major role in determining the marriage of his sister's daughter(s). The Ibo of Nigeria are one of the exceptions in Africa. They are not bound by either system of reckoning descent. In general, patrilineal societies, in contrast to the matrilineal, are patrilocal, in that the new wife is expected to live with the husband's family, more often than not, in the same compound. The matrilocal societies are characterized by the husband taking residence in the compound of the wife's family. The distinction between the two family patterns can be complex, but one could say that, in matrilineal society, "Men find their attention divided between their wives and their children, on the one hand, and their sisters and their children, on the other. While patrilineal societies, particularly those that stress the local lineage, are marked by highly stable local groups, matrilineal descent results in more flexibility, and the membership of matrilineage in any local area is likely to change from year to year" (Azevedo, 2005, p. 376).

Further differential illustrations are appropriate. Austin Ahanotou observes:

> In matrilineal and matrilocal societies, husbands come to live in the wife's natal household, where a long-standing domestic coalition exists between his wife, her mother, sisters, and broader kin who are at hand to defend their sister, daughter, or mother. In patrilineal, patrilocal societies, women do not necessarily have family nearby. The wife enters the husband's family as a stranger with little status. Even female members of the lineage view her as a subordinate. Yet, women in patrilineal and patrilocal societies [can] build important networks of support through their children or the matrilineal family (Ahanotou, 2003, p. 550-551).

These residence arrangements, however, may be altered by the bridewealth agreement, which may determine that the woman will not move to a new residence until the husband has fulfilled his bridewealth obligations. This may happen when the son-in-law has to perform manual labor or hunt for his in-laws or future-in-laws prior to joining or being joined by his wife permanently. Among the Hausa of Nigeria, for example, the married male children would continue to live with parents even after marriage (to one wife only at that point) until he had accumulated enough wealth to sustain his prospective family (Kayongo-Male & Onynago, 1984, p. 4). In the West, unlike in Sub-Saharan Africa, children are emancipated at 18 or 21 years of age and expected to move out of their parent's home. Those who do not abide by this unwritten norm are frowned upon by the rest of society. Moreover, the African extended family is often multigenerational in that people of different generations may live together in the same household or same compound after their marriage.

Bridewealth, rather than "brideprice," a word that may give the impression that the man buys his wife, symbolizes the groom's gratitude to the bride's parents, and bestows upon the husband his rights over the offspring, to the extent that, when he dies, his children become the children of his brother. The latter may even marry the widow. This practice is designed to provide protection, security, shelter, food, and clothing to her and her children. Resembling the ancient Hebrew tradition, this practice is sometimes known as the levirate. Bridewealth is determined following serious negotiations between the two families, and can be fulfilled by the groom's family or himself in the form of money, cattle, as is the case among the Maasai of Kenya and Tanzania, crops, physical labor, and material offerings. Bridewealth is different from dowry in Africa. It is important not to confuse bridewealth with dowry. Dowry is a gift of the parents to their daughter as she begins her life as a wife. Dowry is rare in Africa and occurs only in matrilineal societies. Because, normally, African marriages are alliances between families or clans, the extended family has much to say about divorce. Before the couple decides to break up, relatives will want to know why, and, if the reason is not adultery, infertility, or impotence, relatives will do all their best to keep the two together. Divorce is made more difficult by bridewealth, which may have to be returned if the wife is at fault or cannot conceive, given that her parents had formally guaranteed the husband-to-be that their daughter would give him children.

All writers of the African family further agree that marriage is an obligation of every member of society. Children grow up being told how important marriage is, as it carries on, through time, the name of the family, the clan, and the ethnic group. Specifically-scheduled initiation ceremonies or rites-of-passage, usually organized to fit youngsters' age sets, common to many African societies, reinforce marriage as a social obligation. It is at this time that many other obligations to society, such as sharing, taking care of both close and distant members of the family, observing hospitality, thinking primarily of the community rather than of oneself, respecting the elders and ancestors, and the need to observe cultural norms and traditional values are inculcated in the youngsters. These life training activities and rituals are couched in powerful symbols and threatening ancestral sanctions that are designed to "tame" the unruly generation. Societies and families that practice male or female circumcision, be it infibulation or pharaonic, may subject the youngsters to this painful ritual at this time.

The obligation to marry is demonstrated by the fact that Sub-Saharan Africa has very few bachelors who decide not to marry voluntarily. Celibacy is rare, and Catholicism has always found it difficult to attract young males to enter the priesthood, especially if the family has only one male child. Indeed, in Africa, every male or female has strong dreams about his/her future family. The collective nature of the African families is thus noted by Winston Burton and Roger Winsor:

> The West...values individualism. The individual is supreme, and property is individually controlled. In contrast, Africans perceive the individual as a member of a group or society organized around lineage and the extended family. Often, property is collectively controlled by the larger groups [which is, often, the root of conflict when modern or Western-adopted laws are applied]. Thus, in Swahili, there is no word for "I own," the closest to it being "I am with." In the West, marriage is an agreement between two people, whereas in Africa marriage

involves a whole set of collective procedures, with families from both the man's and the woman's side having to give approval (Burton and Winsor, 1993, p. 6).

The importance of marriage in Africa is also underscored not only by rituals, constant daily admonitions, and the tendency to emphasize it as an alliance between families, but also by the persistence in the remote areas and villages, even today, of pre-arranged marriages, despite the rebellion of those youngsters who have tasted the social freedom introduced by colonialism and globalization.

Another important feature of the African family institution is the right of a man to marry more than one wife (bigamy, if two wives, polygamy, if more than two wives). Even though most African males (over 70 percent) do not avail themselves of this "right," which, nevertheless, they are keen on maintaining at all cost, the practice has been one of the family's structural elements most difficult to eliminate. Christianity and colonialism tried to wipe it out, at times by force and intimidation, or by showing favoritism to monogamous individuals in civil service employment. The effort did not completely succeed. Unable to accomplish their goal, all colonial governments and post-colonial states had to resort to a compromise by instituting three kinds of marriages: Civil, religious, and common law. In the words of Therborn, the Western "legal peace" left for the African family traditions has remained a "complex pluralism of colonial statutory law, a wide ethnic palette of 'customary law,' and Islamic, and, in East Africa, for instance, Hindu law" (Therborn, 2004, p. 28). The most pervasive of the three legacies has been the common law, whereby one can marry according to traditional custom, which does not require the sanction of the central government. The government, however, does not bestow upon marriages consummated through customary law the same rights it guarantees to civil marriages.

Therborn further notes regarding multiple wives that "Africa is above all the world's polygyny. It is not unique [he adds], as Muslim law allows polygyny, but the prevalence is incomparably high," as even one-fourth of married Christian men were engaged in "polygynous unions" during the 1990s. As a result, wives and the society-at-large sanction this old tradition. In fact, there are African theologians today who disapprove the celibacy required of Catholic priests and are looking for a compromise solution that would allow the Church to accept polygynous men's active membership. Women involved in these types of Western "forbidden" unions or triangular unions, are at times referred to as "bureau wives," "kept wives," or "outside wives."

Social scientists have tried to explain why polygamy persists in Africa regardless of one's education and religion. For example, the Christian and Western educated, former professor, and President of Kenya, Mwai Kibaki, is married to two wives: One whom he travels with and attends national functions, and the other whom he sees when he goes to his village. It is known that societies that live on subsistence agriculture have the need for adequate manpower to survive. Since fertility in one woman becomes finite after reaching a certain age, one way to ensure adequate availability of man-power, especially males, to work in the fields is to raise many children. However, this cannot be accomplished effectively, except through polygamy. Indeed, in a region of high fertility, a man with five wives can easily have a household or a compound of 30 children.

Africa is known for its high fertility rates. The root of fertility differences among populations has attracted the attention of many anthropologists, paleontologists, and sociologists. John Caldwell and Pat Caldwell (1976, p. 321-366; and 1990, p. 118-125) have advanced an interesting theory about why, in Africa, high fertility rates are desirable. They theorize convincingly that Euro-Asian societies emerged on alluvial basins, where the use of plows enabled a few people to produce agricultural surpluses sufficient to feed entire families. Thus, those controlling the land became wealthy, an occurrence and process that led to stratified societies, as in India. As parents, these "nouveau riches" and families, through their ability to regulate inheritance and dowry, ensured that all children married within their social class. The opposite occurred in Africa. Here, in the words of Winston and Winsor, societies emerged

> On upland soils unsuited for both plows and irrigation, and yielding only small agricultural surpluses. Sub-Saharan Africa was protected from the diffusion of Eurasian type agriculture by the desert and disease, and so a different system evolved, with agricultural technology based on the hoe. The more agricultural laborers, the greater the yield. Consequently, the system that evolved in Sub-Saharan Africa had to emphasize fertility to meet the heavy labor demand...The Sub-Saharan African system became thus more egalitarian, lacking rigid stratification" (See Winston & Winsor, 1993, p. 13-14).

In patrilineal societies, having many wives is seen as a sign of high social status. Indeed, those households having many wives and children tend to be better off and more respected in the community. This accounts for the unpopularity of contraceptives as family planning in Africa, even though, in certain countries, such as Kenya, Cameroon, Ghana, and Zimbabwe, over 30 percent of married women may be using artificial means to curb fertility. Abstinence, following the birth of a child and throughout the breastfeeding period, has been the most common means of family planning and control of an unwanted population growth. In countries such as Chad, Zaire, Kenya, Mozambique, and Malawi breastfeeding may take as long as three years, which becomes difficult for men not to engage in extramarital relationships. Some researchers have placed much blame on this cultural practice regarding the spread of sexually transmitted diseases, including, and particularly, HIV/AIDS.

Polygamy has also been seen as a type of "social insurance" for old age. In traditional and even modern Africa, families are expected to care for their members, in prosperity and in calamity, in infancy and in old age, the reason why babysitting facilities or senior citizen institutions did not exist then and are rare today. This partly explains why, currently, African governments are slow in responding to the needs of their senior citizens when their families are unable to provide care for them. Some researchers have also claimed that the vulnerability of African children to the disease ecology, accounting for the mounting infant mortality rates in Sub-Saharan Africa, has been another reason why polygamy has persisted and the desire for a large family has endured. However, one can make the point that this may certainly have been one of the major reasons for polygamy and large households in the past, but today, with modern medicine, it seems that the need should be considerably less. Yet, this is not the case. Despite the ravages of HIV/AIDS, tuberculosis, and malaria Africa still holds the highest fertility rates on the globe. Fertility is definitely linked to the primacy of the child in Africa. A child is considered to be a gift from God and the ancestors, demonstrated by the various complex rituals and sacrifices that surround a baby's birth, the conferring of a name, and the formal presentation of the new member to the family and the community. The sacredness of the child is also underscored in many societies in Africa by the fact that it is inappropriate to count the number of children to curious strangers who ask the question.

Thus, a couple that is unable to have children is seen as abnormal, and society may think that it is being punished by the ancestors for known or unknown reasons. As a result, infertile couples will continue to consult the traditional healer until they have exhausted their resources. While impotent men become the village major topic of conversation and, at times, feel compelled to migrate to the city to avoid shame, infertile women may be divorced, creating in them a sense of unworthiness even as human beings. Conservative Westerners have often criticized polygyny as nothing more than promiscuity and a practice of savages. To these critics, Africans respond by pointing to the high degree of divorces and re-marriages in Western societies, and view these social occurrences as nothing more than sexually-promiscuous serial monogamous cases and affairs, not different from African polygyny. In contrast to the Western world, where divorce and re-marriage are still frowned upon, and extramarital affairs are not openly condoned, at least, in Africa, they note, the right to have a second wife is culturally sanctioned and accepted. In this context, interesting and piercing is the point made by an African "social critic," who sarcastically but realistically asked:

> Which one is better, polygamy or walk in, walk out marriages?... Polygamy is a symbol of wealth, of a man of substance and distinction, the reality of polygamy becomes not only sensible but desirable...On the other hand, consider a society that says that polygamy is "illegal." In such a society, unmarried women (not of their own choice but for lack of husbands) take prostitution, brothels signing up...immorality is elevated to business...women marry, walk away, marry, walk away as many times as they wish for all sorts of frivolous reasons including "he cheated on me," "I don't love him or her no more" and all such non-sense...women make a living out of what they call "child support" and proceed to milk several men dry every month. Married men themselves secretly retain concubines in every corner of the city...What is hypocritical is the practice of polygamy in the secret places and avowing monogamy in the open. This is deceit...It makes sense to legalize polygamy (Ahanotou, 2003, p. 542-542).

The love for children and their primacy in the household explain why abortions are not condoned in many African societies. Every government in Africa has made abortion illegal, except when medically the life of the mother is in danger. However, this does not mean that abortions do not now or did not take place in the past. Effective traditional ways of getting rid of unwanted pregnancies or fetuses have been known and used on the continent for centuries. Today, as Ahanotou notes, poverty and attempts to avoid social stigma have contributed to a high rate of unsafe abortions. In Nigeria alone, the rate of maternal mortality rate from abortions was estimated at 1,000 per 100,000 women in 2003 (Ahanotou, 2003, p. 546).

In certain societies in East and Central Africa, as is the case among the Nuer, Akamba, Lovedu, and parts of Dahomey, West Africa, a family practice known as woman-to-woman marriage exists. This practice involves a woman who cannot conceive giving bridewealth to a fertile woman to secure permanent rights to the children her selected prospective wife will conceive, determining in the process which man may be the progenitor. As a result of the contract, all children born of the "woman wife" will belong to the "woman husband." The latter usually commands a good deal of resources for this expensive transaction.

Concubinage in Africa has been mostly a feature of Muslim societies, which is a way of circumventing the Muslim law of four wives only. In the past, in Central Africa, Muslim sultans and powerful men, during their raids for slaves in non-Muslim societies, would often bring home as prizes the most beautiful women who would become their quasi-wives, as the men, in deference to Islamic law or *sharia*, would never marry them, even though the concubines would live side by side with their wives and bear their children. Some of the concubines were purchased rather than captured as slaves but, once concubines, they could not be sold, and their children enjoyed certain rights in society.

One might note a discussion of the African family system here by enumerating what Kayongo-Male and Onyango call the Western stereotypes about the African family, which, according to them, include the following (1984, p. 5-6):

> 1) African families do not show affection in public; 2) in the African family, parents exert strong authority over the children; 3) African families care about the elderly; 4) African family members show a great deal of cooperation; 5) at home, the husband provides very little assistance in household chores; 6) in African families, parents are involved in the selection of their children's choice of a mate; 7) in Africa, women tend to marry at a younger age; 8) African families practice polygamy; 9) it is typical for African large families to live together; 10) Africans have no courtship before marriage; 11) African families have little privacy; 12) within African families, love making is not emphasized; 13) African marriages require bridedewealth; 14) children in African families carry little conversation with their parents; 15) family members are segregated during meals; 16) children in Africa are raised by many relatives; 17) in Africa, marriage is based on economic considerations; and 18) families on the continent of Africa do not share leisure time.

The two sociologists note that, actually, not all of the preceding "stereotypes" are really stereotypes—almost all of them are accurate characterizations of the African traditional and even of the modern family, except for the claim that courtship is absent prior to marriage and that children do not talk to their parents.

Contrary to the latter stereotypes, courtship prior to marriage is common to all African societies, even though the external manifestations may differ and severe restrictions may apply. Families consult with each other once the young man has demonstrated an interest in a girl in the next village or town and has confided this to his parents. This phase is followed by a careful examination of the girl's habits and behavior, her family history, and its standing or status in society. If, for example, it can be proven that her family has had a history of leprosy or other abominable diseases, descends from slaves, or belongs to a certain ethnic group that has not been welcome by the lineages or the clans, then the marriage will not take place unless the two elope and move somewhere else, most commonly to the urban area. In the past, this would render the couple an outcast.

On courtship and marriage ceremonies, Kayongo-Male & Onyango note an interesting practice among the Fulani. Marriage can only take place after a girl has had her first menstruation. The two families reach then a verbal agreement, which is followed by two or three public sacrifices of a cow. Following this ceremony, the two lovers are recognized as husband and wife. Important is to note that, before but not after her first menstruation, she is allowed to see any young men. She is then secluded from everybody. At the right time, the girl is symbolically captured by the groom's brothers. At this point, she is "reluctantly" dragged to the boy's compound, after her family has waged an unsuccessful "mock struggle." Once in the new family, the wife's parents-in-law give her only a mat as her home, a situation that continues until she gives birth to her first child. Just before the child's birth, however, she goes back to her village to join her parents until the child is born and reaches the age of two years. Only then, can she rejoin her husband permanently, is given a home, and becomes a "woman."

Patriarchy, neck-and-neck with polygyny, is, at times, considered the most pervasive feature of the African family institution. According to Mvududu and McFadden, "patriarchy, in its wider definition means the manifestation and institutionalization of male dominance over women and children in the family and the extension of male dominance over women in society in general" (Mvududu and McFadden, 2001, p. 65). The two authors believe that male dominance in the African family is absolute, especially over the children and wife or wives, and add a note on its pervasiveness that, "while the patriarchal family represented by both nuclear and extended family in the African context has not always existed, it has been around long enough to have become the 'natural' family form not only in the African context, but globally" (Mvududu & McFadden, 2001, p. 67).

Matriarchy, in its narrow definition, means the dominance of the woman or wife over the family or household. It may sometimes occur among families in matrilineal societies or when a woman is the family's single head, a phenomenon that is occurring more frequently now that economic conditions and HIV/AIDs are contributing to a large number of widows. It is interesting that, the recent studies of the African American family have claimed that the black family in the United States of America was dysfunctional, one of the explanations being the predominance of matriarchy, particularly prior to the civil rights movement. Some have claimed that matriarchy was an African survival within the US black families. As studies of African societies prove, however, the norm in Africa has always been patriarchy and not matriarchy. Therefore, the so-called matriarchy in the black community in the United States seems to be a hoax. Indeed, Harriet McAdoo has gone on record to claim that the black family was never matriarcal in nature in the first place.

THE SURVIVAL OF THE AFRICAN FAMILY AND THE ACCURACY OF THE DEBATE CLAIMS

The following section briefly examines the merit of the theories that claim that the African family has remained strong despite the challenges of our times and of those who predict or come close to predicting its demise. The best approach is to take those elements that seem to define the African family institution and gauge how they have changed, simply adjusted to the insurmountable stress exerted on the institution, or disappeared. Therborn informs his readers that "Strong patriarchal traditions, albeit with relative sexual promiscuity, large-scale polygyny, institutionalized age cohorts, major cultural weight given to fertility and lineage, and pervasive politico-economic, social and cultural patterning through kinship are some of the most salient features of the African institution" (Therborn, 204, p. 13). How accurate are these statements?

Patriarchy has been described by many as the most important element of the African family, extended (traditional) or nuclear (modern). On this, Mvududu and McFadden write that "The patriarchal, heterosexual family has been the most dramatically affected by all the changes occurring within the societies of Southern Africa," especially the challenges of modernity; industrialization; globalization; wage patterns; the spread of technology; and the family's decreased ownership of land and cattle, normally ascribed to men, both as an institution and a "marker of African authenticity." All of these factors seem to have undermined the "wisdom of fathers and ancestors," to use Therborn's expression. According to him, women, with their new "visa of life," a result of increased educational achievements and steady employment and income, are making more choices now, contributing to the erosion of the husband's and the male elders' authority over them and their children, and helping create new forms of families. Accordingly, presently, the African family is "expanding" and "contracting" at the same time. The New Partnership for Africa's Development (NEPAD) has four essential targets, eradication of poverty, sustainable economic growth and development, halting the marginalization of Africa by the rest of the world, and acceleration of women's empowerment through education and other means. Apparently, this new mindset is contributing to the changing role of women in society and the household.

Female advancement, strongly advocated by feminists the world over, has resulted in what some scholars have termed the 'demographic gift," meaning the creation of "a larger share of working age people, compared to the declining share of young and not yet large share of the elderly" (Boko & Diery, 2008, p. 171-183). These new initiatives combined are negatively impacting the centuries-old authority and privileges enjoyed by men. Some scholars have noted that patriarchy has already been severely eroded as women assume higher profile in society, children refuse being told whom to marry, and the international community pushes for people's and women's rights, which are being slowly accepted in such traditional societies as those in South Africa. Furthermore, many more young Africans are now living as singles in the urban areas and easily engage in irregular unions, or marriages of "shorter duration," performed without bridewealth or ceremonies, as they refuse to commit themselves to the institution of marriage as their parents would want them to. As noted above, the fact that more women now live on wages and salaries and may be the only family bread winners has had some negative impact on children's expected "proper" rearing. The extended family system itself is finding it difficult to fulfill its traditional role, mainly due to hard economic conditions and the impact of ill health, which are draining the family meager resources. Child breastfeeding, for example, is ending earlier than ever before.

Fertility was a major feature of the African family in the past, but, recently, it has gone down from seven children per woman to fewer than five or even less. This trend began even before the ravages caused by HIV/AIDS and sexually transmitted diseases. Perhaps partly due to the film industry, young adolescents, 16 years of age and fewer, are now engaging in unprecedented premarital sex, while at the same time delaying, when they can, the age of marriage. This change has most likely contributed to the high rates of premarital child births in 25 countries of Southern Africa, where "an average of one in five women has a birth before marriage," an occurrence that, in 263 ethnic groups, is determined overwhelmingly by age at first marriage, competing with the higher rates in urban areas and developing countries (DHS, *Comparative Reports 13*, 2006, p.xiii).

It appears that the sexual revolution, which reached Africa during the late 1970s and early 1980s, has caught up with its youngsters. Prolonged adverse economic conditions will continue to send young adults to a life of prostitution, exacerbating, in the process, the rates of sexually transmitted infections (STIs) and diseases (STDs). These new developments have forced Therborn to note that the "Northern notion of 'pure relationships' of intimacy appear to be disappearing." A study conducted in Sub-Saharan Africa in 1993 revealed that the median age at first marriage was between 18 and 19 years, and that between 83 and 97 percent of all women would marry by age 25. This is, of course, a major positive change compared to earlier marriage ages, which, during the 1960s, were 14 and 16 years or less (Adetunji, 2003, p. 107). Also, even by the 1980s, the number of unmarried mothers had begun to increase, and, unlike in the past, they are no longer stigmatized, ostracized, or compelled to get married, especially to old men, as a punishment (Kayongo-Male & Onyango, 1984, p. 14).

Polygamy has certainly declined among certain ethnic groups, such as the Kikuyu of Kenya, but has remained high among others, such as the Luo, and in Zimbabwe among the Shona, in Senegal among the Wolof, and everywhere in Uganda, where the use of contraceptive means is highly recommended and promoted by the respective governments. Recent studies have demonstrated that "contraceptive use, marriage, and post-partum infecundity are the major proximate determinants operating in Sub-Saharan Africa" (Adetunji, 2003, p. 107). Use of contraceptives in Africa has increased over the years and is estimated at one-fourth among married women. In Sub-Saharan Africa, specifically, the contraceptive use rate has risen but not as fast as in other parts of the developing world: 19 percent compared to 70 percent in Latin America and 62 percent in Asia (Adetunji, 2003, p. 108). The causes for the decline of polygamy are many, but, undoubtedly, hard economic conditions have been a major contributing factor because only wealthy men can marry and sustain more than one wife. It is important to know that over 300 million, out of a population of 800 million people who inhabit Sub-Saharan Africa, live below the poverty line, as defined by the World Bank and the United Nations, that is, they make only US$2.00 or less a day (*Africa: South of the Sahara*, 2007, p. 12-24), and, therefore, live a life "devoid of economic, social, and political choices" (Vinik & Tregurtha, 2003, p. 142).

Since the 1970s, divorce has also been on the rise in Africa, most likely, not only as a result of Western influence, but also due to harsh economic conditions. Many families have been unable to sustain the household and have ended breaking up. During the 1980s through the 1990s, the growing rate of divorce surpassed that of Sweden, where, culturally, sex life has been liberalized. Following are some of the divorce statistics: 6.7 percent in Botswana; 8.4 percent in Ethiopia; 7.2 percent in Uganda; 5.5 percent in Tanzania; 9.1 percent in Zambia; 3.3 percent in Kenya; and 3.9 percent in Liberia. During the 1990s and more recently, the rates of divorce in Zambia have risen to 15 percent and to 15-18 percent in Botswana, Kenya, Tanzania, and Zimbabwe, with Nigeria holding at 7.5 percent (See United Nations, 1989 and Therborn, 2004, p. 37-40). There are other factors that have challenged the African family, especially over the past 20 years, which deserve discussion. Unfortunately they cannot be accommodated in this important but limited study.

CONCLUSION

There is no doubt that, during the past 25 years, Sub-Saharan Africa has been facing almost insurmountable problems, especially in the economic and health sector. Both of these have adversely impacted the ability of the extended (and nuclear) family to function effectively. The rate of polygamy has slightly decreased, forcing Ahanotu to declare that "Polygamy in Africa is an institution in decline" (Ahanotou, 2003, p. 541); patriarchy, although still quite strong, is being challenged by both wives and offspring, and is slowly losing ground. Fertility is down, as women avail themselves of contraceptives and begin making independent decisions, their attitudes reinforced by their gained power in the secular and the religious world. Inheritance laws that favor only males and deprive widows are being challenged everywhere in Africa, including the Muslim world; bridewealth has been a target of colonial and post-colonial African governments, even though tradition has succeeded in protecting it—yet, its past exorbitant demands, which left families in difficult conditions, are crumbling; the ability of the family to provide for its extended elderly and poor kin members has eroded considerably; children are bearing children and beginning premarital sex at younger ages; as a result of wars and diseases, families are being overwhelmed by the number of orphans, over 12 million in Sub-Saharan Africa in 2007, most as a result of the AIDS crisis; in 1994, refugees numbered six million (one person in a hundred), caused by internal civil wars and unrest, the largest similar population of any continent; in the same year, displaced persons were estimated at 35 million or one in 15 of the population (McCarthy, 1994, p. 4), even though Africa is home to only 10-13 percent of the world's population. Presently, the number of refugees and displaced persons, fueled by the tragedy of

Darfur, Chad, and Central African Republic, has not improved. Worst of all, despite its small population size compared to its surface area and other continents, Africa is home to an estimated 20 million HIV-positive individuals (Nelson et al.: 2001, p. 540).

Notwithstanding all problems, it cannot be proven that the African family is on the verge of collapse, as most of the judgments are subjective because the variables are both tangible and intangible and cannot gauge or predict people's resilience. As Kayongo-Male and Onyango put it, "In Africa, the extended family is responsible for a lot of strain but we should be more cautious about arguing that the strains signal the death of the extended family system or that the elimination of extended family ties is the last thing that could happen to the African family" (Kayongo-Male & Onyango, 1984, p. 107). Weisner and Bradley echo the same conclusion in their study of Kenyan families, when they write that "…our data suggest that a unidimensional image of the African family as 'breaking down' is unsupported—there is adaptability and continuity" in the African family structure and function (Weisner & Bradley, 1997, p. xxii). In fact the latter believe that migration and fertility have caused more family instability than "a change of values of 'familism' per se." Plon et al. have arrived at the same conclusion and tell their readers that "Throughout the world, the family is in a crisis. Yet, it has its way of adapting in a changing world" (Plon et al., 1997, p. vi). Thus, it is important to realize that most families in the world are experiencing similar problems but for many of them better economic conditions have enabled them to overcome many challenges, including those stemming from ill health. In this context, some scholars point out that the family fluctuates with and just like the economy—it has its ups and downs.

The factors that have forced the African family to adapt to changing circumstances have been many: The colonial legacy that left a complexity of confusing laws many of which the new African governments have been unwilling to change; environmental mismanagement, corruption, unwise and unequal distribution of resources among the population; nepotism; crippling external debt; and acceptance of strangling loans from the International Monetary Fund and the World Bank (Schwab, 2001, p. 143). The huge loans force governments to devalue their currency, scale down resources and funds allocated for health, education, and other essential social services, making the rich richer and the poor poorer. Many informed observers tell us that the reason why many African families face famine and starvation is not solely the unfriendly environment, floods, drought, and locusts' invasion of farm fields, heat, and infertile soil. Much of it comes from governments' unwise decisions. Bernard Schneider notes, for example, "that, often, famine does not come from scarcity of food but from the absence of purchasing power" among the lower class, who are "victims of either exploitation or indifference of other groups, nationally and internationally" (Schneider, 1987, p. 29-34), exacerbated by the workings of the economy, which man has the ability to control, and society break-down (McCarthy, 1994, p. 4).

Globalization has been both criticized and applauded by those who look at its impact on Africa and, for our purpose, the African family. Globalization's good side may be the sharing of new technology, the rapid expansion of health care advances across the world, and genuine interdependence and cooperation among nations. Its ugly side, however, as seems to be the case now in Africa, has been the tendency on the part of the Western governments and their protected multinational corporations to impose on the rest of the world their sometimes decadent values and their capitalist economic system, while fostering, in the process, crippling dependency on the weaker states and societies. Says Offrong: "What one can expect for is that the globalization of the international economy will lead to a true economic dependence (not dependence of some countries on others as is now the case), among all nations and that this will lead to more cooperation rather than conflict" (Ofrong, 2000, p. 245). Currently, most people in the developing world are not optimistic about the positive impact of the one-sided globalization movement. This world situation, combined with the global trade imbalance, is already causing untold suffering and despair, strangling families both in the rural and urban areas of Sub-Saharan Africa.

As a result of many years of experience and autonomy following colonialism, the solutions to the family challenges are well known. Students and observers of the African scene as well as advocates of the African masses have consistently "demanded" that government policies and programs be human-centered, focusing on collective strategies designed to feed the populace through the improvement of agricultural resources; accelerated and equal access to education for all children; "liberation" of the woman from the shackles of patriarchy; expansion and improvement of primary health care services, with equal access to all citizens; rebuilding of the crumbling developmental infrastructure; ceasing the cycle of international begging and demeaning hand-outs; and promoting continental self-sufficiency.

Obviously, many positive occurrences have reinforced the bonds of the African family, including the following: Laws against domestic violence directed against women and children; an environment that has enhanced husbands' and wives' opportunities to travel and spend more time together;

a changing social atmosphere that has allowed couples to enjoy greater intimacy not just for the purpose of procreation; enactment of policies that have enabled a larger number of female children to attend school; promotion of women's health; election and appointment of women to legislative assemblies, political office, and civil service; creation of more children's programs that have allowed mothers to work; and provision of greater opportunities in which men and women can formally and informally interact. One must also acknowledge that, in Africa, when compared to other continents, few children, including the growing number of street children, most of whom are recent orphans, commit violent crimes. A negligible number of African children and adolescents are on drugs, are prostitutes, abuse the elderly, or are teen-age mothers, all of which speak to the positive role the family continues to play and the caring social and physical environment the extended family has provided. Thus, it is important to remember that the support system, even though weakened, is still there. Successful brothers and sisters are still supporting their siblings in school, cousins search jobs for other cousins and kin, and grandmothers still share scarce resources with their grandchildren. Urbanites still feel guilty when they do not visit their kin in the villages on holidays.

Where does the family stand amidst all this? In Ahanotu's point of view, "African kinship and marriage in modern Africa, from all social and class spectra, are in trouble" (Ahanotou, 2003, p. 551). This is true but being in trouble does not necessarily mean defeat or demise. Just as in America, where the black family has been able to adapt and survive, so will, in the long-run, the African family. Finally, one ought not to forget the role played by religion, traditional or otherwise, and spirituality, which have always been an intrinsic part of African family life, providing solace, hope, and meaning to life, particularly in times of crisis. As anthropologist Paul Bohannan and historian Philip Curtin wrote years ago, in spite of all problems, "loneliness is not an indigenous African problem." This was true yesterday and it will be true tomorrow.

References

Adetunji, J. (2003) Population. In E. Nnadozie. (Ed.) *African Economic Development* (pp.99-118). New York: Academic Press.

Africa: South of the Sahara. (2007). London: Europa Publishers.

Afulezi, O. (2001) Polygamy: The Hypocrisy of Society *The African Herald,* March.

Ahanotou, A (2003). *Culture and Society: Kinship and Marriage in Modern Africa.* In Falola, T. (Ed.) *Africa: Contemporary Africa* (pp. 533-552). Durham, NC: Carolina Academic Press.

Azevedo, M. J. (2005). The African Family. In M.Azevedo (Ed.) *Africana Studies: A Survey of Africa and the African Diaspora* (pp. 371-381) Durham, NC: Carolina Academic Press.

Azevedo, M. & G. S. Prater. (1982) *Africa and its People.* Dubuque, Iowa: Kendall/ Hunt Publishers.

Bledsoe, C. & G. Pisson (Ed.) (1994). *Nuptiality in Sub-Saharan Africa.* New York: Oxford University Press.

Bohannan, P. & P. Curtin. (1988). *Africa and Africans.* Prospect Heights, IL: Waveland Press.

Burton, W. & R. Winsor. (1993) Society, Culture, and Kenyan Family. In M. Azevedo (Ed.) *Kenya: The Land, the People, and the Nation* (pp. 5-34). Durham, NC: Carolina Academic Press.

Caldwell, J. (1976). Toward a Restatement of the Theory of Fertility Decline, *Population and Development Review*, 2 (3/4), 321-366.

Caldwell, J.& P. Caldwell. (1990). High Fertility in Sub-Saharan Africa. *Scientific American*, 262, 118-125.

Das, M. S. (Ed.) (1993). *The African Family.* New Delhi: M.D. Publications PVT.

Dodson, J. (2007). Conceptualizations and Research of the African Life in the United States. In H.P. McAdoo (Ed.) *Black Families.* (pp.51-56) Thousands Oaks, CA: Sage, DHS. (2006). *Comparative Reports 13. Premarital Fertility and Ethnicity in Africa.* Calverton, MD: DHS.

Kayong-Male, D.& P. Onyango. (1994). *The Sociology of the African Family.* New York: Longman.

McCarthy, S. (1994). *Africa: The Challenges of Transformation.* New York: I.B. Tauris and Company Publishers.

McAdoo, H. P. (Ed) (2007). *Black Families.* Thousands Oaks, CA: Sage.

Mvududu, S. & P. McFadden. (2001). *Conceptualizing the Family in a Changing Southern Africa Environment.* Harare, Zimbabwe: Women and Law in Southern Africa, Southern Africa Research.

Nelson, K., C. Williams, N. Graham. (2001). *Infectious Disease Epidemiology.* Boston: Jones and Bartlet.

Offrong, D. (2001). *Globalization, Post-Independence and Poverty in Africa.* Enugu, Nigeria: Fourth Dimension Publishing Company.

Plon, M., T. Locoh, E. Viginikin, & P. Vimard. (1997). *Menages et familles en Afrique.* Paris: Centre Francais sur la Population et Development.

Popenoe, D. (1988). *Disturbing the Nest: Family change and Decline in Modern Societies.* New York: Aldine de Guyter.

Rugumamu, S. M. (2005). *Globalization Demystified: Africa's Possible Development Futures.* Dar-es-Salaam: University of Dar-es-Salaam Press.

Schneider, B. L'Afrique *(1982). Afrique face a ses priorites.* Paris: Economica.

Schwab, P. (2001). *Africa: A Continent Self-Destructs.* New York: Palgrave.

Therborn, G. (2004). Introduction: Globalization, Africa, and African Family Patterns. In G. Therborn (Ed.) *African Families in a Global Context.* (pp. 9-46) Gutenberg, Sweden: Nordics Afrikainstitut.

Winch, R. F. (1961). *The Modern Family.* New York: Holt Rinehart and Winston.

Winch, R. M. P. Gracia, M. Gordon, & G Kitson.(1979). Familial Organization: A Quest for Determinants. *Contemporary Sociology* 8 (3), 352-355.

Vink, N. & N. Tregurtha. (2003). Poverty and Development. In E Nnadozie (Ed.) *African Economic Development* (pp.121-145). New York: Academic Press.

Weisner, S. T. & C. Bradley. (1997). Introduction: Crisis in the African Family In S. T. Weisner, C. Bradley & P. L. Kilbride (Eds.) *African Families and the Crisis of Social Change.* (pp. ix-xxxii.) Westport, CO: Bergin and Garvey.

CHAPTER *2*

REFLECTIONS ON MOTHERHOOD IN NUCLEAR AND EXTENDED FAMILIES IN AFRICA AND IN THE UNITED STATES

Niara Sudarkasa

INTRODUCTION

One of the most significant contributions of anthropology, dating back to the 19th century theorists, is the proposition that all kinship is cultural. The early comparative studies of kinship in various societies around the world, carried out by scholars such as Lewis Henry Morgan (1870) and W.H.R. Rivers (1924), demonstrated that kinship positions and kinship terminologies did not bear a one-to-one relationship to biology. As a matter of fact, the biological acts of mating and procreation might be termed nature's *precursors* to culturally defined kinship. In all known human societies, kinship was and is created and terminated by rules and regulations reflected in behavior that was, and is, culturally prescribed, proscribed or preferred.

Thus, in human societies, when we speak of kinship, we cannot oppose "nature" to "culture" because nature itself has become *enculturated*. Even "motherhood," which many might assume to be an obvious *fact of nature*, is in reality a *facet of culture*. Admittedly, *mothering*, in the sense of conceiving, giving birth, and nurturing dependent offspring, derives from and is found in nature. However, in human societies, *mothering* is encased in culturally variable rules, regulations, expectations, and patterns of behavior.

The "encasing" of motherhood in culture is illustrated by the fact that everywhere *giving birth to children* is only one of a number of culturally accepted patterns by which women become mothers. They may have children who are "adopted", and from the African researches that I conducted, I added that they may have children who are "assumed" or "assigned." In indigenous African societies where adoption as known in the West was not common, women often assumed responsibility for the care and upbringing of one or more children of their relatives. Or, without asking for a child, they might have children "given" or "assigned" to them. In the West, with the exception of paid relationships such as foster- parenting, the practice of "assigning" children to women is uncommon, if not unknown. Yet, in Africa, women may be assigned or "given" children who are not "theirs" in an exclusive sense, but to whom they relate "as a mother." Women who have not given birth, or those whose children are no longer living with them might be "given" (or "assigned") a child who will remain in their care for an unspecified period of time in return for the usual affection and assistance parents receive from their children when they are growing up. As a matter of fact, when I was in Nigeria conducting my first field work, as an unmarried woman in my early 20s, I was an oddity in the small town where I lived, and various people wanted to "give" me a child for whom I would take on the assigned role of mother.

Thus, when we speak of "motherhood", we are not speaking of something "natural", in a strictly biological sense. We are not focusing exclusively on "giving birth." We are speaking of a set of behaviors, expectations and responsibilities that constitute culturally defined kinship roles. Of course, we know that even the act of childbirth itself varies according to culturally prescribed rules and expectations. Where and how a woman gives birth varies according to the cultural norms in her part of the world. From mating, through conception, to birth and beyond, *motherhood is a cultural phenomenon.*

Approaching the comparative analysis of "motherhood" as one aspect of culturally defined kinship, the present paper focuses on the impact of contrasting types of family structure in explaining some of the differences in behavior and ideologies associated with motherhood in the United States and on the continent of Africa. Specifically, it examines motherhood in the context of nuclear and extended family structures as these developed in the West and in Africa, respectively, and suggests some of the ways that motherhood has changed as those family structures have been transported to other cultural contexts. (Sudarkasa, 1980, p. 198).

A NOTE ON THE CONCEPTS OF NUCLEAR AND EXTENDED FAMILIES

The typology used in this paper, namely that of *nuclear and extended families,* is that of George Peter Murdock (*Social Structure,* 1949) but the definitions of the terms also incorporate Ralph Linton's concepts of *conjugal and consanguineal families. (Study of Man,* 1936). Nuclear and extended families in this discussion are ideal types more than they are strictly empirical phenomena. Furthermore, the difference between ideal and reality has only grown since Murdock and Linton wrote their books in the mid 20th century.

Basing his typology on *structure or composition*, George Peter Murdock (1949) proposed two basic types of families, of which the *nuclear family*, comprised of a husband and wife and their children, was proclaimed a type that was basic and universal in all human societies. Assuming the nuclear family to be the building block for all other types of families, Murdock re-defined *extended family* (a term used previously by 19th and early 20th century scholars) as two or more nuclear families linked by the parent-child tie or the sibling tie. (Murdock, 1949, p. 2-3).

Earlier, Ralph Linton had proposed a typology of families based on *principles of group formation* rather than on group structure or composition (Linton, 1936). Linton used the term "conjugal family" to describe a family built around the conjugal or marital relationship, whether monogamous or polygamous. Thus, the group that Murdock termed the "nuclear family" had been termed "the conjugal family" by Linton because it was built around the marital relationship. Linton used the term "consanguineal family," to describe large groupings built around a core group of "blood relatives," as would be the case with families built around a clan or lineage.

By emphasizing principles of formation rather than structure, Linton's typology had a flexibility that Murdock's typology lacked. For example, Linton's "conjugal family" could be monogamous or polygamous, so long as the marital tie was the relationship around which the unit was built. Murdock, on the other hand, had to describe a polygamous family as "two or more nuclear families with a spouse in common." As will be shown later in this paper, such a formulation often distorted the realities in African societies. Similarly, Linton's "consanguineal family" emphasized the fact that in many societies, large family groupings are not built around the husband-wife relationship, but around large groups of consanguineal relatives, such as segments of a lineage or clan.

The present paper makes *some* use of the concepts of both Murdock and Linton. As mentioned earlier, the concept of the "extended family" pre-dated Murdock's usage, and, in fact, was "developed from studies of African peoples" (Aldous 1965; Tetteh 1966). Hence, it would be confusing to try to introduce any other concept to describe Africa's large family groupings. Nevertheless, the reader must be reminded that *extended families in Africa are built around consanguineal cores (*usually around lineages, whose members are related by descent). Therefore, African extended families differ significantly from the European model of "two or more nuclear families linked through the parent-child or sibling tie," which formed the basis of Murdock's definition.

The term "conjugal family" is used when referring to indigenous African families based on marriage. This concept has broader applicability than the concept of the "nuclear family," because it can be used in reference to families built around either monogamous or polygamous marriages[1]. Throughout the paper, the term "nuclear family" is used only in reference to the European and American families that conform to the Murdock model or to this type of family when it has been transplanted, adopted, or re-created in Africa.

Talking about the spread of nuclear family, it is ironic to note that at the same time that these structures and ideologies are spreading from Europe and America to Africa and elsewhere, in the various countries of origin, we are witnessing a dramatic decline in the incidence of "in tact" nuclear families themselves. In the United States, for example, increases in rates of divorce, and in rates of parenthood outside of marriage, have made single-parent and sole parent households, "blended families" and "step families" the fastest growing family structures in the nation. In many areas, and in some ethnic groups, fewer than half of all households conform to the nuclear family model. The impact of these changes on motherhood is particularly profound. Low-income, single mothers are especially disadvantaged, both economically and socially, by the dwindling assistance from public agencies and by the absence of reliable support from adult partners and other kin. Many of these single mothers represent what is termed "the feminization of poverty" in other parts of the world. In studying the future of motherhood and other aspects of family organization, investigation of changes *away from* traditional nuclear families as well as changes *away from* traditional extended families will be required in order to discern the possible outcomes of the processes underway.

MOTHERHOOD IN NUCLEAR AND EXTENDED FAMILIES

This paper proposes that a number of differences in patterns of motherhood can be traced to the constraints and elasticities in nuclear and extended family structures as these have evolved in Europe and its Diaspora, on the one hand, and in Africa and its Diaspora, on the other. The paper draws some contrasts between motherhood in nuclear and extended families by examining the following topics:

1. Household composition and residence of newly-wed couples
2. Dimensions and expectations of women's roles as wives and mothers
3. Power and influence in the roles of wife and mother
4. Differing concepts of "real" mothers and "half" siblings
5. The differing relationship of "marital stability" to "family stability"

1.
"Establishing a separate home" versus "joining a compound": Patterns of residence as sources of constraints and elasticities related to motherhood

As an ideal, and at its most basic, the nuclear family is built around a newly-married couple. Ideally, nuclear family residence is "neolocal." That is, after marriage, the husband and wife are expected to establish a separate household, unto themselves, and to maintain a separate dwelling as long as the family exists as a unit. Even when nuclear families are located in spatial proximity to other nuclear families, they are distinct, inwardly-focused residential units. This is the model, to which Murdock refers, and which was more of a social reality in Europe and the United States in the 1950s than it is today.

Historically, this relative isolation and insularity of the nuclear family had a special impact on women as wives and mothers. As the writings of many early Second Wave feminists have shown, mothers in nuclear families who did not work outside the home spent much of their time with their children, rather than with other adults. Without getting into the debate over the "value" of women's work as wives and mothers within their homes, I simply want to note the constraints on the interaction with other adults that the structure and relative isolation of nuclear families imposed on mothers operating within the home. As one of the two adults in the home, a woman as wife and mother was traditionally subject to these constraints more so than her husband, who was the traditional breadwinner, interacting more regularly with a network of other adults.

Obviously, mothers in nuclear families had (and do have) networks of people, particularly women, with whom they interact frequently, or infrequently. Some of them live near their kin; others have clubs and associations to which they belong. This, however, is quite different from the position of the African mothers living in a dwelling where they are literally surrounded by other people, and where there is a very different notion of "privacy" than obtains in nuclear families.

Also as an ideal, which today is only partly a reality, in many indigenous African societies the common residential grouping was a large extended family, built around a lineage, which is a unilineal descent group comprised of relatives who trace their relationship to each other, and to a common ancestor, through a line of fathers (patrilineal) or mothers (matrilineal), but not both. The lineage is *exogamous*, meaning that members must take their spouses from outside their own patrilineage or matrilineage, depending on the rule of descent in the society concerned. In the old days the lineage collectively owned and allocated properties, such as land and titles, among its members. Thus, it was a corporate, property-owning and property-holding group, intended to exist in perpetuity (Fortes, 1953; Lloyd, 1955). Members of a lineage owned and shared a large dwelling or group of dwellings, commonly known as a *compound*, in which they lived with their spouses and children. This group made up the co-residential extended family. I insert the word "co-residential" because some members of the lineage or the extended family might reside in different towns, or even in different countries, but as members of that lineage or as spouses in the extended family built around that lineage, they regarded that compound as their residential home base.

In a patrilineal society, *the extended family* was comprised of the adult male members of the lineage, along with their wives and children. Historically, many or most of this group would reside in the compound belonging to the lineage. Each married daughter or sister of the men in the patrilineage would reside in the compound owned by her husband's lineage. In cases of divorce, and sometimes for other reasons, these sisters and daughters might exercise their right to return to live in their "father's house", i.e. in the compound belonging to their own patrilineage. (Sudarkasa 1973, p.102, passim).

The main point to establish here is that according to indigenous African patterns of residence associated with lineages, compounds and extended families, newly married couples did not, and many still do not, establish separate residences apart from their families.

In patrilineal societies, the groom usually had his own room in the compound, which he may have had before marriage, may have built or may have been assigned in anticipation of marriage. Only rarely would a new wife have her own room when she first moved into her husband's compound. She might initially share a room with her husband's mother or with a wife of another man in the compound. Of course, she would sleep in her husband's room in accordance with the prevailing customs surrounding marital cohabitation. Matrilineal residential patterns might include more options in terms of where the newly married couple will reside, but in matrilineal societies as in patrilineal ones, when a couple gets married normally *they also did not establish a separate isolated household.* They would reside in an existing compound with members of the extended family of the bride, or in separate compounds with their respective matricentric extended families.

Thus, African conjugal families, unlike Western nuclear families, were not structural and spatial isolates. There are many behavioral correlates of this residential pattern, but I will mention only a few that specifically pertain to motherhood. First of all, virtually everything that a mother does during her waking hours is done in the presence of others who reside in her compound, are visitors to the compound, reside in compounds where she is a visitor, or interact with her at her place of work, such as in the market or at the site where she carries on her craft. In contrast to nuclear families, therefore, where much of a mother's behavior goes unobserved by other adults, in African extended families, a mother's behavior is observed (and, if necessary, scrutinized) by other women including her mother-in-law, co-wives, members of her husband's lineage, and an unpredictable number of people throughout the community.

Her actions as a mother, including the way she relates to, interacts with, teaches, and disciplines her children, are all carried out under the watchful eyes of others.

Westerners may think of this as a "lack of privacy" or a potential loss of individuality, and some of these views have indeed been transplanted to Africa as a result of the influence of nuclear family ideologies spreading from the West. But, the Yoruba mothers I studied in Nigeria in the early 1960s, in Ghana in the late 1960s and in the Republic of Benin in the 1980s, valued the companionship of their female relatives, co-wives (when relations were cordial), friends, and female Elders. They shared information helpful in the upbringing of their children. And even though mothers normally carried their nursing babies everywhere with them, if they needed baby sitters for their other children, their mothers-in-law and other women in the compound—or their own mothers, sisters and friends from other compounds—provided trustworthy childcare providers, who knew the children well, and willingly looked after them.

When I reflect on recent incidences in the United States, where American mothers took their own children's lives while the children were in their care, it occurred to me that in an extended family setting such a thing would be unimaginable. If, as reports suggest, one of the guilty mothers was suffering from severe stress and other emotional or mental disorders, someone in the compound would have observed this and would have taken steps to help the mother or to remove the children from her care. Moreover, such observers would not have felt that they were "intruding" if they intervened when a mother was doing something they considered to be potentially harmful to her children.

In general, mothers' roles in the socialization of their children were (and are) significantly different in extended families and nuclear families. In extended families, the care and upbringing of children is never left exclusively to their parents. The extended family is always involved. In fact, members of the extended family, and particularly women in the extended family, are seen, and see themselves, as resources for each other in the rearing of their children. (See, e.g., Sudarkasa, 1973, p. 132-144). Only societies with extended family structures, and supporting ideologies and values, could have produced the proverb that "it takes a village to raise a child."

Among nuclear families, parents generally regard themselves as the only ones who "have the right" to decide on how to bring up their children, especially the right to decide when and how to discipline them. In nuclear family ideology, even though parents may delegate some of the responsibility for looking after their children, they never really see themselves as delegating or even sharing their *authority* over those children. (I must insert the caveat that the State or the nation, through its law enforcement apparatus, has always had the final authority over its citizens. And, in the second half of the twentieth century, in the United States and some other Western countries, the judicial system has virtually replaced parents as the final authority over what can and cannot be done with, and to, children.).

2.
Dimensions and expectations of women's roles as wives and mothers in nuclear and extended families

An adult woman has two kinship roles in the nuclear family she and her husband form at marriage (i.e. within their "family of procreation"), namely those of wife and mother. Of course, she has other kinship roles, such as those of daughter and sister, in relation to the nuclear family in which she grew up (i.e., within her "family of orientation"), but the focus in this discussion of women in nuclear families is on the family of procreation, in which a woman and her husband constitute the core relationship. There are many contrasts between the two "straightforward" roles of wife and mother in nuclear families, and the complexity of the wife and mother roles in African conjugal and extended families.

- An African woman is wife to her husband, which I term the conjugal role of wife.
- A woman is co-wife to the other wives of her husband, and is ranked according to the order of her marriage to their common husband. This co-wife role is a derivative of her conjugal role of wife.
- A woman is symbolically a wife to all her "in- laws", that is, to all the male *and* female members of her husband's lineage. This I have termed her affinal role of wife.
- A woman is one of the entire group of wives in the compound, and as such, is ranked according to the order of her marriage into the "house" (i.e. the compound). This is also an aspect of the affinal role of wife. With respect to lineage affairs in patrilineal settings, wives are the "out-group" whereas their husbands and members of his lineage, including her children, are the "in-group" or "core group" within the compound.
- Within the conjugal and extended family, a woman is mother to the children to whom she has given birth.
- She is also "mother" to all the children for whom she has assumed, or been assigned, responsibility.
- Depending on her relationship with a co-wife or co-wives, a woman may be viewed as a "co-mother" to some or all of her husband's children by his other wives. Most descriptions of polygamy in Africa (actually referring to polygyny, i.e. plural wives) emphasize competition, friction and discord among co-wives, however, cooperation among co-wives often exists. To the extent that a wife is a "good mother" to all the children of her husband, she may appropriately be described as a co-mother, as well as a co-wife.
- Within the wider community, a mother assumes part of the collective responsibility for all children in her husband's lineage and extended family, as well as for children in the lineage, compound and extended family into which she was born, and others to which she is related.
- As mothers reach the age and status of *Elder Mothers* or *Mother Elders*, their roles as mothers seem to eclipse all others, except those associated with Chieftaincies, and they are among the most honored persons in their compounds and communities.

To appreciate the implications of women's various roles as mothers and wives, let me review the structure of African extended families and their sub-divisions as these can be found in patrilineal societies, such as that of the Yoruba.

African extended families could be subdivided in two ways. First, there was the division between the nucleus formed by the lineage members (the "in-group" or "core group"), on the one hand, and the group formed by the in-marrying spouses (the "out-group"), on the other. In many African languages, the in-marrying spouses in patrilineal societies are collectively referred to as "wives" by both females and males of the lineage and compound. Thus, for example, among the Yoruba, the in-marrying women are collectively known as the wives of a particular compound. As wives of the compound, their membership is *rooted in law* and *can be terminated by law*, whereas membership in the patrilineage that owns the compound is rooted in descent and exists in perpetuity.(Sudarkasa, 1973, chap. 5; and 1980). Thus, the position of a wife in the compound is fundamentally different from that of her husband and her children.

Second, African extended families could be divided into conjugal family units, comprising parents and children. In fact, that is the unit that many scholars have focused upon as the building block of the extended family (using Murdock's model), but the error of this conception is revealed by a number of significant facts. (a) Whether a man's marriage was monogamous, with one wife and children, or polygamous, with more than one wife and children, his was *one* family among the conjugal families in the compound belonging to his lineage. The mother-child units were not conceived of as separate *families*, only subgroups within the one family. Both the husband and his senior wife played important roles in integrating the family (Fortes, 1949, chaps. 3, 4; Sudarkasa, 1973, chap. 5; Ware, 1979). (b) Even though each mother and her children constituted a sub-group within the polygamous family, no mother could think of her husband (i.e. her children's father) as being "sometimes attached to her group" and "at other times attached to another group." At all times a wife realized that her husband was the head of the entire family, and she had to think of herself and her children in relation to all the wives and children in their family. (c) The very existence of the extended family as "an umbrella" group for all of the conjugal families within it, meant that even though the *monogamous* families resembled nuclear families in terms of composition, their dynamics differed significantly from nuclear families. They seldom included only children of the couple themselves, but often included children of other members of the lineage, such as children of a husband's "brother" (who could be any male member of the lineage in his generation) or children "given" or "assigned" to the wife by her sisters or other members of her lineage. These examples indicate that even the monogamous conjugal families did not have the typical nuclear-family ethos or the rigid boundaries that could enable them to "just say no" to relatives in need or turn down requests to take in children of their kin simply because they wanted to save their resources for themselves.

In other words, the various "mothers and fathers" in the extended family could not focus solely on caring for their "own" children as is expected in more inwardly-focused nuclear families. Parents within the extended family often assumed responsibilities for children "other than their own, as if they were their own." During my studies of Yoruba traders in Ghana, I found that many of them were rearing the children of their brothers and sisters back in Nigeria. These children were treated "as if they were their own" because, in fact, the principles of joint responsibility and reciprocity within the family, meant that those children were indeed "like their own."

This is reflected in the Yoruba kinship terminology, which falls in the category of what we anthropologists call a "generational" system. The terms "mother" and "father" are extended to the siblings of the mother and father, i.e. to those whom most Westerners would term "aunt" and "uncle." The terms "mother" and "father" are also extended to a wide range of other kinsmen and kinswomen in the mother's and father's generation. Reciprocally, the term for "child" or "offspring" refers not only to one's "own" children but to the offspring of all those who are considered to be one's siblings. The category of siblings includes not only those whom most Westerners term "brothers and sisters," but also those Westerners call "half-brothers, half -sisters," and cousins. In other words, kinship terms which most Westerners use only in reference to "close relatives" are extended to "more distant relatives" in the same generation. In my view, by collapsing relational distance within these large kin groups, the terminology serves to reflect and reinforce the values of social cohesion, shared responsibility, and intergenerational reciprocity, thereby enabling these groups to survive even in the most adverse of circumstances.

3.
Some dimensions of power and influence in the roles of wife and mother in nuclear and extended families.

Motherhood enhances the position of wives in African conjugal families as well as in the overall extended family. As a *wife*, a woman is an "outsider" vis-à-vis the patrilineage and its affairs. (Of course, as a daughter and a sister in her own patrilineage, she is one of the "insiders."). As a *mother*, although a woman is still one of the "out-group" vis-à-vis her husband's lineage, through her children she has contributed to the perpetuation of that lineage. As soon as a wife has her first child, her husband no longer views her primarily as a wife, but as a mother of his children. Among the Yoruba, henceforth, he does not refer to her, or address her, by the term "Iyawo" (wife), but rather by reference to the name of her first born. For example, she may be referred to and addressed as "Iya 'Tunde" or "Mama 'Tunde" (Mother of 'Tunde). Even Westernized husbands and wives who address each other by their given names will use the indigenous forms of address in certain situations.

When a wife becomes the mother of a child, and preferably of *many* children, who will contribute to the continuity of her husband's lineage, or to that of her own lineage, in the case of matrilineal societies, she joins the ranks of the most revered women in Africa. After a wife becomes a mother, she is *expected* to have power and influence over her children, but she also aims to have increased power and influence over her husband *as the father of her children*. A first wife may expect to have such influence over her husband because of her role as his chief confidant, as well as coordinator and peacemaker within the conjugal family. However, a lower ranking wife may also gain considerable influence over her husband because of the number of children she has, or because her husband is especially fond of one or more of her children. If the first wife does not have children at all, or has children only *after* the second wife has already borne children for their husband, considerable strain might be placed on the co-wife relationship as well as on the relationship between the husband and the first wife.

All mothers want to have the maximum possible influence over the fathers of their children, and this is reported by virtually all observers as the greatest source of competition and discord in polygamous families. It should be noted, however, that such discord is not inevitable, and would not be of concern to a husband and his wives alone. Others in his lineage, such as his father or senior brothers, would step in to advise him as to the appropriate and expected behavior toward his wives and children. The man's mother, who also would be one of the senior wives in his compound, and who would be in a position to observe and listen to his wives, would also give him (and his wives) advice as to how to peacefully settle the discord among them.

No doubt, the constant concern by African mothers for the welfare of their children *is* partly a response to the realities of polygamous marriages, but common wisdom might say that mothers everywhere are noted for "putting their children first." Yet, in nuclear families, where the husband-wife relationship holds the family together, women are often portrayed as being concerned first and foremost with protecting their statuses as wives, rather than as mothers with a concern first and foremost for securing rights and resources for their children. In fact, in the United States, it is not uncommon for mothers in nuclear families to be portrayed in literature, or reported in the press, as competing with their children for the attention, affection or favor of their husbands. They are also portrayed as taking the sides of their husbands against their children in various situations. Only when nuclear families are being terminated by divorce, and women no longer have the possibility of deriving power, prestige or resources through their positions as wives, are there reports of women waging "all out war" as mothers to secure rights and resources for their children. Even so, in divorce settlements, what the woman herself receives is based on her claims as the former wife, rather than her claims as the mother of her ex-husband's children. The latter constitute a separate claim altogether.

This contrast between the way mothers are viewed, and view themselves and their children in African conjugal families as opposed to Western nuclear families stems from the differential power attached to the roles of wife and mother in the two family structures. *Whatever power a woman has within the nuclear family derives mainly from her position as wife.* In the ideal situation, she is an equal partner with her husband at the core of the family, but even where she is treated as subordinate to her husband, she still derives status in the eyes of her family as well as in the outside world, from her position as "the wife of So and So." *Motherhood,* particularly in the early years, does not confer on her the special power and influence that attaches to motherhood in Africa. In fact, in nuclear families, women sometimes are reported as resenting the onset of motherhood because it "ties them down" with children, and limits their ability to function socially as wives to their husbands. Such a view would be almost unthinkable in African families.

Of course, in African conjugal families, a wife also derives some power and influence in the outside world from the position of her husband. However, because her conjugal family exists within the umbrella of the extended family, a wife realizes that her husband is subject to the influence of his lineage, his mother, and his other wives. Hence, unless she is the senior wife, a woman can only expect to have limited power or influence, *based on her position as "wife"*. Even the influence of a senior wife or a favorite wife is constrained by the influence of their husband's lineage and that of their mother-in-law. As previously discussed, a wife's chances of increasing her power and influence within the conjugal family are enhanced by motherhood, and particularly by the example she sets in carrying out her role as mother.

Another contrast between women as mothers in Western nuclear families and those in African conjugal families has to do with the expectations in regard to their roles as providers in these two different family contexts. From my researches, I would suggest that whereas traditionally, motherhood encouraged women to become more economically *independent* in African conjugal and extended families, motherhood may encourage some women to become more economically *dependent* in Western nuclear family settings.

As has been noted for women throughout indigenous Africa, in both monogamous and polygamous households, motherhood not only confers prestige, it creates the responsibility to bear a major share of the cost of bringing up one's children. (Sudarkasa, 1973; Hafkin & Bay, 1976; Pala-Okeyo, 1976; Amadiume, 1987; Mikell, 1989; 1997)

In indigenous West African conjugal families, husbands and wives normally keep "separate purses." As a rule, they do not co-mingle their incomes; they do not have joint accounts, and they make separate contributions to the expenses associated with their family. Husbands and wives have their own occupations or businesses, which they usually manage independent of each other. This is a way of minimizing economic risks in situations where spouses have limited capital to invest in their small scale commercial or agricultural enterprises. But this pattern also exists in middle class, wage-earning households, suggesting that over time a cultural pattern has developed where women as wives and mothers value their right to accumulate, manage and allocate their own resources, just as men do theirs. (Sudarkasa, 1973; 1981b; Sims, 1981; Amadiume, 1987; Mikell, 1989).

Undoubtedly, this is partly a function of the fact that lineages are keystones in the social structure, and each spouse is expected to take on certain responsibilities associated with their respective lineages without encumbering the resources of the other. As wives, mothers, daughters, and sisters, women have economic obligations that are independent of their husbands and they take pride in their ability to earn the monies to meet these responsibilities. Most of all, mothers want to be in an economic position "to do their utmost" for their children. And they often assume most of the responsibility for their children's day to day expenses, especially in their early years.

In nuclear families, as I suggested above, motherhood often makes a woman more economically dependent on her husband, especially in the early years. If she had not been employed before the birth of her first child, a mother might choose not to enter the labor force at all while her children are pre-school age. The decision as to whether a working wife will continue to work after she has a child usually depends on whether the formerly two-income household can be supported on her husband's income alone. In the US, the ideal that the husband should be the sole breadwinner is still sufficiently entrenched in the nuclear family ideology that both the husband and wife might be encouraged to "get along" on the husband's income, rather than have a new mother "go out and get a job" or continue in a job after her child is born.

In contrast to preferences within African conjugal families, nuclear families do not emphasize a need for wives to seek to become as economically independent, or self-reliant, as possible. In fact, even if wives do work outside the home, joint accounts and joint management of the family purse are promoted as "best practices" within the nuclear family. This ideology also means that a wife does not have to have an income in order to feel that she is joint owner of the resources generated by her husband. In fact, what might be characterized as a wife's dependence on her husband, from the perspective of the African conjugal family, would be characterized as their *co-dependence* on each other, from the nuclear family perspective. Indeed, over the past few decades when Western feminism has stressed the economic value of women's work inside the home, their contribution to the household may be seen as having equal or nearly equal value as that of their husbands whose contributions come from earnings outside the home.

This section of the paper opened with the observation that *motherhood enhances the status of wives in African family and community contexts.* Based on my researches among the Yoruba, I would add that *the longer a mother lives, the more her status as mother literally overshadows her status as wife.*

Of course, this speaks, in part, to the importance of seniority in Yoruba society, a fact which a number of scholars have noted, but which has been given new prominence through the work of Oyeronke Oyewumi (1996). (See also Fadipe ,1936, 1970; Bascom, 1942, 1951; Marshall, 1970; Sudarkasa, 1973, 1987). Among the Yoruba, as a mother ages, she becomes an Elder- Mother or Mother- Elder (*Iya Agba*). Within her husband's compound and extended family where she resides, an *Iya Agba* is one of the seniormost wives, but more importantly, she is one of the seniormost *mothers* of the adult men and women of the lineage. Progressively, her status as a mother has overtaken and encompassed her status as wife.

In Western nuclear families as a woman grows old, her status as a *wife* is usually enhanced, especially as long as her husband is alive. The husband and wife relish "growing old together", oftentimes far away from their children. Visits from their children and grandchildren on holidays are considered adequate and appropriate. As *mothers*, elderly women from nuclear families often suffer in their old age because they are left on their own by their children. If elderly mothers cannot live out their days in their own homes with their husbands, or by themselves as widows, they usually end up in nursing homes or other assisted living situations. If an adult child visits his or her mother in a nursing home on a daily basis, that is considered a great accomplishment, and a show of utmost caring and concern. (A similar point can be made with respect to the lives of elderly fathers).

In African extended families, elderly mothers are cared for by at least one of their children and some of their grandchildren. They are usually either in the compound where they have lived since marriage or in the home of one of their children. Occasionally, elderly mothers might have returned to their natal compounds where their own lineage resides. But wherever they are, these *Iya Agba* are expected to live out their days among their children, grandchildren or other relatives.

Of course, in some families in Western countries, the same is still true as well. Nevertheless, in the West, care for the elderly in institutions outside the home has greatly expanded in the twentieth century in response to changing residential patterns, changing demographics, changing approaches to health care, and changing values regarding family obligations to aging parents and grandparents.

4.
"Real mothers" and "half siblings": Some contrasts in conceptions of motherhood in nuclear and extended family traditions

One area that deserves to be explored in the comparative study of motherhood has to do with distinctions made between motherhood resulting from childbirth and motherhood resulting from the adoption or acceptance of children who are reared "as one's own." In the United States, I have always been struck by the popular distinction between a person's "real" mother and his or her adoptive mother. And it is still not uncommon to hear persons being asked: "Is that your *real* mother?" Although in some circles, the term "real mother" has been replaced by the more professionally acceptable term "birth mother," the emphasis still implies that the "birth mother" is the "real mother," regardless of the quality of the relationship between a person and his or her "adoptive mother." Interestingly, this distinction between "real" mothers and other mothers that is a part of the nuclear family tradition in the United States, is a distinction rarely made in the parts of West Africa with which I am familiar.

Similarly, one rarely if ever hears a West African mother being asked: "Is that your *own* child?" These two questions, which implicitly extol the biological link between mother and child, are inappropriate in the context of extended families where many children are brought up for at least part of their lives by women other than their biological mothers. In some circumstances, such as when a woman has never given birth to children, it would be embarrassing, hurtful and insensitive to ask if the children she is rearing are her "own" children. Similarly, to ask a person whether a woman is his or her "real" mother, could raise a number of issues that would be considered an invasion of privacy by both the person queried and the woman who is the mother "in deed", if not the biological mother "in fact." This does not mean that such topics cannot be discussed, but the reasons for doing so and the way in which they could be raised are different than in nuclear family contexts, where people matter-of-factly define and discuss "real" mothers and women's "own" children, as if biology alone confers that status.

Just as there are differences in the ways nuclear families and extended families conceptualize motherhood, so too are there differences in the way children of the same mother are categorized in relation to one another. The nuclear family-derived kinship terminology in the United States, for example, divide children of the same mother by reference to their fathers. Children by the same mother but different fathers, are referred to as "half-brothers," or "half-sisters", concepts which are intended to describe precisely the biological relationship of the children concerned. This terminology has gained widespread usage today when "blended families", based on divorce and re-marriage, are increasingly common. Interestingly, Americans also insist on using this terminology in speaking of people from other cultures where the concept of "half" siblings is not a part of normal usage. Americans tend to think of kinship as a strictly biological phenomenon, rather than recognizing the overriding importance of culture in defining kinship relationships. African Americans are one group in the United States who do not normally use the terms "half-brothers or half- sisters" in describing their siblings, particularly when they are born of the same mother, a reflection of the persistent matri-centric emphasis in African American kinship over the centuries.

In African kinship terminologies, which reflect the realities related to extended families and lineage systems, the terms "half-brother" and "half-sister" are not a part of the indigenous usage, even when referring to siblings who share only one parent in common. With respect to the relative importance of motherhood or fatherhood in distinguishing among siblings, it should be noted that the lineage principle determines the way children who share one parent are characterized vis-à-vis each other. In matrilineal societies, where descent is traced through the motherline, a woman's children belong to her lineage, regardless of who their fathers happen to be. In matrilineal societies, children of one mother are not considered to be "partible" in the same way that a mother's children by different fathers would be in patrilineal societies. In those societies, children of the same mother but different fathers belong to different patrilineages and the sociological, legalistic and biological (or presumed biological) links to the father and his descent group are considered more important than the biological link to the mother in determining a person's identity.

The contrasts between the way a mother's relationship to her children are conceptualized according to nuclear family and extended family ideologies show that the nuclear family ideology places the greater emphasis on biology in matters of kinship. This greater focus on biology is indicated, in part, by the use of concepts such as "real mothers" and "half-siblings." In seeking an explanation for the greater emphasis on biology in Western conceptions of kinship, I was reminded of Oyeronke Oyewumi's discussion of what she terms the "somatocentricity" in Western culture. She makes a compelling case for the centrality of biological explanations and emphases throughout Western Culture (Oyewumi, 1996, esp., pp. 1-17). Many of the points made in this paper, provide evidence of this somatocentricity in the ideology and behavior associated with nuclear families.

5.
The differing relationship of "marital stability" to "family stability" in nuclear and extended families

Up to this point in discussing motherhood in nuclear and extended families, the paper has focused on formative and on-going family relationships, without reference to the break-up or break-down of these relationships. Yet, we know that the severance of family relationships, as much as the establishment and maintenance of these relationships, is a regular part of family histories and domestic cycles. This is particularly the case with marital relationships based *in law*, in as much as these are relatively easily severed *by law*. In the remaining section of this paper, I want to briefly comment on the dissolution of marriage and its implications for motherhood in nuclear and extended family systems.

In nuclear families, marital stability and family stability are regarded as one and the same. When a marriage is dissolved, families are considered to be "broken," and children of divorced parents are often characterized as children of "broken homes." When a legal divorce occurs, the ties between mothers (and fathers) and their dependent children are affected by the terms of the divorce as decided in a court of law. For most of the twentieth century, the courts favored awarding custody of minor children to their mothers, with terms of support and visitation by the fathers also being stipulated in the divorce decree. The dissolution of the marriage relationship also officially dissolves all affinal ties between a woman and her former husband's family, even though some of those affinal relationships (such as between former mothers- and daughters-in-law) might be informally maintained, especially "for the sake of the children."

Until recently, in nuclear families in America (and perhaps elsewhere), the ties linking parents to their children have been presumed to be life-long ties. In the United States, in the past one or two decades, however, *children have been allowed to "divorce" their parents* in courts of law. In keeping with nuclear family ideology, the family is not dissolved as a result of a parent-child divorce, as it would be in the case a divorce between the parents. In fact, ironically, the nuclear family might be seen as having been strengthened by the divorce action initiated by a child because it might have "brought the parents [and their other children] closer together." The point is, the marital bond between a husband and wife is that which keeps the nuclear family together, and it does not officially "break-up" unless that bond is severed.

In African extended families, the ties around which the family is built are lineage ties based on descent, and these are presumed to be unbreakable. This has important implications for what happens when there is a dissolution of a marriage within one of the conjugal families that make up the extended family. It also has implications for the relationship between divorced hus-bands and wives. In a patrilineal situation, it has special implications for the continuing affinal relationships between a mother and the lineage and compound (i.e. the extended family) of her children and their father.

To anticipate the main point here: in African extended families, because of the continuity provided by the lineage, *marital stability and family stability are not one and the same.* Family stability rests upon the lineal descent ties which , as previously noted, are presumed to exist in perpetuity. A divorce cannot break these ties, and when divorce occurs, the marriage is broken, but the family is not. The conjugal family to which a divorced wife previously belonged remains a part of the compound. When the marriage was polygamous, the family continues with little disruption. If the marriage was monogamous, the man takes another wife as soon as possible. The family continues, and there is no sense of "a broken home."

In patrilineal societies such as the Yoruba, when a divorce occurs, older children continue to reside in their father's compound, while younger ones would most likely remain with their mothers until they are considered old enough to return to their fathers. In the compound, the children will be cared for by the father's mother, one of his other wives, a brother's wife, or another woman in the compound. (An entirely different set of actions would probably occur when the marriage is across cultural or interna-tional lines, and especially when the departing wife comes from a Western nuclear family tradition.)

Some of the most important aspects of extended family organization are revealed by studying what happens after divorce. Again, referring to patrilineal societies, the extended family ideology emphasizes that the ties between a man and the mother of his children can never be broken. Thus, even though a man and woman may sever their conjugal ties as husband and wife, they have continuing ties as parents of their children.

In the case of the Yoruba, this is most clearly demonstrated by the ties a mother maintains with the patrilineage, compound and extended family of her children, which, of course, are also those of her former husband. These ties will be less visible when the mother remarries, but they may still be manifest. Unless her separation from the compound has been under very acrimonious circumstances, at important ceremonials, such as weddings or funerals, a mother (and former wife) will usually return to her former husband's compound to "do her part" on behalf of her children. This underscores the importance of distinguishing a woman's conjugal role as wife, from her affinal role as wife within the compound and extended family of her husband and children. In other words, motherhood compelled (and compels) a Yoruba woman to continue some of her affinal duties as wife (i.e. duties to those whom Westerners would describe as her *former* in-laws) even after her conjugal role as wife had been terminated

CONCLUSION

The spread of nuclear family structures and ideology from Europe and America to other parts of the world is having an impact on extended family ethos and organization in Africa and elsewhere. With the accelerated spread of Christianity and Western education, the nuclear family has been promoted as the type of family structure that conforms to the "will of God," is most compatible with modernization, and advances economic and social development. By the end of the twentieth century, as a result of the global impact of the West through the visual media, especially through television, most of the world had been exposed to programming that promoted the nuclear family ideal.

How much the spread of the nuclear family ideology has affected the world is indicated by the fact that heads of state, heads of government, diplomats and other senior officials from nations and cultures all around the globe choose to put "*a nuclear family face*" on their domestic arrangements whenever they are in public, particularly when they are functioning in the international arena. In the nineteenth and early twentieth centuries, monarchs from non-Western countries could be seen in public or in pictures with multiple wives and many children. Today, if one observes social activities at the highest international levels, it would appear that all men and women are married monogamously, and living in nuclear families.

Among Western educated African women, the nuclear family is reported to be particularly appealing because the ideology of "one man, one wife," with its commitment to the conjugal family over the extended family, is seen as a vehicle for liberating women and modernizing their societies. Several studies describe the increasing tensions between conjugal families aspiring toward the more closed, inwardly-focused nuclear family model, on the one hand, and the traditional "demands" of extended families on the other. Various scholars are also studying the changing laws that lend greater support for the rights of women as wives and mothers within their conjugal families. Not surprisingly, when studies examine the tensions between conjugal and extended families, and the call for stronger protection of women in their conjugal families, they mainly describe aspirations and complaints of *women as wives,* who desire more "freedom" from the "interference" of their in-laws in matters affecting their conjugal families. It should be noted, however, that African women's desire for change in the direction of nuclear families stem from the fact that they see in these structures benefits for their children as well as themselves. In particular, women are said to want more exclusive access to their husbands' resources during their marriage; and more protection for themselves and their children in cases of separation or divorce. They also want to lower the incidence of polygamous marriages and "outside wives." (Oppong, 1974, Sudarkasa, 1983, McAdoo & Were, 1987, Mikell, 1997; Toungara, 1997, & Manuh, 1997).

No doubt, other sides of the picture will emerge from research that considers other questions concerning the impact of changes in the direction of nuclear families. For example, when African women in both patrilineal and matrilineal systems are asked to consider the impact of such changes on older mothers, and on women in their roles as sisters and daughters, we may expect to see different perspectives on the reciprocal responsibilities associated with extended family membership. Moreover, when advocates of change in the direction of nuclear families are asked to look closely at the documented realities of nuclear family systems, as opposed to the idealistic portrayals which usually serve as the basis for comparative analyses, they will find much to discuss and debate concerning the advantages and disadvantages of this type of family structure. In the policy arena, we can predict that the increasing demands for public assistance to care for the elderly and infirm, the needy and neglected, and others suffering from poverty and deprivation, will prompt many to think about ways in which the extended family can be adapted to meet some of these social services needs.

Parenthetically, it must be remembered that some of the most profound changes affecting families in Africa and other parts of the world are resulting from the scourge of the HIV-AIDS pandemic. Although a discussion of this phenomenon is beyond the scope of this paper, we know that conjecture about future changes in motherhood and other aspects of family organization in Africa (and elsewhere) must allow for the unforeseen demands that this disease and related health challenges will impose on these families. We already see a blurring of the distinction between generations of mothers and grandmothers, as other older women assume more and more responsibility for young children in their families and communities. We can expect that far into the future the AIDS pandemic will compel communities to find ways of adapting their indigenous family structures to the requirements of this relentless scourge. How motherhood will emerge from the decimation left in the wake of this disease is bound to be a major aspect of future research on the topics under discussion here.

In the United States, we see that mother-centered single parent and sole parent family units are taking the lead in intentionally creating new types of residential, familial, and friendship networks that take on some of the responsibilities for assisting with childrearing and other functions of the traditional extended families. These networks signal the fact that mothers do not hold out the unrealistic expectation that two-parent, "in tact" nuclear families will reemerge as the predominant type of household in the United States. (Sudarkasa, 1993). No doubt, research on these emerging mother-centered families and networks represent one of the new frontiers for research on motherhood.

References

Aldous, J. (1965). Urbanization, the Extended Family and Kinship Ties in West Africa. In Pierre Van den Bergbe (Ed.) *Africa: Social Problems of Change and Conflict*. San Francisco: Chandler Publishing.

Amadiume, I. (1987). *Male Daughters, Female Husbands: Gender and Sex in an African Society*. London and New Jersey: Zed Books Ltd.

Bascom, W. R. (1942). The Principle of Seniority in the Social Structure of the Yoruba. *American Anthropologist*, 44(1), 37-46

_____. (1957). Social Status, Wealth and Individual Differences among the Yoruba *American Anthropologist*, 53 (4), 490-506.

Colson, E (1936). Family Change in Contemporary Africa. In *Annals of the New York Academy of Sciences* 92, (2), 641-652 (cited from *Black Africa*, John Middleton (Ed.) New York: The Macmillan.

Fadipe, N.A. (1990). *The Sociology of the Yoruba*. F.O. Okediji and O.O. Okediji (Ed.) Ibadan: Ibadan University Press, 1970 (originally written in 1936)

Fortes, M. (1949). *The Web of Kinship Among the Tallensi.* Oxford: Oxford University Press.

_____. (1959). Kinship and Marriage among the Ashanti. In A.R. Radcliffe-Brown & D. Forde (Eds.) *African Systems of Kinship and Marriage,* Oxford: Oxford University Press.

_____. (1953). The Structure of Unilineal Descent Groups. *American Anthropologist,* 55 (1), 17-41.

Goody, J. (1976). *Production and Reproduction: A Comparative Study of the Domestic Domain.* Cambridge: Cambridge University Press.

Hafkin, N. J. & E. G. Bay (Eds) (1976). *Women in Africa.* Stanford: Stanford University Press.

Linton, R. (1936). *The Study of Man.* New York: Appleton-Century, 1936.

Lloyd, P.C. (1955). The Yoruba Lineage. *Africa,* 25(3), 235-251.

Manuh, T. (1997). Wives, Children and Intestate Succession in Ghana. In G. Mikell (Ed.) *African Feminism: The Politics of Survival in Sub-Saharan Africa.* (pp.77-95) Philadelphia: University of Pennsylvania Press.

Marshall, G. A. [Niara Sudarkasa]. *Women, Trade, and the Yoruba Family.* [Ph.D. Dissertation] New York: Columbia University

_____. (1968). Marriage: Comparative Analysis. In *International Encyclopedia of the Social Sciences,* New York: Macmillan Co./The Free Press.

_____. (1970). In a World of Women: Field Work in a Yoruba Community. In P. Golde (Ed.) *Women in the Field: Anthropological Experiences,* (pp.165-191) Chicago: Aldine Publishing Co (Reprinted in Sudarkasa ,1996)

McAdoo, H. P. (Ed.) (1993). *Family Ethnicity: Strength in Diversity.* Newbury Park, California: Sage Publications, Inc.

Mikell, G. (1989). *Cocoa and Chaos in Ghana.* New York: Paragon House. 1989.

_____., (1997). *African Feminism: The Politics of Survival in Sub-Saharan Africa.* Philadelphia: University of Pennsylvania Press. 1997.

_____. (1997). Pleas for Domestic Relief: Akan Women and Family Courts. In G. Mikell (Ed.) *African Feminism: The Politics of Survival in Sub-Saharan Africa* (pp. 96-123). Philadelphia: University of Pennsylvania.

Morgan, L. H. (1997). *Systems of Consanguinity and Affinity of the Human Family.* Lincoln, Nebraska: University of Nebraska Press. (Orig. pub. 1870).

Murdock, G. P. (1949). *Social Structure.* New York: The Macmillan.

Oyewumi, O. (1997). *The Invention of Women: Making an African Sense of Western Gender Discourses.* Minneapolis and London: University of Minnesota Press.

Pala-Okeyo, A. (1976). *African Women in Rural Development.* Washington, DC: Overseas Liaison Committee, American Council on Education.

_____. (1997). Gender and Democracy: The Unfinished Agenda. In *Report of the Third International Conference of the New or Restored Democracies* (ICNRD), United Nations.

Rivers, W.H.R. (1924). *Social Organization.* New York: Alfred A. Knopf.

Schwab, W. B. (1955) Kinship and Lineage Among the Yoruba. *Africa,* 25 (4), 352-374.

Shimkin, D., E.M. Shimkine & D.A. Frake, (Eds.) (1978). *The Extended Family in Black Societies.* The Hague: Mouton Publishing.

Shimkin, D. & V. Uchendu. (1978). Persistence, Borrowing, and Adaptive Changes in Black Kinship Systems: Some Issues and Their Significance. In D. Shimkin, et.al. (Eds.) *The Extended Family in Black Societies.* The Hague: Mouton Publishing.

Shorter, E. (1975). *The Making of the Modern Family.* New York: Basic Books.

Sims, R. (1981). The African Woman as Entrepreneur: Problems and Perspectives on their Roles. In F. C. Steady (Eds.) *The Black Woman Cross-Culturally* Cambridge, Mass: Schenkman Publishing Co.

Stone, L. (1975). The Rise of the Nuclear Family in Early Modern England: The Patriarchal Stage. In C.E. Rosenberg (Ed.) *The Family in History* (pp. 13-57). Philadelphia: University of Pennsylvania Press.

Sudarkasa, N. (1973). *Where Women Work: A Study of Yoruba Women in the Marketplace and in the Home.* Anthropological Papers, No. 53. Ann Arbor: University of Michigan Museum of Anthropology.

_____. (1996). *The Strength of Our Mothers. African & African American Women and Families: Essays and Speeches.* Trenton, NJ: Africa World Press.

_____. (1980). African and Afro-American Family Structure. *The Black Scholar,* 12 (2), 37-60. (Reprinted in J. B. Cole (Eds.) *Anthropology for the Eighties [and Nineties], New* York: The Free Press, 1982 and 1991; also in Sudarkasa, 1996)

_____. (1981a). Interpreting the African Heritage in Afro-American Family Organization In H. P. McAdoo (Ed.) *Black Families,* (pp.37-53) Beverly Hills, California: Sage Publishing Co. (Reprinted in Sudarkasa, 1996).

_____. (1981b). Female Employment and Family Organization in West Africa. In F. C. Steady (Ed.) *The Black Woman Cross-Culturally,* (pp.49-63) Cambridge, Mass: Schenkman Publishing Co. Inc. (Reprinted in Sudarkasa, 1996).

_____. (1986). The 'Status of Women' in Indigenous African Societies. First version in *Feminist Studies,* 12 (1), 91-103, expanded version in T. Terborg-Penn (Ed.) *Women in Africa and the African Diaspora.* Washington, D.C: Howard University Press (Reprinted in Sudarkasa, 1996).

_____. (1993). Female-Headed African American Households: Some Neglected Dimensions. In H. P. McAdoo (Ed.) *Family Ethnicity: Strength in Diversity,* (pp. 81-89). Newbury Park, California: Sage Publications, Inc. (Reprinted in Sudarkasa, 1996).

_____. (1995). African American Families and Family Values. In H. P. McAdoo (Eds.) *Black Families,* 3rd Edition, Newbury Park, California: Sage Publications, Inc., 1995.(Cited from Sudarkasa, 1996, pp.41-74)

_____. (2000). Towards More Equitable Participation of Women and Youth in Democracy and Development. Presented to the United Nations Fourth International Conference of New or Restored Democracies, Cotonou, Republic of Benin, Dec.

Tetteh, P.A. (1966) Marriage, Family and Household. In W. B. Birmingham, et. al. (Eds.) *A Study of Contemporary Ghana*, London: Allen & Unwin (also Evanston: Northwestern University Press, 1966).

Tilly, L. & J. W. Scott. (1978.) *Women, Work, and Family.* New York: Holt, Rinehart & Winston.

Toungara, J. M. (1997). Changing the Meaning of Marriage: Women and Family Law in Cote d'Ivoire. In G. Mikell (Ed.) *African Feminism: The Politics of Survival in Sub-Saharan Africa* (pp. 53-76). Philadelphia: University of Pennsylvania Press.

UNIFEM Biennial Report. (2000). *Progress of the World's Women 2000.* New York: United Nations Development Fund for Women.

Ware, H. (1979). Polygyny: Women's Views in a Transitional Society, Nigeria 1973. In *Journal of Marriage and the Family*, 41 (1),183-195.

CHAPTER 3

A TIME OF TRANSITION: CONTEMPORARY EXTENDED FAMILY NETWORKS IN GHANA

Osei-Mensah Aborampah

INTRODUCTION

Among the most significant influences in a person's life is the family, which is the basic unit of human social organization. The family of the past influenced decisions people made. Certainly, it continues to do so in the present and Ghanaian families are no exception to this pervasive conditioning effect. Like other peoples of the world, the behavior of Ghanaians have been influenced by families through their intersection with the lineages of which they constitute a segment, as well as their intersection with other social institutions. The family is charged with not only the responsibility of bearing and begetting the next generation, but also sponsoring its members into productive adulthood.

Prior to Ghana's encounter with Europe, the task of nurturing, training and sponsorship in various communities occurred within the context of the lineage and extended family, as well as specialized institutions. A system of kinship prescribed what kin group members of the immediate family belonged. It prescribed the general linkages between one member of a kin group and the rest of the community. Extended families were created as a result of alliances between different kin groups through marriage. Extended families not only provided a sense of identity, but also cultural capital of ideas, concepts and general knowledge for personal enrichment and fulfillment. Even though the role of the extended family in the lives of

Ghanaians has undergone profound changes, its pervasive influence is still apparent. Indeed, extended families in Ghana have been pivotal in ensuring the economic stability and psychological well-being of their members.

Members continue to assemble and act as a corporate group in at least, two of life's most crucial events—in marriage and in death. Those driven by a sense of obligation and sincere concern for the welfare of extended family members continue to support needy members in any way they can. Thus emerging middle class families continue to participate in their extended family networks, partly as a result of the continuing ravages of poverty afflicting the majority of Ghanaians, and partly because of the rapid changes taking place in the country. In this essay, I examine contemporary Ghanaian extended family networks, focusing on the matrilineal Akan of Ghana. First, I provide a historical overview of the structure and functioning of Akan matrilineages. Second, I present diagrammatically the structure of my own Akan matrilineage and describe the day-to-day functioning of a segment of this lineage. The data for this section of the chapter forms part of a broad project to collect kinship information from my elders. All in all, kinship links formed the basis of daily interactions and for the expansion or contraction of the maximal matrilineage, besides the vital events of birth, death and migration. Third, I report a portion of a study conducted by a colleague and the present author on intergenerational cultural transmission among the Akan of Ghana. The portion employed here focuses on youth perceptions about the viability of extended family networks in Ghana today. Finally, I discuss the impact of social changes that are taking place and suggest areas that appear to offer challenges and opportunities for further research about contemporary extended family networks in Ghana and elsewhere in Africa.

BRIEF LITERATURE REVIEW

The widely held view among social scientists is that the disappearance of traditional institutions like the extended family would be just a matter of time. According to this view, in the course of modernization, changes in socio-economic conditions may cause changes in a society's social organization in such a way as to render traditional institutions obsolete. For example, Addai-Sundiata (1996, p. 68) observes that changing family patterns in Ghana include "conjugal or nuclear family as the basic unit of residence and domestic functions, intense involvement of spouses, parents and children with each other within the nuclear family unit, and the development of egalitarian relations within the nuclear family." Addai-Sundiata reinforces these observations with a summary of Nukunya's delineation of similar changes deemed to be taking place within the Ghanaian family

(Addai-Sundiata, 1996, p. 69). The summary highlights the strengthening of marital bond at the expense of kinship bond, non-adherence to traditional kinship practices both in rural and urban settings, but especially in the latter, and the gradual breakdown of the sanctions sustaining kinship behavior.

Observations and assumptions about the demise of the extended family are derived from theoretical discussions presented by such earlier anthropologists and sociologists as George Murdock (1949), Talcott Parsons (1943, 1953), Louis Wirth (1938), Carl C. Zimmerman (1947), William J. Goode (1970), A. R. Radcliffe-Brown and Daryll Forde (1950), and Meyer Fortes (1949, 1963). The propositions articulated in the studies just cited can be summarized as follows:

- The development of the isolated nuclear family is a product of structural differentiation accompanying industrialization;
- Industrialization undermines the existence of the extended family as a result of a combination of factors, including physical mobility, social mobility, and erosion of family functions;
- The elementary or simple family is the most advanced form of family organization that is compatible with industrialized societies;
- The nuclear family is universal and;
- The nuclear family is the building block of all other family structures so that the extended family may be viewed as two or more nuclear families linked through the parent-child relationship.

The picture of a lineal progression from extended to nuclear families appears not to hold for a cross-section of developing societies as many studies have shown (Camilleri, 1967; Marsh & O'Hara, 1961; Skolnick 1973; Inkeles & Miller, 1974; Olsen, 1979; Morgan and Hirosima, 1983; Miller, 1984; Stokes, LeClere & Yeu, 1987; Ram & Wong, 1994). Concerning the necessity for paternity, one may argue that legitimate paternity in many African societies was/is not necessary for social placement. Certainly, paternity was not necessary for the social placement of children born in matrilineal societies. Additionally, bilateral affiliation was/is not universally necessary. African extended families served as a critical mechanism for social reproduction and continuity. Families were built around consanguineal core of relatives rather than around conjugal core of relatives (Sudarkasa, p. 1996). These social realities notwithstanding, the factors alleged to account for the disappearance of the extended family in Ghana, for example, are many. Industrialization, Western education, new faiths, and the construction of single family homes designed for conjugal life-styles have conjoined with other factors to produce the alleged changes. Mensa-Bonsu (1996, p. 233) points out that "as residence patterns change, and internal and international migration become a permanent feature, the weakness of a reliance on the extended family becomes manifest." She suggests that "the strengthening of the nuclear family holds a greater prospect of family survival and stability than the system represented by the extended family."

In order to appreciate the present dynamics of Ghanaian families, it is important to understand past family traditions that continue to show their influence today. The expected overall changes may not occur at the same rate as the changes that occur within other socio-economic institutions. As indicated earlier, a very powerful institution like the extended family may strengthen its position even more, over time, being reinforced not merely by religion and custom, but also by the ordinary day-to-day processes of living. In African rural settings, economic activities and childbearing practices are largely governed by what Caldwell (1982, p. 134-135) calls "family morality and theology." At least in the past, the individual was subordinated to the larger domestic unit and the moral person was one who thought in terms of the needs of the extended family. The standards by which an individual's activities were judged were cast in religious terms and the ancestors were the jealous guardians of the highest moral values. The task, then, is to ascertain the extent to which these socio-religious principles and values continue to exert their influences on Ghanaian families.

HISTORICAL OVERVIEW

The rule of matrilineal descent is the key to understanding the social organization of the Akan of Ghana. Akan people presently occupy the Ashanti, Brong Ahafo, Central, Eastern and Western regions of Ghana. Specific culture clusters of the Akan include groups like the Asante, Fante, Bono, Akyem, Akuapem, Asen, Denkyira, Twifo, and Wassa. Historically, the institutions of kinship, marriage and the family provided the collective mechanism for the societal and cultural continuity of Akan people. Kinship evolved through marriage and reproduction, and over time, individual family members established and recognized a variety of social relationships. Among the Akan of Ghana, a unilineal system of kinship and descent emerged out of the variety of ties of biological and social relationships that were recognized.

A person's line of descent was traced unilineally through females so that a woman, her brothers and sisters, as well as her sisters' sons and daughters belong in the woman's matrilineal kin group. Conceptually, this kin group included the living members, the dead members, and the unborn members. The living adults formed the core of blood or consanguine relatives around whom extended families were built.

Extended family members cooperated in social, cultural and ritual activities which helped a growing child to fulfill community expectations of his or her own social development. The extended family network made it possible for a child to be nurtured, trained and sponsored into adulthood. It is apparent from the presentation thus far that an underlying principle that guided Akan community life was cooperative effort. Collective responsibility and pro-socialization were articulated in their daily behaviors. Sanctions for breaches of family rules were perceived to disrupt the social order. Breaches of social relations were viewed to possess what Basil Davidson would call "spreading moral effects" (Davidson, 1969, p. 243), which could result in a misfortune to the wrongdoer, the wronged or the matrilineage. To this end, the socializing influence of the wider community was pervasive. The wider social context could influence socialization in the sense that child rearing practices were shaped and influenced by the beliefs and values widely held in the community or by the community consensus on how children ought to be treated. Sanctions for violations of community norms could be applied not only to the individual wrongdoer, but also to his/her entire family/lineage/clan.

Among the Akan, the prevailing political system was a centralized social structure, in which kings, chiefs, queens, and councils of elders managed a community's political, social and religious affairs. A web of kinship already described as matrilineal was spun in this system. It must be stressed that this web, along with the rites of passage as well as religious rules and restraints, constituted the machinery for maintaining social order. The efficacy of this machinery would seem to explain, in a large measure, the absence of standing armies and police forces in pre-colonial Africa. Additionally, and as Davidson points out, this complex web of kinship networks operated to prevent the development of small groups of landowners.

An Akan had a deep-rooted sense of belonging, loyalty and emotional attachment to his/her matrilineage. In practical terms, the matrilineage served as what Davidson (1969, p. 113) calls instruments of collective welfare. One of the measures of the strength of a matrilineage was its numbers. This partly explains the premium placed on the reproductive capacity of Akan women in the past, if not at present. Older men were known to be more polygynous than younger men and the former tended to marry younger women. The practice of polygyny, along with child spacing, helped women to realize high levels of fertility. The core group of blood relatives exercised authority over marital and reproductive decisions affecting members. In the past, for example, betrothal and preferential marriages were arranged by the lineage core. As a result of marriages with other lineage members, necessitated by the rule of exogamy and the incest taboo, as well as the need for kin group cohesion and solidarity, extended families became more complex than nuclear families. Economic and other forms of cooperative efforts allowed for the creation of a security system of mutual obligations. Thus the nuclear family became embedded in, and subordinate to, the extended family.

In terms of the processes of living, property was collectively owned by the matrilineage, not the nuclear family. As already pointed out, decision-making in many spheres of life rested with the lineage core, although its effectiveness depended on such factors as residential arrangements and availability of arable lineage land for subsistence agriculture. Where individual members migrated to establish farms elsewhere, the movement did not imply severance of membership in their matrilineage. Rather, the latter's core group continued to exercise its authority over such "migrant" family members. The historical analysis just presented can be illustrated with a schematic representation of the author's own matrlineage. The genealogical history was collected from my elders in the summers of 1993 and 1996, the fall of 1999, and the summers of 2001, 2005, and 2007. I have used numbers rather than names to conceal members' identity as promised.

The genealogical depth shown in Figure 3.1 is seven generations. In actual fact, the depth reported by the elders is nine generations. Only seven are represented in the diagram for purposes of this analysis. Members of the first six ascending generations saw themselves as one family and helped one another in good and in bad times. By definition and practice, descent was traced through the female line so that 1, 2, 3, 6 and 7 were the females in the first four ascending generations whose reproduction ensured the perpetuation of the matrilineage. In the fifth generation, 9, 13, and 17 were the "torch bearers," so to speak. This responsibility devolved on 20, 23, 26 and 29 in the sixth generation. Even though the reproduction of female members ensured the perpetuity of the lineage, the decision-making body included men and women. To illustrate with the fifth and sixth generations, members of the consanguineal core group included 9, 13, 17, 19, 20, 22, 23, 25, 26, 28, 29 and 31. In classificatory terminology, 9, 13 and 17 were "sisters" to one another, and collectively "mother" to all lineage members in the sixth generation. The illustrations provided thus far capture the essence of the "principle of consanguinity," for which emphasis is placed on blood relations.

Figure 3.1: Schematic Representation of an Akan Matrilineage

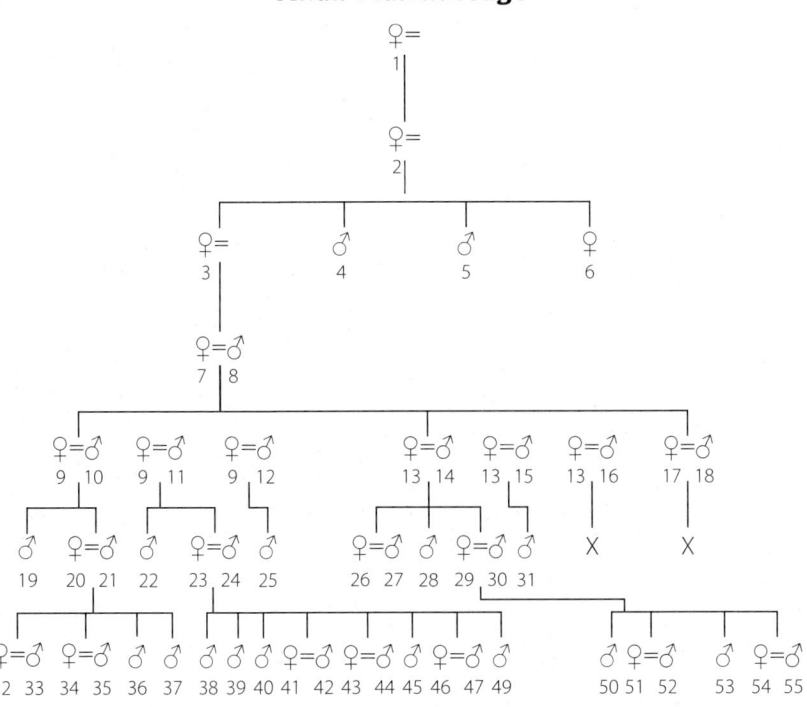

Key: ♀ = represents a female; ♂ = represents a male; X= represents no offspring

As Sudarkasa (1996) has suggested, it is important to diatinguish two contrasting basis for membership in African families if this institution is to be understood. First is the principle of consanguinity, just mentioned. This refers to kinship based on blood ties or a pattern of social norms that regulate the relationships that exist among people who descended from one another (parent-child) or who have real or fictive common descent (siblings). Second is the principle of conjugality, which refers to kinship based on marriage or a pattern of social norms that regulate the relationships between two individuals for whom a mating arrangement has been socially sanctioned. In different societies of the world, families tend to be built around a consanguineal core or a conjugal core. In either case, one tends to be subordinate to the other. As Sudarkasa observes, families in Europe clearly demonstrate the predominance of conjugality over consanguinity, certainly ever since the industrial revolution if not before.

On the other hand, consanguinity seems to have been the predominant form of family organization over time in Africa, certainly during and after the period of colonization. A. R. Radcliffe-Brown and his cohort of anthropologists who studied African kinship and family attest to this point. These two principles underlying kinship and family formation were widely accepted in the different societies in which they emerged as a result of the long history of social evolution, as well as the appearance of permanence and stability attached to them. In Africa, family formation involved marriages among different lineage members. As a result of such unions, extended family networks evolved. Thus, while lineages were based on descent, extended families were based on descent as well as marriage. The extended family produced by the marriage of 7 and 8 in Diagram 3.1 would include all the living members comprising numbers from 9 through 55.

As Sudarkasa explains, the extended family could be subdivided into two distinct entities: one formed by the consanguineal group, and the other, formed by the in-marrying group. Using the fifth generation as an example, numbers 9, 13, and 17 would form the consanguineal group and numbers 10, 11, 12, 14, 15, 16, and 18, the in-marrying group. For Akan societies, people lived in their compounds with their kinsmen and women. Spouses were not isolated in single family homes. They lived in their own lineage compounds or in those of their spouses. People depended on one another to utilize land, to produce, to distribute and to consume. Many spheres of interdependence were woven inextricably into the fabric of Akan societies. All relatives by marriage and those by blood constituted the proper focus of relations of enduring sorts.

THE STRUCTURE AND FUNCTIONING OF A MINIMAL MATRILINEAGE

In order to understand the structure and functioning of the selected minimal matrilineage, it is important to make distinctions between the concepts of "family," "household," and "extended family." For example, in Diagram 3.1, the domestic group identified by numbers 20, 21, 32, 34, 36, and 37 constituted a *nuclear family* in the sense that it was made up of husband, wife and children and all were co-resident in one compound, although they formed part of a larger group. As the children became adults, 34 moved to reside in the house of 19, the rest of the children married, continued to reside in the compound (family home of orientation), but prepared their meals separately. In effect, four separate *households* evolved at this point but their members continued to reside in the same dwelling unit. Thus the households consisted of all persons who occupied a common dwelling and shared a common food supply. While the wives of 36 and 37 joined them, the husband of 32 lived in his own compound with other members of his own matrilineage. The latter relationship constituted a visiting union, but of a legal sort.

When we isolate 9, 19, 20, 22, 23, 25 plus the children of 20 and 23, we have what might be considered a *minimal* matrlineage. Notice that the spouses are not included. Again, the latter constitute the *affinal* or *in-marrying* group. The living members of the affinal group together with the living members of the minimal matrilineage constitute a non-co-resident extended family. A few more extended families can be identified in Diagram 3.1. One is formed by two classificatory sisters, 34 and 51, who presently reside in the family compound of 19 (now deceased), with their children and grandchildren. Another one was formed by 32 who lived alone with her grandchildren until she passed away. Her children have matured into adults, living with their husbands or separately in their own homes. However, her grandchildren were fostered into her care and they shifted back and forth between their parental and grand-parental homes. Prior to the death of 32, her family structure represented one that would be described as *matrifocal*. This concept will be explained in a later section.

After the spouses of 9 and 13 died, both moved into the base compound of 19. Later, 34 and 40 were fostered to the care of 9 who resided together with 13 in the home of 19, as just indicated. When 34 married and produced children, the domestic group became a four-generational extended family structure. Reciprocal assistance was provided among all members of this extended family. Indeed, 34, 40, and other siblings often provided their labor for the work on the farms of 9, 13, and 19. Reciprocally, 34 and 40 ate from the bowls of 9 and 13. However, decisions affecting the welfare of the matrilineage were made by the lineage core, that is, the consanguineal group, consisting of 9, 13, 19, 23, 25, and 31, as recalled by this author.

A single man married to several women, each maintaining a separate household, would constitute another type of family. This structure is what anthropologists have labeled as a *polygynous* family unit. A typical African polygynous compound may be considered as a single family, but may consist of different households. The latter is delineated by the "uncommonness" of the food supply within the single dwelling unit. For example, 50 currently is married to two women who are not represented in the diagram. Each woman maintains a separate household , but all reside in the same compound. Again, reciprocal assistance is provided among all members of this domestic unit. An analytical problem discernible from the structures described thus far is that if a list of members within the households and family units were to be drawn, they may or may not coincide. This is because of the multiple and shifting household memberships often created by the practice of fosterage or informal adoption, which is characteristic of Ghanaian families, including the Akan.

As Fortes (1949, p. 63) has described in relation to the Asante of Ghana (a matrilineal group), "not only do the dwelling groups (*fie*) vary in composition at any given time, but their membership fluctuates from month to month as people move to and fro from farming and trade." The extent of residential flux may be illustrated with examples from Diagram 3.1. As already pointed out, 34 and 40 were fostered to 9. Prior to that, 40 was informally adopted by 25. It was after the latter died that 40 was fostered to 9. In another instance, when 20 died, 36 and 37, then still young, were fostered to the care of 23. It must be pointed out that aside from events like death triggering the movement of members from one household to another, "a person has a moral, if not legal, right to stay and/or sleep in the house of any member of his/her matrilineage." (Fortes, 1949, p. 70). Those who do so would be counted as full members of their "new" households. If there are multiple spouses within the single dwelling unit, common food supply or pooling of resources for common support would not be the norm, yet food and assistance would be freely given and received among members in those separate households.

Today, all the male members of the seventh generation of the matrilineage represented in Diagram 3.1 occupy separate households with their spouses and children. A few of the women either live with their husbands or live alone with their children. The base household of 19 for example, is now occupied by 34, 51 and their children, as indicated earlier. As in the past, whatever mutual aid system that prevails among members of this dwelling unit "is an obligation of kinship, not as part of domestic social organization." (Fortes, 1949, p. 64).

Concerning the day-to-day functioning of a matrilineage, the essence of mutual aid comes alive in times of the greatest stress like death or marital disruption when members become actively involved in the mortuary and traditional marriage rituals. In general, the roles of the heads of a matrilineage are pivotal in ensuring members' economic well-being and psychological health. As Fortes (1949, p. 255-257) has described for the Asante,

> The lineage head watches over the welfare of the group, settles disputes among members, organizes lineage events [like funerals], receives bridewealth for a marrying female member, and serves as the custodian of the male ancestral stools The male lineage head has a female counterpart (obaapanin). She watches over the morals of the women and girls, supervises such feminine matters as puberty rituals, helps in settling family disputes, and preserves consecrated stools of family queenmothers. The female head is often the best genealogical authority and this gives her considerable authority within the matrilineage.

During the celebration of an annual festival in the area where my research was conducted, members of the matrilineage in Diagram 3.1 assembled in the base household of 19 to give thanks to God and their ancestors for the year's good health and bountiful farm produce. The pouring of libation and sharing of food constituted key moments in the period of the festivities. The occasion also provided an opportunity for family members who resided elsewhere in the country and abroad to visit folks at home, exchange gifts as well as gossip. In the spirit of lineage solidarity, the festival provided members a convenient means to resolve outstanding disputes.

A child growing up in any of the larger family units could be influenced by several role types: uncles, grandmothers, step or surrogate mothers, etc. The child is likely to come in (daily) contact with relatives who may stand to him/her as substitutes for parents, or as brothers and sisters. The interaction enables the child to imbibe the collective values of the group --- obedience, respect, generosity, responsibility, etc. Collective socialization is the process through which the child learns the language of the ethnic group to which s/he belongs, and incorporates the attitudes and behaviors considered appropriate by the group. This type of traditional education is often criticized for stifling individualism and creativity. The critical point ignored in such discussions is that extended family socialization, at least in the past, operates to conceal invidious competition and self-assertion. Instead of competition, the extended family or kin group provides a growing child with scope for his/her deepest interests and ambitions to be realized. The larger group makes it possible for some members to acquire the training and skills necessary for adult life. This point may be elaborated with extended family involvement in formal education.

EXTENDED FAMILY INVOLVEMENT IN EDUCATION

The key to occupational mobility during the colonial period and the decades following political independence, was education. Consequently, this powerful incentive induced many extended families in Ghana to sponsor members to seek higher education both at home and abroad. In several cases that I am aware of, lineage heads, in consultation with other significant members, selected talented individuals for formal education in missionary schools. The first few generations of educated family members in many parts of the country received education through lineage/extended family resources. Those lineages that understood the potential returns on the investment in their members' education took advantage of the situation. Over the years, especially since Ghana's political independence, the responsibility of educating talented lineage members has gradually shifted from the use of lineage resources to sponsorship by the older generation of educated lineage members.

Many studies (Fortes, 1963; Goody, 1966; Nukunya, 1969) indicate that it was (and still is) common among the educated lineage members or "middle class" families throughout Ghana to sponsor their junior siblings, nephews and nieces living in their households. Oppong (1969) has recently demonstrated the extent to which the modern urban elite, the senior civil servants of Ghana, educate their relatives' children. She found that "senior civil servants spend a considerable amount of their salaries on accommodating, maintaining, assisting, and educating their kinsfolk, as well as their conjugal families." According to Oppong, an important part of this expenditure is the payment of secondary boarding school fees and maintenance of school children. Oppong notes that relatives' children are supported through elementary school, secondary school and even training college and university. In the summer of 2001, I organized a focused group discussion on the extended family and education in Ghana. The discussion was facilitated by a senior research fellow at the Institute of African Studies of the University of Ghana. The consensus was that the extended family remained vital not only for the education of its members, but also for members' economic and emotional well-being. One participant had adopted (informally) five nephews and one niece and had sponsored their education through the senior secondary school level. In the course of their education, he provided them food, clothing and accommodation. As adults, the nephews and niece consult him for advice on personal matters.

Although education in Ghana, as elsewhere in Africa has historically been biased against women, Robertson's (1984) study of women and class in Accra (capital city of Ghana) suggests that women play a prominent role in financing family members' education. Women in the Accra survey paid the school expenses for a majority of children of both sexes. Coming back to the matrilineage represented in Diagram 3.1, the formal Western education of 40 was sponsored by a number of members in his matrilineage, including 19, 25, and 50. In turn, 40 has sponsored and/or is currently sponsoring the education of a number of his nephews and nieces from elementary through secondary school to the university. The vocational/technical training of another nephew is being sponsored by 49.

A TIME OF TRANSITION

While educational sponsorships appear to continue unabated, profound social changes are taking place in Ghana as indicated earlier and these changes are definitely affecting the operation of the Akan matrilineage. For example, members of the seventh generation, as well as two descending ones not represented in Diagram 3.1 are the ones alive today. Lineage headship for both males and females has devolved on individuals within other segments of the maximal matrilineage. Of the members alive today, 50 is the most senior of the males, but 53 is the substantive head of this segment, with 51 as his female counterpart. While members meet occasionally for family events, there is a general perception of changed times and the diminishing influence of lineage heads. The latter do not necessarily vacate their own homes to reside in the lineage compounds of the deceased heads as in the past. Number 53 could move to live in the base compound of 19 but has chosen to reside in his parental home of orientation. The exercise of authority over women and children is now significantly influenced by one's socioeconomic status. Individuals in the seventh and descending generations not represented here have built their own single family homes to accommodate their spouses and children.

At present, the resolution of the perennial problem of balancing opposing loyalties to the descent group and one's conjugal unit is increasingly in favor of the conjugal unit. Although marriages are still fragile arrangements for members of this matrilineage, their nuclear families are held together more by affectionate ties than lineage instrumental concerns. The amity and solidarity that are now binding within the matrilineage are limited to a small number of kin that are selected for intimate relationships. Thus, the uterine children of 23 engage in daily contacts and more intimate relationships than between any one of them and the uterine children of 20, 26 or 29. In general, striving members must now achieve on their own with some support from the extended family, as indicated earlier. As a result of diminishing resources, the lineage heads can do little beyond moral support for those individuals.

The forces generating these changes, including education, religion, urbanization, the information in cyberspace and biotechnology, are making it possible for individualistic, materialistic and other secular values to compete with the lineage and moral solidarity that once prevailed. Although the fact of birth continues to provide one with a chain of socially recognized relatives through females in the matrilineage, the current competition for status has given personal achievement much prominence. Since respectability and reputation are increasingly associated with one's education, wealth and other status symbols, adherence to the instruments of collective survival is waning. What, then, is the prognosis of extended family networks among Ghanaians of the twenty-first century and beyond?

This issue was partially addressed in a nonrandom survey of twenty-eight adults that a colleague and I conducted to study intergenerational cultural transmission among the Akan of Ghana (Adjaye & Aborampah, 2004). Questions were developed around an array of cultural themes to determine the elder's role in everyday life as well as specific roles such as life cycle transitional events. Concerning the Akan matrilineal system and transitional rituals performed by elders of the kin group, no less than 60% either strongly agreed or agreed with the following propositions:

- The matrilineal principle of descent should continue to operate as the basis for unity and solidarity: 64%;
- Social capital (education, training, etc) should continue to be invested in all members of the matrilineage: 76%;
- Puberty rites (*bragoro*) should continue to be practiced: 60%;
- Customary marriage should continue to be practiced: 93%;
- Bridewealth should continue to be given upon marriage: 86%;
- Marriage ceremony should continue to be practiced: 100%;
- Members of the matrilineage should stick together in times of stress: 93%;
- Childbirth should continue to receive top priority from all members of the matrilineage: 71%.

We also attempted to ascertain respondents' opinions about changes perceived to be occurring within the Akan matrilineage. For example, while 93% agreed that marriage should be viewed as an economic duty to the matrilineage, 91% agreed that it should be based on individual love. While all agreed that individuals should marry persons of their own choice, at the same time, 78% agreed that inter-ethnic marital relations should be encouraged among members of the matrilineage. There is a clear preference for small family sizes (78%) and a clear opposition to large family sizes (46%) as the mechanism for building the political base of the matrilineage.

Given that the traditional compound housing structure of the Akan tends to promote face-to-face interaction and caring, and serves as the physical space for the major cultural activities of the matrilineage, we wanted our respondents to react to changes perceived to be occurring in that area as well. As expected, 82% agreed that members of the matrilineage should continue to maintain family compounds for the lineage ceremonies. However, 57% disagreed with the proposition that members of the matrilineage should be obligated to build their homes in their matrilineal homelands, and 71% agreed that single family homes should be preferred to traditional family compound units. Moreover, 57% disagreed with the suggestion that single family homes as a housing structure tends to undermine lineage solidarity.

When asked whether, over the past year, respondents provided and/or received assistance from other members of the family, 75% responded in the affirmative. The types of assistance provided/received included the following: money (71%); medicines (32%); advice (71%); clothing (39%); food (57%); house care (36%); and free transportation (18%). This would seem to suggest that members of the matrilineage continue to provide for economic wellbeing and psychological health of other members. Majority of the respondents continue to perceive each of the eight pair bonds (dyadic relationships) within the family as strong, which provides a strong basis for the prevailing mutual/reciprocal assistance. However, all agreed that the co-wife to co-wife relationships in multiple-spouse marriages are weak, which is to be expected given the earlier indication of a strong preference for marriage based on individual love as well as individual choice.

It can be discerned from the responses reproduced here that social changes are indeed occurring in the Akan matrlineage. However, in spite of the reported variations in the operation of extended family networks, the institution may be adaptable to the changing conditions in Ghana. Although, more and more single family structures are being built to accommodate nuclear, rather than extended, families, kinship ties extend beyond individual single family homes. Upwardly mobile families in the cities and towns continue to foster the children of other relatives either formally or informally. Even though the highly educated members tend to organize their lives around their nuclear families more so than their rural counterparts, many of these educated individuals participate very actively in their lineage and extended family affairs. As indicated earlier, two of the most significant transitional events in a person's life that tend to bring members into networks of alliance and cooperation are funerals and weddings. On such occasions, members congregate to mourn and ensure the safe passage of the departed member into the spirit world or to celebrate the coming together of two lineages through the ties of marriage. Many members who have traveled abroad still maintain interest in their intimate kin group, perhaps as a result of the continued belief that caring for, and sharing with kin are proper things to do.

THE NATURE OF CONTEMPORARY EXTENDED FAMILY FUNCTIONING IN GHANA

In Ghana, as elsewhere in Africa, many exclusive and complementary rights and obligations extend beyond the marital couple or consensual union. This usually happens when other relatives are present in the household or when a couple sees itself not as an independent entity but part of a larger group. Much of the previous literature has tended to emphasize the composition of the household to determine whether the family is extended or not. However, extensions of obligations can also serve as useful clues to assessing the nature of extended family networks in Ghana. As I have explained elsewhere (Aborampah, 1992/93, p. 56), interdependence in the Akan communities of Ghana made cooperative behavior a sine qua non for collective survival. Concerning ties of kinship, Siegel (1992, p. 175) quotes Blaine Harden as making the following observation:

> The significance of such ties was dramatically illustrated in 1983 when 1.3 million migrant workers from Ghana; nearly one-tenth of all Ghanaians were suddenly deported from Nigeria. Things looked bad, for severe drought had only worsened the chronic crisis that is the Ghanaian economy. Western relief agencies drew up plans for emergency camps to feed and house the deportees. Yet, this particular crisis soon evaporated, for within two weeks, the Ghanaian deportees had all disappeared into their families at home.

These types of extended family mutual aid prevail in many Ghanaian communities. They occur in ways described as expressive aid and instrumental aid (Billingsley, 1968). The former relates to the moral, emotional, and spiritual support that members of the extended family share with one another. Expressive aid can also come in the form of self-esteem building. Expressive aid is important because it helps members of the family to cope with the vicissitudes of everyday living or provide them with the raison d'être for their continued existence. The latter pertains to the sharing of material goods and money among members. In contemporary Ghana, family members living abroad remit substantial sums of money to needy family members. Instrumental aid is very important to the extended family because it has become a vital survival mechanism for many Ghanaians. Whether rich or poor, struggling or not, the mutual aid system provides security to those who need it and builds family unity because those who do not need support continue to support those that do.

Strains on the mutual aid system do occur from time to time that may produce "a mixed sense of cynicism, dread, and guilt" (Siegel, 1992, p. 175). Siegel quotes Harden who reports the story of a Ghanaian sociologist to underscore this feeling:

With his mother's support, he became the first university graduate in his family. In spite of his enviable teaching job in Accra, his government salary cannot properly support his wife and five children. Yet he shares his three-bedroom home with eleven home-village cousins (his classificatory brothers and sister) and, during his rare visits home, cannot refuse his mother's, mother's sister's, and sister's desperate requests for cash. 'I want out of the extended family trap,' he says, 'and when my mother dies I don't think I'll go back to the village anymore.

The old have their misgivings about the young as well. There seems to be a felt uneasiness about contemporary social changes and the elders' loss of grip on the young. Nonetheless, continued reliance on the instrumental and expressive aspects of the mutual aid system would seem to suggest its viability even in urban settings. The extended family, as a network of interdependency, is still widespread among Ghanaians. As Siegel (1992, p. 175) would put it, "family ties are sometimes strained, and Africans do not always honor the ideals of family loyalty. Yet it is important to note that such cultural ideals are as common to African societies as those of personal autonomy are in our own [Western] societies."

On account of shifting household composition and extensions of obligations and mutual aid, five extended family networks may now be identified. It must be noted, however, that there is a sixth type of structure that will be alluded to and left for later research. Where appropriate, examples will be drawn from Diagram 3.1. First, there is a long standing practice in Ghana where two or more brothers and/or sisters with their children set up a household of their own or are the only ones left in a family compound after their parents die off. The household of 34 and 51 (in Diagram 3.1) with their respective children and grandchildren fit this description. Although they both reside in the compound of 19 (long deceased), they maintain separate and distinct domestic functions, albeit reciprocal in many respects. The two individuals are classificatory sisters and belong in the same matrilineage. Structures of this sort were identified in the ethnographic studies of Ashanti by Forde. Nowadays, situations have emerged where men who are able to migrate do so by choice or relocate out of their families of orientation or die off so that their sisters are left behind to fend for themselves, of course with assistance from other kin members. Type two is a rapidly growing family structure involving Ghanaians who reside abroad and their parents who reside at home in Ghana. Those abroad send their kids home to be raised by the kids' grandparents. The grandchildren may be fostered to their grandparents for a variety of reasons. The working parents abroad may send their children home for economic or disciplinary reasons. Others may want their children to acquire the basic culture of the ethnic group to which the parents belong. Sometimes, parents abroad may simply want an opportunity for their children to connect with the parents' own lineages back home in Ghana so that the past is not entirely lost to the children.

The third type is the more common extended family. In this example, the typical household is the three or four generation extended family members. It could be a segment of a matrilineage, consisting of a male head and his children, his sisters and/or their children, as well as his own and his sisters' grandchildren. The extended family structures of 37 and 50 (not shown in Diagram 3.1) represent this type. In Ghana, a segment of a patrilineage may also form a multigenerational extended family. This structure usually consists of a male head, his wife and children, plus sister(s) and/ or brother(s) and their children, as well as their patrifilial grandchildren. The fourth type of multigenerational extended family network, emerging out of the increasing trend in single-parenthood, is the *matrifocal* family alluded to earlier. This type consists of a mother, her daughter(s), and her daughter(s)' children. This is illustrated by 51 in Diagram 3.1, who resides with her children and grandchildren. The primary reason for the focus on the mothers results from the non-acknowledgement of paternity and/or care by the grandchildren's fathers. Fathers' failure to take responsibility for their children may be due to their own marginalized positions in a society in which gainful employment is difficult to come by. Economic support for the women may be provided by other individuals, including sons, uncles and brothers, most of whom may be resident abroad or elsewhere in Ghana.

The fifth type of network consists of a husband and two or more legally married wives and their children. Polygynous family structures are now more commonly associated with rural dwellers engaged in agricultural production. In the past, the practice of polygyny served, in part, as a structural devise to obtain labor for subsistence agriculture. An existing nuclear family could be transformed into a polygynous one if the husband was selected to succeed to a deceased brother's estate and the widow(s) was/were inherited or agreed to marry the successor. All the different household units are kept together as a single family by the man or husband. Members of this type of extended family structure may engage in networks of alliance and cooperation that can allow co-wives to derive maximum satisfaction in their relationships. Besides farming, trading can be an essential part of the household economy. On the other hand, if and when favoritism and petty jealousies are allowed to prevail, life can be emotionally strenuous for all involved.

There is another emerging family structure in Ghana and elsewhere in Africa that needs a close scrutiny. This family structure consists of a legally married man or "husband" and one, two or more consensual partners or concubines. The man or "husband" sets up separate housing units for his concubines and visits them on a regular or periodic basis. Children may be born to such unions. Urban anonymity and the marriage squeeze currently faced by many Ghanaian women force the desperate ones to serve as unofficial second or third "wives" of gainfully employed married men who possess the ability to cater to their needs. In such *"polynuclear"* structures, there is a high degree of segregation, with each woman or "wife" constituting a semi-autonomous unit. The man or "husband' in a polynuclear extended family unit is the link between the separate households made up of each woman or "wife' and her children, as well as other relatives who may be fostered to the care of the "wife." The implication is that the emotional bond between a woman and her children is likely to be the most secure. With assistance from the man or "husband," a woman in this type of relationship can generate an independent income through trade for her own support, as well as fulfill her obligations to her own family. This type of structure needs further investigation to determine its prevalence and incidence within the general Ghanaian population.

DISCUSSION/CONCLUSION

A lot has been written about kinship as a social reality, about its persistence, about its disappearance. I proceeded from the assumption that it is a meaningful social entity for Ghanaians, although the nature and content of kinship may vary from one community to another. To begin somewhere, we can agree that parents constitute a convenient starting point and over time, children may be born and so on. Thus, there is a universe of kin and this can be determined through genealogical reckoning as presented in the preceding sections. For Ghanaian extended families, as in other African societies, the nucleus is the consanguineal group that includes the living, the living-dead (Mbiti, 1969) and those yet to be born. This nucleus is reckoned unilineally for the most part. There also is the outer group (i.e., the affinal group or in-marrying members and their consanguines). The living-dead are relatives who are physically dead but remain in the memories of the living. Libation and food are often offered to them because they serve as the immediate pillars and roots of the extended family. They solidify and mystically bind the whole lineage. Every Ghanaian lineage makes sure that its own existence is not extinguished. Pressures on the unmarried, marital arrangements, and other traditional practices provide for the perpetuation of the lineage. Parents especially in the traditional setting, are anxious to see that their children also bear children. Failure to do so implies the death of the unborn and depletion or diminishing of the extended family or lineage. On almost every occasion of the pouring of libation, supplications are made for the replenishing of the lineage with more children yet to be born.

There is always a dominant family figure regardless of the structural type. The dominant family figure occupies the leadership role. Among the Akan of Ghana, for example, there are clearly defined rules for the selection of this figure. The dominant figure is the guardian of the ancestral stool which is considered the soul of the matrilineage. The dominant figure is the custodian of all lineage property, and with the help of the lineage core, land and other lineage resources are allocated to members. According to Clark (1994, p. 95), Asante lineage elders still allocate considerable property and financial assistance through decisions on inheritance, loans or gifts, residence and schooling, with women participating as elders and as recipients. Concerning gender differentials in access, Clark further observes that "principles of leadership and inheritance give women less access than men to lineage-controlled resources, but ensure women's access at a token or minimal subsistence level. Nonetheless, loyalty to the lineage remains a fundamental moral principle and emotional commitment for most Akan of both sexes. This appears to be the case for the patrilineal groups as well. At the level of functioning on a day-to-day basis, individual family heads act as the minor dominant family figures. As illustrated with Diagram 3.1, extended family bases like those of 19, 37 and 50 are a characteristic of various structures. These extended family base households are the centers of extended family activities. Among the Akan, the dominant family figure may or may not reside in the lineage base household.

Thus, the new factors making for changes in kinship, marital and other relations and their precise interaction need to be thoroughly investigated. For example, in what manner and to what extent has the process of family nucleation affected residence at the base household, as well as the circle of intimate kin in the context of extended family networks? To what extent does the emancipated status of educated women militate against the practice of polygyny? It would be worthwhile to clearly understand emerging familial adaptations to the changing conditions. Another area is whether market women are converting their income-earning opportunities into ideological criticism of relationships among them and their spouses. My conversations with a few men in my research area reveal some bitterness felt toward their wives because of perceived changes in the latter's attitudes. Incidentally, these women have become successful traders. Could their economic self sufficiency serve to undermine their marital relations? These are issues of empirical validation.

A careful research on the changing attitudes toward mortuary rituals and funeral celebrations are needed. Have ancestors and deities outlived their usefulness in safeguarding extended family members and community welfare? The dread once held for the spirit of the deceased appears to have waned. Have Christian interpretations of death come to supersede traditional ones? Within the context of contemporary funeral ceremonies, nonkin bases of social alignment seem to have emerged to supplement kinship relations. Market women's groups and church choir groups have become significant participants in Ghanaian funeral ceremonies as a whole. Again, more careful research is needed to empirically ascertain the interactions among these contending forces.

Throughout this presentation emphasis has been placed on relationships with kin and ancestors. Together, they served as the pivots on which most interactions, most claims and obligations, and above all, most loyalties and sentiments were expressed. This was captured in the Akan saying: *Mogya bi ye dom* (blood is thicker than water.) Also, the individual was entirely subordinated to the lineage, and by extension to the extended family. As indicated earlier, the moral person was one who thought and acted in terms of the needs of the family, lineage, and community. There is no question that new forces are contending with these old principles that undergirded family institutions. More careful research is needed to empirically ascertain the impact of the structural transformations. It is my hope that the various features highlighted in this presentation would provide useful bases for further research.

References

Aborampah, O. M. (1992-93). Religious Sanction and Social Order in Traditional Akan Communities of Ghana and Jamaica. *Journal of Caribbean Studies,* 9(1 & 2), 41-58.

Addai-Sundiata, J. H. (1996). Family Dynamics and Residential Arrangements in Ghana. In Ardayfio-Schandorf (Ed). *The Changing Family in Ghana.* (pp. 64-85). Accra: Ghana Universities Press.

Adjaye, J. K. & O. M. Aborampah. (2004). Intergenerational Cultural Transmission among the Akan of Ghana, *Journal of Intergenerational Relationships,* 2(3/4), 23-38.

Caldwell, J. C. (1982). *Theory of Fertility Decline.* New York: Academic Press.

Camilleri, C. (1967). Modernity and the Family in Tunisia. *Journal of Marriage and the Family,* 29, 590-595.

Clark, G. (1994). *Onions Are My Husband. Chicago*: The University of Chicago Press.

Davidson, B. (1969). *The African Genius: An Introduction to African Cultural and Social History.* Boston: Little, Brown

Fortes, M. (1949). Time and Social Structure: An Ashanti Case. In M. Fortes, (Ed.) *Social Structure: Studies Presented to A. R. Radcliffe-Brown.* (pp. 54-84). Oxford: Clarendon Press.

Fortes, M. (1963). *Kinship and the Social Order. Chicago*: Aldine.

Fortes, M. (1975). Kinship and Marriage Among the Ashanti. In A. R. Radcliffe-Brown & D. Forde (Eds.) *African Systems of Kinship and Marriage* (pp. 252-284). New York: Oxford University Press, Eleventh Impression.

Goode, W. J. (1970). *World Revolution and Family Patterns.* New York: Free Press.

Goody, E. (1966). The Fostering of Children in Ghana: A Preliminary Report. *Ghana Journal of Sociology*, 2 (1)

Harden, B. (1988). Torn by Tradition and Modernity: In Africa, Family Ties are Binding too Tightly. *Washington Post National Weekly Edition* 6(December 5-11), 6-8.

Inkeles, A. & K. A. Miller. (1974). Construction and Validation of a Cross-National Scale of Modernism. *International Journal of Sociology of the Family*, 4, 127-147.

Marsh, R. M. & A. R. O'Hara. (1961). Attitudes toward Marriage and the Family in Taiwan. *American Journal of Sociology*, 67, 1-8.

Mbiti, J. (1969). *African Religions and Philosophy.* New York: Praeger.

Mensa-Bonsu, H. J. A. N. (1996). Family Law Policy and Research Agenda. In E. Ardayfio-Schandorf (Ed.) *The Changing Family in Ghana* (pp. 221-241). Accra: Ghana Universities Press.

Miller, K. R. (1984). The Effects of Industrialization on Men's Attitudes Toward the Extended Family and Women's Rights: A Cross-national Study. *Journal of Marriage and the Family*, 46(1), 153-160.

Morgan, S. P. & K. Hirosima. (1983). The Persistence of Extended Family Residence in Japan: Anachronism or Alternative Strategy? *American Sociological Review*, 48, 269-281.

Murdock, G. P. (1949). *Social Structure. New York*: Macmillan Company.

Nukunya, G. K. (1969). *Kinship and Marriage Among the Anlo Ewe.* London: Athlone Press

Olsen. N. J. (1979). Changing Family Attitudes of Taiwanese Youth. In R. Wilson, S. Greenblat & A. Wilson (Eds.) *Value Change in Chinese Society.* New York: Praeger.

Oppong, C. (1969). Education of Relatives' Children by Senior Civil Servants. *Ghana Journal of Child Development*, 2(2), 43-47.

Parsons, T. (1943). The Kinship System of the Contemporary United States. *American Anthropologist*, 45, 22-38.

_____. (1953). A Revised Analytical Approach to the Theory of Social Stratification. In R. Bendix & S. M. Lipsett (Eds.) *Class, Status, and Power.* (pp. 92-128). Glencoe, IL: Free Press.

Radcliffe-Brown A. R & D.Forde, (Eds.) (1950). *African Systems of Kinship and Marriage*. Oxford: Oxford University Press.

Ram, M. & R. Wong. (1994). Covariates of Household Extension in India: Change Over Time. *Journal of Marriage and the Family*, 56, 853-864.

Robertson, C. (1984). *Sharing the Same Bowl: A Socioeconomic History of Women and Class in Accra, Ghana*. Ann Arbor: The University of Michigan Press.

Siegel, B. (1992.) Family and Kinship. In A. A. Gordon & D. L. Gordon (Eds.) *Understanding Contemporary Africa*. Boulder, CO.: Lynne Rienner Publishers.

Skolnick A. (1973). *The Intimate Environment: Exploring Marriage and the Family*. Boston: Little, Brown.

Stokes, C. S., F. B. LeClere, & S. H. Yeu. (1987). Household Extension and Reproductive Behavior in Taiwan. *Journal of Biological Science*, 19, 273-282.

Sudarkasa, N. (1996). *The Strengths of Our Mothers*. Trenton, N.J.: Africa World Press.

Zimmerman, C. C. (1947). *Family and Civilization*. New York: Harper and Row.

CHAPTER 4

FAMILIES IN CAMEROON

Zacharia N. Nchinda

INTRODUCTION

In Cameroon, as in all other societies, the family is the basic unit of social institutions. Family relations form the basis of how the society is organized and shape the activities of the people from marriage and birth celebrations to divorce and death ceremonies. However, families in Cameroun, as elsewhere in Africa, are extended families rather than nuclear ones, and the whole society is tightly integrated. To better understand the changing pattern of extended families in Cameroon, I will place them in their historical, social, and religious context and explain how the society has changed over time. Indeed Cameroonian families can be found in a number of forms, and not all families share the same living conditions or life chances. While visiting Cameroon in 2008 for a research project on poverty in the urban centers, I realized that gradual changes were emerging in the structure of families even though extended families remain universal. These changes were gradually reducing the commitments to relatives beyond the nuclear family.

This chapter is focused on families in Cameroon for three reasons. First, the complexity of Cameroon mirrors the complexity of Africa. The country has been referred to as Africa in "miniature," for it is endowed with more than 200 different ethnic groups, possess a mixture of Christianity, Islam, and traditional religious adherents, has the legacy of three colonial powers (Germany, Britain, and France), and a family structure which is reflective of what can be seen across Africa. Second, the country offers a framework to examine the class and power relationships within various families, the challenges individuals and families face, and the nature of kinship ties. Finally, the Cameroonian family structure provides a lens for viewing broader social changes, in the country from the pre-colonial, through the colonial to the independent and con-temporary periods.

BRIEF BACKGROUND TO CAMEROON

Cameroon is located in West-Central Africa.[1] With a population estimated at over 18 million and covering a surface area of 475,440 sq. km, it is slightly larger than California.[2] It is diverse geographically, culturally, and socially. Its relief, vegetation, soil, and climate vary from region to region and stretch from the dense mangrove swamps and thick equatorial rainforest along the Atlantic coast in the south, to the thinly vegetated plains of Lake Chad in the north (Le Vine, 1964, p. 3-4). The country is culturally diverse with more than two hundred different ethnic groups speaking over 250 different languages and vernacular. Cameroon was colonized by three European powers: Germany (1884-1916), France (1916-1960), and Britain (1916-1961) and because of the absence of a national language, English and French are taught as the official languages.

During the First World War, joint Anglo-French expeditionary forces defeated the Germans in the country. Britain and France partitioned Cameroon between them with Britain colonizing one-fifth and France four-fifths of the former German Colony. British Cameroons was divided into two portions, Northern and Southern Cameroons. Britain integrated the administration of the areas as part of its colony of Nigerian. In 1922 the League of Nations confirmed Anglo-French partition and allowed them to control the territories as Mandates. In 1946, the United Nations Trusteeship Council reaffirmed Anglo-French control and this time as Trust Territories. In January 1960, France granted independence to its portion of Cameroon as the (first?) Republic of Cameroon. In February 1961, Britain organized a plebiscite in its sectors of the Cameroons to find out if the people wanted to gain independence as part of the independent Federation of Nigeria or French Cameroons (Percival, 2008: p. 114; Chem-Langhëë, 2004, p. 110-111). British Northern Cameroons voted to join Nigeria and British Southern Cameroons voted to reunite with French Cameroons. The reunification took place on October 1st, 1961 to create the Federal Republic of Cameroon. In 1972, the government changed the country's official name to the United Republic of Cameroon and in 1984 it was changed again to the (second?) Republic of Cameroon. The country is divided into ten administrative provinces (headed by governors appointed by the President) and has been ruled by two presidents since independence, Ahmadou Ahidjo (1960-1982) and Paul Biya (1982-). Despite Cameroon's huge ethnic diversity, strong kinship ties unite the people.

KINSHIP TIES

The kinship system common in Africa today can be traced in history to the various ethnic groups that settled the continent. In Cameroon, the diverse ethnic groups fall into broad groups such as: from south to north, the Coastal Bantu (Duala, Bakweri, Basa, Bakundu), Equatorial Bantu (Bèti- Fang Bulu), Semi-Bantu (Bamilèkè, Tikar, Chamba, Bamoun), Pygmies, Nigritic (Mbum, Vute), Kirdi (Matakam, Fali, Masa), Mandara (Kotoko), Foulbe, and Arab Choa (Le Vine, p. 5-14; Ardener, 1956, p. 11). It is within these broad categories that smaller ethnic units, lineages and families were formed. Families in Cameroon, as in other parts of Africa, are made up of two types of membership: those that are related by "blood," consanguine, and those that are related through "affinity" customary or civil law (Sudrkasa, 1998, p. 93-94; Mbaku, 2005, p. 140). While in the West the concept of family revolves around nuclear family (husband, wife, and children), in Africa family does not distinguish between conjugal and consanguine relations. The notion of family is more extensive and covers kinship relationships between and among the nuclear family and the external families on both the mother's and father's side. Members of the lineage in Africa are all those who can trace decent to a common ancestor, and some families can be large. These enlarged families form clans. Members of the same lineage or clan are prohibited from marrying one another. Lineages in Africa serve major functions. They act as points of reference to individuals; showing their genealogy, where they belong within the society, and the place they proudly call and identify as "home". In addition, lineage tracing makes it easier for individuals to reconnect with their ancestors and to pinpoint the unique place where they can seek highly needed "blessings" in case something goes wrong, for example childlessness in a marriage.

Historically, when members of two different lineages get married, the ramifications of their actions expand far beyond the individuals involved. Marriage brings together the extended families that are now considered *de facto* "brothers" and "sisters." It unites the lineages of the husband and those of his wife/ wives and ties the in-laws in a social bond. It is because of the close ties within families that marriage proposals are carefully examined. In rural areas such lineage scrutiny is easier and links can be traced quickly. In recent years migration, rapid urbanization, the expansion of western education, and globalization have all acted as vital agents of change and affected the nature of family relations in the country. It has not made the task of tracing lineages easy. However, whether in urban centers or abroad, when two Cameroonians of the same region declare their intension of getting married, their lineages (mostly those in the rural areas) scrutinized each closely to make sure they are not "brothers" and "sisters."

Thus marriage in Cameroon, as in most parts of Africa, is a social knot that binds together not only the individuals but also all the families involved. It is an entanglement that unites all the forces of the extended family structure: parents, grandparents, uncles, aunts, cousin, nieces, nephews, and even the spirits of ancestors.

MARRIAGES

Marriage in Cameroon, as in all other human societies, is one of the most fundamental social institutions. It is the main structure not only for family formation and procreation, but also for guaranteeing social and economic status, maintaining social order, and transmitting the beliefs and customs from one generation to the other. Marriage is a major corner stone of the society and so important that few adults rebuff the institution and from birth, African boys and girls are pre-pared and encouraged to look forward to it. It confers on the couples involve social prestige and status, and prepares the way for their transformation into motherhood or father-hood.

The official marriage age in Cameroon as stipulated by a June 1981 law is fifteen years for girls and eighteen years for boys and in theory only the President of the Republic can grant an exemption to this rule.[3] In practice this law is not followed in rural areas and among Muslims in the north, where a girl can be forced into or given into marriage at lower ages, generally without their consent (Adams, 2003, p. 89). The marriage process in Cameroon is a lengthy one which extends over years. In rural areas where there are no schools, from the moment of birth, a young girl can be betrothed and prepared for marriage. In that case, when the girl is seven or eight years of age, she is allowed to visit or even live with the family of her future husband.

During this period, both families undertake the task of studying each other and testing if the marriage is workable. It provides the opportunity for the future spouse to familiarize herself with her future in-laws and study their ways. In rural areas with schools, such arrangements may be postponed until the girl completes primary school. At that time, at the age of about thirteen or fourteen, more formal marriage arrangements can be made. Early marriage is still common in the West and Northwest regions of the country partly due to customs and traditions and among the *Kirdi* and Fulani of north Cameroon, because of the slow expansion of western education and their high "traditional attachment to female virginity at first marriage" (Calvès, 1999, p. 294).[4] It was the duty of future mother-in-laws to closely monitor the future bride, and make sure that premarital sex did not place. Having sexual contact with a pre-pubescent girl is considered a taboo and an abomination in many parts of Cameroon.

In urban centers and among the educated and wealthy families, such early or traditional marriage arrangements have been abandoned. In such families, girls are protected and allowed to grow at home and continue their education beyond the primary and secondary school levels before marriage is considered. Brighter girls are even encouraged to pursue higher education.

In Cameroon, the prospective husband's family provides bridewealth (marriage-price, bride-price) to the future bride's family, though the amount and/or nature varies according to the region and ethnic group. The provision of bridewealth does not imply that the future husband is paying for a property or buying his wife. As Mbaku has pointed out, it serves mainly as: a) token donation to the family of the bride for the loss of her labor; b) thank you to the bride's family for raising their daughter success-fully to the point of marriage; c) a sanction that the marriage is recognized and granting permission to the couple to freely consummate their union; d) formal legalization of any off-spring that may result from the marriage. In the event a girl conceives when the bridewealth has not been paid, the resulting child belongs to the girl's family and not the husband's (Mbaku, 2005, p. 147).

Bridewealth can at times be expensive because it involves "settling" in kind and / or cash, many members of the extended family of the future wife. The wedding gifts that are exchanged include livestock (goats, pigs, sheep, chicken, and cattle), foodstuff (varies with the region), wrappers (cloth skirts), clothes, kola nuts, palm oil, alcohol, cigarette, farm tools (machete, hoe), and building materials. Cash payment is often demanded by some members of the bride's family, but the amount to be exchanged and the period allowed (whether before, during or after the marriage) is agreed upon mutually by the two parties. It varies from one family to the next. While one poor family with a bright daughter may demand more for nurturing such a child, another does not, and is pleased to see their daugh-ter get married. The indebtedness of the groom's extended family to that of the bride can never be repaid and they are always reminded of that by the bride's extended family members whenever the occasion presents itself.

If a girl abandons or refuses to accept a future husband, her family, or any future husband she chooses to marry is obliged by tradition to refund the bridewealth. If not, then any child resulting from such a union belongs in principle to the first husband. The extended families will always consider the runaway wife as theirs.

The amount to be refunded is not fixed but negotiable mostly if the runaway wife left behind a child and the more the children the lesser the refund. This idea of refunding the bridewealth gives husbands an upper hand over their wife/wives, mostly if the latter comes from less wealthy families that the husband knows cannot easily afford the refund.

There are three main regimes of marriage in Cameroon, and they are determined by the nature in which they are established: the customary or traditional marriage, civil or legal marriage, and religious (Christian or Islamic) marriage (Johnson-Hanks, 2003, p. 158). Customary marriage, which prevailed prior to the advent of Christianity, colonial rule, and the introduction of Islamic religion in northern Cameroon, still exists today. A traditional marriage is generally the first to be performed in most weddings before the civil and/or religious types complement it later. In rural areas, most marriages are of the customary type.

Civil wedding is one of the foreign practices introduced into Cameroon by colonial authorities. It gradually developed roots and co-exists side-by-side customary marriage. It is the kind of marriage preferred by Cameroonian elites and many of those living in urban centers. However, even after performing customary marriages they will still follow with civil marriages. Since June 1981 marriage settlement in Cameroon is regulated in accordance with Ordinance no. 81-02. The law requires that the husband at the time of marriage to declare the type of antenuptial settlement that he prefers, whether monogamy or polygamy.[5]

The colonial powers and Muslim invaders introduced Christianity and Islamic religious traditions respectively in Cameroon, along with its profoundly patriarchal structures. Religious wedding ceremonies depends on whether the individuals involve came from traditional, Christian or Muslim families and their educational level. Christian weddings takes place in churches and is widespread in the South, while Islamic marriages are common mostly in northern Cameroon, and in those parts of the country where there are large Islamic worshipers.

Gender inequality remains imbedded in marriages in Cameroon. Husbands generally have more powers in the household than their wife/wives. Polygyny, where a man marries more than one wife, is common but polyandry, whereby a woman marries more than one husband, is rejected outright. Plural marriage is more rampant in rural areas than in the urban centers. The practice persists for various reasons. First, some people interpret having more than one wife as a sign of prestige, wealth, and status, and the more wives the higher the status (Brian, 1972, p. 143). For example, according to J.A. Mope Simo (1991, as late as 1987, the *fons* in the chiefdoms of Ndop Plains had wives as follows: Bamessing 21, Bamali 19,

Bamunka 40, Babungo 49, Babessi 23, and Bam-balang 29 (Mope Simo, 1991, p. 419).[6] Second, in rural areas, a larger family is seen as a source of strength and for economic reasons, more children meant more hands to do farm work. Thus some wealthy men believed that having more wives could result in more children.[7]

Third, some husbands practice polygyny in cases where their wife cannot conceive or where their wife procreates only girls and they are in need of a son as heir. In addition, having more children could serve as insurance against old age and death and the higher mortality rate in the rural areas make it necessary to improve the chance of survival. Fourth, women in Cameroon, mostly in the rural areas breast feed babies for a long time, about two years in some cases. During this time sexual intercourse with their husband is a taboo due to the belief that any such act can threaten the growth and well-being of the infants or toddler. Because of this, polygyny offers the man the opportunity to satisfy his sexual desires until the child is weaned. Finally, polygyny assures the man that in case there is any separation or divorce with one wife, he will always have others to take care of his home. However, the practice of polygyny has often deprived many young men who are not rich from having wives; it has forced them to migrate from the villages to the cities.

While Christianity permits a man to marry only one wife, Islamic law permits a man to marry as many as four wives; but on condition that the husband is certain he can love all his wives evenly and provide for their wellbeing. However, knowing how difficult it is to treat or handle potentially jealous co-wives equitably, it is obvious that silent tension persists in all polygynous homes. Such tensions in the compound often peaks when the husband is about to bring in a new bride. The first wife in polygynous homes has more power than the other co-wives, with the newest arrival having the least power. But none of the women has any power that is comparable to their husband's.

The living arrangement in a polygynous family is simple. In rural areas, and among the Fulbe in the north, the husband provides a separate house for each co-wife but they all live together within the same compound. The husband has his own house considered the family dwelling and his wives take turns passing the night with him. In urban centers, the husband may rent separate apartments, or if he is wealthy, build separate houses for his co-wives and alternate his nights between or among them.

In the rural areas of Cameroon, mostly in the Christian south, there is another form of marriage, the "woman marriage," that can be practiced by a wealthy woman. In this case, a rich woman in need of a son or who cannot procreate decides to act as a "female husband" by "marrying" her own wife who is fertile. She pays the necessary bridewealth just as a man will. The "female husband" then encourages her wife to go out and bear a child or children by any man she loves. All children of such union belong to the "female husband."

While many girls in rural areas have little choice over their future husband, their counterparts in urban centers, along with those who are educated and of higher socio-economic status, have the advantage not only of selecting their fiancées but also deciding whether to enter into polygynous marriage relationships or not. The marriage process under Islamic law is highly dictated by the father, and the wife (wives) and daughter (s) have little say.

CHILDBIRTHS

In most African societies children are the *raison-d'être* for marriage and are considered highly valuable. The future of the lineage and society depends on them and they must be protected and trained to understand and perform their roles. Because of this, the first duty of any woman getting into marriage is to bear a child. The birth of a child in a family is often greeted with jubilation. As the child comes of age, he/she is expected, as part of the training process, to help the parents in various activities whether on the farm or at home. The number of children a couple decides to have is not fixed but their decision may be influenced by various factors such as the environment, whether rural or urban, their fertility status, their educational level, or the sex of the siblings

Though healthcare centers are widespread in urban centers in Cameroon, they are scarce in rural areas and many children are born at home by experienced older mothers. In some areas women give birth alone at home before calling on neighbors for help (Regis, 2003, p. 95). The birth of a child is often accompanied by the provision of gifts and/or good wishes to the mother from the extended family. Because a child is highly treasured, the desire to have one is so strong that couples are ready to go to extremes. For example, couples that are unable to have children do not shy away from consulting both modern and above all traditional doctors to realize their dream of having a child. Families exert huge efforts to protect, maintain, and train their children according to the ways of the lineage. In rural areas where the rate of infant mortality is highest, some parents use talismans and traditional medicines to protect their children from possible "evil spirits." In many parts of the Islamic north, infants and toddlers are protected by their families from "dangerous evil spirits" in the society and outside world with amulets.

In most cases when a couple fails to have a child, the woman is to blame. Cameroonian men believe that infertility is generally a woman's problem and that they are immune from it. As a result of this erroneous belief, girls whose mothers have other children are highly desirable by prospective suitors. Arranged marriages are common among many groups

The initiator of such a venture may come from the girl's or the boy's family. In either case, both sides weigh the quality of the family and the quality of the prospective bride or groom. An easy match is identified in cases where for example there is no "witch" in either family, the girl comes from a respectable family, and her family does not have a history of children dying early. Furthermore, the family of a young man may want to find out if the future bride is a flirt or if her lineage is too large. A large lineage is an indication of extra cost and responsibilities which can be avoided. Parents of daughters still encourage them to marry from wealthy or high ranking families in the society even if it is a polygynous family.

Premarital sex is a common practice in many urban areas and some ethnic groups such as the Bèti-Bulu-Fang accept the practice as "an important element of normal adolescence...[and] an important component of physical well-being" (Johnson-Hanks, 2003, p. 170). The sexual activities of young girls are not severely supervised and they are not punished for engaging in premarital sex. With rapid urbanization and the spread of western education, the attempt by parents to select possible marriage partners for their children is increasingly met with resistance. However, a man and woman who fall in love in the city or college and want to get married must seek the approval of their parents. Each side must give consent to the marriage after carrying out their own investigations of the suitability and future prospect of the marriage. Even if a boy and girl have been living together with or without a child, it is to their best interest to seek the "blessings" of their parents. If they refuse to gain their parents' consent before marriage or defy their objections, they face the prospects of rejection by their families and hovering around them will always be the fear of isolation and "bad luck" in their marriage.

FAMILY RESPONSIBILITIES

Ideally, marriage is really a union of two personalities into one. In practice, this is not the case. Despite the wishes and efforts of the Christian church to unite two personalities (husband and wife) into one, difference in personalities, action, and desires do persist. As Jessie Bernard posits, within each marriage you can always find "his-and her version" of things making the union "her marriage" and "his marriage" (Bernard, 1998, p.

450-451). However, though the need for children may be at the forefront of marriages, men and women in Cameroon, as in other parts Africa, enter into marriage with other diverse objectives and expectations in the household and which are often shaped by their lineage affiliations.

In Cameroon, "her marriage" and "his marriage" activities are defined in the household. The gendered division of labor is such that women and me have different responsibilities and this varies with the locality, the educational level, and wealth. Most wives have their duties clearly defined and they face the double burden of production and reproduction. As agents of production in rural areas, many wives in Cameroon cultivate food crops on the farm and back in the household they cook and take care of the children. They own the food crops they grow, but the land is owned by their husbands (Goheen, 1996; Brian, p. 153). As children grow, girls and boys are trained to follow different career paths mostly chosen by their parents. While boys are encouraged to pursue education, girls are often guided to be future mothers. In the Islamic north husbands and wives also occupy different worlds at home. Among the Fulbe for example the men and women occupy separate spaces and "have remarkably different ways of talking about their lives, marriage, fortune, scarcity, well-being, and disease" (Regis, p. 45). While an Islamic man can call his wife by name, she cannot do so for him. Men make most of the major decisions at home. However, wives in rural areas are not totally submissive to men or voiceless at home. For example, among the Coastal Bantu and Semi-Bantu, they can sell the surplus crops they harvest to earn money that they can spend as they deem fit. They have a voice when it comes to issues such as taking care of a sick child, the daily menu, family planning, and welcoming family guests.

Contrary to western standards where the wife (and some husbands) prepare and serve meals and the nuclear family sits around the same table to eat, in many parts of Cameroon, a mother feeds and eats with her children; while the husband is served and often eats his meals alone. This separation at meal time is another sign of power and manifestation of authority by a husband over his wife /wives and children in a family (Martin, 1970, p. 68). However, some men, especially the highly educated, share in the responsibilities of taking care of the children. For example, dropping and picking them up from schools and participate, as westerners do, in sharing breakfast and dinner at set table with their wives and children.

In Cameroon urban centers the division of responsibilities does not generally follow the "breadwinner father" and "stay-at-home mother" pattern. Wives are still responsible for cooking and taking care of the children but they also seek and attain an "upgrade" of their status by not depending solely on their husband. They try to educate their husbands about their right to participate in decision making in the family mostly in areas such as choice of spouse for their daughter/son, choice of wedding dress, and entertainment of wedding guests. Urban wives have more non-agricultural job opportunities open to them and many perform professional and white collar jobs, engage in commercial activities, and continue their education. They have higher status and feelings of higher standard of living in the family than rural women.

However, whether in the rural or urban areas, the extended families have a lot to play in maintaining the stability of marriage. They can intervene on behalf of the wife or husband depending on who is at fault. It is in their interest in cases of misunderstanding to make sure the family functions and so any of the friendly in-laws can act as a mediator in cases of disputes.

FIDELITY TO PARTNER(S)

In Cameroon, the desire for faithfulness in marriage is not shared equally by men and women. Men have an upper hand. In rural areas, some urban centers, and among Muslims, men continue to practice polygyny. The reception and accommodation of an "illegitimate child" or child born out of wedlock varies with the place, the family, and individuals concerned. In rural areas, a child born to an unwedded girl belongs to the family of the girl. If a woman is divorced and her parents have not repaid the bride-wealth, then any child she conceives belongs to the former husband. In the event that a child is born out of an adulterous relationship, the child belongs to the legal husband. However, such a relationship is frown at and rejected. In the urban centers and among some educated classes and Christians, the introduction of an "illegitimate child" into the family is a cause for concern and source of trouble. However, some husbands, who know that they are impotent, can allow their wife or wives to go out and bring "illegitimate children" whom they accept as legitimate. The children belong to and are welcomed in the family.

Trusting men in Cameroon is a difficult exercise for many wives. Many wealthy and upper class husbands in urban centers have "deuxième bureau" or mistress, sometimes even more than one.[8] They keep mistresses partly as a display of wealth and partly as an exploitation of power. These "deuxième bureaux" most often are younger girls who need "sugar daddies" to supply their daily material needs.[9] Married women respond to their husband's adultery in various ways: some physically attack their husbands or mistresses, other seek divorce, others ask their husbands to bring their mistress home as co-wives, and others call on the extended family network to intervene and attempt to resolve the issues.

There are few cases where older women, "sugar mammies" also seek younger boyfriends. These women for various reasons are not satisfied by their husband and want to fulfill their sexual desires with younger men.

DIVORCE

Though divorce is not a common phenomenon in Cameroon, some marriages break up. Since both couples are married into lineage, it is the wish of extended family members to make it work. Thus whenever there is tension and conflict in a marriage, the extended families of both couples intervene and pressure then to resolve the issue. For example in-laws, neighbors, mutual friends, and religious authorities can mount pressures. Women are often reminded to persevere, and that they should not abandon their children.

The frequency of divorce varies with the area. In rural areas where most marriages are conducted following customary laws, the extended families intervene in cases where couples are having problems and seek ways to preserve the marriage. Pressure mounts on the guilty party to make amends. In the urban centers and among educated Cameroonians, divorce is readily acceptable.

In the event of divorce, the father takes total control of grown children. The mother may have control of infants and toddlers until they are of age, at which time they will join their siblings in their father's house (Adams, p. 90). The causes of divorce varies and includes repeated violence against one's wife, adultery/cheating by a man or woman, repeated bad behavior by the woman or man, failed murder attempts by one spouse, financial hardship, spouse's accusations of witchcraft, disagreement and constant arguments with in-laws, and childlessness. In almost all societies in Cameroon, divorced women are generally viewed more unfavorably than divorced men.

DEATH

Birth is the beginning of death, and death is present the moment a child is born. How to prolong life has always been the challenge of mankind. In Cameroon, the response to death in the family varies with the age of the deceased and the circumstances of death. In the event of miscarriage or stillbirth, there is no crying and the dead child is buried quickly. The belief is that the unborn child did not love or want the family; because if it did, it would not have died. Any crying may lead to further bad luck as the deceased child may mistake that for love and decide to return. The family must show the child all aspects of rejection and hatred. When the deceased is an infant or a toddler, there is some crying but not much. Burial takes place early and there is little death ceremony. For grown up children there is much weeping and wailing and this varies with the family. Poor families may not have money to entertain mourners for long. In the rural areas the corpse is stripped and dressed in its best attire before burial. In the urban centers the corpse can be preserved in the mortuary for more than a week.

In Cameroon, families do not feel the death of a husband or wife in the same way. When a husband dies, the response varies in rural and urban areas. For the Semi-Bantu, e.g. the Bamoun, a widow in the rural areas is obliged to sit on the floor and not lie on a bed till the husband is buried. She cannot join the group in eating and does not shake hands with anybody. She has to remain bare footed and may not take a shower (Maillard, 1984, p. 201). After burial, she can sew mourning attires that may be of blue, black (sign of sadness) or white (sign of new beginning) color with matching headscarf, ear-ring, and shoes. In the urban centers, the mourning period is much shorter and the preferred mourning dress for widows is often white. Widows in towns face another huge challenge. Those who had rich husbands face the risk of being accused of killing their husband in order to inherit wealth. Many such widows in Douala and Yaoundé are referred to as "happy widows" and some of them for their own safety may have to sever ties with the family of their deceased husband. When a wife dies, the husband does not undergo the same widowhood ritual.

The death celebration of important personalities in Cameroon is a grand affaire and can involve the whole lineage, friends, well-wishers, and provide a social occasion for people to meet and exchange ideas and gossips on a wide range of issues from local to national and international events. For example, in the grassfields region of the country, the death of high ranking economic, political, social, or traditional individuals calls for weeping, feasting, dancing, eating, and drinking. It is a time for the families to unite and cooperate, and the head of family often seize the occasion to meet, organize, and assists other members with problems (Jindra, 2005, p. 362). The manifestations of gender are often present during such solemn occasions and are marked by the gender division of labor, for while women make arrangement for the cooking, men take care of drinks and sitting arrangements (Maillard, p. 199). Great feasts (which may last for several days) are often carried out after the burial and the final "cry die" or "second funeral ceremony" which may be prolonged for a year or more depending on the finances, remain important opportunities to cement and reattach family links with ancestors, pour libations to avoid bad luck, and thus secure family unity. Such "cry die" ceremonies assume collective characters for the lineage and the ancestors are always remembered during important traditional rituals.

Suicide in Cameroon is frown upon and considered taboo. It is interpreted as an offense against self and a shame to the family for which purification is necessary. If this occurs in a family, the members have to seek traditional way to "wash off the bad luck." In rural areas when a suicide occurs by hanging children are shielded from seeing the corpse and special individuals are called to take it down.

However, recent death ceremonies in Cameroon has taken on a different turn mostly for those families with children overseas. It is assumed that families with children abroad mostly Europe and the U.S. have lots of money. Thus in the event of an important death in the family, burial can be delayed for a long time awaiting the arrival of a son/daughter. Such death ceremonies have become flamboyant occasions for lineage members to display wealth through the purchase of rich caskets, elaborate traditional and/or church ceremonies, the disruptions of traffic flows, suspension of work, and prolong ceremonies after burial. The presence of sons/daughter from abroad at death ceremonies provide favorable occasions for extended family members to exchange views, gossip, entertain, and request more visits from them and not only when death occurs.

With the birth of multiparty politics in Cameroon since the early 1990s, the death of important personalities in urban centers has taken another dimension. This is so because multiparty politics and the widespread formation of political parties in various regions and towns have come along with a stronger support for autochthon politics. This local and ethnic development of politics has had huge impact on death celebrations for the wealthy or upper class individuals in urban centers. They provide occasions for immigrants' urban families to manifest to the public what Peter Geschiere (2005) refers to as the real place where they came from, that is, to display where they belonged.

This was again more important because given that the dead in African were not really gone, burial sites took added meaning as special locations for rituals. The decision of where to bury a deceased immigrant often provide an occasion for family members to prove to the public whether he/she (and by extension the family left behind) belonged to the city where he/she died or belonged to their village of origin. In cases where the home town of the deceased is chosen as place of burial, the family indirectly displays to the public the importance of lineage and the need to cement social ties both with the living and with the ancestors. While some village lineage members may not be happy with the deceased for coming to the village only when dead, others see burial as occasions to reaffirm family bond and unity. Because villages have adopted fixed geographical boundaries, once a body is buried, it cannot be exhumed easily without some elaborate traditional rituals, and burial sites have become locations for ceremonies in association with the worship of ancestors.

INHERITANCE

Most Cameroonian society follows the patrilineal line of decent in inheritance. When a husband dies, the eldest son or any other designated son becomes the successor. In rural areas, a father may inform his family members and friends about his successor before his death. In families with no male child or where the son is considered useless, a daughter may be designated to inherit but on condition that she never marries and remains in her parent's compound. She is free to have as many children and with any person she wants. Also, widows are tied to their husband's village and marital home, mostly if they have children (Guyer, 1979, p. 10-11). A brother of the late husband can take the widow and remarry or give her out to another husband. The widow has to remain with the family, but a widow with no child may prefer to return to her natal kin. In urban center, the educated and upper class have established wills.

SEPARATION AND SINGLE PARENT HOUSEHOLD

All efforts are made by the members of the lineages to keep married families intact. Yet, separations do occur. In the event of a temporary separation, the woman does not take the children with her, but leaves them behind with the husband. This often puts the man in a delicate situation mostly when the children are small. With an "empty" compound (due to the absence of his wife), the man must depend on other members of the extended family to help him take care of the children.

There is no uniform tradition in Cameroon in dealing with single parenthood. While some villages frown at the practice, others welcome it. Single parenthood is rare in the rural areas. Citing studies carried out by Abéga et.al. (1994) among the Béti-Fang, Ewondo, and Eton ethnic groups of the Center and East Provinces of Cameroon, Calvès (1999) points out that premarital pregnancies and births were part of a strategy carried out by young couples who wanted "to force their parents to accept and recognize their union" (Calvès, p. 292). However, for the Semi-Bantu groups such as Bamilèkè or Tikar, it is a family shame for a girl to get pregnant before marriage. In case of unwanted pregnancy, the girl may be sent away to the family of the boy responsible to take care of her. However, the poor economic conditions, rapid urbanization, and the expansion of western education have all transformed the marriage pattern in Cameroon. While many young men and women have postponed marriage with the hope of doing so when conditions improve, they have not given up pre-marital sex.

In the urban centers, premarital sex, and premarital pregnancies and births and thus single motherhood are more common among the western educated groups and Christians (ibid., p. 292-297). Many western educated girls do not interpret the stigma attached to unwedded mother-hood in the same way, and yet their chances of getting married either to the father of their child or a new suitor diminished as the years go by.

Few Cameroonians will accept to start a family with a woman who already has older children. They are reluctant under the pretext that the woman may still have love for her child's father and so will be unfaithful, that the child may not take instructions from them, that the cost of bringing up someone else's child may be excessive, that disputes may erupt in future over inheritance, and the fear that friends may ridicule them for not being able to marry a "fresh" wife.

In Cameroon urban centers there are many working women who are single parents. They want to enjoy life and have children at the same time. Many of the children born to these single mothers are accepted and accommodated by the mother's lineage and brought up within the extended family network.

SOME RECENT FAMILY TRENDS IN CAMEROON

Cameroon, as many other African countries, began the mid-1980s with huge difficulties that affected and increasingly shaped the extended family as an institution. Due to the economic difficulties facing the country and other African countries since the mid-1980s, many of them turned to the IMF and World Band for help. These Bretton Woods institutions intervened with Structural Adjustment Programs (SAPs) aimed at instilling austerity, jolting African economies into sound footing, and facilitating their repayment of foreign debts. However, these programs failed to yield the intended results and instead plunged the recipients of foreign loans more into poverty (Mbaku, 2004, p. 404-409). For example, in Cameroon civil servants had their salaries slashed by more than fifty percent and this caused enormous suffering to families. Second, the wind of globalization blowing through African countries required the liberalization of their markets and economies for foreign competition. This unfair competition not only led to unemployment for many workers, but it also lowered the income of many employed Cameroonian by reducing the value of export commodities on which the people depended for revenue. Furthermore despite the reduced earnings, the country had to service its foreign debt, thus forcing the government to cut back on many economic and social services.

Apart from these external forces, major internal dynamics in Cameroon have made the poverty situation worse. The high rural-urban migration, political instability, excessive corruption, the absence of broad higher technical and professional education, the failures of agricultural production, the increased reliance on unstable oil, and the rapid spread of HIV/ AIDS have not only created difficulties and destabilized families but have also strained lineage relations. Historically the Cameroonian and African traditions has been to close ranks and help a brother or neighbor in need, mostly children. However, the high unemployment rate and lack of social infra-structures have all made support by other family members difficult.

The poverty generated by the external pressures of the IMF/World Bank policies, western dominated globalization, and the internal failures of the Biya regime have all generated much strain on Cameroonian families and led to unintended consequences. They have caused a fracture in the extended family safety net and transformed family responses and reactions to various issues such as street children, orphanages, parenthood, abortion, and internet dating. Children and family ties that used to be the bedrock of the society are gradually being transformed and nowhere is this more visible than in the nation's two larger urban centers of Yaoundé and Douala. In Cameroon, as in other parts of Africa, there is pride in having children, but walking through the streets of the heart of Yaoundé and Douala I could not help observing many children wandering the streets. Increasing numbers of children, ages six through eighteen can be seen abandoned in the streets of these major cities, and their numbers are growing (Balaam, 1997). These street children include refugees, handicapped, HIV/AIDS victims, the exploited and abused, rouges and thieves (Nyobe, 2006, p. 14).

Many of these street children, if asked, tell or describe their despair and painful experiences with homelessness.[10] These are signs that the extended family structure, formerly reputable and cherished of holding together African families, is gradually losing its grip and some Cameroonian families are increasingly turning their backs on their neighbors, above all on children, the pride of the future. Some children lack the immediate and extended family support and care and as a result, live in fear of tomorrow.

Within the urban centers the marginalization of children is illustrated by another phenomenon: the growth of orphanages. But the development of orphanage in Cameroon began during colonial rule and the number has only increased. For example, as far back as 1935 when the Baptist mission opened their first maternity center in Shisong (Njinikom) they began registering their first orphans: children whose mothers died during or shortly after birth and by 1938 when the number increased to 20, a separate room was provided for their care and a sister appointed to take charge (Lafon, 1988, p. 166). A new orphanage building attached to Shisong medical center was opened in 1953.

As the number of orphans increased after independence to more than a hundred in 1963, Father Leo Van Son constructed a new/modern orphanage with "kitchens, laundries, refectories, and sleeping quarters both for the orphans and the women who help the sister take care of the orphans" (ibid., p. 166-167). The economic crisis affecting Cameroon and the outbreak of HIV/AIDS have, on the one hand, only increased the problem of orphans, and on the other hand, the expansion of private and mission centers in urban centers such as Douala, Yaoundé, and mile fifteen, close to Buea to respond to the needs of these children.

With the goals of preventing malnutrition, educating families to extend a hand to their needy ones, and to provide more support to the children, these centers are increasingly acknowledging the gradual erosion of the extended family institution in Cameroon. The traditional pattern of parenthood in Cameroon is gradually being washed away in another area: an increase in the rate of premarital sex and children born out of wedlock. In the urban centers all over the country, more young men and women are sexually active and facing the challenge which comes with pregnancy (Calvès, 2002, p. 445).

In addition, poverty has increased the rate at which younger girls go after "sugar daddies" with the goal of squeezing out money to make ends meet. While the sense of financial power has made a few wealthy men develop insatiable sexual appetite that "only more women" can fulfill, their failure to financially satisfy one partner had led to their mistresses developing insatiable financial needs that "only more men" can provide. Thus the rate of infidelity is high. In these urban centers also, economic hardship has again affected family formation in the sense that the age at first marriage is increasing more and more.

Furthermore, another sign of increasing family changes in Cameroon can be seen in the increased number of abortions. Young men and women are not very enthusiastic to have children and depend on their extended families to help them. Thus though not legalized, abortion is a common practice among teenagers and unmarried women in Cameroon and many sub-Saharan countries. It is often carried out in secret and can be performed in a crude manner by the girl herself mixing local herbs, by relatives and friends, by "native doctors," and in hospitals by trained nurses and physicians. As Calvès (2002) point out, the reasons why young men and women in Cameroon carry out abortion are diverse. They include the desire to complete their education, the lack of future prospects in the relationship with their partners, fear of parent's reaction if the pregnancy is discovered, the risk and fear of childbirth by teenage girls, the desire to postpone having another child when a sibling is still too young, economic hardship and poverty, poor health, and fear of abandonment by the father of a child (Calvès, p. 254-255). Though the order of the reasons may vary for boys and girls, the general outline applies to both. Despite efforts by governmental and non-governmental agencies to educate the public and young men/women in particular about the use of condom as a means to prevent unwanted pregnancies, STDs, and HIV/AIDS, condoms are still not widely used (Meeker & Klein, 2002, p. 2). Yet in cases of unwanted pregnancies, the young women along with their friends in most cases make the decision to abort the child and proceed to carry it out. They cannot fully trust the lineage system to stand by them.

Finally two most recent trends and attempts at family formation in Cameroon are common among elite women in the urban centers such as Douala and Yaoundé. First, many of them are no longer carried away with the need for elaborate bridewealth. What they need most is simply to have a husband who will accept monogamy, love them, and both are able to have financial security (Johnson-Hanks, 2007, p. 648). Second, some elite women are looking for marriage partners over the internet. As the marriage rates in the country falls due partly to economic hardship, many educated women in the urban centers have turned to cyberspace looking for foreign husbands. The internet offers a theoretical possibility for them to resolve the practical local reality of scarcity of husbands (ibid., p. 643).

Nevertheless, within this cyberspace, it is obvious that their quests for husbands are not limited this time to Cameroonians alone but to whoever their fortune may bring mostly from the European or American world. Moreover, successful marriages of this nature calls into question the structure and issues of traditional laws and customs, bridewealth, marriage relations, and the extended family as an institution. In addition to offering the prospect of winning a new husband, the internet has opened a new world for Cameroonian women, provided an extraordinary awareness of marital possibilities, exposed new "modern" feminine roles, and empowered them to know and fight for their rights and not accept second place. It offers Cameroonian women the dreams of experiencing western style marriage and seeing it as the ideal way of treating/dealing with future husbands. In this new context family lineage can be extended but in a transformative way. Whether internet acquired husbands will respect traditional African lineage institutions is an open question. On the other hand, the internet has also reinforced the idea that marriage is not all and that divorce is normal as seen on the "net."

CONCLUSION

Families in Cameroon as in other parts of Africa remain the institution around which the society revolves. They have tried to stay traditional, holding firm to the tenets of the extended family structure and manifested these efforts in the whole fabric of circumstances that generates, maintains, and promotes its survival. From birth through marriage, distribution of household roles, staying faithful to each other to divorce and ultimately death, the arms of the extended family are always nearby, and ready to provide help to keep families, and the future of the society together. Yet, as social institutions, the structure of families has not remained immune to changes. The rapid rate of urbanization and globalization are all leaving their impact on the family. It is increasingly evident in Cameroon, as in other parts of Africa, that while at the center their traditional extended lineage institutions are struggling to hold tight to their cherished cultural norms and social values, the individualistic trends of the west is fast knocking on their doors, chipping and roughing them at the edges, and seeping in gradually. Moreover, most of those chipping away these extended African family values are Africans.

Notes

1. Cameroon's location varies according to authors: some place it in West Africa, others in Central Africa, others in Central-West Africa, and still others in Equatorial Africa. This variation stems from the fact that the country is located between west and equatorial /central Africa, and as a result, it shares the major characteristics found within these regions, and has been referred to as "Africa in miniature."

2. Central Intelligence Agency (April 2010). *The World Fact Book: Cameroon.* Retrieved from https://www.cia.gov/library/publications/the-world-fact-book/geos/cm.html

3. United States Bureau of Citizenship and Immigration Services (October 2002). *Cameroon: Information on Forced or Marriage.* Retrieved from http://www.unhcr.org/refworld/docid/3f51ec864.html

4. A large part of the northern population is non-Islamized, and referred to by Muslims as pagans, *Kirdi.*

5. These instructions can be found on marriage certificates issued at the various Civil Status Registration centers in most urban areas in the country.

6. The rulers of the centralize chiefdom or kingdom in the Northwest and West Provinces of Cameroon are referred to by titles such as *fons,* or *fo.*

7. Having more wives does not guarantee having more children with each one of them.

8. Some men have interpreted polygyny as license to flirt and at each moment they step out, they claim they are looking for another bride.

9. John Mukum Mbaku (2005), *Culture and Customs of Cameroon*, (Westport, Connecticut: Greenwood Press), 145; Nanche Billa Robert (July 2009), *Marriage in Cameroon, Douala Cameroon*. Retrieved from http://www.cho-pachoplive.com/2009/07/marriage-in-cameroon-by-nanche-billa.html

10. See for example the reports of activities of the center taking care of street children in Yaoundé: Foyer de l'Esperance, (2007), *Rapport d'Activités, 2007* (Yaoundé: Presses de l'Université Catholique d'Afrique Centrale); Foyer de l'Esperance, (2002), *Historique du Foyer de l'Esperance* (Yaoundé: Presses de l'Université Catholique d'Afrique Centrale).

References

Adams M. (2003). Cameroon. In L. Walter & A. M. Tripp (Eds.) *The Greenwood Encyclopedia of Women's Issues Worldwide, Sub-Saharan African* (pp. 81-107). Westport: Greenwood Press.

Ardener, E. (1956). *Coastal Bantu of the Cameroons*. London: International African Institute.

Balaam, Y. (1997). *Enfants de la Rue et de la Prison dans une Ville Africaine (1975-1992)*. Yaoundé : Presses de l'Université Catholique d'Afrique Centrale.

Bernard, J. (1998). Two Marriages. In V. Hansen & A. I. G. Karen (Eds.) *Families in the U.S. Kinship and Domestic Politics* (pp. 449-457). Philadelphia: Temple University Press (reproduced from Jessie Bernard, *The Future of Marriage*, New York: World Publishing, 1972).

Brain, R. (1972). *Bangwa Kinship and Marriage*. Cambridge: Cambridge University Press.

Calvès, A.E. & D. Meekers. (1999). Advantages of Having Many Children for Women in Formal and Informal Unions in Cameroon. *Journal of Comparative Family Studies*, 30 (4), 617-639.

Calvès, A. E. (1999). Marginalisation of African Single Mothers in the Marriage Market: Evidence from Cameroon. *Population Studies*, 53(3), 291-301.

_____. (2002). Abortion Risk and Decision Making Among Young People in Urban Cameroon. *Studies in Family Planning*, 33 (3), 249-260.

_____. (2000). Premarital Childbearing in Urban Cameroon: Paternal Recognition, Childcare and Financial Support. *Journal of Comparative Family Studies*, 31 (4), 443-461.

Chem-Langhëë, B. (2004). *The Paradoxes of Self-Determination in the Cameroons Under United Kingdom Administration, The Search for Identity, Well-Being and Continuity*. Lanham: University Press of America.

Geschiere, P. (2005). Funerals and Belonging: Different Patterns in South Cameroon. *African Studies Review*, 48 (2), 45-64.

Goheen, M. (1996). *Men Own the Fields, Women Own the Crops: Gender and Power in the Cameroon Grassfield*. Madison: The University of Wisconsin Press.

Guyer, J. J. (1979). *The Economic Position of Bèti Widows: Past and Present*. Boston University: African Studies Center.

Jindra, M. (2005). Christianity and the Proliferation of Ancestors: Changes in Hierarchy and Mortuary Ritual in the Cameroon Grassfield. *Africa*, 75 (3), 356-377.

Johnson-Hanks, J. (2007). Women on the Market: Marriage, Consumption, and the Internet in Urban Cameroon. *American Ethnologist*, 34 (4), 642-658.

_____. (2003). Education, Ethnicity, and Reproductive Practice in Cameroon. *Population* (English Edition, 2002), 58 (2), 153-179.

Lafon, N. J. (Faay Lii Wong). 1988) *A History of the Catholic Church in Kumbo Diocese (1912-1988)*. Anomalous.

Le Vine, T. V. (1964). *The Cameroons from Mandate to Independence*. Berkeley: University of California Press.

Maillard, B. (1984). *Pouvoir et Religion Les Structures Socio-Religiouses de la Chfferie De Bandjoun (Cameroun)*. Berne: Peter Lang.

Martin, J. Y. (1970). *Les Matakam du Cameroun Essai sur la Dynamique d'une Société Pré-industrielle*. Paris: ORSTOM.

Mbaku, M. J. (2005). *Culture and Customs of Cameroon*. Westport, Connecticut: Greenwood Press.

_____. (2004). Economic Dependence in Cameroon: SAPs and the Bretton Woods Institutions. In J. M. Mbaku & J. Takougang (Eds.) *The Leadership Challenge in Africa, Cameroon Under Paul Biya*, (pp. 394-423). Trenton, NJ: Africa World Press.

Meeker, D. & M. Klein. (2002). Determinants of Condom Use among Young People in Urban Cameroon. *Studies in Family Planning*, 33 (4), 335-346.

Mope Simo, J.A. (1991). Royal Wives in the Ndop Plains. *Canadian Journal of Africain Studies / Revue Canadienne des Études Africaines*, 25 (3), 418-431.

Nyobe, J. C. (2006). *Réinsertion Socio-économique des Enfant de la Rue: Projet Conjoint MINAS/Croix-Rouge de Belgique*, Master 2 Thèses, Université de Yaoundé II, Cameroun and Université de Rennes I, France.

Percival, J. (2008). *The 1961 Plebescite: Choice or Betrayal*. Mankon, Bamenda: Langaa Research & Publishing.

Regis, A.H. (2003). *Fulbe Voices: Marriage, Islam, and Medicine in North Cameroon*. Boulder, Colorado: Westview Press.

Sudrkasa, N. (1998). Interpreting the African Heritage in Afro-American Family Organization. In K.V. Hansen & A.I. Garey (Eds.) *Families in the U.S. Kinship and Domestic Politics* (pp. 91-104). Philadelphia: Temple University Press (reproduced from H.P. McAdoo (Ed.) *Black Families* (2nd ed.), Sage Publication, 1988).

CHAPTER 5

PROCREATION AND MARRIAGE HERITAGE AND SOCIAL CHANGE AMONG THE ABAGUSII OF KENYA

Alfred T. Kisubi

INTRODUCTION

This chapter attempts to salvage and appraise what remains of *gusii* traditional beliefs and practices after an encounter with British colonialism for 155 years. It takes a brief look at the Abagusii in their historic and present daily, secular existence in the Kisii Highlands of Kenya. Because the study was carried out in Ogembo Division, Southeastern Kisii, close attention is paid to conditions in that region at the time of the study. It is a qualitative look at the functions of family, drawing contrasts between more traditional (but rapidly changing) and contemporary *gusii* society.

The goal here is to present what remains of traditional *gusii* culture as witnessed and recorded by the investigator between 1982 and 1985, with significant updates between 2003 and 2006. In Ogembo I attended many *gusii* rituals and obtained material from many student informants, who participated in the rituals as natives. Gradually, I became aware of the vast and complicated system of ceremonial practices going on around me. It was an astonishing and enriching experience to note the contrast between the modern economic life and the ordered arrangement and the colorful symbolism of *gusii* life, which included the extended family.

In the course of the research, student participants were encouraged to physically hunt for occasions such as birth, initiation, marriage, funeral and so on. We discussed why oral literature was dramatized at such occasions. We tried to compare Kisii performances with those of other parts of Africa, especially East Africa. Expressed in literature was the evidence that there are cultural links between the peoples of Africa. We observed also that members of the extended family keenly attended all performances. Very few people turned up just because they were enthusiastic fans like they do to a concert in the West or in African urban areas. Students were also assigned extensive readings and exposed to existing literature about the Abagusii.

In all the following overview is based on two sources: oral evidence based on several interviews in my private possession, conducted among the elders and students in Sameta location; scholarly studies recorded about various themes of *gusii* life between the 1940s and the 1980s in which accounts of the main features of *gusii* local and kinship organization have already been presented (Mayer, 1949, 1950; LeVine & LeVine, 1959; Knowles, 1956; LeVine, 1975).

Gusii society is organized on the basis of lineage, and polygamy is practiced in the region. Thus, the word "family" as used here does not refer to a restricted environment characterized by an intense relationship between parents and children also called nuclear family. It refers to an infinitely wide-ranging social environment—an extended family, more properly termed a "domestic unit" or a set of conjugal groupings living in close association and being bound to one another. In this context, it is argued that family must be construed in its broadest sense, involving a variety of forms depending on the social-cultural environment in which it emerges.

STUDY THESIS AND STUDY GOALS

In the United States, most people regard a family unit as a social group of two or more people, related by blood, marriage, or adoption who live together. (Macionis, 2006). There are several family structures like the extended family, the nuclear family, the blended family and the single family, to mention a few. In Kisii and many parts of Africa, extended family is a more familiar family unit to the natives than any other form. It consists of three or more generations of biologically and socially related individuals, who usually live in the same vicinity. Some may not live together, but keep very close relations with their kin. Due to industrialization, geographic location and social mobility, the nuclear family is becoming more common in Kisii (Ziehl, 2002). However, it is not yet as widespread or as idolized as in U.S. culture.

The *gusii* extended family still acts as a support group to many children. For example, if a child lost his or her father, other men like his paternal or maternal uncles, grandfathers, grandmothers, and older brothers may act as "social fathers." The child has many more adult mentors actively involved is raising him or her than a child growing up in a nuclear family or single family. Many Africans would agree that male and female relatives of the child help the child's parents with discipline, provide financial support and facilitate the child's education (Jayakody & Kalil, 2002; Masmas et. al., 2004; Nyamukapa & Gregson, 2005). Hence an African proverb says, "It takes the whole village to raise a child," a point already made in the chapter on motherhood by Sudarkasa, as well as those on Caribbean families.

In the U.S. African immigrant and African–American communities, single parents are supported in many ways by many relatives and friends helping out for free in child rearing (Roschelle, 1997). In addition, grandmothers help with baby sitting, offering guidance and warmth. (UNESCO, 1980; Hill, 2003). The extended family provides emotional support during mourning of a loved one, divorce, job loss, birth of a new born, holiday celebrations and numerous occasions like graduations, and weddings. It provides a variety of relatives whom one can confide in. Some are always available to call, visit or plan family gatherings, which in turn prevents loneliness. In addition an extended family may help with accommodation in times when one has been laid off or one is having marital problems. Extended family members might help their kin with employment if they have a family business. Unfortunately this ideal is under attack by forces of urbanization and globalization. As the young move to cities in their own country or even migrate to other countries in search of economic opportunity, or just fleeing other push factors such as war, natural disaster and oppression, geographic isolation adversely impacts the extended family. Physical and free social connection with extended families may be difficult. The more impersonal cyberspace communication replaces it. Members have to travel long distances on very expensive jet planes to visit with other members of the extended family, or pay at least the equivalent of five US dollars for a prepaid phone card to make just one phone call to connect with them.

It means that connections between members of the extended family are increasingly maintained in fewer ways than they were in the past. Foster (2000) notes that despite its weakening, the extended family remains the predominant caring unit for orphans in Africa. He laments that as the extended family crumbles under the forces of globalization increasing numbers of children are slipping through the safety net leading to increased risk of physical, social and psychological morbidity.

In this chapter, I will concentrate more on showing the traditional family values of the Abagusii, than on discussing the changes it has undergone. I do this in order to: educate the public and policy-makers about the cultural dynamics among a native people; suggest changes to existing disempowering and ineffective family policies; highlight the aspects of the extended family that still work in spite of the onslaught of current social changes so as to help stem the tide of alienation from the institution.

ORAL HISTORY: EARLY IMMIGRATION AND MIGRATION

While *gusii* oral history can help us understand how the *gusii* extended family came about, British colonial history in Kisii can explain the inception and dynamics of the forces of change that have impacted *gusii* practices, especially in the functioning of all *gusii* social institutions, including the extended family.

Abagusii belong to a larger group of Bantu peoples of Africa, but they have the closest linguistic connections with the Logoli section of the Luyia, the Kikuyu of central Kenya, and the Kuria (Batende) of central Kenya with whom they share some myths of origin (Oluoch, 1957). There are many versions of the Gusii creation legend but here we discuss only two versions, which generally point out a common origin but differ in the direction of migration. Generally, I was told that the Kisii migrated from a place called Misri (probably Egypt), due to population pressure on the arable and pastoral land. Southward they moved along the River Nile finally reaching East Africa through the Great Lakes region (Lakes: Albert, Kioga, Kivu, Tanganyika and Victoria) or by way of Mount Elgon in Eastern Uganda into Kenya. Here are the two versions:

One version says that once upon a time, the ancestors of the Abagusii lived in Misri (Egypt) and moved southward following the River Nile. They came to the north of Uganda, then moved eastward to Mount Elgon, then later on moved to Nandi Hills. Later they came to Kano plains, but because of Luo invasions, they moved farther southeast into the Kisii Highlands. (Charanah, 1982; Nyambarora, 1983; Onwonga, 1984). It is also believed that before the Abagusii came to Nyanza, especially the Kavirondo, they sojourned around Mount Elgon, and some might have been in the Sudan (Omwenga, 1984).

The second version differs from the first as to what direction they followed from Misri. It says that under the leadership of their patriarch, Omogusii, they left Misri and went westward into the Congo Basin in about 1000 A.D. They left the Congo forest where they first sojourned, because the tropical rainforest climate was not suitable for their agriculture and pastoral needs. They then moved eastward through Uganda, across Lake Victoria eastward to Uasin Gishu, but they did not stay because the land there was not suitable for their sedentary purposes either. On they pushed into Kisumu area but were repelled by the Luo. They decided to search further south. Eventually they climbed the Kisii Highlands, and saw that the land was fertile and the rainfall sufficient but not as torrential as in the Congo rainforest. So they settled to produce and reproduce to nurture and expand their lineage (Mumbo, 1985).

Both versions agree that the Abagusii migrated from their original habitat in search of land for pasture and farming. Their population had outgrown the land capacity of Misri. On their way to the Kisii Highlands, they mixed with Luos. Though they fought many battles, the Abagusii intermarried with the Luo to produce the present Abagusii and the Mowagori of Western Kenya. That is why these two ethnic groups have Luo influences in their culture, such as the round shape of their traditional huts.

Concerning Gusii clans, it is said that Omogusii had four sons from his wives Kemunto, Moraa and Kwamboka. The sons usually misunderstood each other, though they spoke the same language. They feuded over land and the game that they hunted. To break the conflict, each son decided to leave his family and wander off into the wide world. Wherever he went, each son got married and started not only a new family, but also a new lineage. Thus the various sons became patriarchs of the Gusii clans: Mogetutu, Nyaribari, Mobasii, Mochari and Mogirango. Each lineage changed the original Bantu language to suit the new environment and create a new identity. This led to the diversity of the Bantu languages that are closely related to Ekegusii, such as Kuria and Mowagori. When he settled in Kisii, Omogusii had many other children before he died. All the Abagusii cerebrate him as their patriarch (Onsombi, 1985).

BRIEF COLONIAL HISTORY

In 1908, the British colonial government of Kenya sent an expedition against the Abagusii of Kitutu, who were opposed to the establishment of a government station at Kisii (Getembe), opened in 1907. Their disapproval was demonstrated by the murder of two constables, an Indian trader and several Luo men.

Again in January 1908, an attempt was made to kill Northcote, the local Assistant District Commissioner. A British punitive expedition took place twelve days later and lasted for two weeks. As a result, over 200 Abagusii were killed, 7000 head of cattle and 5000 sheep were captured and huts burned.

121

The Abagusii did not yield easily. Six years later the Abagusii of Kitutu and Nyaribari searched the deserted administrative headquarters at Kisii. This had been evacuated on September 9, 1914 as a precaution against German attacks from Tanganyika in the south, during the First World War. At the same time, the Roman Catholic Mission at Nyabururu and the Indian shops at Riana were looted. For these outrages the colonial government fined the Abagusii 10,000 head of cattle, and 1,600 young men were sent to work on public projects.

Eventually the British subdued resistance. Their early administration aimed at establishing their own type of law regardless of the native customs that had bound Abagusii together for centuries before (Were & Wilson, 1960; LeVine, 1959). By the time Kenya got independence in 1963, the Abagusii were torn between two worlds: their own and that of the departing colonials.

KINSHIP AND SOCIAL STRUCTURE: PEOPLE IN COMMUNITY

Individual and group interaction within and between the Gusii clans: Mogetutu, Nyaribari, Mobasii, Mochari and Mogirango occur over and over again in a similar way. There is a network of statuses or positions, roles and role expectations whose interactions are regulated by social norms. It is this social structure, this kinship system in its traditional context that we describe next.

A deep sense of kinship with all it implies has been one of the strongest forces in traditional African life. Among the Abagusii everyone was part of this system. Each one of them knew what was expected of him or her and what he or she could expect in return. One important characteristic of a kinship group is its "corporate nature." Members tend to be loyal to their lineage. They strive to meet the standards of conduct established by the head of the group and following his or her directives.

In a community, one should show a deep sense of kinship, which is one of the strongest forces and outstanding features of traditional African life. It is the ties that bind relatives together. Kinship is established through consanguinity (birth), affinity (marriage) and blood (clan). The importance of kinship to the community is that it controls the way people or individuals behave in society (Mbiti, 1985; Mazrui, 1991; Kobiane et. al., 2005). It controls social relationships; it governs marital customs (incest taboos). This means that each individual is a brother, or a sister, father or mother, grandfather or grandmother, cousin, brother-in-law or sister-in-law, uncle or aunt. An old wise saying goes, "One Man (person) is no Man (person)."

It is in this context that Jomo Kenyatta (1965, p. 119, 195) identifies the African as 'first and foremost several people's relative and several people's contemporary," expected to speak as a member of a certain group rather than in the first person singular. Noni Jobavu (1960, p. 51) agrees that as an African "you represent others or others represent you so that you are ever conscious even of relative status, classification and independent relationship in terms of which your conduct is being judged." Only by living together within our families and with our fellows organized under established (agreed) and recognized (respected) rules and relationships can the extended family truly become a community of charity and justice. What society requires are "transparent lives," according to Victor Uchendu (2007, p. 14-18). Solitude is therefore regarded as a "mark of wickedness," and "secretive persons are held in contempt." A deep sense of kinship with all it implies has been one "technology" Africa can transfer to those societies which are affluent but poor in family values.

Since everyone was related in someway to everyone else, each one of them was expected to know what was expected of him or her and what he or she expected in return. To provide closer human co-operation especially in hard times of crisis and conflict or even in good times of feasting and celebration was one of the expectations and obligations of the individual (Charles, 2006). Unity in all walks of life was another. Respect, co-operation and charity, were values that Abagusii highly regarded and expected of an individual. In return, the lineage provides "security, protection, and companionship for the individual."

MARRIAGE CEREMONIES:
ADOLESCENCE AND YOUNG ADULTHOOD

Gusii Marriage Customs and Ceremonies

The parents of the young man are responsible to select a suitable wife for him. Or if he has decided on a particular girl he wishes to marry they may be willing to accept his choice and then approach the parents of the girl on his behalf. Or if the parents choose and either of the couple is unwilling, their parents may not force the marriage. Cases of conflict of interest have been known between the children's choices and their parents' choice, resulting in elopement. In most cases a friend or relative of the young man, acting as an intermediary go-between (*esigami*), introduces the matter of marriage to the parents of the girl. (For other groups, the father and the mother of the girls are approached separately by the paternal uncle and the mother of the young man respectively).

Both monogamous and polygamous marriages are found among the Abagusii. Eighty-eight percent of the Abagusii couples allowed some form of polygyny, in traditional society. In such instances, the first wife will have a more formal marriage ceremony than the second, and as for monogamy, a divorced woman will fetch less bride wealth and have a less elaborate ceremony than a virgin. However, this trend is changing rapidly as Christianity and the money economy become the order of the day. The practice of polyandry, where a woman may have more than one husband, has never occurred among the Abagusii. The proverb: *Basacha babere mbakoba nyomba emo* warns that there cannot be two husbands in one house for the same wife.

However, Abagusii practice woman-to-woman marriage. A widow whose husband left no son because she was barren or had only girls will woo a young girl to marry her. If the girl consents, the widow will pay bride wealth just as the male suitor would do. However, the woman-to-woman marriage ceremony does not have the same structure as the heterosexual marriage. It is not separable between ritual seclusion, liminality and reaggregation. It is an incognito contract. The young girl will come to live with her woman-husband. If she gets pregnant by any man in the neighborhood, the child will belong to the widow, who by tradition is the pater. In the past, the genitor did not have a right to this child. In fact, if the child was a boy, he would be named after the widow's late husband. However, these days the genitor can invoke Kenyan law to claim the baby.

Woman-to-woman marriage played an important role in traditional Kisii. As discussed by Sudarkasa in Chapter two of this volume, it ensured that the barren widow had a chance to have a child. It also enabled the widow to get a son who assured her ownership of her late husband's estate in this patrilineal society. Women who did not have sons usually had no property rights, especially to land. So to ensure her stay after her husband's death, she had to get a son through a woman-to-woman marriage.

Courtship (Ekerorano): Dramatic Transition

It is proper now to look at traditional *gusii* marriage rites pertaining to *ekerorano* as a period of transition that has considerable importance for the individual and society. *Ekerorano* is the most dramatic part of the long liminal adolescence. It is the climax of this transitional drama. It is episodic because it includes rites of separation and transition. It terminates with rites which insure a preliminary incorporation into marriage and adulthood. Above all, it marks the separation of the individual from transitional adolescence.

The father of the boy is responsible for looking for a good go-between (*esigani*) who is informed about his son's intention to get married. He also tells the *esigani* how many cows he can afford. The go-between goes to a family with a good daughter--good not only in looks, but also in manners, attitude, industry and temper. He usually crosschecks his knowledge of the would-be affinal family by clandestine investigations. In many cases however, people in traditional society know each other very well.

The go-between is regarded as a trustworthy orator, who can use his art of persuasion to convince the girl's parents. Both parties actually depend on him (there are no women go-betweens) as he is supposed to be an impartial, mutual emissary. If anything crops up to threaten the negotiations, he is expected to converse and reconcile the parties.

After the news has been broken to the girl's parents, and only if the father (not the mother) agrees to the proposal, a day is fixed for the go-between to take the suitor to the girl's home for the maiden courtship visit (*ekerorano*). A friend or relative of the young man acting as an intermediary, together with the boy's peers, go to the girl's home for *ekerorano*. If the girl rejects the boy, she does not give his company chairs to sit on, and she does not give them porridge to drink. So they go home and the marriage proceedings stop.

If the girl's father wants the relationship to continue, he forces the girl to accept the boy. He arranges for the bride wealth negotiations. After the payments are made, strong boys from the suitor's family come and take the girl by "force." A night is secretly arranged when the young man and his friends will come to fetch the girl by mock-fighting the brothers of the girl symbolically. The fetching of the girl is called "catching of the bride". She is, however, not stolen but is given away under mutual agreement between the two families. The girl cries, because she is sorry to leave her parents. In this way she shows how much she loves them. In her heart the girl maybe very happy she is going to marry the man of her choice and her crying takes on the character of pretension. The entire episode is known in Kisii custom as '*omoyaba*,' meaning first meeting with husband.

When both father and daughter accept the proposal the *ekerorano* is a happy moment. As the young men visit with the girl's family, a small feast is given to them. A bull is slaughtered in the cowshed (*boma*) to be eaten by both parties in a kind of communion. On this night, they eat, drink and dance until morning. Songs are sung by maids, colleagues, women and men of the bride's consanguinity, while parents give her gifts, such as saucepans, mingling stick, a small pot and other cooking utensils; some kind of dowry but not as elaborate as among the Indian castes, where brides take a lot of wealth from their homes to the grooms' homes.

Usually there is drinking and rejoicing with *ekerorano* songs. The girl is allowed to participate in whatever deliberations the two families make. She has to give her consent, after which the boy's party will return home after fixing a day for the boy's parents to come to the girl's home to negotiate the bride wealth and draw the program for the wedding (*enyangi*). The following are the lyrics of some *ekerorano* songs that are sung on various occasions that mark courtship and betrothal between a man and a woman:

Table 1: Ekerorano (Betrothal) Mate selection Song

Ekegusii	English
Bono Ntorigeti Gochora, Gochora	We Want to Choose, to Choose
Bono ntorigeti gochora, gochora	We want to choose, to choose
Bono toregeti gochora omoiseke omuya	We want to choose a beautiful spouse
Nigo oranyare komoira, komoira	Who will suit, suit
Nigo oranyare komoira omomura omuya	Who will suit the handsome suitor
Nyaboke torigeti gochora gochora	We have chosen Nyaboke, chosen
Nyaboke torigeti gochora nere omuya	Nyaboke the village belle
Bamura ba seito nabarumu, nabarumu	Our young men are heroic, heroic
Bamura ba seito nabarumu, nabakora egasi	Our young men are heroic, they work hard.

Table 2: Ekerorano (Betrothal) Values Song

Ekegusii	English
Narora banto bange bakongaina abaiseke babo	There're those who stop their daughters
Kakongaina abaiseke babo tibachi ase abataka	Stop their daughters marrying the poor
Baiseke babo baboboria ninkia ase abataka?	Their daughters ask, why not the poor?
Abataka mwanya banto,	The poor are human beings
Nabanda mwanyabanto!	The rich are just human beings too,
Abataka nabasacha,	The poor are men
N'abanda nabasacha!	As the rich are men too
Abanto abataka nabanyasae	Poor people belong to God
Niabanto abanda nabanyasae!	Like the rich are God's people too!

Bride wealth: A Symbol of Exclusion

There are different marriage forms in Kisii, some more dominant than others. Marriage arrangements (*ekerorano*) entail some form of consideration or value provided by the groom and/or his group of kin, friends and supporters of the girl and her group. This pertains in almost forty percent of *gusii* society. The consideration is comprised of eighty percent bride wealth payments and ten percent bride service arrangements. Only one percent of the sample material used in this report indicates that marriage arrangements are accompanied by a dowry by the girl instead of bride wealth payment or bride service.

Marriages are legitimized in the first place by a bride wealth transaction (Mayer 1950). The young man and his friends go to the girl's home to negotiate with the parents of the girl. (The fixing of the bride wealth is actually done by the uncles of the girl, but these uncles have been instructed beforehand by the parents of the girl how much they should ask). A small feast is given by the parents of the girl. The girl is present at the negotiation talks and must give her consent. After the girl has given her consent the friends of the young man will return to their homes. Male and female goats are sent to the parents of the girl to symbolize the bond between the young man and the girl. Moreover, the parents of the young man accompanied by elders take a pot of *busaa* beer brewed at their homestead to the parents of the girl. The first part of the bride wealth is taken to the girl's home by friends of the young man. Later the second or the third part of the bride wealth follows, after which the young man asks the parents of the girl to give him their daughter.

Those boys who cannot pay bride wealth are denied the fruits of legitimate marriage such as respect and status among adults. They are separated and are excluded from marriage privileges. If they cohabitated, like some of them do, the general public does not recognize their marriage until they have gone through *ekerorano*, a period of transition and *enyangi*, which is the period of reaggregation. This case study illustrates how serious bride wealth is among the Abagusii. Their oral arts stress the importance of this practice. The following song laughs at a young man who cannot afford to pay bride wealth or a girl who elopes, without bride wealth.

Table 3: The Cow Song

Ekegusii	English
Ngombe	Cow
O oyaye oyaya	Oh oh you, you
Oyaye uyaya	Oh you
Oyaye uyaya	Oh you
Moisia koraniba	Uncircumcised boy, buy a cow first
Moisia koraniba	Boy, buy a cow first
Omoisia koraniba	Uncircumcised boy buy a cow
Omoisia, omosia koraniba	The cow gives sorrow and great joy
Ngombe neyobororo	The cow is of great importance.
Ngombe, ngombe neyobororo	

(Onwonga, 1984; Kisubi, 1985).

Cattle are of importance for bride wealth. If there are no cattle, there is no wife for the young man, although he may be circumcised. So it is fine for the uncircumcised to plan for cattle. The cow is also important for milk and breeding herds. The bull, too, is handy for this breeding, while oxen pull the plow in this predominantly agrarian culture. Beef and draught cattle are as important to the Abagusii as dairy though for lack of grazing ground each homestead keeps less than ten heads.

Among the Abagusii, the bride is of value. Her value lies partly in her fecundity as a mother and partly in her contributions to the workforce of the group she joins through marriage. Oral arts are full of songs that stress this fact:

Table 4: Obweri (Bride wealth) Song

Ekegusii	English
Obweri	Bride wealth
Aliririririri...	*Aliririririri...*
Anyomba yomosangore	The house of the bride
Tobwate toyesangore	Let's praise it
Omokungu nomosacha	Wife and husband
Toumarane bweri	Let's meet them
Obweri nabwo	For with bride wealth
Omokungu na bana	Come a wife and children
Onye tobwati obweri	No bride wealth,
Tokwenyorera mokungu	No wife.
Karwe obweri mosarare	Give bride wealth, save your name
Ekero mwabwatanigwe	Have some descendants, keep your name

(Onsombi, 1984; Mumbo, 1985)

Bride wealth therefore, is an expenditure of the groom's family and conversely, an income for the bride's family. It was marriage insurance among the traditional Abagusii, especially when marriage arrangements were exclusively the function of the boy's family in cooperation with the girl's family.

The groom's family gave the bride's family goats and cattle along with other gifts (LeVine and LeVine, 1955-57). Abagusii women are traditionally considered to be of value to the prospective spouse and his group, and, to obtain such value, some compensation must be made to the group giving up the girl. Sara LeVine narrates the plight of Suzanna Bosibori, a young *gusii* girl, whose bride wealth was not paid. "Bosibori says vehemently "my father has not come to greet Ogaro, my son; he has not sent even a shirt.

He won't do anything for my son until Ongaki has paid cattle, and Ongaki had paid nothing at all, not even a chicken. Ongaki dares not go there to greet his in-laws. He would not be welcome there." (LeVine, 1979, p. 43).

First marriages for both partners are expensive and demand chastity of both the boy and girl. Virginity of both is required (Luluaki, 1997; Shell-Duncan et. al, 1999). However, subsequent unions of people who have for some reason been separated or divorced from former spouses are not seriously regarded by the community and even by their parents. These unions are less formal, less expensive, and depending on age and social status, an individual has more freedom to contract the union on his or her own.

These days, bride wealth deters the adolescent who doesn't have cows or goats or money to think of getting married immediately after circumcision. In the past, the boy worked hard to help his father get the cows. Today, the boy goes to school in search of a certified career. Bride wealth legitimizes sexual activity in a marriage which is expected by society to produce children. Virginity is also expected of the girls. She who is not a virgin, fetches very little bride wealth.

The requirement to pay bride wealth necessitates that adults closely participate in the marriage arrangements. It is the father's cows to be used, so he arranges the marriage. It is the girl's parents to receive bride wealth, so they, too, arrange her marriage with keen expectation.

Of course, there are more than economic reasons for paying and receiving bride wealth, but I have stressed its economic implications to show how it prevented the adolescent from arbitrary marital behavior. Adolescents are expected to keep good rapport with their parents. The bad boys or bad girls always have it rough or never manage a decent marriage.

Reaggregation or Incorporation: By the Wedding (Enyangi)

Enyangi completes a marriage. Besides emphasizing the substitution of husband's for father's authority and the transition from one set of lineage allegiances to another, *enyangi* marks the entry into a new stage of life: in this aspect it follows on a series of earlier rites of passage of which circumcision is the most important for boys and clitoridechotomy for girls (Mayer, 1950, p. 113-125). A woman of any age who has not made *enyangi* is technically a "girl." She is distinguishable in everyday life by not having the marriage ankle rings or a Christian marriage band or one of the special *enyangi* names. Such a woman cannot pass to higher religious or social status. She cannot, for instance, be initiated as a female circumciser, a diviner or a marriage priestess (*omokundikane*). Similar rules apply to boys who have not made *enyangi* (Mayer, 1950).

Enyangi (wedding) is the only ceremony at which the usual separation between men's and women's activities is waived. The *gusii* traditional *enyangi* (wedding) has four important ceremonies: (a) *Egekwano*, (b) *Egasabo*, (c) *Egetaorio*, and (d) *Echorwa*. These are the rites of marriage which consist chiefly of rites of permanent incorporation into the new environment.

Egekwano is the occasion when elders (men) from the girl's home come to meet the elders (also men) in the suitor's home to negotiate the bride wealth. The father of the boy has to offer one or two cows. Sometimes someone in the boy's paternal extended family, who appreciates the marriage of their boy, will offer the cows.

Egesabo is the occasion the suitor and other young men again go to the girl's home for a more intimate visit with their affines. They normally go at night. With their affines, they drink *busaa* beer, chat and feast the night away. Early in the morning, their company returns home.

Egetaorio is another interesting occasion. The suitor and some sturdy young men of his acquaintance or clan go to the girl's home taking *obokano* (a harp) with them for a night of music and dance. They also drive a bull along with them. *Echorwa* is the occasion when the wedding procession leaves the girl's home to go to the boy's home.

At *enyangi* the hero and heroine of the day figure with equal prominence in all the rites performed. In theory, the priest and priestess, and all male and female in-laws on either side also participate equitably in a modality of social relationship or *communitas*. This ceremonial equality of sexes is in keeping with the underlying meaning of *enyangi*. Since at a stage of marriage *enyangi* emphasizes the personal bond between a certain man and a certain woman, the goodwill of the two partners has to be reckoned equally important (Mayer, 1950).

As a rite of passage, *enyangi* serves to punctuate at one and the same time a male and female life, both husband and wife being elevated to a new status. Marriage rituals and ceremonies then, dealing with a sphere of life in which women and men become adults and acquire higher statuses in society, are appropriate settings for the emphasis of emotional and de jure relationships among the Abagusii, regardless of other changes they may have gone through over the years.

The suitor and five young men go to the girl's home, taking a harp with them. The suitor wears a crown (*esumati* or *ekore*), and carries a shield and spear. They are accompanied by a young boy called a heresy witness (*omongwasi*), who carries a horn (*chintere*). That night they eat, drink and dance the night away.

Before they enter the main gate of the girl's home, they clash with strong men from the girl's clan in a mock fight. This is to test the strength of the boy and his group. After the "fight", which the suitor's group always wins, the suitor and his company heroically storm into the girl's compound, where somebody will welcome them and usher them into a house.

At 8:00 a.m. they are given the girl by her father. Most memorable of all rituals on this occasion is the matrimonial ceremony between the suitor and the girl by one of the elders on the girl's side (*omokundekane*). And so during this *enyangi* night the young man and the girl become husband and wife in the presence of the brothers of the young man, old women and sisters of the bride. If during their first sexual intercourse blood is produced, due to the breaking of the hymen, this blood is collected on pebbles by witnesses and these pebbles are brought to the parents of the bride, showing that their daughter was a virgin. There is great rejoicing and the young man will thank the parents of the bride for the fact that their daughter was a virgin and that she was well looked after. He will send the parents of his bride a big bull as a token of his gratitude.

The suitor, leading the marriage procession, wields his spear and shield; symbols of manhood. The bride carries a small *calabash (enkondo)* as a sign of womanhood. Two witnesses from the girl's side (*abomoimari*) also carry horns like the *omongwasi* and walk with the young girls from the bride's side that carry maize or millet flour for the newlywed woman to her new home.

Customarily, on their way to the suitor's home, they are not supposed to meet anyone walking along the paths. Nobody should precede or try to overtake a wedding procession. Anybody caught doing so is booed or even assaulted. The bridegroom controls the procession. If he stops, they too stop. The bride keeps a close eye on her small *calabash (enkondo)*, until she enters her new compound where her new mother-in-law greets her with honor and respect.

After the mother-in-law takes the bride's *calabash (ekondo)* from her hands, the procession enters the bridegroom's parents' house, only through the front door into the front or living room (*eero*). After this, they go into the suitor's circumcision house.

Three days later, the heresy witnesses are sent by the boy's mother to go into the newlywed's house and check on the bridegroom's potency. Normally they are an old woman and a young girl. They come with food which the bridegroom should not touch. It is to be eaten only by women, while they consult with the bride on matters concerning her husband's potency.

After their investigation, the heresy witnesses go to report the matter to the boy's mother. If the report is positive, then amid happiness, the bride is given marriage bands (anklets) to wear. The anklets symbolize the state of being married and off limits. Usually the day she starts wearing anklets she takes a new nick name such as one of the following: *Chierosoia, Chiebunga, Chietunda* and so on.

Wearing anklets is not enough to fully integrate a woman into her husband's community. People look forward to the day when she will bear a child, especially a son who will perpetuate the clan and extended family. Childbearing is an important custom among the Abagusii. Though it is natural and controlled by biological conditions, society regards it as if it were caused or even prevented by society.

The new wife will stay at her husband's home for a period between one week and a month. (For other ethnic groups, when the girl enters the house of the young man her feet are washed by a member of the young man's family to show she is welcome). During the period of a week to a month at the homestead of her new husband, a team of girls visit her to keep her company. Boys from the homestead of the new husband will also visit and there will be dancing and feasting for two or three days. After the celebration the girls will return to their homes and only one girl will remain behind. She is called *'omokobi.'* After living at her husband's home for a month the new wife returns to her parents' home and she is welcome at the gate, by one of her relatives who waits for her by custom. A chicken is killed and its beak is tied on a string and put around her neck. This is considered to be a blessing.

She is accompanied by many relatives of her husband's clan and there is a great feast at the homestead of her parents. The feast is offered to her husbands relatives and her parents pay for the feast. The beer offered is a symbol of friendship, communion, unity and acceptability. The parents question their married daughter about her stay at her husband's home. The new wife waits at her parents' home till the goat gift for menstruation is brought to her by her husband, accompanied by his friends. The goat, or sometimes a cow in rich families, is slaughtered and dished out to the parents of the new wife, and the remaining part of goat-meat or beef is given to the new husband and his friends. They eat everything including the head, which must be consumed last. After the feast ends the wife returns to her husband's home in the company of her husband and his relatives. Now husband and wife are ritually ready to settle down to their new life, where they are expected to bear and raise children, so that the new couple may be remembered when they die and their family and clan will be secured. Below is an assortment of, *Enyangi* (Wedding) Songs:

Table 5: Enyangi (Wedding) Witness Song

Ekegusii	English
Rero Twensi Tobeire Kirori	Today We Bear Witness
Rero twensi tobeire kirori	Today, we bear witness
Ase abaminto aba babere	To you our brother and sister
Omomura no moiseke	Going to be a family...
Naimwe kemokogenda timogechana	Never ever hate each other
Mwanchane ase obogima bwaino	Love your husband as you love yourself
Morokia abana cheniora chingiya	
Aye omoiseke osike iso nanyoko biara	Love your wife for life
Naye omomura osike iso na nyoko	Teach your children good manners
	Honor your parents-in-law.

Table 6: Enyangi (Wedding) Virginity Song

Ekegusii	English
Omoiseke Kero are Sobo	A virgin Girl At home
Omoiseke kero are sobo	A virgin comes tonight
Ni are buna enyomba yerigena	She is a house of stone
Omoiseke kero are sobo	A virgin girl at home
Ni are buna enyomba yerigena	Is a house of stone
Aaee aaee nigare buna enyomba yerigena	Aheh, aheh, a house of stone
Aaee aaee nigare buna enyomba yeri-gena omoiseke kare sobo nigo akoyorerwa Amaguta nesabuni	Aheh, aheh, a house of stone A virgin girl gets cosmetics and soap from parents
Omoiseke kare sobo nigo akogorerwa Amaguta nesabuni	A virgin gets cosmetics and soap from parents
Aaee aaee nigare buna enyomba yerigena	Aheh, aheh, a house of stone
Aaee aaee nigare buna enyomba yerigena	Aheh, aheh, she's a house of stone

Table 7: **Enyangi *(Wedding)* Solo-Chorus Happy Song**

Ekegusii	English
Omongina n'Omugaka Goka Rende	Mother And Father Are Happy
S:Omongian n'omogaka goka rende	S: Mother and father must be happy
C:Ero mbande... !	C: Behold, the succulent banana sucker!
S:Mwanyorire oyorabakonye rende	S: You have got one to fetch water for you
C:Ero mbande...!	C: Look, the Sappy Sucker!
S:Nainde nere orabachiere roche rende	S: You have got one to help you
C:Ero mbande...!	C: Behold, the banana sucker!
S:Mwanyorire oyarabowugere rende	S: You have got one to cook for you
C:Ero mbande...!	C: Behold the succulent sucker!

Table 8: **Enyangi *(Wedding)* Bride's Duty Song**

Ekegusii	English
Omokungu Omoriakaria Ache Inka	Welcome Home Our Bride
Omokungu omoriakaria ache inka	Welcome home our Bride
Achenka ee, ee	Welcome home, eh, eh
Akore egasi yaye mono,	To work hard and well,
Akonye abana baye,	To bear children,
Taba omworo gaki gaki	Never to be lazy at all, at all

Table 9: **Enyangi *(Wedding)* Multiply Song**

Ekegusii	English
Osarare Osarare Osarare	Multiply, Multiply, Multiply
Osarare osarare osarare	Multiply, multiply, multiply
Osarare osarare osarare	Multiply, multiply, multiply
Mobe buna chiinyeke chianyancha	Be sand grits of the sea
Mobe buna chinyeke chianyancha	Be the sand grit of the sea shore
Moirende nababisa baino nase	Watch out for foes against your seeds
Ebisakwe bionsi	All sides, watch
Ebisakwe bionsi	All days, watch...
Tigara buya	Stay well
Nyasae abarende buya	God, keep you well
Emiaka yonsi	All the years
Abarende buya	Keep you fit
Emiaka yonsi	All years.

Table 10: Enyangi (Wedding) Processional Song

Ekegusii	English
Abwo Gocha	They Are Coming
Abwo gocha	They're Coming
Abana Baminto Eeh	Our Children, eh
Abwo gocha	They are coming,
Gocha,	Are coming,
Abana baito, eeh	Our children, eh
Abana baito abaya	Our good children
Abwo gocha abana baito eeh	They are coming, our children eh
Gocha abana baito abaya eeh	Are coming our good children eh
Mbono nkare gochia egari naririra baba	They are coming in a car, mother
Mbono nkare gochia egari naririra baba	They are coming by car, mother
Nkare gochia	They are coming
Gocha.	Coming.

Table 11: Enyangi (Wedding) Bride's Consanguine Farewell Song

Ekegusii	English
Bono Gwachire	Now You're Gone
Bono gwachire	Now you're gone
Kaweri omongwana	Goodbye good girl
Chiombe chiagera	Because of the cattle
Kwaeri omwana oito	Goodbye our daughter
Korende tojumia	But don't worry
Naboigo ense ere!	That's what the world is!
Nyasae akorende	May God guide you
Onyore abana	So that you get children
Ntobe togogokwania abwo-bwoo	We will be greeting you later.
Kwaeri oyominto.	Goodbye our daughter.

To announce that she is married and deter would-be suitors, Omo-gusii married woman wore anklets on her legs, and kept it on till she died Divorce was not permissible those days. However, these days, this custom is very faintly found among very old spouses, about one per square kilometer, with population density of seven hundred thousand people. The following song is about the anklet:

Table 12: Enyangi (Wedding) Anklet (Moraa) & the Leg (Omari) Song

Ekegusii	English
Ekio Negetinge	The Anklet and the Leg
Ekio negetinge kiamwabo omorondo	The anklet and the leg know each other
Oyayeee, ekio negetinge	Oh yeah, yeah, anklet and leg
Ekio negetinge kiamwabo omorondo	The anklet and the leg know each other
Oyayeee, ekio negetinge	Oh yeah, yeah, anklet and leg...
Oyio Moraa, oyio Moraa	Moraa, oh Moraa
Ooyomwabo Omari	And Omari will too,
Oyayeee, oyio Moraa	Know each other
Oyio Moraa oyomwabo Omari	Moraa the bride of Omari
Oyayeee, oyio Moraa	Yeah, oh Moraa

The Dynamics of Gusii Marriage & Family

As pointed out earlier, the colonial challenge to and disintegration of Abagusii traditions have resulted in some changes in marriage and other practices. Attitudes have changed today as a result of western propelled "modernization" and many of the elderly feel alienated and sometimes insulted by the onslaught of Western influence (Bascom 1959; Little, 1959; Mere, 1976; Chetty, 1980). For example, *ekerorano* (courtship) and *enyangi* (wedding) practices have changed. Marriage is becoming less a function of the extended family and more of a responsibility of the individuals and their nuclear family. These days, one can marry in church, court or follow the traditional way. Bride wealth is losing its strong traditional role as marriage insurance. Today, some marriages are consummated without bride wealth. In towns, many modern marriages are ending in divorce. Sarah LeVine (1976) illustrates the demise of bride wealth with the Suzanna Bosibori case. Although Ongaki had not paid bride wealth, Suzanna "was still living with him." (LeVine, 1976). LeVine argues that ten years before her research in the 1970s, a very large portion of marriages were still taking place according to traditional practices. However, with the extreme shortage of land, fewer and fewer farmers have space on which to graze cattle. In the past, Abagusii took ownership of cattle as a matter of course. These days, however, the majority have no cattle at all or have them only briefly when they have received some in payment of bride wealth or bought them prior to making such payments themselves.

The cost of cattle has risen so enormously, young men do not have the resources to buy them, unless those young men come from modern (i.e. educated) families with high paying jobs. As a result, the custom of bride wealth payments when girls go from their consanguineal to their affinal home has diminished rapidly. The traditional practice is now very rare indeed. As a result most of the oral arts that mention bride wealth are not taken seriously as they used to be in the past.

Bride wealth, is payable in money and in installments. The prospective bridegroom (not necessarily his family) saves a lump sum of money, and then he buys goats and cows. The balance of the bride wealth is paid in money to the bride's family over a long period of time. These days, in order to fully enter into adulthood, one has to spend half a life time in formal educational institutions to acquire the status and skills of the new economy. Economic pressures do not allow young people to follow the procedures of marriage that their parents and grandparents followed (Van Den Berghe & Pierre, 1965; Steklov, 2002). Marriage alone does not make one an adult either. Both men and women need a job or business outside the home to be able to afford and sustain a marriage and family relationship.

As a result of the increasing living expenses in the modern sector, Christianity, Islam and secularization of institutions by education, urbanization and the new nation state, polygyny and woman-to-woman marriages are giving way to monogamy (Gugler, 2002). New forms of sexuality have emerged: cohabitation, prostitution and mere friendly relations between senior bachelors and spinsters are rapidly taking over the more traditional forms (Ogionwo, 1975). Around Ogembo town only a minority of the people actually lived in polygynous families, while well over half of all marriages were monogamous. This is because the Seventh-Day Adventist Church is very strong in the area. However, I noticed that some married men may sneak to an outside mistress or prostitute. Many of the transients, government workers and non-farming casual workers depend on the newer forms of sexuality: cohabitation, prostitution and friendships for convenience. The marriage ceremony which is structured into separation liminality and reaggregation (Van Gennep, 1960) is no longer the only access to a spouse and children.

In many cases, young people are not prepared to wait until the boy has earned the money to buy the cattle. Almost every *gusii* girl elopes. She often secretly leaves her parents' home and goes to her lover's home without ritual or ceremony. She immediately starts to behave like a married woman. The parents are often most indignant when this occurs. Neither the girl's parents nor the boy's or any extended family member involved regards the marriage as legitimate until the cattle have been paid. Regardless of the many children she might bear and regardless of the many years she might cohabit, her marriage is null and void until the cattle have been paid. In most cases, the parents of the girl are disappointed. The bride wealth is never paid, yet they cannot take their daughter back, so they let her continue cohabitating.

Migrant workers always visit bars where night *malayas* (prostitutes) wait to solicit drinks and cash. Many women in the neighborhood married or not, also seek other men even when their own husbands are at home. On two occasions, women were caught in adultery (LeVine, 1976). These new sexual relationships have altered the ceremonies of marriage. So much that the older generations think their society is losing the old family values, replacing them with unstructured forms.

Whatever change has occurred, *gusii* marriage still plays a role of enabling *gusii* boys and girls to move from adolescence to adulthood. Whether it is done in the church or traditionally outside the church, the bride and groom go through periods of separation, transition and reaggregation, the universal structure of the rites of passage (Van Gennep, 1960). The oral arts are therefore a record of the marriage expectations of the past, though some songs have been changed to suit the present.

CONCLUSION

Our research confirmed that for the Abagusii the extended family has both secular and religious symbolic meanings. At both the secular and religious or metaphysical levels, the elaborate rites of marital initiation anoint the boys and girls with the privilege to be active members of the extended family of the living and the dead and introduce the youth to the challenges, pleasures, subtleties and expectations of the family. Then and only then are the young regarded as mature enough for membership in the family of their contemporary relatives and ancestral relatives.

Although the study shows that traditional *gusii* family system is still practiced in the hill countryside, the progress of urbanization is systematically causing some changes and the old family values are in transition. *Ekerorano* (courtship) is steadily losing the strict community controls and instead couples are controlling their own romance. Gusii parents once dominated mate selection based on bride wealth economic concerns, but now romantic considerations are looming larger. Intimacy between husband and wife is replacing community surveillance. Young *gusii* couples now can decide to have an uxolocal home, sometimes outside their district, where they are employed in the modern Kenyan economy. Although back in the hills the mainstay is still the growing of coffee, tea, and pyrethrum, these agrarian activities and the village oriented social life are giving way as the young in large numbers move into urban areas for good and all.

However, I think since culture is more dynamic than static, a hybridization of the traditional, Islamic and the modern Western cultures is occurring through powerful processes of diffusion, invention and adaptation to the new peripheral capitalist economy in Africa. In Ali Mazrui's (1991) "triple heritage," African family values are not dying out under the onslaught of Islamic and Western values. The three are clashing for turf like the lion, the cheetah and hyena do over a fallen wild-beast carcass in the wilderness. So far none of the three cultures has complete control of the African social institutional terrain, but each of them is a mirror of its original form (Fatou 1985). As Plato would say, just the essence remains of each.

Notes

1. *Dictionary of Modern Sociology*, p. 127
2. Ibid., p. 281
3. Facing Mt. Kenya, p.309 also p.119 and 195; see p. 179 for the saying: "It is witch-doctors who live and eat alone."
4. Drawn in Color, p. 51. At the occasion of consulting with her relatives on the subject of her father's remarriage, all other interested parties expressed themselves to her through the proper "mouths" or intermediaries; and she herself was spoken to collectively because she stood for her absent sister and brother.
5. The Ibo of Southern Nigeria, pp. 14-18.

References

Bascom, W. R. & M.J. Herskovits. (1959). *Continuity and Change in African Cultures*. Chicago: University of Chicago Press.

Charana (1982). Nyambarora, (1983). Onwonga (1984). Omwenga. (1984). Mumbo. (1985). Onsombi (1985), and Kisubi (1985). Creation Myths, Courtship and Marriage Songs. In R. L..Perry & A. T. Kisubi (Eds.) *The Sametan*. Kisumu, Kenya: Kisumu Press.

Charles, N. (2006). Family Support Networks: Intergenerational Exchanges. *International Sociological Association*, Durban, South Africa (ISA).

Chetty, R. (1980). The Changing Family: A Study of the Indian *Family* in South Africa. *Suid-Afrikaanse Tydskrif vir Sosiologie/The South African Journal of Sociology*, 11(2), 26-39.

Fatou, S. (1985). The Muslim Family and the Modern World: Papers from an International Symposium. *Current Anthropology*, 26 (5), 555-580.

Foster G. (2000). The capacity of the extended family safety net for orphans in Africa. *Psychology, Health and Medicine*, 5 (1), 55-62.

Gugler, J. (2002). The Son of the Hawk Does Not Remain Abroad: The Urban-Rural Connection in Africa. *African Studies Review*, 45 (1), 21-41.

Hill, N., N. Bush, K. R. & M. W. Roosa. (2003). Parenting and Socialization Strategies and Children's Mental Health: Low Income Mexican-American and Euro-American mothers and children. *Child Development*, 74, 189-204.

Jabavu, N. (1960). *Drawn in Color: African Contrasts*. London: Murray.

Jayakody, R.& A. Kalil. (2002). Social Fathering in Low-Income, African-American Families with Pre-school Children. *Journal of Marriage and Family*, 64 504-516.

Kenyatta, J. (1965). *Facing Mount Kenya*. New York: Vintage Books.

Kobiane, J. F., A. E. Calves & R. Marcoux. (2005). Parental Death and Children's Schooling in Burkina Faso, *Comparative Education Review*, 49 (4),465.

Levine, R. A. (1965). The Gusii Family. In R. Gray and P. Kegan (Eds.) *The Family Estate*. London: Routlage.

LeVine, R. A. (1959). An Attempt to Change the Gusii Initiation Circle. *Man, 59*, 117-20.

Little, K. (1959). Some Urban Patterns of Marriage and Domesticity in West Africa. *The Sociological Review*, 7(1), 65-97.

Luluaki, J. Y. (1997). Customary Marriage Laws in the Commonwealth: A Comparison between Papua New Guinea and Anglophonic Africa. *International Journal of Law, Policy and the Family*, 11 (1), 1-35

Macionis, J. J. (2006). *Society*. Upper Saddle River, NJ: Prentice Hall.

Masmas, T. N., H. Jensen, D. da Silva, L. Hoj, A. Sandstrom & P. Aaby. (2004). The Social Situation of Motherless Children in Rural and Urban Areas of Guinea-Bissau. *Social Science & Medicine*, 59(6), 1231-1239.

Mazrui, A. (1991). The Polity as an Extended Family: An African Perspective. *International Journal of Sociology of the Family*, 21 (2), 1-14

Mayer, P. ((1951). Bridewealth Limitation Among the Gusii. *Colonial research Studies: Two Studies in Applied Anthropology in Kenya*. 3, 19-33. London.

Mayer, P. (1950a). Privileged Obstruction of Marriage Rites among the Gusii. *Africa*, 113-25

Mayer, P. ((1950b). *Gusii Bridewealth Law and Custom*. Cape Town: Oxford University Press for Rhodes-Livingstone Institute.

Mbiti, J. S. (1985). *African Religions and Philosophy*, London: Heinemann Educational Books.

Mere, A. A. (1976). Contemporary Changes in Igbo Family System. *International Journal of Sociology of the Family*, 6(2), 155-160.

Nyamukapa, C. & S. Gregson. (2005). Extended Family's and Women's Roles in Safeguarding Orphans' Education in AIDS-Afflicted Rural Zimbabwe. *Social Science & Medicine*, 60 (10), 2155-2167.

Ogionwo, W (1975). Family Structure And Development: Cart And Horse Or Chicken And Egg? *International Journal of Sociology of the Family,* 5 (1), 53-65.

Oluoch, J. (Sept. 1957) Tribes of Kenya-Kisii. *Kenya Today 3,* 1820.

Roschelle, A. R. (1997). *No More Kin: Exploring Race, Class, and Gender in Family Networks.* Thousand Oaks, CA: Sage.

Shell-Duncan, B. & M. Wimmer (1999). Premarital Childbearing in Northwest Kenya: Challenging the Concept of Illegitimacy. *Social Biology,* 46, (1-2), 47-61.

Siquana-Ndulo, N. (1998). Rural African Family Structure in the Eastern Cape Province, South *Africa. Journal of Comparative Family Studies,* 29(2), 407-417.

Steklov, G. (2002). The Economic Boundaries of Kinship in Cote d'Ivoire. *Population Research and Policy Review,* 21 (4), 351-375.

Uchendu, V. C. (1965). *The Igbo of Southeast Nigeria.* New York: Holt, Rinehart, and Winston.

UNESCO. (1980). Role of Parents in the Education of Children of Pre-School Age in Tropical Africa, India and the Maghreb Countries, Report: UNESCO-ED-80-WS-97, p.47.

Van der Merwe, P. & Greeff, A. P. (2003) Coping Mechanisms of Unemployed African Men with Dependents. *The American Journal of Family Therapy.* 31 (2), 91-105.

Van Den Berghe, P. L. (1965). *Africa: Social Problems of Change and Conflict.* San Francisco, California: Chandler Publishing Co.

Van Gennep, A. (1960). *The Rites of Passage,* Chicago: University of Chicago Press.

Ziehl, S. (2002). Black South Africans Do Live in Nuclear Family Households-A Response to Russell. *Society in Transition,* 33 (1), 26-49.

CHAPTER 6

HEALTH AND THE SURVIVAL OF THE EXTENDED FAMILY IN AFRICA

Mario. J. Azevedo

INTRODUCTION

For centuries, the African family has experienced tribulation and turmoil but has stood as the bedrock of security, comfort, and hope for its members and those surrounding it. Whether facing adverse internal dynamics or external pressures intent on radically changing or completely destroying it, the African family withstood its ground and survived the onslaught of major wars, slavery, and colonialism. On the one hand, unable to alter it radically, Islam, when possible, adapted the African's family cultural traditions, including acceptance of multiple wives beyond the accepted four, veneration of ancestors, and the use of charms. As a result, this imported religion has essentially lived with Africans in harmony for centuries. Christianity, on the other hand, either used its charm or novelty or showed its intolerant side by forcing changes and making inroads whose ultimate goal was to radically alter the African family's structure, function, and values and simply replace it with the Western European concept of family. Where it could, the colonial state, as well, allied with its Church, imposed monogamy, fought the continent's traditional ways of educating and raising children, declaring, in the process, that the concept of the ancestors and extended kinship were senseless and superstitious.

However, where Christianity thought it had completely transformed the African traditional family, in most cases it encountered only disappointment. Missionaries realized that the African was like a genius in his search for an eclectic system that would accommodate the old ways to the West's new impositions on the family. Thus, while a Catholic family would go to Mass on Sunday morning, the same household would offer sacrifice to the ancestors in the back of the house in the afternoon. Where a newly-converted African Baptist family seemed to love listening to the sound of music in a clean, white-painted church, the same family might be seen dancing to the tune and the rhythm of the drums in the village accompanied by Church-forbidden songs. In sum, no matter what Christianity attempted to accomplish its goal quickly, it failed to erase completely the family values and practices traditionally imprinted in the new converts, even after two or three generations. In the end, the Church, too, gave up the idea of totally destroying the family or its centuries-old structure. Learning from past experience, currently, every foreign religion, including Islam and Christianity, is attempting not to replace the African family but, to the extent possible, tolerate it and adapt it, the reason why the two foreign faiths have spread so fast during the last four decades following independence.

Colonialism and its violent system of forcibly conscripting men into labor projects and its intermittent military recruitment and migratory settlements caused a major disruption of the African traditional family but did not destroy it either, nor did pestilence, endemic or new epidemic diseases, or the harsh environment of drought, flooding, and bad weather irreparably weaken the pillar of African society, the traditional family. Indeed, colonialism brought with it the curse of new diseases, such as influenza, syphilis and other sexually transmitted diseases, measles, and unwittingly spread endemic and new diseases of trypanosomiasis, tuberculosis, yellow fever, diarrhea, malaria, and typhoid through forced settlements of people hitherto perhaps immune to these ailments (Patterson et al., 1978, p. 11-12) or the opening of the forests to make room for roads, railroads, and imposing administrative posts. At times, the colonial projects would directly or indirectly affect and undermine Africans' immune system against foreign diseases to the point of depopulating entire communities and districts. Throughout the transformation, the African family adapted itself and seemed to be here to stay. Yet, more recently, the health community has been seriously asking whether the institution can withstand the burden of the old and emerging diseases that are taking an unprecedented toll on its women and children and threatening the very foundations of people's livelihood and lifestyles. Every informed student of Africa agrees that what the continent is experiencing today is unprecedented and could lead to the destruction of the traditional as well as the modern family as we know it. Never before has the world seen anywhere the severe human devastation that malaria, HIV/AIDS, tuberculosis, the Ebola virus, meningitis, and other infectious and chronic diseases are causing to the continent of Africa.

STRUCTURE AND FUNCTION OF THE AFRICAN FAMILY

Anthropologists, historians, geographers, and sociologists agree that, for centuries, Africa has traditionally accepted a family that was more extended than nuclear, more accepting of polygynous (polygamous) than monogamous marriage, more patrilineal than matrilineal, and more consanguineal than simply conjugal, its strength and survival lying on kinship solidarity, language, and territorial origin. Except in urban areas, colonial legacy, Christianity and Western globalization have not altered the meaning of marriage in Africa, which essentially has remained an alliance between two families or two clans, hence the involvement of relatives and kin to prevent frivolous divorces. Arranged marriages are still performed in the countryside and the village setting. The rate of polygamy ranges from 30 percent in such countries as Nigeria and Kenya, among certain ethnic groups, to 36 percent in Chad, Congo, Benin, Ghana, Mali, Senegal, and Tanzania, with two wives being the pragmatic norm.

Circumcision, along with the rites-of-passage to adulthood, motherhood, fatherhood, and the status of an elder, is still practiced in most African family households, especially in West Africa. Likewise, the extended family, be it conjugal or consanguineal, is still the most important source of security and socialization for the child and members of the family. Indeed, take the extended family away, particularly in the villages and rural areas of the continent, and you will also deprive Africans of their sense of belonging, direction in life, and their very humanity. As Kayongo-Male and Onyango write, "The most significant feature of African family life is probably *the importance of the larger kin group* [authors' emphasis] beyond the nuclear family...Households in urban areas have extended kin members in residence for years...Children may go to live with distant relatives for schooling or special training courses...Relatives may also have much influence over the decisions of the couple" (Kayongo-Male & Onyango, 1984, p. 6).

It is still true in Africa today that the primacy of the child is paramount, and it still takes a "village to raise a child." In the context of the African extended family, the role of the elders is still relevant; elders are held as more experienced and therefore wiser, whose advice deserves to be listened to and followed. Most often than not, the African extended family tends to be consanguineal in the sense that people who share the same blood (mother, child, and relatives) may live together in the same household or compound or close to each other in surrounding households.

Obviously, Christianity and colonialism have compelled Africans to accept nothing but the nuclear monogamic family structure. Yet, even Christian households tend to be extended, and, unlike the West, all adults are responsible for the well-being of the whole family. Solidarity and support of and from kin have, therefore, remained the major features of African families, whether "modern" or traditional. However, the most recent disease environment, especially HIV/AIDS, threatens the very core of the fabric of Sub-Saharan African society, causing unprecedented demographic shifts of potentially catastrophic consequences. Almost 20 years ago, Popenoe argued that the African family was becoming "internally deinstitutionalized carrying out fewer traditional functions, losing power relative to the state, and becoming smaller and more unstable and that the cultural value of familism [was] weakening in favor of self-fulfillment and egalitarianism" (See Bradley & Weisner 1997, p. xix). How prophetic were and still are these statements, as Africa faces the HIV/AIDS, tuberculosis, and malaria crises?

One of the first problems the researcher of health and the state of the African family, especially in Sub-Saharan Africa, encounters is the lack of adequate information and writings linking the two themes. Health has been attracting the attention of several researchers more recently. However, most of the health studies have been conducted not by epidemiologists or health behavioral scientists but by pure social scientists or medical anthropologists-sociologists with little or no academic background in public health. As a result, the available studies often lack the depth, the scope, and the legitimacy to be credible. The theme of the African family was popular during the 1960s and 1970s but has received less attention from scholars more recently. Instead, studies of Africa have tended to focus on politics, the impact of globalization, urbanization, industrialization, secularization, issues of human security as defined by the United Nations since 1994, and economic development, in which the family is dealt with in sweeping generalities, quite often zeroing in only on the impact of HIV/AIDS based on a few empirical and inferential studies.

The preceding remarks do therefore present limitations to the following study. Consequently, the chapter is intended to do the following: expose and sensitize the reader to the unprecedented heavy burden of disease on the African continent, with emphasis on Sub-Saharan Africa; assess its impact on what is currently holding the African family together, paying special attention to the extended family; and discuss the practical and immediate policy implications the situation seems to warrant.

146

THE BURDEN OF DISEASE IN AFRICA

The Epidemiologic Factor

The international community is in agreement that Africa, of all regions of the world (Haan, 2005, p. 130), presents the most challenges regarding the disease burden and human ability to cope with it and experience health as defined by the United Nations (UN). The UN defines health as "…a state of complete physical, mental, and social well-being and not merely the absence of disease or infirmity." To this definition, epidemiologists would like to add the sentence "the existence of conditions that promote fulfilling and satisfying lives." Unfortunately, less than 10 percent of Africans qualify when this UN measuring stick is applied to the continent. Given that almost 80 percent of the continent is located within the tropics, the natural and man-made environmental risk factors causing or contributing to disease are many. While the climate tends to be warm and hospitable to insects and vectors that carry unimaginable infectious disease micro-organisms, the frequent floods provide a fertile breeding ground for mosquitoes, snails, and flies that are detrimental to Africans' health, especially infants and children. Added to the infectious and communicable ailments are the chronic diseases, at times known as the diseases of "opulence," "affluence" or "lifestyle," spurred by Western influences, industrialization, and globalization. The latter include obesity, diabetes, cardiovascular disease, stroke, alcoholism, rheumatic fever and rheumatic heart disease, hypertension, cancer, genetic disease, sickle-cell anemia, drug and tobacco addiction, chronic obstructive pulmonary disease, such as asthma, and untold respiratory ailments that unnecessarily increase exponentially morbidity and mortality rates by about 40 percent in the developing world and 27 percent on the continent of Africa (Haan, 2005, p. 130).

These conditions have affected the continent to the point where life becomes harder every day that passes. Civil wars, unrest, violence, vehicle crashes—Africa has the highest number of deadly vehicle crashes on the planet (*Encyclopedia of African History*, 2005, 2,623), corruption (which, in Nigeria, is said to have contributed to the decline from 90 percent of the children's immunization rate in 1990 to the currently reported 20 percent), misguided policies, and external dependency, all make Africans wonder where they have gone wrong and ask whether they will ever be able to reclaim their continent and provide a modicum of good life to the millions of the poor walking in their polluted cities and decaying infrastructures. These conditions have contributed to high mortality rates on the continent. Health and scientific research circles reveal that "out of 100 [natural] disasters [epidemics, endemic diseases, drought, and floods, which often interact with man-made disasters] reported worldwide, only 20 percent occur in Africa. Yet, Africans suffer 60 percent of all disaster-related deaths" (Ojekutu-Macauley, 2003, p. 104). Deforestation has continued at full speed for decades. Thus, while, in West Africa, 75 percent of the forest has disappeared since 1950, in Nigeria, Kenya, Burundi, Cote d'Ivoire, and Madagascar the rate of deforestation is 90 percent, a considerable loss to agriculture. In addition, in Africa, lack of industrial development and the absence of certain natural resources, such as gas and petroleum, force 90 percent of the populace to rely on "biological resources" for almost all major necessities: Food, shelter, clothing, income, and "herbal medicine."

Malaria, Diarrhea, Malnutrition, and Other Ailments

For centuries now, one of the major threats to the survival of Africans and their families has been and continues to be malaria, a disease transmitted mainly by a female vector mosquito of the species called *Anopheles gambiae,* which carries the nefarious disease micro-organism known as *Plasmodium falciparum.* Endemic in 15 of the 17 countries covered by WHO in Sub-Saharan Africa, malaria infects and kills more than a million Africans each year and contributes to one in five children's deaths, one-third of all visits to health care or hospitals, and from one-quarter to one-third of all hospital admissions in Sub-Saharan Africa. Its most common clinical symptoms are chills, fever, anemia, and enlarged spleen in the victim. Today, malaria infects 300 million people worldwide (270 million in Africa). Despite the "Roll Back Malaria" initiated by the World Health Organization and philanthropic international organizations and agencies in 1998, as well as the various vaccine trials undertaken in various parts of the continent, malaria seems to continue to be the number one killer in most African countries, challenged only by AIDS in certain regions of the continent. Insecticide-treated sleeping nets, home insecticide sprays, new and standard anti-malarial drugs (e.g., quinine, chloroquine, perymethamine, sulfones, and lariam) have provided some reprieve, but not enough to stem malaria's death toll. In Kenya, it kills 34,000 under-five children per year or causes 93 deaths a day (*Republic of Kenya*, 2006-2007, p. 20).

It is often said that, when reported cases only are considered, in the course of one year, an African experiences an average of 300 mosquito bites, which at times may affect 80 percent of the population simultaneously, as is the case in some East African countries, such as Kenya (Azevedo, 2003, p. 183). Diarrhea, defined as at least five bouts of watery stools a day, which at times may contain pus, mucus, blood (called dysentery), as well as excessive fat, contributes to close to a million (800,000) deaths, especially among infants and children under five years of age, aggravated, as it were, by mal-nutrition, under-nutrition, and lack of essential vitamins that strengthen the immune system. Diarrhea leads to dehydration, electrolyte imbalance (i.e., insufficient potassium, calcium, phosphates, and magnesium), and death, if not treated. It is estimated that, in Africa, "a child less than five years of age faces five times the risk of having diarrhea per year, a 10 percent probability of contracting the disease in a given year, and a 14 percent probability of dying from it" (Azevedo, 2003, p. 183). According to the UN, 37 percent of diarrhea cases in the world occur on the African continent. Despite its potential ravage, however, simple oral re-hydration therapy (ORT), which any mother can perform even in the remotest village, is enough to save a child's life. Unfortunately, only one-half of the Sub-Saharan African children are treated with ORT, contrasted to 74 percent in North Africa and Asia.

In absolute numbers, mal-nutrition, or lack of food intake that is essential to growth and good health, is highest in Asia (47 percent of the world's total), followed by Africa at 35 percent. However, while the rate of mal-nutrition has been declining rapidly in Asia during the past 20 years, in Africa it has been increasing, especially during the last 10 years. In fact, according to Labonte and Schrecker (2004, p. 103), "Of all African countries, 18 showed some improvement in recent years, three showed no changes, and 10 showed increased rates." Currently, diarrhea is the fourth leading cause of death in Africa and is predicted to become the ninth leading cause by 2020 worldwide from second in 1990, and constitutes 10 percent of the African continent's overall disease burden. According to the African Medical and Research Foundation (AMREF), diarrhea, along with other diseases and nutrition deficiencies that affect children more heavily, makes Sub-Saharan children "five times more likely to die before their fifth birthday, 10 times to die before their 10th birthday, and nine times to die from an infectious disease" (*Africa: South of the Sahara*, 2007, p. 24). The rainy season is particularly hard on children, as it is the harbinger of new pathogens, colds, and humidity, which are responsible for higher morbidity rates. A study conducted in 2000 in a small Komindou Health Center, Guinea, West Africa, staffed by a nurse and one assistant nurse, illustrates the point.

Season	Number of Children Treated	Number of Children with Malaria	Number of Children with Diarrhea
Dry			
January	25	8	6
February	24	7	6
March	38	11	12

Season	Number of Children Treated	Number of Children with Malaria	Number of Children with Diarrhea
Total	87	25	24
Rainy			
June	55	18	12
July	66	34	21
August	52	13	11
Total	172	65	34

Source: Andrew J. Gordon et al., DHS, 2004, p. 24.

Adding insult to injury, the rainy season is also the time when food provisions become problematic and malarial and mosquito infestations are at their highest.

Tuberculosis, HIV and AIDS

Immunization against tuberculosis (TB), a respiratory disease caused mainly by the acid-fast bacillus micro-organism *Mycobacterium tuberculosis* (and less so by the two related *mycobacteriae africanum* and *bovis)* is on the rise on the continent and affects over 170 million people as a result of global conditions, lack of enforcement of immunization protocol and dosage, and resistance to hitherto effective drug therapy and antibiotics. Transmitted into the lungs from person to person through inhalation or ingestion of infected droplets, TB is responsible for 25 percent of related deaths occurring in the developing world including Africa. Its symptoms include chest pain, inflammation of lung membranes, loss of appetite and weight, fever, sweats, coughing up sputum with pus, and shortness of breath. The Global Tuberculosis Control Program of the World Health Organization (WHO) reports that Sub-Saharan Africa is one of the "six regions" of the globe that is still experiencing the highest number of TB infections (*Africa: South of the Sahara*, 2007, p. 25), with an incidence rate of 272 per 100,000 population, 10-fold higher compared to that of 27 per 100,000 in Europe. It is responsible for close to 500,000 deaths a year. In Africa, the highest rates, estimated at 200,000 or 300 cases per 100,000 population, are clustered in such countries as Democratic Republic of Congo, Kenya, Ethiopia, Nigeria, and South Africa. In Kenya, one of the most developed countries in Africa, the mortality rate due to TB is 133 per 100,000 population from an infection rate of 610 per 100,000. A few years ago, in Burundi and Malawi, for example, TB cases rose by 180 percent and 140 percent, respectively, as opportunistic infections of HIV/AIDS (Azevedo, 2003, p. 184).

The sudden rise in TB morbidity and mortality rates compelled African Ministries of Health to declare the disease a "continental emergency" in 2005. The results of the declaration are yet to be felt. Unfortunately, TB can remain latent for 50 years in 60-70 percent of the population of the developing world before it shows its clinical symptoms (Nelson et al, 2001, p. 419-420). As noted, TB is also an opportunistic disease that tends to co-infect easily HIV/AIDS infected persons and together (the reason why, at times, it is labeled "the twin evils" or "Bonnie and Clyde"), are decimating thousands of people over the globe daily. Indeed, studies have shown that persons co-infected with TB and HIV experience an annual risk factor for developing TB in excess of 10 percent, while those with a TB infection have a 20-30 percent life-long risk of developing full-blown tuberculosis (Southerland, 1976, p. 1-63; Vynnycky, 1997, p. 183-201). Pneumonia, bronchitis, asthma, cholera, and other diseases affecting the respiratory system are very common in Africa, even though the diagnosis is often inaccurate. Experts say that an African child faces "at least 10 infectious respiratory ailments (IRAs) each year and has a 25 percent probability of contracting one some day in his childhood" (Azevedo, 2003, p. 184). IRAs are believed to be responsible for 55-60 percent of children's diseases as well as for 17 percent of their doctors' or hospital visits, and account for 20 percent of childhood deaths in Sub-Saharan Africa.

The globe has seen the frightening rise and spread of the human immunodeficiency virus (HIV) and the resulting acquired immunodeficiency syndrome (AIDS) disease since the 1980s. Mainly heterosexually transmitted in Africa, HIV and AIDS have created a crisis that some have called the "silent holocaust," the "killing field," or the "slow genocide" (Bongmba, 2007, p. 19). Currently, some 25-30 million Sub-Saharan Africans are believed to be HIV/AIDS-positive, with infection rates of more than 10 percent in 16 countries (20 percent in South Africa, 36 percent of adults in Botswana, and 25 percent in Swaziland and Zimbabwe), killing some 6,030 people in the region a day, with this number predicted to double in 2010. Since 1997, the world community has known that, even though Africa accounts only for 13 percent of the world's inhabitants or close to 900 million people, it is home to 68 percent of the world's HIV/AIDS cases, with women accounting for 82 percent of the total prevalence (Thiuri, 1997, p. 11), a situation that does not seem to have changed radically a decade later. Studies in Africa have also shown that HIV patients "contract malaria more easily and certainly have a poorer prognosis" of survival (Barnett & Whiteside, 2002, P. 45). According to some reports, AIDS killed 17 million people in Sub-Saharan Africa in 2000 alone and orphaned 12 million children in the region.

Trypanosmiasis (Sleeping Sickness), Onchocerciasis (River Blindness), Yellow Fever, Schistosomiasis (Bilharzia) and Other Diseases

Trypanosomiasis or sleeping sickness in humans and rinderpest in animals, which is caused by the dreaded tsetse fly, is still blinding and killing hundreds of Africans every year and decimating cattle where the fly is endemic. The tsetse fly infection is deadly if it is not treated early enough with prophylactics and allowed to reach the brain. During the colonial period, consistent sleeping sickness outbreaks occurred in such countries as Chad and Cameroon, often compelling entire villages and communities to abandon their habitat on orders from both European and African authorities. In 1932, for example, the Catholic Mission at Kou, near Doba, in Southern Chad, under orders from medical and missionary personnel, had to be completely evacuated to a safer place, located hundreds of miles away (Azevedo, 1978, p. 124). Apparently, the number of trypanosomiasis cases has been reduced to close to 25,000 a year, but outbreaks are not uncommon in West and Central Africa.

Even though much progress has been achieved in Burkina Faso, along the West and Central African rivers, in such countries as Cameroon, Gabon, Nigeria, and Chad—constituting one of the few success stories in Africa's epidemiological ecology—the black fly, which causes onchocerciasis or river blindness, has depopulated several communities and prevented agricultural activity in the proximities of river banks. Worldwide, river blindness affects 17 million people, but most of the victims are found in Africa. A concerted action by the world community and African governments has eliminated the vector in most areas, allowing people to return to the fertile lands along the rivers (Zewede, 2005, p. 518-519). The vector of river blindness is a black female fly that sucks worm-infected blood from patients, subsequently spreading it to healthy individuals. The parasite prefers shallow river banks where it breeds and latches itself onto the human body, in which its eggs hatch and breed, eventually resulting in unbearable eye itching and the host's blindness.

The impact of the almost one hundred percent deadly Ebola and Marburg viruses in Central Africa and Sudan, respectively, the seasonal outbreaks of meningitis, and the ubiquitous measles, are maladies that affect many Africans in their daily lives, notwithstanding the availability of vaccines for many of the common but fatal infectious diseases on the continent. Who is to blame for the situation?

Luckily, smallpox has been eradicated from the continent. Yet, the viral paralysis-causing polio or polyomyelitis, which during the early 2000s was almost a thing of the past, has not disappeared completely mainly due to resistance from some Northern Nigerian and Nigerien Muslim leaders who saw vaccination as a conspiracy to render their female children infertile. Transmitted from person to person, polio causes severe irritation of the brain membranes or meninges as well as back pain and stiffness and paralysis in the affected individual. Reportedly, on August 17, 2007, polio cases had been reduced to only 80 in the Nigerian-Nigerien border compared to the area's 756 in August 2006 and 1,125 in Nigeria alone.

Yellow fever is another deadly disease that has been very difficult to eradicate from the continent. It is caused by a parasite carried by the *aedis egypti* mosquito vector and transmitted through a bite on the human body. Yellow fever can be transmitted from person to person, as the mosquito may carry the infected blood and bite another host. Yellow fever symptoms include headache, fever, and liver damage, vomiting, and bleeding. Mention ought to be made also of Lymphatic filariasis, which can result in elephantiasis. Filariasis affects 90 million people worldwide, but it is overwhelming on the continents of Africa and Asia. Elephantiasis is the enlargement of the lower body, such as legs, from blockage of the lymphatic ducts by parasitic worms.

Apart from the various diseases discussed here, the African continent is one of the two regions of the world that suffer serious water shortages resulting from the destruction of forests and the creation of new dams, as is the case with the Aswan Dam on the Nile River and those built on the Volta River, exacerbating the scarcity of drinking water and causing flooding as well as the spread of worms, insects, and snail-related diseases. Schistosomiasis or bilharziasis, whose extreme symptoms may include blood urine, is caused by the infiltration of river snails into the human body when the two come into contact with each other in infected waters. It is a common disease in Africa.

Parasitic and Water-Born Nature of Africa's Diseases

Currently, most of the killer diseases in Africa are of a parasitic nature and water-borne—yellow fever, cholera, tetanus, typhoid, diarrhea, malaria, onchocerciasis, trypanosomiasis, and malaria—and can be either eradicated or effectively controlled through sanitation, water cleanliness, immunization, surveillance, pharmaceutical intervention, and policy strategies. Yet, during the mid-1980s, parasitic and infectious diseases alone were responsible for 4.25 million deaths in Africa (Azevedo, 2003, p. 185). Luckily, while in Kenya, malaria deaths decreased by 44 percent between 2004 and 2006, in Zimbabwe, the rate has gone down by 40 percent during the same period. Luis Gomes Sambo, the Angolan WHO Regional Director for Africa, notes that, in 46 African countries with a population of about 718 million people, HIV/AIDS, tuberculosis, and malaria are the three most deadly diseases responsible for six million deaths annually. Leprosy, a disease caused by the *Mycobacterium leprae*, less infectious as was once thought, still shows its ugly face even in the African cities of West, East, and Central Africa, with no end in sight. Leprosy affects thousands of Africans every year. Because of the deformities it causes in a patient, prior to HIV/AIDS, leprosy was traditionally considered to be the most abominable disease on the continent. In fact, just as in Biblical times, people in Africa used to run away when a leper approached a village. The stigma associated with it has somewhat abated. Visible symptoms of leprosy are skin lesions, eye inflammation, destruction of nose cartilage and bone, testicle atrophy, and, sometimes, blindness.

Water availability and sanitation in Africa are issues of life and death for most people. As a result of the natural environmental conditions and man's misguided policies and habits, it is estimated that 300 million or one-third of the continent's inhabitants does not have "reasonable" access to water. In Sub-Saharan Africa, for example, only 51 percent of the population has access to clean water and only 45 percent to sanitation. In Ethiopia, for example, while only 10 percent of the population has access to clean water, 46 percent of child mortality is due to unclean water supply and lack of sanitation (*Environmental news*, February 29, 2000). In Lagos, Nigeria, of the eight million people living in the city, only 30 percent (2.4 million) have access to potable water. Many of the rivers are beginning to "die" as a result of man's careless habits. To provide a graphic example of what is happening to African rivers, *Environment News* (February 29, 2000) thus characterized the sorry state of rivers in Ghana, where people say that there is "water everywhere, but not a drop to drink": "Tons of untreated human and industrial waste wash into sources of drinking water. Two hundred dams, wells, and boreholes in the Upper West Region are polluted with an amalgam of sewage, high colonies of fecal coliform and used engine oil. Bloating carcasses of cows, sheep, dogs, and cats float in the contaminated water."

LITERACY AND POVERTY

Literacy has always been cited as an important factor in the elimination or containment of disease. Environmental degradation, unwise social and economic policies, and loan-related conditionalities from the International Monetary Fund (IMF) and the World Bank have all contributed to a low level of adult literacy on the continent, estimated at 35 or 45 percent, according to some sources. Low literacy rates have also contributed to a huge number of people who are forced to live below the absolute poverty line. If one takes the World Bank's own definition of poverty as "a multidimensional phenomenon, encompassing inability to satisfy basic needs, lack of control over resources, lack of education and skill, poor health, malnutrition, lack of shelter, poor access to water and sanitation, vulnerability to shocks, violence and crime, lack of political freedom, and voice," Africa is at the bottom of the ladder, with 340 million of its people expected to be labeled poor, living at less than US$2 a day, by the year 2015. Currently, 75 percent of the people living in Sub-Saharan Africa make less than US$2 a day (*Africa: South of the Sahara*, 2007, p. 12-24). Illiteracy is highest among females, even though it has been proven that one year added to the education of a mother results in an 8.8 percent reduction in childhood annual mortality rate. It also raises the level of health awareness and the standards of hygiene within the family and the community and contributes to the reduction in the number of children's deaths in particular.

Africa's infrastructure continues to crumble, while corruption remains unabated, including in those countries, such as Nigeria, Mozambique, and Kenya, which, during the past election cycles, have vowed to fight graft with all means at their disposal. In Kenya, the appointed Corruption Czar was forced to resign and flee the country in 2005 when he started a systematic assault on the corrupt practices of government officials. The government also shut down a newspaper that reported the pervasive rapacious habit at the highest levels of power. Just the year before, it appeared that Kenya was serious about the campaign to rid the country of corruption when the National AIDS Control Council (NACC) Director, Margaret Cachara, was indicted on charges of having enriched herself "with HIV funds." However, the crusade was just a façade to appease the population.

Africa will have to marshal all its resources if it expects to stem the high tide of old, emerging, and re-emerging infectious (and chronic) diseases. Unfortunately, if one considers global warming to be a reality, the El Nino and La Nina phenomena will occur more frequently, and our globe will become more of a breeding ground for insects, mosquitoes, and plague-causing rodents. It is well to remember that epidemiologists have warned that:

> As the lower altitudes of our troposphere become warmer, insect vectors such as mosquitoes, house and river flies, tse-tse flies, and moths will climb up to higher altitudes and latitudes, hitherto some of the safest havens for many Africans who live on the highlands of Ethiopia, Eritrea, Kenya, Uganda, Zimbabwe, Mozambique, South Africa, Malawi, and parts of West Africa, including Cameroon, Gabon, and Northern Nigeria, rendering our ecosystem more dangerous to human habitation (Azevedo, 2003, p. 201).

Such real and potential health hazardous conditions seem to augur an ominous scenario bound to have an impact on the structure and function and, ultimately, the survival of the African family and its "extended web of kinship," as we know it today.

IMPACT OF DISEASE ON THE AFRICAN FAMILY

HIV/AIDS and the Family

The following section examines in detail the impact of the health crisis on the African family, with particular reference to extended kinship as a distinctive feature of its structure and function. It must be noted that the impact of disease on the African family is an evolving theme that researchers only now are taking seriously, especially in light of the ravages of HIV/ AIDS in Sub-Saharan Africa. To the extent possible, the following discussion highlights the impact of diseases, such as AIDS, malaria, and trypanosmiasis on the family and the family household that have received more attention from researchers recently. More than any other disease, including malaria, seen in some quarters in Africa as a normal and acceptable social phenomenon, AIDS has become a concern of every government and related institution on the continent, both preoccupied ultimately with the issue of the survival of the African extended family as we know it. As a premise to the next pages, it pays to echo the words of Cameroon Catholic author Elias K. Bongmba, when he writes that: "Although it attacks one person at a time, HIV/AIDS is a public disease that disrupts families and communities. The fact that it afflicts many people in Africa through the privacy of the sexual act does not negate the sociopolitical character of the AIDS crisis" (Bongmba, 2007, p. 6).

From the specific studies conducted on AIDS and the African family, the following discussion focuses on those examples and studies that seem to have a wider valid application to the continent. We need to agree first that "poor health shackles human capital, reduces returns of learning, impedes entrepreneurial activities and holds back growth and development."

Malaria and the African Family

Studies in Rwanda, Burkina Faso, Togo, and Congo (Brazzaville) during the 1980s and 1990s revealed that a single bout of malaria results in 12 days of direct and indirect costs to the family or the individual. Schistosomiasis, on one hand, when it strikes, forces many families and households to use bride-wealth to pay for the treatment of relatives. In Cote d'Ivoire, when illness hits a household, the average cost of treatment often supersedes the full-time salary of a family member. In Kenya, among the coastal people, one-fourth of the land is being sold to cover the exigencies caused by various illnesses. The same seems to be happening in Sudan, where a study of 250 smith families affected by malaria and schistosomiasis proved that the smith professionals were forced to abandon their occupations in order to attend to sick family members (Azevedo, 2003, p. 198). It is also reported that families are selling their cows, plows, land, bicycles, and dead people's clothes (a taboo in many societies) to others or giving them to the traditional healers, some of whom are becoming wealthier as the crisis grows in the villages (in some countries, 50 to 80 percent of the population that is unable to use modern health care goes to the traditional healer).

Experience has demonstrated that the African extended family serves as a support system to members at all times, but especially when they are in need. In patrilineal societies, for example, the children belong to the husband's clan, so that, when the husband dies, both the offspring and the widow, whom the brother might marry, are taken care of by the family, ensuring the well-being of all involved. The system has been described as "elastic," always able to "stretch" to find food, shelter to sleep, and clothing for the child and the widow. However, recently, as a result of AIDS, in many parts of Africa, the system is being overwhelmed and has begun to crumble, "reducing the number of adults in their prime and piling fresh responsibilities on elderly people" (Kaleeba, 2004, p. 277). In Africa, the *de jure* or *de facto* "extended web of kinship" provides a "ready-made source of companionship and carries with it a certain degree of acceptance. Hence, kinsmen are not usually turned away" (Falola, 2006, p. 179). Today, however, things are beginning to change radically.

The Orphan Phenomenon

One of the new major responsibilities of the traditional extended family in Africa has become the care of orphans. HIV/AIDS is creating an untold number of orphans as a result of one or both parents' deaths, usually the mother going first. Today, Sub-Saharan Africa is home to some 12 million AIDS orphans (more than 900,000 per country, in Nigeria, Ethiopia, and Uganda, and some 500,000 in Tanzania) (Robinson, et al, 2007, p. 190), and predictions were that the number would reach 20 million by the year 2010. Studies have shown that the needs of these children, usually left at the care of the extended household and grandparents, are tearing the family fabric at the seams. The older people, to whom the children are usually entrusted, need added care themselves, and are therefore unable to provide for the community and the family as a result of illness and the demise of the most productive family members (Bongmba, 2007, p.

19). UNICEF has expressed great concern about the ability of families in Africa to care for the orphans as a humanitarian and kinship priority and noted that the AIDS orphans are "overwhelmingly cared for by relatives, including especially grandmothers, but the capacity of the extended family to cope with this burden is stretched very thin and is, in places, collapsing."

Death and the Weakening of the Family Support System

In Zimbabwe, many of the entrepreneur men and women selling goods at the city market are returning home to the villages because the "family breadwinner is gone" or adults are sick. According to some experts, in some Sub-Saharan countries, the system of solidarity and hospitality and the "values that reflect and depend on a large extended family" have already collapsed due to AIDS, and orphans are either taking care of themselves and their brothers and sisters or live away from home as "street" children, where they get involved in illegal and risky activities. Sadly, it has been noted that "survey data from eight countries [in Sub-Saharan Africa] revealed that one, Zimbabwe, had school enrollment rates higher for orphans than non-orphans and then only orphans who had lost both parents" (Kalipeni et al., 2004, p. 292-293). In Zambia, statistics show that 25 percent of the children are orphans, mostly as a result of the AIDS crisis. Barnett and Whiteside note that, in the past, politicians and international agencies representatives would stress that the extended family in Africa would easily absorb orphans. Today, in light of the ravages of HIV/AIDS, the two authors note, such talk is "heard less as the full effects of the epidemic [AIDS] become apparent" (Barnett & Whiteside, 2002, p. 187). The logical consequence of what is happening in Africa today is that the high death toll among mothers not only contributes to a high number of orphans but it also erodes the family household and causes extreme economic and social hardship.

The high death rates of infants and children due to the diseases discussed above should be particularly disconcerting to African leaders because they have a direct impact on the survival of the family and the future of the entire continent. As more mothers vanish from the continent as victims of infectious diseases, particularly AIDS, wrote Laurie Garrett a few years ago, "Hope [has] to rest with the children of Africa, the continent's next generation of potential bankers, lawyers, economists, farmers, business financiers, and planners. But studies in Zambia, Zaire (DRC), and Malawi revealed [at the time] that many AIDS orphans died shortly after their mothers' demises, even though the children were not themselves infected" (*Encyclopedia of African History*, 2005, p. 527). The situation has, of course, gotten worse.

As a result of the search for employment and the lure of the big cities, as is the case in Zambia, where more than 51 percent of the population lives in the cities, the burden of village life and family responsibility rests on women. Indeed, says Graham about rural life and women's health:

> Many women are left in the relatively unhealthy rural areas without support while men head to the cities for work. Women are also hit harder by food shortages and famine, and illness in a community increases the burden on women because they are the primary caregivers for sick family and neighbors. Maternal mortality, including deaths from unsafe abortions, is higher in Africa than anywhere. In Sub-Saharan Africa, a woman has one chance in 21 of dying of pregnancy-related causes during her reproductive life, compared with one in 54 in Asia and one in 2,089 in Europe (*Encyclopedia of African History*, 2005, p. 623).

Among the Yoruba, the extended kinship system is said to be weakening because of the "break-up of the kin groups and the emergency of the family system in which nuclear family members are released from wider kin obligations and obligations between spouses are more emphasized," all exacerbated by the impact of industrialization, urbanization, cultural diffusion, the economic crisis, and HIV/AIDS (Falola, 2006, p. 186-189). A study of 21 caregivers (15 women and six men) of 51 AIDS patients in a community in Tanzania revealed that male relatives would accept helping family members only when their sisters, wives, mothers, or daughters were not available. As a result, such necessities as food, soap, water, firewood, cleaning, and cooking become the responsibility of neighbors and women's self-help associations. The patients' needs at the site were so many and requiring so much time that the caregivers found no time to attend to their own personal needs, such as engaging in their own agricultural work (Monique, 2004, p. 36).

In many areas of Sub-Saharan Africa, the high maternal mortality resulting from the deadly ravages of HIV/AIDS and other diseases has contributed to the dissolution of a great number of family households over the past few years. A study conducted in Zimbabwe in 2000 among 215 family households confirmed this occurrence. Forty percent of the sampled households had absorbed orphans who had lost both parents. However, "65 percent of the households where the deceased adult female used to live before her death were reported to be no longer in existence in both the urban and rural sites" (Barnett & Whiteside, 2002, p. 188). The United Nations reports that Sub-Saharan Africa is home to the highest rate of maternal deaths in the world, 241,000 per year, or 264 per 1,000 population, accounting for almost one-half of the world's maternal mortality or greater than four times that of high-income countries (Boko, 2008, p. 175). Indeed, the UN notes also that a woman in this part of Africa has one chance in 16 of dying during pregnancy or childbirth, contrasted to one in 4,000 in the developed world. Unfortunately, as studies have shown, at least 80 percent of the tropical ailments in women and their families are preventable or can be effectively treated at the primary health care facilities. It is also important to stress that, while the average rate of adult maternal mortality rate in Sub-Saharan Africa is 3.6 times that of Latin America and middle-income countries, South Africa's, Swaziland's, Botswana's, and Namibia's exceeds 500 per 1,000 population (Boko, 2008, p. 175).

In 16 Sub-Saharan countries, 10 percent of reproductive age women are HIV-infected, reducing their life expectancy to 50 years in the hardest-hit countries (Falola, 2006, p. 179-182). Generally, in such countries, life expectancy at birth (LEB) has been reduced by five to 10 years over the last decade (Chen, 2003, p. 127). Botswana, for example, was expected to have a life expectancy at birth of 38 years by 2010. Worse is the realization that, on average, women are infected at six to eight years younger than men and "fall sick and die at younger ages" (Chen, 2003, p. 133), thus decreasing fertility among childbearing age women in the region. This finding is worsened by the fact that the chance of a woman who loses a husband through AIDS to re-marry is virtually none (Thiuri, 1997, p. 97). Known is the fact that men in Sub-Saharan Africa still wish to marry a virgin as a part of their tradition and the belief, among some, that sexual intercourse with a young virgin can cure AIDS.

Disease and Its Economic Impact on the Household and the Nation

Until 2002, almost no studies had been conducted on the economic impact of disease in Africa. According to some sources, only eight serious studies had been completed, and they all focused on disability-adjusted life years (DALYs) or lost years as a result of ill health that caused absenteeism from the workplace. Today, the situation has changed but most of the studies refer to malaria and, more recently, to HIV/AIDS, in terms of both direct and indirect financial losses to the family and the nation. Summarized below are some of the findings.

While, on the average, we are told that malaria seems to siphon at least one-quarter of a family's income for treatment alone, in Tanzania, a household is expected to spend a minimum of 25 percent of its income on treatment. For a country in Sub-Saharan Africa, the loss to GDP is about 1.3-4.0 percent as a result of malaria. Malaria's overall impact on the national budget is said to be as much as 40 percent of public expenditures, 30 to 40 percent of inpatient admissions, and as much as "50 percent of outpatient visits" in areas where the infections are higher (April 24, 2007 figures). Lynne Rienner notes that, in Sub-Saharan Africa, the "direct costs of AIDS per case exceed per capita GDP" as well as the "per capita public expenditures of \$5 on health care" (Falola, 2006, p. 234). In Nigeria, for example, agricultural output during the past few years seems to have declined by 77 percent as a result of a 50 percent farmer's absence from work due to illnesses attributed to malaria, meningitis, onchocersiasis (river blindness), guinea worm, tuberculosis, and schistosomiasis (bilharzias or bilharziasis) (Falola, 2006, p. 242). This is significant because extended African families tend to be engaged in subsistence agriculture, one of the major reasons for polygyny. Agriculture provides jobs, "food security, generation of health, a stemming of rural-urban migration, and the raw materials necessary for industry."

Estimates of direct costs for Zimbabwe, Malawi, Kenya, Tanzania, and Rwanda have ranged, according to Rienner, from 23 percent of the 1990 public health spending in Kenya to more than 65 percent in Rwanda. On average, she writes on the impact of AIDS, "for countries shown, the total annual treatment cost per AIDS patient was 2.7 times per capita GDP" (Rienner, p. 297). This means that funds reserved for education and other social programs that are designed to strengthen the family are being diverted to other programs to stem the threat posed by HIV/AIDS. Interestingly, Rienner further notes, prevention of one case of HIV infection seems to save 8.8 discounted healthy life years, "a number that ranks fifth after sickle-cell anemia, neonatal tetanus, birth injury, and severe malnutrition in the number of healthy life years saved" (Rienner, 2003, p. 297).

In an article published in 2006, using a simulated model spanning 20 years, Tediosi et al. found that the "total number of undiscounted DALYs lost to malaria in [a] population of 100,000 people is approximately 481,000, which corresponds to a rate of 0.24 DALYs per capita per year" (Tediosi et al., 2006, p. 90-93). In direct costs, notes the study, the total undiscounted direct costs would amount to US\$485,793 over the 20-year period, corresponding to US\$4.86 per capita and, on average, US\$0.24 per capita per year. Likewise, outpatient treatment at the health centers would account for 35 percent of total direct costs, drug treatments 7 percent, hospital admissions 58 percent, severe cases 40 percent, and patient costs 22 percent. The study ends by noting that, "The marginal cost, i.e., additional financial opportunity costs that would be incurred, when introducing a new control intervention, is approximately 58 percent of the average cost" (Tediosi et al., 2006, p. 90-93). Other studies show that Sub-Saharan Africa loses some \$2 billion a year from the negative impact of malaria. This amount is considerable, especially for the families, overall, in hardest-hit countries.

Virtually no similar studies have been conducted on the financial impact of trypanosomiasis or sleeping sickness on the African extended family. This researcher was able to identify one conducted by five researchers in the Buma community near Kinshasa, Democratic Republic of Congo, following a trypanosomiasis outbreak in 2000-2002. The study involved a total of 57 patients, with the median average age of 26 years (4-72 years range), 57 percent female. The outbreak directly affected 47 people or 21 percent of the households. The researchers found that the cost per household or families living together in one household was "equivalent to a five months' income for that household" (Lutumba et al., 2007). Furthermore, the trypanosomiasis related DALYs was 2,145, while interventions to control it averaged 1,408 DALYs, corresponding to US$17. The median hospitalization period for the sick was 10 days (ranging from 30 to 270 days); the care givers spent 10 days each with the patients after hospitalization. Following were the indirect costs: For the 47 patients 94.55 percent; hospitalization 4.16 percent; treatment 1.11 percent; consultation 0.10 percent; laboratory tests 0.09 percent. The study also revealed that all direct and indirect costs represented 43 percent of the annual revenue of a family or household or an estimated US$384 in Buma (range US$0.00-US$1,980). The estimates were based on agricultural and small trade activities. Obviously, the financial burden, setting aside the physical and mental anguish, was enough to bankrupt all affected families in the community.

Estimates are that, in Botswana, AIDS-related ailments will cost one-third of the country's economic potential during the next 10 years, if the rates do not come down soon enough. The layoff of 200 percent of the "economically active adults will result in a budget deficit of 21 percent." This is expected to result in severe skilled worker shortages which will further reduce the GDP growth by 1.5 percent per year. Studies in Kenya have revealed that the country loses 10 years of discounted productive life years or more than three-fourths of an individual's undiscounted productivity years (Rienner, 2003, p. 297). Also, estimates are that each reduction of the workforce affects economic performance and reduces the GDP from 4.3 percent in a non-AIDS economy to 2.4 percent in the AIDS simulations. These conditions are said to have happened in Cameroon from 1987 to 1991, where an annual loss of 10,000 skilled and unskilled workers in rural and urban areas took place.

Fertility, Family Planning, and Population Growth

From another angle, the premature death of young girls due to HIV presages a bleak future for Africa. In Tanzania, for example, 60 percent of the girls aged between 15 and 19 years, who are future potential mothers, are said to be HIV-positive, and girls in that country have an infection rate five times higher than that of boys of the same age. As experts further note, female vulnerability to HIV/AIDS is determined by age and marital status. Baylies (200, p. 11) notes that "The particular vulnerability of young married women follows from the way the desire for children makes protection problematic, the fact that men tend to have more partners in the early years of marriage and husbands may be particularly prone to wander during their wife's pregnancy or in the post-partum months." Conversely, abstinence in post-partum, which may be as long as three years, constitutes a grave danger for the wife, as husbands tend to be more sexually "mobile" and, in the process, contract sexually transmitted infections (STIs) (Laurent, 2000, p. 98), as clearly demonstrated in Kigali, Rwanda. We know that high rates of STIs in a population contribute exponentially to the spread of HIV. Thus, for example, in Uganda, studies have shown that HIV-positive girls between 13 and 19 years of age were "twice as likely to be married as those who were negative," resulting in catastrophic consequences for the families involved.

The impact of fertility in HIV/AIDS infected households and families can also be devastating. As Barnett and Whiteside (2002, p. 187) stress on the cultural and physical impact of female infections in a nuclear or extended family in Africa:

> Households with adult female infections experience lower birth rates and higher infant and child mortality rates. In households where a parent or both parents have AIDS, the likelihood is that fewer children will be born and that a significant proportion of those who are born will die in infancy or early childhood. Inevitably, this means that the personnel of the household are not replaced and that the life ways and traditions of that household are not carried forward.

A major HIV/AIDS misfortune on the family in Africa is that, throughout the rest of the globe, the disease affects mostly the uneducated and the poor. The paradox in Africa is that poverty alone does not account for the casualties. In fact, the number of educated people, urban dwellers succumbing to the disease is staggering. The disease is hitting family breadwinners, the educators, the prosperous, the leaders, the most powerful, and the well-to-do parents of young children, at times forcing these important family members to return to the villages to die, the reason why in Africa, HIV/AIDS is known as the "disease of the educated and the townspeople." Writes Kunitz (2007, p. 179) poignantly:

> Nonetheless, across the continent mortality among the political and other elites remains high, so much so that it is further jeopardizing already unstable political regimes and the possibilities of future economic growth. Thus, while poverty may be a fundamental cause of AIDS in wealthy countries, it is not so obvious that it is equally fundamental as an explanation of differences in vulnerability within Africa. Victimizers may themselves be victims.

In Zambia, estimates reveal that "educated women past their teens" are three times more likely to contract HIV than their uneducated counterparts. It is also well documented that the risk factor of contracting HIV is "higher among women whose husband or partner has a higher salary and higher education level, among monogamous families, and among those with an alcoholic partner" (Laurent, 2000, p. 96). In Malawi, it is estimated that at least 12 government ministers and members of the national parliament have died over the past few decades. In Central African Republic (CAR), apparently 85 percent of the teachers who died over the recent past have died from AIDS, a major blow to the families and kin. It has also been estimated that 107 primary schools in CAR have closed due to teachers' shortages as a result of AIDS deaths, leaving only 66 percent of the schools functioning throughout the country. The migratory movement has been one of the major invisible "highways" for the spread of STIs. However, in Sub-Saharan Africa, the urban-to-rural areas migratory pattern has become the most common direction and pathway of HIV/AIDS infections. Most often, when the city can longer sustain the sick, people simply move back to the countryside to die near their extended families or kin.

The health situation in Africa is also severely aggravated by the "brain drain" caused by the flight of doctors and medical personnel to such countries as the United States of America, United Kingdom, and Canada. South African officials, who have had much to lose from the medical personnel flight, unsuccessfully accused the Canadian government of intentionally luring its best physicians. Yet, in 2002, the number of South African physicians employed in Canada rose from 174 to 1,738 (Labonte et al., 2004, p. 59). Currently, in Sub-Saharan Africa, the shortage of doctors, nurses, midwives, and other essential health personnel totals 800,000, with an overall shortfall of almost 1.5 million health workers. In fact, overall 25 percent of Africa's doctors and 5 percent of its nurses were employed in Europe and North America in 2006. Partly as a result of the medical personnel flight, 38 of the 47 countries in Sub-Saharan Africa do not meet the WHO's recommendation of 20 physicians per 100,000 population and 13 have only 5 physicians or fewer for 100,000 people. Malawi has only some 266 physicians for a population of 13 million, which is equivalent to 2.1 per 100,000 population unit (http://en.wikipedica.org/wiki/global_health, p. 3, Retrieved 12/10/07). Overall, the WHO notes that Africa has only 590,198 health workers, with 36 countries suffering a severe shortage. For coverage of 80 percent of its health needs, the continent would have to increase the number of its health workers (doctors, nurses, and midwives) by 140 percent. In the words of Shula Marks, "Economic collapse has affected the lives of doctors and nurses, undermining their status and at times even their sense of professionalism, as transport infrastructures have collapsed, drugs have been in short supply, hospitals have deteriorated, and corruption has found a ready foothold among poverty-stricken health demands" (Marks, 2007, p. 546-547).

The New "Variant," "Bang Bang" Famine and the "Accordion Effect:" Causes and Impact

African families, especially those in the Sahel region and in Southern Africa, have had to cope with cyclical drought and famine virtually every five or seven years and with annual floods, the hard-hit being such countries as Mozambique, Zimbabwe, Zambia, South Africa, and Kenya. However, the severity of the resulting famine that displaces hundreds of extended families living in the flood areas is often man-made. Yet, notwithstanding the cyclical pattern of the natural disasters, African leaders make no provisions to prepare the people for these eventualities and have implemented no serious or effective strategic plans to ensure that the impact is minimized. The Southern Africa Coordinating Conference (SADC), made up of such countries as Zambia, South Africa, Mozambique, Tanzania, Swaziland, Angola, Botswana, Lesotho, and Zimbabwe have done little of import to predict the droughts, store enough food, or plan how the people living along the banks of the Zambezi, Limpopo, Rovue, and Rovuma Rivers might be able to evacuate quickly and rebuild in areas that do not put them in the harm's way of the constant flooding.

The health crisis in these regions, particularly in the wake of HIV/AIDS, which are sometimes aggravated by civil wars, civil unrest, and unemployment, has created what Barnett and de Wall have called the "new variant famine," which is characterized by "the inability of poor, AIDS-affected households to cope with the demands of securing sufficient food during a time of food crisis." AIDS is said to play a major role in famines that have occurred recently in such countries as Lesotho, Malawi, Mozambique, Swaziland, Zambia, and Zimbabwe. Since September 2002, according to the United Nations, some 14 million people have been at "risk of starvation," with the spread of AIDS being "understood as a 'root cause' for the decline in agricultural production" (Monique, 2004, p. 33). Monique thus further elaborates the reasons of the intermittent famine in Sub-Saharan Africa, its relation to the unhealthy environment, and the lack of political will on the part of the leaders:

> The circumstances that have led to the AIDS "famine crisis" are complex. But certainly what must be considered is the historical relationship between the imposition of export monoculture and the decline in subsistence production and small-scale farming; the effects of agricultural pricing policies and the severe cost/price squeeze felt by small local farms; the impacts of the instability.

On the "new variant famine" and the anthropologists' image of the "accordion effect" strategy among African farmers, for example, de Waal notes that it has become a habit in some communities for a family not to grow "nutritious" crops that are easily visible to relatives, which would force them to share food from such crops as corn or maize. Some are now focusing on "invisible" tubercular crops such as cassava, "the selfish crop," whose production in some areas has skyrocketed two-fold. In Zimbabwe, the Farmers Union claims that corn or maize production dipped by 61 percent and vegetable output by one-half as a result of the death of the family "breadwinner." In other words, as de Waal puts it in reference to Africa from India's famine experience, "one demographic insult predisposes to another, to the extent that students of India's population history have diagnosed the phenomenon of 'bang bang famines'" (de Waal, 2003, p. 134). This is also happening in Africa. A related issue is breastfeeding, which is fast becoming a true dilemma for African families, as an infected pregnant mother can transmit the infection to the fetus. Breastfeeding has been proven to transmit the virus from mother to the born child through maternal milk. Currently, however, the benefits of breastfeeding outweigh the risks of HIV transmission, and mothers are urged not to stop the practice (*Encyclopedia of African History*, 2005, p. 624).

Finally, when one considers that most families have had at least one person to die from diseases such as AIDS and tuberculosis, one realizes the impact on the personal and household level. However, when one adds to the family the easily controllable disease burden from measles, meningitis, yellow fever, and diarrhea, which can hit a household at the same time, one cannot fathom the anguish and hopelessness that befall couples and the "extended web of kin," often with no government assistance in sight, once their meager resources are depleted.

HEALTH, HEALTH POLICY, AND THE AFRICAN EXTENDED FAMILY

Demographic Considerations

The natural and man-made causes of disease in Africa are no longer a mystery, particularly in reference to the most deadly infectious illnesses. HIV/AIDS is slowly being managed worldwide with anti-retrovirus drug treatment and through sex education, even though in Africa only a handful of countries (e.g., Senegal, Uganda, Kenya, and Botswana) have made some inroads into the containment of its rapid growth. Demographers tell us that, even though the population of Africa is still growing and is predicted to reach 1.8 billion by 2050 from today's 900 million—representing an increase of 34 percent in 50 years—the rate of increase is slowing down, the disease burden being one of the major factors. From the 3-4 percent growth the continent experienced during the 1960s-1980s, the rate has been reduced to 2.3 percent on the average, with small variations between country and country and between region and region.

Several experts have claimed that AIDS is the number one predictor of population decline in Africa. Studies have further shown that, in Zimbabwe, for example, the rate of fertility has declined by 33 percent over the past 10 years. Others predict that, in South Africa, home to five or six million people or 15 percent HIV-positive citizens out of a population of 40 million—about 12.5 percent of all people living with HIV/AIDS in the world (Chen, 2003, p. 142-143)—the population growth will decline by 71 percent, negatively affecting 18 percent of the labor force. Lincoln Chen adds that Africa's most developed country, South Africa, will have only 31 million people by 2050, corresponding to one-half of what it would have without AIDS. In Mozambique, the demographic consequences of AIDS are dire, and the situation will continue to be so for the next 10 years. With a population of over 19 million, this former Portuguese colony has seen its population growth reduced from 4 percent during the 1980s to 2.1 currently, with 26 percent of its under-five children expected to have died from AIDS between 2002 and 2005, while another 26 percent was "diagnosed" as living under weight. It is unknown whether the mortality rate did, in fact, hit the country as predicted.

Unfortunately, while family fertility has been going down, premarital fertility has being rising in 25 African countries where data have been collected, showing an average of one in five women giving birth before marriage (DHS, 2006, p. iii). This confirms other studies that claim that, in Sub-Saharan Africa, the rate of premarital sexual intercourse is on the rise despite the HIV crisis, representing, on the average, 40 percent or more the impact of the "sex revolution" among the 20 to 24-year old women. In certain poor sections of Lusaka, it is estimated that 25 percent of the 10-year-olds and 60 percent of the 16-year-olds have already had sex. In Malawi, about 65 percent of the women get pregnant before the age of 20 years. At times, this is attributed to men searching for virgins not just for the lure of it but convinced that virgins are cures for HIV/AIDS.

As expected, over 22 million women in Africa would like to have another pregnancy to sustain a large family, which explains why most family planning is still done in the traditional way. However, spacing children, an "insurance" for old age, through breastfeeding may prevent sexual intercourse in the household for three years among certain ethnic groups. Currently, only 25 percent of the African countries have a working family planning in place designed to reduce growth, despite the fact that economic growth is not keeping pace with fertility. Fertility now stands at between 3 and 5 children per woman between the ages of 15 and 49 years. Since its introduction by the West during the mid-seventies, family planning has had its problems. One study conducted among some communities in Tanzania revealed that people believe that it causes female infertility, deformities in babies, and cancer or "itching of private parts." The lack of condom use is also responsible for the still relatively high fertility in Africa, even though access and costs of contraceptives are variables to be considered. For example, in Kenya, a condom costs US$4 compared to $0.15 in the United States. In Zambia, about 74 percent of married women use no modern contraceptives. Ironically, the African Union Conference of September 19, 2007, in Maputo, was devoted primarily to the use of contraceptives and family planning. Will anything come out of the resolutions approved at the gathering?

Health and Africa's Leadership

Notwithstanding all predictions and the deplorable health conditions on the continent, African leaders have not lived up to their pledges to make health care a right of all their citizens. In fact, only two countries in Africa have followed through on the 2002 Abuja, Nigeria, pledge by all heads of state and government that each country would allocate at least 15 percent of total government expenditures to health, with the realization that the

AIDS crisis alone called for a minimum continental budget of $3 billion a year, while counting on $10 billion of assistance from abroad. The African Union, in its session of April 9-13, 2007, in Johannesburg, South Africa, the third of its Ministries of Health, announced the "Africa Health Strategy 2007-2015," pledging, among other things, to lower maternal mortality from 500-1500 to 228 per 100,000 population and reduce under-five mortality from 171 to 61 per 100,000. Yet, Labonte and his colleagues' study claims that "Only six African countries spend more than US$60 per annum, only nine countries spend more than US$34 to cover essential health services. Even using the US$12 per capita per annum package proposed by the World Bank (1973) for minimum necessary health services, 19 African countries of 46, for which data are available, spend this amount or more. These figures have profound implications for health policy in Africa" (Labonte et al., 2004, p. 178).

In Tanzania and Malawi, for example, the maternal mortality rate stands at 529 and 620 per 100,000, respectively, and it is even higher in such countries as Chad, Niger, Burkina Faso, and Swaziland. For families or women that would like to have an abortion, the odds of the mothers-to-be to come out of the ordeal alive are not reassuring. Sadly, while, in Africa, 22,000 women die each year from "unsafe abortions," 40 percent of pregnancy-related deaths in the world occur in Sub-Saharan Africa. In Ethiopia, "backstreet abortions are second only to tuberculosis as the highest killer of pregnant women, accounting for 22-54 percent of the mothers' annual mortality rate" (*Environment News*, February 29, 2000). It is unlikely that the projected African Union reductions for maternal and child mortality rates will occur on the continent even during the next 15 years. On a related matter, one author makes this revealing statement: "In Sub-Saharan Africa, poor reproductive health practices, especially inadequate birth spacing, contribute as much or more to maternal and child mortality than HIV/AIDS. Unfortunately, the rate of modern contraceptive prevalence in Africa is only 13 percent among married men" (http://www.advanceafrica.org/what_we_do/Repositing_family/index.html, Retrieved 12/15/2007).

Health facilities are still inaccessible to many poor families, especially in the countryside, due to distance or failure of the population to realize how important primary prevention is. The existence and popularity of the traditional medical system prevent many from walking or traveling to health care centers or to follow referrals to city hospitals, except as the last resort, sometimes spreading the rumors that "hospitals kill people" (Slickerveer, 1990, p. 25). According to the WHO and UNICEF, in the developing world, and more acutely in Africa, "only 15 percent of the rural and non-privileged urban population" have access to health care services (Slikkeveer, 1990, p. 25). In Ethiopia, for example, among the Oromo peasants, there is "less than one visit per year per person" (Slikkerveer, 1990, p. 31). Lack of health facilities, distance to the nearest health post, and resilience of the traditional system explain these conditions.

African leaders must be concerned about what the HIV/AIDS case load is doing to Africa's hospitals, health centers, and dispensaries. Prior to the AIDS crisis, one could still see, even in some urban hospitals, two patients, at times with infectious diseases, sleeping in the same bed for lack of a sufficient number of beds. Today, the situation has turned into a greater crisis because over half of the beds (60 percent in Burundi and South Africa) are taken by HIV/AIDS patients. This means literally that patients with other afflictions who may need to be hospitalized are being turned away to die in their compounds or in their villages. At Kenyatta National Hospital in Nairobi, Kenya, the number of patients affected with AIDS-related diseases and admitted at the hospital "doubled" from 1988 to 1992, while the admission of patients with other illnesses dropped by 18 percent (Rienner, 2003, p. 293). In Mozambique, people say that when the doctors hear a patient coughing and realize that he is returning from work in the South African mines, they do not even diagnose him. They simply tell him he has AIDS and give him some placebo, so dire the situation has become.

The social stigma attached to HIV/AIDS in Africa has certainly caused untold psychological suffering. Suffice at this point to quote one scholar writing on a married woman named Sara who contracted HIV through blood transfusion in one region of Nigeria. Once she had accepted her condition, the young woman decided to visit her sisters and extended family relatives for moral support. To her dismay, the negative reaction from family members was unprecedented and unbelievable, as described below:

> Family bonds run deep in Africa. So, when your family turns on you, there are few other places to go. The stigma of HIV in Nigeria freezes people with fear. Some HIV-positive Nigerians tell stories of villages scattering upon the arrival of an HIV-positive member. Husbands have been known to dump wives and leave home (http://crs.org/nigeria/hiv-second-chance/, Retrieved 12/1/2007, p. 4 of 6).

Likely, a similar story is repeated over and over again in Sub-Saharan Africa. One author put it this way: When AIDS became a known disease elsewhere, "All sorts of belief systems were constructed to attach the disease to anything but the real cause—uninformed and unprotected sex with multiple partners. Instead of curiosity about the nature and modes of transmission, a great deal of social and medical stigma developed. Those infected, therefore, hid and denied their status until they succumbed to the disease" (Zewde, 2005, p. 522-523).

War and Health in Africa

A nation's health care system can only flourish in an environment of peace and stability. Since the 1980s, at the onset of the HIV era to the present, numerous wars, mainly civil wars, have either been ravaging the countryside and the cities of Africa or have recently ended, but only following massive destruction of the health care infrastructure and the deaths of millions of lives: Angola, Mozambique, Sudan, Chad, Algeria, Ethiopia-Eritrea, Namibia, Somalia, Democratic Republic of Congo, Central African Republic, Guinea-Bissau, Liberia, Sierra Leone, Cote d'Ivoire, Uganda, Rwanda, and South Africa. Suffices to reiterate here what epidemiologists, historians, and sociologists have said about wars and their impact on health:

> War accounts for more death and disability than many major diseases combined. It destroys families, communities, and sometimes whole cultures. It directs resources away from protection and promotion of health, medical care, and other human services. It destroys the infrastructure that supports health. It limits human rights and contributes to social injustice. It leads many people to think that violence is the only way to resolve conflicts—a mindset that contributes to domestic violence, street crime, and other kinds of violence. And it contributes to the destruction of the environment and overuse of nonrenewable resources. In sum war threatens much of the fabric of our civilization (Levy & Sidel, 2008, p. 3).

Civil wars have also made Africa the "refugee capital" of the world, currently with close to six million and displaced persons of its own. The conflict in Darfur alone has caused 280,000 refugees, with thousands of other persons living as internally displaced. While the war in Sudan is estimated to have cost three to five million lives since its inception during the 1970s, the recent civil war in Central African Republic has already resulted in thousands of deaths and 40,000 refugees and displaced persons. In the Democratic Republic of Congo, the five-year war has already caused a maternal mortality rate of 1,800 per 100,000 population live births, and, according to the United Nations, its toll ranks as "the third or fourth highest death toll in the world." In Guinea-Bissau, Sierra Leone, and Liberia, hundreds of health care centers were destroyed by the wars and never replaced. In Guinea-Bissau, the number of doctors (2.3 per facility) dropped by 50.4 percent to 1.4 per facility during the first year of the conflict and to 1.03 by 10 percent during the second year (Soyibo, 2005, p. xxi). The synergy of war and AIDS makes for a terrible human predicament. In the words of one scholar, "The impact of HIV/AIDS in Africa is no less destructive than that of warfare itself," as it overwhelms the health services and leaves millions of unprotected orphans (Falola, 2006, p. 183). The killing and the raping of women by armed forces in times of war and armed conflict have all been well documented by the conflicts in Kosovo, Democratic Republic of Congo, Rwanda, Chad, Darfur, and other places. Since the 1980s, the negative impact of war has been heightened by HIV/AIDS, carried and transmitted by soldiers to the helpless women in the countryside and the cities. Indeed, according to some accounts, the rate of HIV infections among the African armed forces has been extremely high. In 1999, following seems to have been the prevalence of HIV among soldiers in the various countries:

Country	Size of Armed Forces	Percentage: HIV Prevalence
Angola	113,000	50
Botswana	7,800	33
DRC	31,100	50
Lesotho	2,050	40
Malawi	10,800	50
Mozambique	6,000	—
Namibia (1996)	8,100	16
South Africa (2000)	90,500	15-20
Swaziland (1997)	3,000	48
Zambia	21,500	60
Zimbabwe	36,000	55

Source: Adapted from Chen, 2003, p. 150.

Death from all sources in Africa has created so much social and demographic distortion that many demographers have abandoned representing populations with the usual pyramidal structure where the young occupy the greater part of the national, community, or family demographics. Currently, demographers and epidemiologists prefer to picture the structure and shape of Africa's population more as a chimney than a pyramid because children and women are dying in larger numbers than the old, with fewer babies being born, conditions that decrease the population numbers and age sets (Chen, 2004, p. 147).

CONCLUSION

Health and External Pressures

African leaders and health professionals know exactly what needs to be done both in terms of policies and strategies to reverse the disease trends on their continent. In the final analysis, it is a matter of setting the priorities straight and having the will to enact changes that are obviously needed if the continent, its people, and its cherished family traditions are to adapt to and survive the crisis for decades to come. HIV/AIDS has certainly been the greatest challenge Africa has ever had to face. The etiology of the disease is now known and, even though ethnocentric notions have been advanced to explain the crisis, the causes of the rapid spread are more or less clear, though more research on cultural and ethnic risk factors seems to be needed. Monique (27) has summarized the causes or factors advanced since the 1980s to explain the phenomenon: Traditional ritual practices; sexual activity at young age; high level of premarital sex; high level of extramarital sexual intercourse; polygamy; wife sharing; widow inheritance by patrilineal brother; funeral rites; scarification; use of infected and contaminated instruments; most recently, lack of widespread circumcision, which is being heralded now as the savior of the continent and rejected by others (See Nicoll, 1997, p. 194-195); and alleged general "sexual promiscuity" of African societies when compared to Western and other world societies.

Quite often the protagonists of these sometimes dubious or exaggerated claims rarely look at the root causes and the domestic and international factors that make it very difficult for Africa to come out of its health quagmire, including: The colonial history and the legacies of dependency under which Africa is still operating in many aspects of its daily life; the negative impact of the structural adjustment conditionalities attached to the loans from the International Monetary Fund and World Bank, which perpetuate Africa's debt dependency. According to most researchers, the loans and the debt have created more inequalities among the poor and the rich; the added inequalities and the nefarious impact of globalization, which has eroded African leaders' independence in foreign policy; and unfair terms of trade that impact negatively on Africa's economic growth and development and favor in general Western governments and in particular multinational corporations whose assets are sometimes greater than the gross domestic products of African nations. Sadly, of the 40 most indebted countries, 32 are in Africa, suffering from a debt that has more than doubled for most of them since 1980. Sylvia Ojutuku-Macauley adds that, while 12 of these countries show a GDP-debt ratio of "between 100 and 350 percent," 13 show a ratio of between 20 to 40 percent (Ojukutu-Macaule, 2003, p. 111). Evidently, no family or business could survive if it managed its business the way African leaders have managed their countries' finances. In countries such as Ghana, originally heralded as a success story for the IMF and the World Bank, Kenya, Sierra Leone, Nigeria, and Zimbabwe, studies have recently shown that the "loans were granted under almost impossible terms, the most devastating of which were the cuts in government spending and the devaluation of the currencies," which led to "the postponement or total abandonment of development programs where African governments could not afford to build new hospitals, schools, or roads, and where existing institutions were perpetually short of supplies" (Ojukutu-Macauley, 2003, p. 111).

On globalization, Monique once again summarizes the picture when she writes:

> The actual success of global institutional response to AIDS in Africa, particularly to alleviate the impact of the epidemic in hardest-hit communities, likely lies outside the AIDS epidemic multi-sectoral strategies, but more firmly in the evolution of a just global order that sees the protection of the exercise of basic human rights not just as the responsibility of the individual nation-state. In our increasingly globalized world, it is the far-from-invisible hand of the market—the decisions of a particular epistemic community, which views both patriarchy and capitalism as 'natural'—that shapes the local conditions which determine who has access to the exercise of basic human rights (Monique, 2004, p. 177).

The new global "order" has increased the levels of poverty and inequality in the world, making the rich richer and the poor poorer. The system has, for instance, allowed the world's 200 richest people to more than double their "net worth in the four years to 1998 to more than $2 trillion." Interestingly, one fifth of the wealthiest individuals on the globe come from the developing world (*World Health Report*, 2005, p. 4), including Africa. As the World Health Report adds, "An 'equity lens' is important because political and economic institutions are shaped in ways that can reinforce unfair advantages and widen socioeconomic disparities" (*World Health Report*, 2005, p. 4).

Inequalities and Inequities:
The Role of Women in the African Family

While there are, definitely, inequalities in Africa brought about and perpetuated by international economic and political conditions, there are undoubtedly others that are internal to the continent, and they evolve around the role and place of men and women in the family and household, the community, and the nation. In this context, a need arises to probe deeper into the role of a culture that seems to perpetuate the patriarchic system that renders females almost powerless when it comes to decisions in matters of conjugal sexual activity, seems to condone domestic rape, physical abuse and violence against wives and adult and young females, and "sanctions" husbands' affairs outside the family social perimeters, all of which impact not just HIV transmission but the transmission of other communicable sexual diseases. Obviously, these patterns of behavior are more pronounced in certain societies and clans than in others, which call for more careful research on ethnically-based cultural traits and practices that might favor an ecological environment favorable to the spread of sexually transmitted diseases. In the plain words of two African scholars:

> To break this chain, women must be empowered to be able to say no to men without suffering sexual or physical violation, social ostracism, or economic destitution; this calls for a redefinition of gender and sexual behavior codes and for the drawing and implementation of policies, directives, and programs that will eventually conscientize both men and women to accept gender equality and behave and live as equal partners (Kalipeni & Thiuri, 1997, p. 114).

Applied to health, it is clear that the excessive rate of maternal mortality is one of the consequences of gender inequality, because maternal deaths are "entirely preventable, yet remain unchecked due to lack of emergency health services for the poor," who, in Africa, are mostly women, "and to the historical neglect of women's broader reproductive health needs" (Ostin et al., 2003, p. 138).

Health Care Improvement Strategies

The policy choices for African leaders are clear and simple. They should include:

- Enacting and enforcing laws that address the disparities in access to health by women, the poor, and the disabled both in the cities and the rural areas
- Ending the inequalities that make women sexually and otherwise powerless in the family, the household, and the nation
- Enacting all health strategies African leaders themselves have agreed over the years on health care for all by providing funds and financially ensuring that preventive primary health care and community-based services, safe water, sanitation, and environmental protection remain the strongest means to stem the ravages of infectious (and chronic) diseases on the continent
- Taking every measure to lessen dependency on international hand-outs that make them subservient and ineffective globally, especially in their inability to influence the terms of trade, debt alleviation, and economic development
- Accelerating the education and promotion of women
- Ending the culture of corruption through transparency and accountability and
- Incorporating the knowledge of traditional healers and enlisting their assistance in the delivery of health care and the rehabilitation of the patient in the community.

Clearly, Africa faces a health crisis but the challenges are not insurmountable. Adetokumbo Lucas thus summarizes the strategies to improve health on the continent: "A combination of radical reform of health systems to improve efficiency, cost effectiveness, and equity; capacity strengthening to help policymakers and health workers manage diversity and change; promotion of health research to guide decisions on local issues and to participate with the global scientific community in efforts to develop new and improve technologies; and rationalization of international technical cooperation that is designed to promote self-reliance" (Lucas, 2002, p. 15). Throughout this process, social science and scientific research must go hand in hand with the effort to improve health care on the continent. Thus, regarding the survival of the family in all its manifestations, the theme of this study, African leaders might need to listen to Nana Apt who admonishes that: "If the family is expected to continue to serve as the primary safety net it once was, we must know more about how social changes have affected the family's ability to undertake such responsibilities" (Apt, 2007, p. 194-195) and find the right path to its brighter future.

A few years ago, experts talked about the prospects of the African continent undergoing the epidemiological transition from an infectious to a chronic disease environment. This is no longer a topic of serious conversation, as endemic infectious diseases continue to take their toll, while emerging new ones and drug-resistant others make it appear that, when Africa makes one step forward, it makes two steps backward. Obviously, the present work, for lack of data, omitted discussion of mental health. Mental or cases of psychological impairments are many in Africa, and dementia and schizophrenia have certainly increased given the difficult conditions families and members are currently experiencing. Since African governments have consistently paid virtually no attention to the problem, the extended family has had to take care of its sick. One can only point out that, as defined by the United Nations, good physical health also implies and requires good mental health, or, as the Romans used to say centuries ago, "mens sana in corpore sano" (a sound mind in a sound body).

An all-out assault on HIV/AIDS will require a concerted effort to make available anti-retroviral drugs to all patients through provision of funding and exertion of pressure on pharmaceutical companies to sell their drugs at a cheaper price on the market. As a strategy against HIV/AIDS, Africans should not rely only on providing individual sex education or putting emphasis on abstinence and behavioral changes, as the West seems to expect of them, while it focuses its resources on drug provision for its own people (Monique, 2004, p. 9) and lets its communities decide whether or not sex education and sex behavioral change ought to be a mandatory part of classroom instruction. These strategies, along with meaningful policies on health care management and declared war on corruption, which has siphoned the very funds allocated to combating the HIV/AIDS crisis, will improve the odds that poor people, women, children, and those who do not work for the government have a fair share of the national pie. However, this is a tall order because ending corruption cannot happen overnight since it is intertwined with the international market and the structure of the post-colonial state. Mbaku suggests that eliminating corruption will require radical institutional changes that must seek to "modify incentive structures and force market participants to engage in behaviors that produce the outcomes that society desires" (Mbaku, 2003, p. 157).

Survival of the Extended African Family

When all is said and done, it is one thing to say that the African nuclear and extended family is experiencing a crisis and another to claim or "predict" that it will not survive the test of time and disease. So far, what is evident is that more adult family members are dying prematurely and at a faster rate than ever before due to ill health and other factors, natural or man-made; more breadwinners are succumbing to AIDS and other diseases; more young adults—males, but particularly females, the future mothers—are dying at younger ages as a result of STDs and TB; and an unprecedented number of orphans are "clogging" the streets, while grandparents and the extended web of kinship, either due to disease or economic misery, are unable to care for them.

Furthermore, while disease-related social stigma is turning parents against children and husband against wife, politicians, statesmen, computer specialists, bankers, teachers, university professors, and lawyers return to the villages to die when their anti-retrovirus drugs are unable to keep them alive in the city. Certainly these conditions have weakened the traditional family values of solidarity, compassion, hospitality, provision of unselfish financial assistance, support of household harmony, care of the elderly and children, advocacy for the mentally ill, and hope in one's future. Whence will these challenges lead the African family? No one can predict, especially if the economic conditions continue to deteriorate and the social and physical infrastructure goes on crumbling. Yet, one has to keep the faith, in the hope that, as was the case in the past, this basic social unit, nuclear or extended, will weather the storm, adapt itself, and survive and thrive in the decades to come.

References

Africa: South of the Sahara. (2007). London: Europa Publishers.

African Union. (2007). *Africa Health Strategy 2007-2015.* Johannesburg, April 9-13, 2007, Third Session of the AU Conference of Ministers of Health. Addis Ababa, African Union.

Apt, N. A. (2007). Health and Aging in Africa. In M. Robinson, W. Novelli, C. Pearson & L. Norris. *Global Health and Global Aging.* San Francisco: Jossey-Bass.

Azevedo, M. & G. S. (2005). *Africana Studies: A Survey of Africa and the African Diaspora.* Durham, NC: Carolina Academic Press.

_____. (2003). Health and Development in Africa. In E. Nnadozie (Ed.) *African Economic Development.* (pp. 181-206) New York: Academic Press.

_____ (1978). Epidemic Disease among the Sara of Southern Chad, 1890-1940. In D. Patterson & G. Hartwig (Eds.) D*isease in African History: An Introductory Survey and Case Studies.* (pp.1118-152). Durham: Duke University Press.

Baliamoune-Luz, M. (2008). Gender Issues and the Role of NEPAD. In S. Boko & D. Seck (Eds.) *NEPAD and the Future of Economic Policy in Africa.* (pp. 171-182).Trenton, NJ: Africa World Press.

Barnett, T. & A. Whiteside.*(2002). AIDS in the Twenty-First Century.* New York: Palgrave.

Baylies, C. & J. Bujra (2000). Perspectives on Gender and AIDS in Africa. In C. Baylies & Janet Buzra.(Eds) A*ids, Sexuality, and Gender in Africa.* (pp. 1-24). New York: Routledge.

Boko, S. & D. Seck (Eds.) (2008). *NEPAD and the Future of Economic Policy in Africa.* Trenton, NJ: Africa World Press.

Bongmba, E. (2007). *Facing a Pandemic: The African Church and the Crisis of AIDS.* Waco, Texas: Baylor University Press.

Bradley, C.& T. Weisner. (1997). Introduction: Crisis in the African Family. In T.Weisner, C. Bradley & P. Kilbride (Eds.) *African Families and the Crisis of Social Change.* Westport, CO: Bergin and Garvey.

Brown, L. R. (2004). Economic Growth Rates in Africa: The Potential Impact of HIV/AIDS. In E. Kalipeni, O.N.Z. Shisana & W. Shisana. (Eds.) *HIV and AIDS in Africa.* (pp. 191-303). New York: Blackwell Publishing.

Chen, L., J. Leaning & V. Narasimhan (Eds.) (2003). *Global Health Challenges for Human Security.* Cambridge: Harvard University Press.

Cooper, E., C. E. Pearson, & M. R. Schwartz. (2002) *Critical Issues in Global Health.* San Francisco, CA: A Wiley Imprint.

Encyclopedia of African History, 2. (2005). Health: Medicine and Disease—Post-Colonial. New York: Taylor and Francis Group.

Falola, T.& M. Heaton. (2006). *Traditional and Modern Health Systems in Nigeria.* Trenton, NJ: Africa World Press.

Falola, T. (Ed.) (2008). *Africa 5.* Durham: Carolina Academic Press.

Garrett, L. (1994). *The Coming Plague: Newly Emerging Diseases in a World out of Balance.* Baltimore, MD: Penguin.

Gordon, A.J,.P. S. Yoder & M. Camara. (2004). *Signs of Illness, Treatment, and Support for Young Children: A Perspective Community Study.* Baltimore, MD: Measure, DHS-USAID,

Haan, de M. (2005) *The Health of Southern Africa.* Cape Town: Juta Academic;

Hofrichter, R. (Ed.) (2003). *Health and Social Justice: Politics, Ideology, and Inequity in the Distribution of Disease.* San Francisco: Jossey-Bass.

http://www.worldband.org/html/extdr/pb/pbaidsactivities.htm, p. 3, Retrieved 12/10/2007.

http://crs.org/nigeria/hiv-second-chance/ , Retrieved 12/15, 2007, p. 4 of 6.

http://www.advanceafrica.org/what_we_do/Repositing_family/index.html, Retrieved 12/15/2007

Kaleeba, N. (2004). Excerpt from We Miss You All. In E. Kalipeni, S. Craddock, J. R. Oppong & J. Ghosh. (Eds.) *HIV/AIDS in Africa: Beyond Epidemiology.* Oxford: Oxford University Press.

Kalipeni, E. & P. Thiuri. (1997). *Issues and Perspectives on Health Care in Contemporary Sub-Saharan Africa.* Lewiston, NY: Edwin Mellen Press.

Kalipeni, E., S. Craddock, J. Oppong & J. Ghosh. (Eds) (2004). *HIV/AIDS in Africa: Beyond Epidemiology.* Oxford: Blackwell Publishing, Ltd.

Kayongo-Male, D. & P. Nyango. (1984) *The Sociology of the African Family.* New York: Longman.

Kunitz, S. J. (2007). *The Health of Populations: General Theories and Particular Realities.* Oxford: Oxford University Press.

Labonte, R., T. Schrecker, D. Sanders, & W. Meeus. (2004). *Fatal Independence: The G8, Africa and the Global Health.* Ottawa, Canada: Ottawa University Press.

Levy, S. B. & V. W. Sidel. (2008) *War and Public Health.* Oxford: Oxford University Press

Lutumba, P., E. Makieya, A. Shaw, P. M. Shula. (2008). Health Since the 1970s. In *New Encyclopedia of Africa.* London: Thompson Gale.

Meheus & M. Boelaert. (2007). Human African Trypanosomiasis in a Rural Community, Democratic Republic of Congo. *EID Journal.* 13(2)

Mbaku, J. M. (2003) Corruption. In T. Falola (Ed.) *Africa, 5.* (pp. 131-159) Durham: Carolina Academic Press.

Monique, O. C. (2004). *Neoliberalization and AIDS Crisis in Sub-Saharan Africa.* New York: Palgrave.

Nelson, K., C. M. Williams & N. Graham. (2004). *Infectious Disease Epidemiology: Theory and Practice.* London: Jones and Bartlett Publishers.

Nicoll, A. (1997). Routine Male Neonatal Circumcision and Risk of Infection with HIV-1 and Other Sexually Transmitted Diseases, *Arch. Dis. Child.* 77, 194-195.

Nnadozie, E. (2003). *African Economic Development.* New York: Academic Press.

Ojukutu-Macauley, S. (2003). Health in Africa. In T. Falola (Ed.) *Africa: Contemporary Africa, 5.* (pp. 103-130). Durham, NC: Carolina Academic Press.

Ostin, P., A. George & G. Sen. (2003). Gender, Health, and Inequality. In R. Hofrichter (Ed.) *Health and Social Justice: Politics, Ideology, and Inequity in the Distribution of Disease.* (pp. 132-156). San Francisco: Jossey-Bass.

Patterson, D. & G. Hartwig (Eds.) (1978). *Disease in African History.* Durham, NC: Duke University Press.

Republic of Kenya. (2006-2007). *Reversing the Trends: The Second National Health Sector Strategic Plan of Kenya.* Nairobi: Government Printer.

Robinson, M., W. Novelli, C. Pearson & L. Norris. (2007). *Global Health and Global Aging.* San Francisco: Jossey-Bass.

Ross, A. & M. Tanner. (2006) An Approach to Model the Cost and Effects of Case Management of Plasmodium Falciparum. *American Journal of Medical Hygiene,* 75, 90-93.

Slickerveen, L. J. (1990). *Plural Medical Systems in the Horn of Africa.* New York: Kegan Paul International.

Soyibo, A. (2005). *Health Care Delivery Under Conflict: How Prepared is West Africa?* Ibadan: University of Ibadan Press.

Sutherland, I. (1976). Recent Studies in Epidemiology of Tuberculosis, Based on the Risk of Being Infected with Tubercle Bacilli. *Advances in Tuberculosis Research.*,19, 1-63.

Tediosi, F., N. Maire, T. Smith, G. Hutton, J. Utzinger, S. Craddock, J. Oppong & J. Ghosh. (2004). *HIV and AIDS: Beyond Epidemiology.* New York: Blackwell Publishing.

Thiuri, P. (1997).The Threat of AIDS to Women in Africa. In E. Kalipeni & P. Thiuri. *Issues and Perspectives on Health Care in Contemporary Sub-Saharan Africa* (pp. 85-114) Lewiston, NY: Edwin Mellen Press.

Weisner, T., C. Bradley & P. Kilbride (Eds.) (1997). *African Families and the Crisis of Social Change.* Westport, CO: Bergin and Garvey.

Vidal, L. (2000). *Femmes en temps de SIDA: Experiences d'Afrique.* Paris: Presses Universitaires.

Vynnicky, E. & P.E. Fine. (1997). The Natural History of Tuberculosis: The Implications of Age-Dependent Risks of Disease and the Role of Infection. *Epidemiology and Infection*, 119, 183-201.

Waal, de. A. (2003). HIV/AIDS: The Security Issue of a Lifetime. In L. Chen, L. J. Leaning,& V. Narasimhan (Eds.). *Global Health Challenges for Human Security.* Cambridge: Harvard University Press.

World Health Report. (2005).*Global Health Watch.* London: Medact,

Zewde, A. (2005). The Health of Africa and its Diaspora: Confronting Crisis and Charting New Directions. In M. Azevedo (Ed.) *Africana Studies: A Survey of Africa and the African Diaspora.* Durham, NC: Carolina Academic Press.

CHAPTER 7

EXTENDED FAMILY AND KINSHIP NETWORK SYSTEMS FOR CARING FOR CHILDREN

Florence Kyomugisha and John B. K. Rutayuga

INTRODUCTION

The increasing number of deaths from AIDS and civil wars in Africa since the mid 1980s has resulted in astronomical losses of lives and skills, robbing communities of entire generations. The reality of the situation in African societies is that when people are in the prime years of production and just as they get to the age when many are forming families and having children they die from complications of the AIDS disease, leaving behind orphans. The World Health Organization (WHO) and other agencies that work with orphans of the AIDS epidemic define an orphan as a child under the age of 18 who has lost one or both parents. This is an appropriate and practical definition of orphan because in Africa AIDS is mostly transmitted through sexual contact, and when one parent becomes infected with HIV, he or she will in most cases infect his or her partner, and subsequently, children who lose one parent to AIDS are more likely to lose the other parent as well. A UNAIDS and UNICEF joint report on orphans stated that "[I]n 2003, 12.3 percent of all children in Sub Saharan Africa were orphans." (UNAIDS/UNICEF 2004). As the enormous numbers of AIDS deaths among adults increasingly result in large numbers of orphans, interventions and other systems of caring for orphans and other vulnerable children become strained and most importantly systems for caring for orphans vary from country to country based on the country's economic and political situation. Over the years, there has been an on going debate within the academic, political and organizational spheres about the concept of governments' and private organizations' interventions for alleviating the orphan situation in Sub-Saharan Africa. During the earlier period of the AIDS epidemic, it became apparent that institutional solutions such as children's homes were impossible to capitalize and operate. Furthermore, most Africans believed that the establishment of children's homes (formal institutions) promoted a breakdown of the traditional system of fostering and were "a culturally-destructive, last ditch non-solution injurious to children's welfare" (Hunter, 1990). What de facto took place right from the onset of the orphan crisis was the instinctive reaction of members of the community to the cultural African normative mandate that the care of orphans is primarily a shared responsibility among all extended family, kin networks and the local community.

This chapter discusses the traditional economic and social safety networks of the kinship and the extended family that have been resilient to the impact of AIDS on communities, and how these networks are coping with the orphan problem. The discussion focuses on the dynamics of African marriages, kinships and friendships that link people and families creating the networks that pool resources and work together to care for each other in times of crises. We acknowledge that in discussing the dynamics and role of extended family and kin networks, it becomes apparent that we are dealing with variation and change in the social organization based on time and space; but we are also aware of some common characteristics of extended family and kin networks that have been constant cutting across time and space. Our discussion focuses on the rural populations in North Western Tanzania and South Western Uganda because the people (Bahaya, Banyambo, Banyankole) of the lacustrine region of East Africa share a similar language, culture, traditions and claim to have the same ancestors. We particularly focus on rural populations because of the impact of contextual differences in location (for instance urban verses rural) on the dynamics of extended family and kin networks.

METHODOLOGY

In examining how the Tanzanian and Ugandan traditional economic and social safety networks of the extended family and kinship are coping with the orphan problem, we take as our starting point the fact these societies have experienced enormous numbers of AIDS deaths among adults over the years to the extent of robbing communities of entire generations. Furthermore, these societies have been under constant political and economic strain and pressure to cut on social and health services due to structural adjustment programs (Earth, 1996).

The literature is replete with various definitions of extended family and kin, and therefore, we attempt to use the definitions of extended family and kin networks that are more realistic for the social organization in this region of Africa; and we often use the concepts "extended family networks" and "kinship networks" interchangeably (when referred to in consanguineous and conjugal contexts), because these two concepts and their roles in African society overlap and have an intricacy that does not obtain in the western context. Furthermore, the literature focusing on extended family and kinship networks and HIV/AIDS in this region of Africa is recent, and without adequate prior works to build on, we draw from oral traditions and oral histories (Vansina, 1985). Thus, our discussion of extended family and kinship networks is drawn from the system itself; for instance, we utilize proverbs and adage, the old wisdom of our ancestors, because this knowledge of the past is necessary for us to be able to understand the dynamics, strengths and resourcefulness of extended family and kinship networks of the present system. This approach enhances our understanding of the social organization of marriages, kinship and extended family networks, and their significance in the life of an individual especially as we explore this social organization within the concepts that are realistic, established and have transcended changes in time and space.

We also believe that the most practical and realistic approach to our discussion calls for people who are familiar with the society's traditions and language, and whose observations and lived experiences are utilized to provide the description and interpretation of extended family and kin network roles of caring for children in contemporary society. In that context, the authors were raised in this region of Africa and are very familiar with the dynamics of extended families and kin network system. Furthermore, not only have the authors participated in the innovative interventions for reviving the traditional mechanism for caring for AIDS orphans and other vulnerable children, but have also participated in interventions for preventing the spread of HIV infections (Rutayuga, 2004; Kyomugisha, 2006).

MARRIAGE: A PILLAR OF KINSHIP

Marriage among the Bahaya, Banyambo and Banyankole is regarded as a pillar of the kinship. Without marriage there would not be progeny, and thus the continuation of kinship. In the past, parents arranged the marriages *(obushwere)* of their children. One of the fundamental reasons

185

for the arrangement of marriage was to establish alliances between the two concerned kinships (*oluganda*). The significance of marriage was first experienced during the engagement (*okusherera*) period. Unlike in the West where engagement was decreed in 1215 by Pope Innocent III, "*okusherera*", an arduous period of bond and alliance formation between two marrying kinship groups, was a natural product of exchanging and sharing of gifts aiming at building lasting relationships that would ensure the perpetuation of each kinship group. Traditionally, "*okusherera*" lasted over two years during which the affianced couple would not meet but communicate through emissaries until the wedding day. There has always been a strong belief in marriage as a long-term commitment, and while arrangement of the two or more years of the engagement ensured stability of the newly established relations, the actual marriage established far reaching structural, familial and social relations in a continuum of a social process that was regulated by customary laws, taboos and other codes. Furthermore, fundamental to the African marriage are the several rituals that are still performed during marriage ceremonies to formalize and legitimize the union into the larger extended family and kinship which agree to the terms and conditions of the union of the bride and groom. During a ceremony just before the bride leaves her parents' home on her way to her husband's home, she sits on her father's and later on her mother's laps. She is counseled "for the last time as their child" to follow the values and roles she learned from each of her parents (as wife and mother), and especially the values and roles regarding the begetting and raising of children. Then her parents present her to the arbitrator. This is followed by the bride's brother escorting her out of the house, where she gathers a handful of twigs and brings them back to her mother. The twigs ritual symbolizes the bride's parents' assurance to their daughter that she will always remain their daughter despite her leaving her parents' home. She will refer to her birth place as a place where we belong (*owaitu*); and her new family as home (*omuka*). On entering her husband's house, the bride sits on her parents-in-laws' laps to symbolize the level of integration into the new family; the signature to the alliances entered into: she is born again in the new family and subsequently into the new extended family and kinship. The morning after the wedding, the groom's mother prepares a meal for the bride and the groom. After they eat the food, she counsels them about their expected roles and behavior towards each other, extended family, other kin members and the community at large. Other rituals performed during this period of the marriage include the rituals of fertility anointing *(kusiiga amajuta),* and clearing seeds from pathways *(kwihya empambo omu kihanda),* which are essential and significant for solidifying the union directly between the two newly-weds and indirectly enhancing collaboration between the two kin groups and their communities. These ceremonies and rituals are events of celebration by family, kin and other village members to symbolize everyone's participation and support in times of happiness and sadness.

Traditionally there are other forms of marriages besides the one described above. Polygyny, a marriage that involves one man having multiple spouses is a centuries old form of conjugal union and a form of marriage that is of interest and most debated in the west. Although very few ceremonies, rituals and pomp are performed in case of polygynous weddings, relationships and alliances are formed and entered as in monogamous unions. Wife inheritance (almost extinct) was another type of marriage in which a widow married a kinsman of her late husband, often his brother. In case of the husband's death, the widow's paternal aunt took her and handed her over to her brother-in-law who took the widow in his household and cared for her as his wife. There were no ceremonies or celebrations whatsoever. This was a custom that was necessary for sustaining the life of the woman and her fatherless children, as well as for the sustenance of the relationships with the extended family and other kin groups.

Traditional marriages have been diluted by colonialism and the imposition of Western laws, Western education, new religions, new forms of politics and foreign lifestyles. Compounding the transformation is the exodus from rural to urban residences, often to far places from home as unmarried young people go out in search of gainful employment opportunities or schooling; or even those still at home, meet, form relationships and make arrangements to get married without the consent of their parents. Despite the turbulent times witnessing the erosion in the old traditional marriage practices, there is the persistence, durability and survivability of some of the customs. Many young men and young women across economic and educational levels and sophistication, who have married away from their parents' home, often at some point come home so that the essential marriage rituals and ceremonies are performed to ratify the marriage; to calm down the gods' rage; and to ensure the continuum of structural social relations and networks that are regulated by customary laws and traditions.

CHILDREN: A CONTINUUM OF COMMUNITY

Marriage between two people from two kin groups and the formation of families are cornerstones of the community and their existence is a matter of community interest. Childbirth is the seal that cements the bond between husband and wife, and their families. The fact that children are born every day never overshadows a single childbirth as a unique special event to the parents, family, other kin and the community at large. The expectant mother becomes the jewel of the family and of the community. She receives special treatment and pampering from everyone around her as they await the childbirth, which is seen as a seal of the marriage and a new mother's integration into her new family and kinship, especially her integration into women's networks. Childbirth meets the expectations, fulfils hopes, calms anxieties as it completes and binds families and kinship groups together into the future horizons. Every childbirth is a celebration and an assurance, a rejuvenation of the continuum of life existence into immortality not only of the many who claim, in one way or the other, any relationship to the newborn but also of the entire community. An African family "normally" includes one's direct parents, grand and great grand parents, brothers, sisters, uncles, and aunts, cousins, nieces and nephews and their spouses. However, the concepts of family, mother and father, brother and sister, define far more for Africans than what they mean in the contemporary western family model. Normally, an African child refers to any of his uncles or aunts as his fathers or mothers, his nephews and nieces as his or her sons and daughters; cousins as brothers and sisters, and so on. Thus, due to the intricate nature of relationships and networks among all the people in the community, the upbringing of a child becomes a corporate responsibility of the community; in the general sense no one claims the sole parenthood of the child: the child belongs to the corporate body of human beings, and is referred to as our child *(mwana waitu)*, a term of endearment. The dynamics of this corporate child rearing is illustrated by the phrase, "it is not my child but our child" *(Omwana tazalw'omoi -lit. a child is not born by one person)*, a common phrase in everyday language of the people of this region of East Africa.

The immediate family (biological parents and siblings) and extended family provide for the child's physical and emotional needs on a daily basis, and the kinship and community supplement this role by providing for the social needs and any other support in the child's interest. This rearing of children is ascribed by the values, traditions and interests of the kinship. All members of the kinship, therefore, participate in the socialization process; the molding to fashion the child into a full-fledged social and corporate being. For instance, it is common practice for children to leave their immediate parents' home for a variety of reasons to go and live with a relative or a family friend. Many times during the weaning period toddlers are sent away from home to be cared for *(kurerwa)* by other women in the extended family and kin network including aunts, grandmothers, co-wives or female friends. These "other mothers" are chosen because they are reliable, trustworthy and possess certain qualities (or resources) that parents believe are necessary for the upbringing of their children. In other situations involving older children, the parents will temporarily entrust their children to a close mature extended family member who will instill manners, good behavior and cultural values in the children. It is also not uncommon for children to ask their parents to be sent to live with another household among their kinship. This household in most cases will have its own children who will provide companionship for the child. van der Vliet (1974) found a similar socialization of young children in her study of southern African societies. She explains that when children are sent to live with the next of kin,

> they are seldom lonely or lacking companions; the typical house-hold has a number of women of similar age to their mothers, who will themselves have children of about their age. This stage is important in that it lays the foundations for much of his future adult behavior, which will require their co-operation within a group of cotemporaries. Their peer groups, watched over by those just a little older, lay down rules for acceptable conduct and are in a strong position to see that they are obeyed. Sanctions such as mockery and ostracism enable them to deal effectively with displays of bad temper, selfishness and poor sportsmanship (p. 220).

The raising of children by non-biological parents is a common phenom-enon throughout Africa as demonstrated in Sudarkasa's (2004) study in West Africa. She documents:

> women may be assigned or "given" children who are not 'theirs' in an exclusive sense , but to whom they relate "as a mother." Women who have not given birth , or those whose children are no longer living with them might be "given" (or "assigned") a child who will remain in their care for an unspecified period of time in return for the usual affection and assistance parents receive from their children when they are growing up (p.1).

Kinships, the Community and Child Rearing

The traditional African kinship that children are born into is an intri-cate and complex system of a network of human relationships. Kinship ties through blood (consanguinity) or through marriage (affinity) or even friendships are of fundamental importance because they have a moral, ethical and spiritual content, and therefore must be recognized for their role in regulating and maintaining the life of a community.

189

Lineage

Descent from (common) ancest*ors* elevates the human being from the mundane to the cosmic domain near to the creator *(Omutonzi, Luhangai).* Ancestors in their capacity as guardians play important roles, including the role of linking people on earth with their creator, and also interceding for or mediating between earth and the final source of life. The relationship that extends up to the creator through the ancestors is both horizontal and vertical; the ancestors' descent is living kin members' ascent. The relationships among individual members within and without the kin groups are likewise elevated to a higher level and the reciprocal relationship between kin members and extending ultimately to the ancestors and the creator (*Luhanga)* is believed to abide in the recess of human soul, and reside in the subconscious mind of the members; the existence of the relationship is not taught nor passed on from generation to generation; it is believed to be in-born and lived by, by being a member of a kin group (Forde, 1994). That is, the corporate and reciprocal actions which are reinforced by the conceptualization of the lineage unity and through the ancestor cannot be ignored without consequences. The kinship system is therefore elevated and kinship provides an individual with his or her roots and identity. Membership in specific kinship determines an individual's status and role, and duties and rights in society. Mbiti (1970) explains that, "[I]t is kinship which controls social relationships between people in a given community; it governs marital customs and regulations, it determines the behavior of one individual toward another" (p.102). Furthermore, the social recognition of kinship ties, linkages and relationships provide individuals with criteria and dictate people's claims and obligations to each other, for example, they are a source of rights to inheritance. Documenting traditional kinship systems in Africa, Gulliver (1963) explains that the notion of lineage unity and continuity was expressed in the idea of joint inheritance and ownership of resources which enhances a sense of belonging. Also Preston-Whyte (1974) documents that,

> the social recognition of these linkages provides the individual with major criteria upon which to categorize his fellows and with a corresponding set of rules to guide interaction with them. Thus kin and non kin are distinguished and treated differently, while various categories of kin are recognized, and behavior towards individuals falling into them organized, according to a blueprint of kinship expectation (p. 177).

Fictive Kinships

Numerous kinship groups link up to make up communities, sometimes grouped under villages. It is the corporate nature of African communities which are knit together by a web of kinship relationships and other social structures that keep the community life vibrant and going. In that context, there is a distinct phenomenon of a type of kinship, the fictive kin that is prevalent in African societies. Fictive kinships are hospitality groups that are formed and established not necessarily around lineages but become members of the social group. These kinds of units may be formed through friendships. Fictive kinships are heterogeneous but form a basis of cooperation between members and non members of lineage groups. Where lineage kinships are oriented towards the continuity of the lineage, the regulation of inheritance, rituals etc, fictive kinships are oriented towards cooperation and hospitality in the community, which are necessary for the social and economic ends of the distribution of resources such as, land for cultivation, food, access to water, schools, healthcare and many other resources.

Kinship System of Rearing Children

Members of the community (who belong to extended family, lineage and fictive kinship) recognize and acknowledge binding obligations to each other to ensure the solidarity and continuity of the community. Members are obliged to serve the kinship system; in return the system provides the members with a security blanket. The kinship security blanket is likened to the insurance coverage to which members pay premiums by bearing children, and therefore, bearing children is a duty upon every member of the kinship to ensure there is stability, continuity and expanding membership. It is not uncommon to hear older members of the community asking any unmarried younger adults when they will "give" them grandchildren.

There is a strong element and elevated social interaction and cooperation especially among kin who reside close to each other. It is the corporate nature of communities (villages) which are knit together by a web of kinship relationships that keep the community life going. Members of community share life's sustenance intensely. There are no strangers as far as sharing a meal and drink is concerned. There are communal farmlands, economic trees, streams, barns, and markets, common water sources (wells), and common grazing grounds. There are also communal shrines, squares, masquerades, ritual objects and festivals for recreational activities and for social, economic and religious purposes. This is also a system of social control within the group and is conceptualized through elements such as cooperation and social organization of ceremonies, rituals relating to important stages in the life cycle, including marriages, childbirth, child naming, funerals, last funeral rites, inheritance or settling disputes. This may also involve the organization and distribution of scarce resources, such as fertile land for cultivation, labor trees for building and animals; the giving of loans and credit, *"okuhereka"* and *"empano,"* which are significant when people are in distress or crisis. What is significant is that membership in the extended family, lineage and fictive kin networks overlap and often make it complex for a foreigner to understand the dynamics of the African kinship network system. For instance, it is very common to hear a child refer to her neighbors (not biologically related) as uncle and/or aunt. This intricate nature of relationships and the reciprocal duties and obligations among people have binding force.

Similar to many societies in the world, the traditional African child must be taught to accept and reproduce the values, sentiments and behavior of the society (extended families, kinships and communities) into which he or she is born and raised. Early African education emphasizes conservatism and conformity and loyalty to the community's way of life. Unlike the formal western education of children, most of the education of children in traditional African societies was acquired through imitation of the behaviors and skills of the adults in the children's environment. The limited formal education mainly focused on training in social relations, values, ethics and manners. Within the socialization of children was the element of social ascription and from a very early age a child was labeled in terms of the status and predetermined roles he would fill in society. The predetermined roles were based on the child's sex, position in the family and parents' status. The education and socialization of a child was a joint endeavor of adults in the extended family, kinship network and community who are interested and invested in the child's progress and therefore collaborated within a framework of producing an effective and ideal member of the community and society. This system of education and socialization complements western education in contemporary rural African communities. It is these attributes of the kin networks and community that are invoked when children are orphaned.

Orphans' Reintegration in the Kinship and Community

To a young person, the death of a parent is an unfathomable loss of everything; the most stressful event from human, emotional and material perspectives. In such circumstances the extended family and kin have the cultural mandate to step in to shelter orphans from the chilling effects of their parents' death. Presumably, the idea is that children are scattered, have lost meaning of life and alienated after their father's death, for example.

The socialization of orphans immediately after the death of their parents involves the reaffirmation and assurance of the continuation of the belonging and inclusion of the orphans in the kinship and subsequently the community. The first stage of the socialization of the child after the father's death is the ceremony of bringing the children "home" (*okutahya abaana*). Soon after the burial of the deceased person, the head of the kinship group becomes the surrogate temporary head of the orphan household. Toward the end of the period of mourning, the inheritance ceremony (*okusikisa)* is performed. During the inheritance ceremony, the heir-to-be is seated on the "throne," and the head of his kin group hands him his dead father's spear, a long knife and a shield. These instruments are symbols of authority and power that is bestowed on an individual to protect himself and others, and thus through this ceremony the heir (*omusika*) is vested with the authority, power, rights and obligations of the head of family; and assumes his late father's place among his kin and the community at large. This ceremony is followed by the distribution of the parents' assets, including the family banana/coffee farm (*kibanja*). The farm land is the source of food, income, social standing and prestige. Depending on the age of the orphans, members of the kinship put in place a mechanism to help the orphans cope with the consequences of their father's death and his absence. Extended family and other members of the kinship are obligated to pay constant vigil by frequently visiting the orphans to advise them and monitor their progress; and to help in other ways including meal preparation, food production, house repair, and providing many other necessities to help and assist the orphans to cope with their situation.

In the case of a mother's death, the ceremony and rituals of disciplining the children (*okuter' abaana*) are performed. On the appointed day, the "mothers" (aunts or other women in the village) prepare a square meal and drinks for the ceremony at the orphans' home. During the ceremony the women announce, "Here we are, your mothers," after all, the children address each of the women as "mother" (*mawe*); the maternal aunt as, 'my-mother-the-junior' (*maw'ento*); and the paternal aunt as my-father-the-female (*tat'enkazi*). Several rituals are performed at this time to assure and establish the reciprocal caring relationship between the children and the women in the kin network. The ceremony ends with the ritual of bringing all the orphans together in front of the women at the ceremony. The women pledge to honor the fundamental obligation of keeping a watchful eye over the orphans, monitoring their wellbeing and progress in life; they assure the orphans that they will not go hungry or become homeless; and the orphans' needs will be taken care of as long as mothers in the kinship network (and other women who will come after them) live. The leader among the women (mostly an aunt) tells the children: "Your mother is not dead, because here we are to do whatever your mother used to do for you. We will love you, feed you, and take care of you; your mother lives in us…" The women (other mothers) then symbolically touch each orphan with a small twig (*akashanju*) to denote an important duty of a mother to correct her child for character and behavior formation. The common phrase, "spare the rod, spoil the child" (*omwana alerwa n'enkoni*) emphasizes an adult's role in socializing a child into acquiring societal values and good behavior.

Young children who have lost both parents are taken into the household of extended family or other member of the kinship, mostly an aunt, and in some cases a stepmother. Older children stay in their parents home but receive the "mothers" care which involves visiting orphans frequently and bringing them food and other necessities and guiding them into acquiring living skills. The orphans are encouraged to return the visits, especially, when faced with problems. For generations the kinship system of socializing orphans was efficient for absorbing orphans and it is now showing resilience to the impact of AIDS and civil wars on communities (Rutayuga, 2005).

ORPHAN SITUATION IN TANZANIA

Despite a decrease in the percentage of children that was projected to be orphaned between 2001 and 2010, the number of orphans in Tanzania is likely to increase and surpass two million in the twenty-first century (UNAIDS/USAID, 2004). When communities en-mass burry their members at their child-bearing age or even younger, it appears there will be no future for families or the community. The astronomical losses of people, skills and resources due to AIDS deaths in Africa in the past three decades have resulted in large numbers of orphans, and communities have been faced with a very big challenge of caring for orphans. Large numbers of families who may already have children of their own take on new roles and responsibilities as they take in orphans. The changes in roles and responsibilities for members of the household contribute to stress and strain on resources available to the household. Compounding this situation, a significant number of orphans are being cared for by relatives who are no longer economically productive, mostly old and feeble grandparents who have much less time and energy to provide for all the needs (financial, social, emotional) of the children in their care (Rutayuga, 2005). Over the years we have also seen an increasing number of orphan households headed by older siblings (Rutayuga, 2005). Despite the fact that communities had been experiencing these challenges for more than a decade, in 2001 Tanzania's former President Benjamin Mkapa stated, "Tanzanians should use traditional approaches to take care of the orphans. It is important that relatives of the orphans take the responsibility of caring for them. This is important because our country is poor, it cannot build enough centers for the orphans" (The Guardian, 2001). In the absence of government intervention for this enormous orphan problem, there is a concern about the potential of large numbers of orphan households (households that have taken in orphans) living on the margin of established society, and becoming vulnerable to poverty, crime, risk of poor health and dying, which would subsequently lead to the disintegration of communities. This has been a unique situation for concern for African societies, which believe in regenerating themselves through the children born into the community. After years of ineffective governments' response to the situation of orphans, members of the community realized that they must step up to meet the challenges of the AIDS epidemic to save and strengthen their communities. People know that it is the community's responsibility to halt its disintegration and preserve the natural phenomena in which corporate parenting is an obligation to every member of the community; and cultural knowledge and skills, indigenous traditions, customs and life experiences are passed on from one generation to the next. Today members of communities are coming together and utilizing the traditional kin network system and community based care for vulnerable families and households. Communities have developed creative and innovative ways of revamping the capacity of the extended family and kin economic and social networks for caring for orphans and orphan households.

Ukimwi Orphans Assistance

It is upon the innate instinct, strength and capacity of the extended family and kin networks that the model of intervention of Ukimwi Orphans Assistance (UOA) was designed. Ukimwi (*Upungufu wa Kinga Mwilini*) is a Ki-Swahili acronym for HIV/AIDS. Ukimwi Orphans Assistance is a kinship network-based community organization that provides assistance to orphan households in the Kagera region of Tanzania. UOA focuses on empowering and enhancing the capacity of the extended family and kin network system to mitigate and reduce the psychosocial and socio-economic challenges and hardships of orphans. This includes UOA's approach of encouraging people to draw from the cultural strength and resources of kin networks of caring to link local communities to address the concerns of orphans. It's mission states, "UOA is committed to assisting orphans and vulnerable children in Africa to grow up free of HIV/AIDS and develop, in their cultural environment, into mature, self-sufficient, and productive members of their communities" (Rutayuga, 2005). UOA, which was initiated in 1989 at the grassroots level in Tanzania, is now established as a (501(c) (3) international organization (see Figure 7.1).

UOA utilizes a socio-economic development approach to enhance the capacity of the kin networks to reduce the social and economic challenges and hardships that orphans and vulnerable children face, and are experienced by households that care for orphans. Community members are encouraged to draw from the cultural strength of the African tradition in which the entire community organize and pull resources that enable the families and community to raise orphans to be self-reliant adults. Villages are divided into wards and each ward has an UOA program, which involves a team of leaders, mainly elders who are retired professionals. The UOA leaders' aim is to provide guidance to local stakeholders who are caring for orphans and other community members who are concerned about the situation of orphan households and collaborate to develop assistance programs for orphan households. Community members mobilize at village and ward levels, and hold meetings to identify the needs of orphan households and define challenges in their community. The planning, decision-making and implementation of these assistance programs are characterized by community members' accountability, reliability and trust. Resources for running UOA programs are generated from contributions of labor, skills and knowledge of the community members. The principal monetary resources for funding some UOA programs and other activities come from contributions from the people in the community. In addition, UOA utilizes local materials such as land, wood, grass, and members' homes to provide space for convening meetings.

UOA Farm Land Development

Coffee, banana and other food projects involve the rehabilitation of the permanent family land (kibanja) which is a basis for providing for the livelihood and sustainability of the household. Maintaining farm land involves a considerable amount of skill and labor, and therefore, extended family, kin and other members of the community pull together in helping the orphan household to grow food crops and teach them the skills they need to maintain the farm land and sustain themselves in the community. The farm land rehabilitation may include; (1) repairing orphans' houses; (2) growing and maintaining banana groves and gardens of food, such as, maize, beans, peanuts, yams, and vegetables; (3) maintaining coffee shamba, which involves coffee husbandry for shade grown coffee; and (4) maintaining heifers for nutrition and manure. Some of the farm land projects generate income needed for other household necessities.

Figure 7.1. Ukimwi Orphan Assistance community organization in Kagera, Tanzania

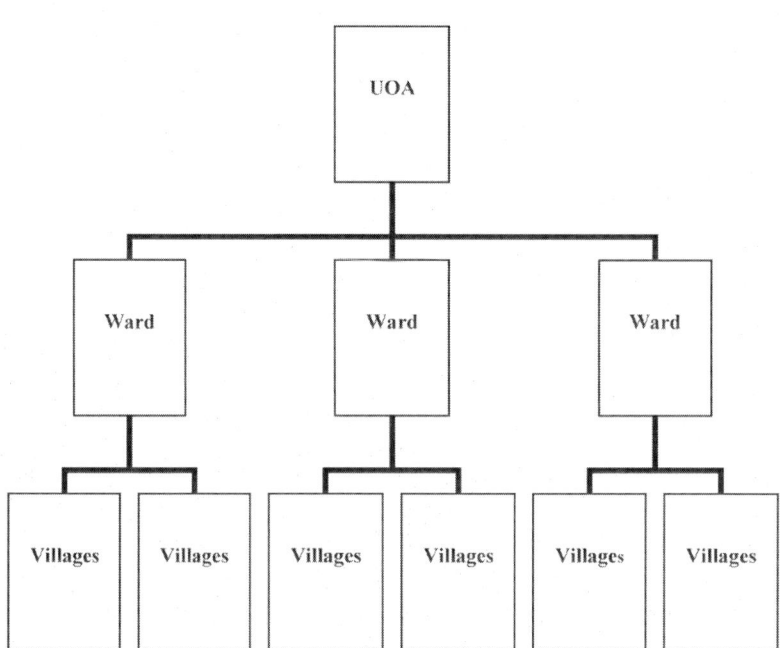

UOA Education and Skill Development

The skills development and vocational training program involves orphans and the adults who care for them. The program is implemented through sending adolescent orphans to vocational training schools and institutes, or pairing them with experienced artisans in the community to receive training in various skills. Through this program orphans acquire the knowledge and skills they will need to be able to sustain themselves in that community. The program may include: (1) metal and carpentry, masonry, arts and crafts, and small business training for the youth and adults; (2) training orphans in indigenous knowledge and skills that are essential for banana and coffee husbandry or raising livestock; (3) home economics training for women and older siblings, which is essential for good health, nutrition and general wellbeing of orphans and other vulnerable people; and (4) maintenance of village primary schools. Assistance for formal education for orphans and other vulnerable children is provided through: (1) providing school uniforms, books and pencils, so that children can go to school to get primary education; (2) building kindergarten schools for children in the community.

The Future of Orphans

The face of African societies and institutions, and the dynamics of kin networks have changed in the course of time, the core, however, has sustained a degree of stability. In the absence of government or other agencies' intervention for orphans, and despite that many households that take in AIDS orphans often are locked in a vicious circle of deprivation and vulnerability to poverty, there is a strong resilience of the traditional African extended family and kinship system of fosterage that has enabled communities to squarely face the awesome AIDS challenge. Communities have shown resilience as they strive to prevent or reduce stress from settling down on orphans. The extended family and kinship network corporate care for orphans assures the orphans of belonging to the community and not feeling alienated from their roots; they provide the assurance and insurance blanket for their future lives. Today, the extended family and kin linkages provide the vast majority of orphans with the care, love, stability, a sense of identity, and practical knowledge and skills that are necessary for adult life. The orphans in these communities know that they have the opportunity to grow and mature into adults among their own people, which will enable them to be responsible and acquire some status and recognition in the community. According to a joint report from UNICEF and UNAIDS, community care at the grass-roots level where orphans remain in their indigenous communities remains the most practical and effective way of caring for orphans and other vulnerable children in most Sub-Saharan countries (UNAIDS/UNICEF, 2004). The reality is that there is a lack of national resources to adopt realistic goals and implement effective interventions and programs to alleviate the poverty, the suffering or other challenges experienced by many families that care for children who have been affected by war or the AIDS pandemic. It is time for us therefore, to rethink our national agenda for the young people in Africa and to acknowledge that the creation or development of comprehensive programs for all children poses a broad challenge for Africa. Our goal should be to implement a range of alternative intervention strategies that meet the needs of children and families in a multi cultural society. Interventions and programs need to be well developed and tailored to the populations of children who apparently, most of the time have different needs because of physical, social, and economic factors. There is urgent need to examine alternatives to what we have in place today.

References

Earth, B. (1996). Structural Adjustments and its Effects. *Canadian Woman Studies/ Les Cahiers de la Femme.* 16(3)

Forde. D., Ed. (1994). *African Worlds, Studies in the Cosmological Ideas and Social Values of African Peoples.* International African Institute, Oxford University Press.

Gulliver, P.H. (1963). *Social Control In An African Society.* London, Rutledge & Kegan Paul Ltd.

Hunter, S. (1990). Orphans as a Window on the AIDS Epidemic in Sub-Saharan Africa: Initial Results and Implications of a Study in Uganda. *Social Science and Medicine,* 31, 681-690.

Kamali, A., J.A. Seeley, A.J. Nunn, A.J. Kengyeya-Kayondo, J.F. Ruberantwari & D.W. Mulder (1996). The Orphan Problem: Experience of a Sub-Saharan Africa Rural Population in the AIDS Epidemic. *AIDS Care,* 8(5), 509-15.

Kyomugisha, F. (2006). HIV, African American Women and High Risk in Heterosexual Relationships. *Journal of African American Studies,* 10(2), 38-50.

Mbiti, J. (1970). *African Religions and Philosophy.* Anchor Books Doubleday & Company, Garden City, NY.

Preston-Whyte, E. (1974). Kinship and Marriage. In W.D. Hammond-Toole, (Ed.) *The Bantu-Speaking Peoples of Southern Africa.* Routledge & Kegan Paul, Boston.

Rutayuga, J. (1992). Assistance to AIDS Orphans Within the Family/Kinship System and Local Institutions: A Program for East Africa, *Special Supplement to AIDS Education and Prevention,* Guilford Publications. Inc.

Rutayuga, J. (2005). The Traditional African Stress Management for Orphans: A Self-healing System. Delivered at the African Healing Wisdom Conference, Washington, DC, July 2005.

Sudarkasa, N. (2004). Conceptions of Motherhood in Nuclear and Extended Families, with Special Reference to Comparative Studies Involving African Societies. *JENDA: A Journal of Culture & African Women's Studies.* Issue 5.

Tanzania HIV/AIDS Indicator Survey 2003-2004.

The Guardian Unlimited Tanzania, October 15, 2001.

The World Bank. (2001). Reaching Out to Africa's Orphans, A Framework for Public Action, Washington, D.C.

UNAIDS, UNICEF. (2004). Children on the Brink 2004: A Joint Report of New Orphan Estimates and a Framework for Action.

UNAIDS/WHO. (2004). Report on the global AIDS Epidemic.

Vansina, J. (1985). *Oral Tradition as History.* Wisconsin: University of Wisconsin Press.

Part II
AMERICA

CHAPTER 8

THE AFRICAN AMERICAN FAMILY: CHALLENGES AND OPPORTUNITIES

Gwendolyn S. Prater

INTRODUCTION

Beginning with the 1940s' publication of E. Franklin Frazier's work arguing that slavery had managed to erase any vestiges of African survivals in the black family, a position that contradicted the thesis of renowned anthropologist Melville Herskovits, the theme of the African American family has continued to receive considerable attention from scholars, especially African American. Franklin's thesis was embraced by many others who claimed that the African American family was dysfunctional and that, a major cause was its matriarchal structure. While a series of other notable African American scholars in sociology, social work, psychology, and history have followed in the footsteps of these intellectual pioneers, some have stressed the black family's strengths and adaptability. Others have focused on the "multigenerational" kinship networks that seem to have characterized the African American family unit from the civil war to civil rights and to the 21st century. However, a plethora of others have criticized the first studies of the institution, which, in their perspective, contributed to the propagation of the stereotypes and the pathological theories advanced about the state of the black family in the United States. A number of scholars have further pointed out that, departing from the wrong premise that the white middle class was the only acceptable model of a functional household, some of the early writers did not make a distinction between marriage stability and family stability. They thus created further confusion in a field already plagued with unsound and unproven methodological approaches.

The debate over the nature and survivability of the African American family has underscored more than any other debate worldwide the complexity of the concept, its definition, and the problems associated with the attempt to apply it to its social manifestations. Scholars and activists have framed the debate around several issues and questions, including: What constitutes a family? How distorted the picture becomes when one adopts as a tool of analysis "median" or a model family, which usually refers to the white middle class family that consists of a mother, father, and one or two children, living together in a visible household? What impact does matriarchy and patriarchy have on the family unit and offspring? Is the nuclear family "superior" to or "better" than an extended family? How does one define family stability? What is the role of education, employment, and income in the emancipation and self-sufficiency of the family? How great is the impact of "class" in determining living patterns and acceptance of the black family in white neighborhoods? What is "the proper" social upbringing of children? How does the living environment determine children's (and adults') abnormal behavior that results in high crime, uncontrollable drug use, a high number of teen-age pregnancy, and high rates of sexually transmitted diseases, high degree of school drop-out, and imprisonment? Is there one family structure acceptable to all or are there many types of families according to cultural traditions and heritage, which are as functional as the one Western civilization has attempted to impose on the rest of the world?

The following discussion in chapter eight attempts to answer some of the preceding questions by focusing on the following: The strengths and shortcomings of the major theoretical assumptions proposed over the past decades; the socioeconomic factors that seem to determine the state of the African American family at the dawn of the 21st century; the changing roles and behaviors of family members; the impact of the seemingly dwindling African American male; and the prospects of the institution's survivability as it continues to face mounting obstacles that have compelled certain academic and political circles to declare its demise or irrelevance within the black communities of the United States of America (and the Caribbean).

CONCEPTUAL FRAMEWORK

The fierce debate over the nature, structure, and function of the African American family resulted from the studies conducted by such intellectuals as E. Franklin Frazier, Melville Herskovits, and W.E.B. DuBois, during the late 1930s and 1940s. The resulting controversies brought to the fore such renowned scholars as John Hope Franklin, Stanley Wilkins, Daniel Moynihan, John Blassingame, Lee Rainwater, Robert Hill, W.R. Allen and Harriett Pipes Macdoo, Eric Lincoln, Andrew Billingsley, Robert Staples, Jualynne Elizabeth Dodson, Delores Mack, Colin Turnbull, Carol Stack, Niara Sudarkasa, and William Julius Wilson. In their study of slavery and its impact on the black family, whose origins were in Africa, historians, such as W.E.B. Dubois, generally concluded that, throughout slavery, African traditional practices, names, folklore, and cultural norms, at times known as "Africanisms," "African survivals," or "African residuals," contributed to the survival of the family among the dispersed and subjugated black people both in the north and the south of the United States (US). In a nutshell, these historians, as they looked at the African family, discerned a continuum but never concluded that the institution was on its way to becoming irrelevant, as some of their later colleagues declared to the world.

Sociologist E. Franklin Frazier was the first to "fire the shot" in 1939 when, using some statistics from slavery and a couple of contemporary records, posited that slaves had lost their African traditions of marriage fidelity and patriarchy, which were replaced by matriarchy due to the absence of the husband, if the black family household ever had one. This resulted in a family institution that was completely new and crippled, constantly striving to emulate and assimilate the values and structure of the white family. Such analysis and conclusion squarely contradicted DuBois' and Herskovits' studies. In the words of one scholar, Frazier decided not to agree, for example, that "African American family structure, marital customs, and sexual practices were derived from African cultures, but considered "African American men indiscriminate and extramarital sexual behavior as a product of their enslavement and unrelated to customs or practices from their ancestral polygynous cultures of Africa" (Dodson, 2007, p.54). In 1938, anthropologist Melville Herskovits, who had carefully studied both the African family as well as the African American family had arrived at a different conclusion, when, dissecting the major features of African culture one by one, he became convinced that Africans and their descendants who landed on the shores of the Atlantic had preserved their culture. Herskovits posited that the resilience of the elements of African cultures or the residuals of African traditions in America and the Caribbean were maintained by the African American community till his own time, detecting them in songs, the clear manifestations of spirituality, folklore, dance, call-and-response in Church services, walking manners, persistence of the essential components of the extended family, foods, magic, healing practices, and the primacy of the child. To him and to others like him, the African American family was a "visible" and not an "invisible" institution, as some have characterized it during slavery. Agreeing with Herskovits, anthropologist Collin Turnbull was forced to say emphatically in 1976 that "the enslaved who were exported to the Americas were Africans before…and Africans afterwards…, and their descendants are still Africans" (McAdoo, 2007, p. 60).

Daniel Patrick Moynihan, Assistant Secretary in the Office of Planning and Research of the US Department of Labor, joined the debate when President Lyndon B. Johnson asked him to prepare a paper on the state of the black family as a part of the President's "War on Poverty Program" in 1965. In his 78-page treaties, titled "The Negro Family: The Case for National Action," Moynihan basically used Frazier's sociological conclusions and Blood's and Wolf's 1960 survey of black families in Detroit, while never conducting an historical analysis of his own. Detroit statistics had shown that 44 percent of the black families in the city were female-headed, in contrast to 20 percent among the white families (Boamah-Wiafe, 2001, p. 119). Moynihan singled out matriarchy, or the dominance of the female in the household, as the major culprit of the challenges to the black family, both in slavery and in post-emancipation, and held it responsible for such problems as high crime, high drug use, high teen-age pregnancy, and high rates of ill health.

Like Frazier, whom he often misinterpreted, Moynihan acknowledged the impact of slavery, racism, and discrimination, but maintained that households headed by women were a major contributing factor to the instability and dysfunction of the black family in the United States. Repeating Frazier's studies, Moynihan wrote of "broken families," "illegitimate marriages" and "illegitimate children," the nefarious impact of "matriarchy," the "economic dependency" of black families, and even noted African American recruits' "failure to pass the armed forces entrance tests," "delinquency," and "crime," all due to the malfunction of the matriarchal African American family (Dodson, 2007, p. 55). Since the 1970s, most studies have attempted to rectify Frazier's and Moynihan's conclusions or to reinforce what they wrote, making the debate over the African American family perhaps one of the most heated and interesting academic exercises but with real social consequences in the American polity, pitting sociologists against historians and anthropologists and psychologists against other social scientists.

The first school of thought, which generally follows the thesis advanced by E. Franklin Frazier, Daniel P. Moynihan, and Lee Rainwater, stresses the negative aspects of the black family or its dysfunction, all of which have been classified as the pathological theory about the African American family. Some have called this conceptual framework the "cultural ethnocentric school," which sees mainstream white American family life and values as the norm and believes that African Americans have, since slavery, attempted to assimilate. Dodson clarifies the nature of this school by noting that its underlying premise is that all immigrants who enter the United States of America wish to and should adopt the "values, attitudes, and behaviors of those property-owning Anglo-Saxons, Protestant men who initially determined the direction of the 13 colonies that became the nation" (Dodson, p. 52).

In this context, most African American families have failed to achieve the goal. Lee Rainwater, after conducting a study of matriarchy in the United States and the Caribbean, concluded in 1968 that such family structure was responsible for the dysfunction of the black family and, while denouncing it as "detrimental to the personality development of African American children," he claimed that it interfered with the African American males' development of "normal heterosexual roles."

The second school of thought tends to dwell on the positive side of the black family, stressing that the institution has always survived under the most trying conditions, such as slavery, racism, and discrimination, and that it has always been able to adapt to changing circumstances. This school is, at times, called "cultural relativity," which emphasizes the unique impact of culture and sees the African American family as embodying its own "cultural integrity" traceable to its African ancestry. The basis of this line of thought is that no single model of family fits all families, and that, therefore, scholars and politicians ought to cease judging African American families and others through the prism of the white Anglo-Saxon model, which they have succeeded in imposing on other peoples of the world.

The next school of thought, propounded mainly by Wilson in his *The Declining Significance of Race: Blacks and Changing American Institutions* and neo-Marxists, has indirectly affected the debate over African American values and the prospects of the survival of the African American family. Wilson argues that class, and not race, is the most important predictor of the well-being and the permanency prospects of the black family. Thus, as many African Americans climb up the ladder of education and wealth as members of the middle-class, Wilson claims that the black family will thrive and prosper as much as the white family has so far. In other words, Wilson holds that race is a disappearing phenomenon in American society and that black middle class families will continue to leave the inner city and move to the suburbs where blacks and whites mingle and raise and educate their children to adopt the best cultural norms and exhibit socially acceptable behavior.

As Dodson notes, this academic and neo-Marxist class of scholars stresses that "the role of social class in determining patterns and characteristics of family life" is paramount and that, "when one controls for social class, no appreciable differences are found between African American and European American families" (Dodson, 2007, p. 53). Wilson, the Dean of the School, has been castigated for underestimating the pervasive role of individual and institutional racism, both covert and overt, and overlooking the courts' lack of enforcement of anti-segregation housing statutes, and for conveniently forgetting the fact that, "as educational and earnings attainments among blacks increase, the degree of racial segregation between blacks and whites does not fall" (Niemonen, 2002. p. 184). In fact, on this issue, says Niemonen (2002, p. 201), "Generally, the higher the educational and income levels of whites, the more likely they are to express socio-class prejudices rather than racial prejudices. The lower the educational and income levels of whites, the more likely they are to express the opposite."

The fourth school is in the process of development, and it has been advanced by such scholars as Ruth Dennis, Harriett Pipes McAdoo, John McAdoo, and Art Mathis, who label it the "reflective analysis." Supposedly, such a proposed theoretical framework does not rely on inferences, as common to studies of the black family, but focuses, in McAdoo's own words (2007, p. 64-65), on the following: 1) looking at the socialization of African American individuals as the process that brings together, in direct and dynamic interactive practice, individuals, the cultural values of the community, and the mores, norms, and values of the larger U.S. society; 2) accounting for the effects and affects—of the general unavailability to African American families of the maximum economic, social, and political resources required by its raison d'etre to provide its citizens; and 3) accounting for the environmental reality that, disproportionately, members of African American families are forced to use relatively minimal and substandard resources in order to achieve an effective socialization process and end product that allows their members to function both in the U.S. social reality of consistent and sufficient social supports and in the African American reality of fluctuating scarcity of resources (McAdoo, 2007, p. 64-65).

To this group of seasoned scholars, the proposed approach "would help as first steps for evaluating, interpreting, and analyzing research data about African American families and yet validate the conceptual needs of research" (McAdoo, 2007, p. 65). Currently, however, it is hard to understand how such a model would differ from the existing models, unless the authors imply that all studies of the black family have been based solely on statistical data and not on added reflection or a critical analysis.

At the center of the continuing controversy, obviously, is the very concept and definition of the family. There is certainly general agreement that the family is the basic social unit where the child is socializaed and where the members receive care and develop a special relationship that transcends other social relationships. Essentially agreeing with many other scholars, Daniel Boamah-Wiafe defined the family as a "group of two or more people who are related to each other by descent, marriage or adoption who live together in the same household" (Boamah-Wiafe, 2001, p. 115). A major problem with this definition is that it assumes that all members of the family must live in the same household to be a family. Most scholars also agree that the nuclear or conjugal family (mother, father, and child) tends to live in the same household, whereas the extended family may live in different households and even thousands of miles apart. The extended family, most common in Africa, is made up of "several nuclear families where members are either biologically or socially-related, brought together by a bond that is "so strong that they are committed to one another and interact among themselves frequently." In general, says Boamah-Wiafe, "members of the second and third generations of extended families tend to maintain closer ties with one another than their nuclear counterparts would to members outside the immediate family" (Boamah-Wiafe, 2001, p. 116).

THE AFRICAN AMERICAN FAMILY DEFINED

Even though the extended kin element is characteristic of African families, many scholars believe that the African American family, especially during slavery and later, survived because it maintained the residuals of the African family support system, which has helped it to weather the physical, political, and social storms over the centuries and adapt. Niara Sudarkasa recalls that, when she was growing up in the South during the 1950s, the extended family, like in Africa, was the norm, with single black women with children out of wedlock living with grandparents, mothers, parents, and grandmothers or relatives. She claims that the welfare policies of the United States went counter to this important feature by forcing single mothers to live alone rather than in a multigenerational household. She therefore advocates a return to the extended family of yester years (Sudarkasa, 2007, p. 175).

Thus, many scholars point out, the most-quoted African saying that it takes a village to raise a child survived among the black people of the New World. To explain the persistence of the extended family, Dodson writes that people with "a high degree of powerlessness were significantly more oriented toward the extended family, perhaps as a defense mechanism against oppression." So did Carol Stack in 1974, when she suggested that "the extended family was, in part, a strategy for meeting physical, emotional, and economic needs of black families." In Africa, of course, there was also another reason: A large family, most often characterized by a polygamous household, was a status symbol and a type of insurance guarantee for old age, at the time society expected children to take care of their kin under any circumstances, a source of readily available manpower in a subsistence economy. Thus, it is also noted by some experts that the lack of outcry among African American wives when husbands go astray sexually resembles the toleration of African wives when their spouses take extra wives, as long as he continues to be a provider and treat their first wives as their lawful spouses.

The most known African American cultural relativists, such as Andrew Billingsley (1968), Virginia Young (1970), and Robert Hill (1971), are in agreement about the presence of African cultural residuals in the black family but do not agree on "their level of impact," even though they are in unison on the proposition that "the distinctive cultural orientation in this community encourages family patterns that are instrumental in combating oppressive conditions of racism in US society" (McAdoo, 2007, p. 50), just as African families have had to withstand the oppression of slavery, colonialism, and, more recently, globalization. Straddling the middle ground, historians U.B. Philips (1929) and Stanley Elkins (1959) concluded that "although significant African cultural traits, such as names and folklore, did initially survive the enslavement experience, these were eventually lost or destroyed" (Dodson, 2007, p. 54).

Obviously, the most traumatic, psychological, and physical oppression the black family has ever experienced is slavery and the slave trade from 1619 to 1865. Historian John Hope Franklin, the Dean of African American historians, has provided a vivid picture of the enslavement saga and its consequences for both individuals and families who were subjected to the ordeal. Enslaved Africans were brought to the New World to work on the plantations, the homestead of white farmers, and white people's businesses after crossing the horrible Middle Passage on the Atlantic. In the process and on the shores of America, families were split often intentionally and other times unwittingly. When the slave master allowed a black couple to wed and have children, there was no guarantee that this budding family would be allowed to remain either as a nuclear or an extended family, as was a practice in their continent of origin. To maximize profit, says John Hope Franklin, the slave master practiced retail sale techniques by selling each member separately rather than the entire family, unless he was going out of business. Forbidding the usage of the original African languages, names, spiritual manifestations, and folklore was one way through which slave masters made it difficult for families to function unimpeded as was the case among white families.

This compelled Eric Lincoln to write in 1974 that the black family in slavery was "essentially an amorphous group gathered around the mother or female head on the plantation" and that, as a result, only a few slaves had a family. The issue, of course, is how extensive this amorphous family actually was and how strong and effective the mother's leadership was allowed to function in terms of regulating sexual relations and human reproduction in the household, maintaining and ensuring "emotional intimacy," caring and socializing (or "taming") the child, providing sustenance to the old and the ill, food, and shelter to all, and protecting its members (Boamah-Wiafe, 2001, p. 116).

The Emancipation Proclamation of 1861 and the subsequent abolition of slavery through the 13th Amendment to the US Constitution in 1865 were welcomed milestones in the lives of enslaved Africans. However, for some African Americans and their families, emancipation, all the way to reconstruction (1865-1877), presented a series of unexpected challenges. Having no means of subsistence, some freed slaves stayed on the plantations, while others sold their work as sharecroppers, or moved north to such cities as Chicago, Detroit, Washington, D.C., and New York, where they were often unable to find the kind of life they were looking for. The 1865 newly-created federal Freedmen's Bureau, whose aim was to find employment, provide land, assist in creating educational opportunities for the freed African Americans, and ensure direct relief to "poor children within their families," did not reach all slaves. Lack of meaningful and sustained assistance forced many to experience greater life insecurity than when they lived under their previously enslaved circumstances. In other words, the promised 40 acres and a mule never materialized, and the Freedmen's Bureau experiment expired in 1871.

Notwithstanding the enactment of the 13th Amendment that freed the slaves, the 14th which declared blacks citizens, and the 15th which made them eligible to vote, former enslaved African Americans in the South began experiencing new forms of discrimination and intimidation, such as lynching, segregation in business establishments and schools, and in public and private facilities. They were subjected to viciously unjust and unfair voting laws, which became known as the Jim Crow Laws. As a result, from 1882 to 1968, close to 5,000 African Americans were lynched in the country, and many thousands of others maimed and imprisoned. These prevailing conditions presented new challenges to the African American family and to those young men and women who wished to establish one. Yet, the existing records and the memory of so many African Americans who underwent this trying experience, the majority of whom could name and describe their families, even after two or three generations, attest to the fact that, even then, the African American family had survived. Thus, although Billingsley characterized the emancipation period as a "catastrophic crisis for the ex-slave" and the Reconstruction as "a colossal period," he could not help but mention that "screens of opportunities" existed, which enabled a large number of families to survive and others to "achieve amazingly stable and viable forms of family life, and a few to achieve a high degree of social distinction." As historian John Blassingame poignantly puts it:

> Although it was weak, although it was frequently broken, the slave family provided an important buffer, a refuge from the rigors of slavery. While the slave father could rarely protect the members of his family from abuse, he could often gain their love and respect in many ways. In his family, the slave not only learned how to avoid the blows of the master, but also drew on the love and sympathy of its members to raise his spirits. The family was, in short, an important survival mechanism (Prater, 2005, p. 386).

The consequences were obvious: Children were separated from parents; parents may also be split, if the master chose to sell one of them, usually the father, leaving everyone behind. Also, quite often, the male slave was so involved in the master's business that he had no time for his wife or children. It is from these conditions that the fierce debate over matriarchy arose. How widespread matriarchy was is still a subject of debate and conjecture. Its existence is dismissed by scholars such as Robert Hill. In those households where the master recognized the marriages of his slaves, which was never protected by law, enslaved wives and daughters may also be taken away from the father and husband to satisfy the sexual desires of the salve master as concubines or simply mistresses, this being done either overtly or covertly not to provoke the wife's ire. Studies have also shown that, by the age of seven, children were often separated from their parents as a way of preventing the development of a bond that might unite the household against the master. The extent of extra marital relations between slave masters and their female slaves in the South have been illustrated and proven by the high number of children that resulted from these sordid affairs.

John Hope Franklin notes that in antebellum (1850), America had a slave population of 3.2 million people, of which 246,000 were of mixed parentage. According to W.E.B. DuBois, in 1860, the number rose to 588,352 (411,000 in Franklin's estimate) out of a population of 3,900,000. Many of the sexual encounters have been considered by African Americans as nothing but a series of rapes of powerless women. This is one reason why many scholars have criticized E. Franklin Frazier, as he paid virtually no attention to rape and other types of forced sexual malfeasance of slave masters. Instead, he made specific references to the fact that, in his view, the mulatto family was stronger because it was not matriarchal but predominantly patriarchal. In most instances, try as he might, the father in the South remained simply a "breeder," especially in such States as Virginia, South Carolina, and Mississippi. Atwood and Genovese, disputing Frazier's and Moynihan's claim that the African American family was ever matriarchal even during slavery, write that the institution was characterized by partnership, flexibility, and "equalitarianism" in marriage resulting in stable families, as was the case among whites in the post- World War II period (Prater, 2005, p. 385).

Herbert Gutman notes that, from the civil war to civil rights, the majority of African American families remained two-parent-households both in the North and the South, even though most were from the lower class, and maintained a multigenerational structure with a well established extended kin network, just as was the case in the land of their ancestors. On this, Billingsley concluded from his studies that, despite slavery, black families kept family ties, maintained solidarity, respected their traditional mores, and never abandoned the mutual assistance tradition, much of which, he added, were African survivals (Prater, 2005, p. 384).

As usual, critics of the studies claiming that the black family in the United States has been dysfunctional have tried to "punch holes" in the methodologies and the data used to advance the glooming forecast about the survivability of the African American family. McAdoo, for example, reminds her readers that a clear distinction exists between the stability of the family and the stability of marriage because a marriage can be stable but not the family and vice-versa. Two parents do not make a household or a family stable. Indeed, notwithstanding divorce or separation, a family may remain stable through love and adequate resources to raise the children.

As noted in the preceding discussions, many dismiss the exaggerated weight given to matriarchy in the black community. Sudarkasa warns that a one-parent household should not necessarily be considered "illegitimate." One has to take into account, she notes, what in the black family tradition constitutes "illegitimate" behavior or an illegitimate child. The ethnocentric mindset discussed above occurs only when Western-Christian values and norms are imposed on people and assimilated. McAdoo also warns that "There are several distinct groups within the African American community, yet, when we are able to relate only to mean or median statistics, the wide diversity of family experiences becomes blurred" (Prater, 2005, p.

384-385). McAdoo goes on to emphasize that there is a common thread in the fabric of the black family and community, which is reflected in the crucial role of such African survivals as the importance of "oral traditions, reliance on extended families [consanguinal relationships or otherwise], spirituality, rhythmic movement expressions, and communalism." Billingsley expressed the same idea when he noted that "black people must not be viewed as a carbon copy of whites, but a people with a different history, a unique place in American society, and a distinctive set of contributions to the larger society."

In this same context, scholars such as W.R. Allen and Harriett McAdoo, have convincingly documented that most of the early studies of the black family were conducted on the lower black middle-class and then, by inference, applied to the rest of the black families. Indeed, in reference to middle-class values and integration in white neighborhoods, which should logically derive from higher education, employment, and income touted by Wilson, for example, Boamah-Wiafe asks whether one can use the norms of a social class created and imposed by the dominant white population to define black families that have been living in an "oppressive, pluralistic, and fluid society such as the United States." Indeed, the so-called neighborhood integration of the black and white family rarely occurs, since, "when the black middle class families move, they do so into neighborhoods that have a relatively high percentage of blacks" (Boamah-Wiafe, 2007, p. 122, 191). In the words of Niemonen, housing desegregation that would allow black families to enter white neighborhoods has been impeded by "the attitudes and actions, past and present" of already constituted white neighborhoods, which accept the laws of open housing in "principle but not in practice" because "...race cannot be ignored as a salient dimension of significance of American society" (Niemonen, 2002, 194, p. 207). Higginbottam considers class to be an imperfect tool of analysis of the African American family, which needs to be reinforced by others, because "we cannot predict the survival and dignity of African American families without understanding the socioeconomic and cultural context of their functioning" (see McAdoo, 2007, p. 63), which Wilson's model seems to imply. In her critique of the pioneering analysts who predicted the demise of the black family, McAdoo stresses the point that "the majority of African American families are neither in dire poverty nor among the affluent. They are not on the nightly news as having been shot, and they are not featured in *Jet Magazine* among the elite families" (McAdoo, 2007, p. xiv). This reality prompted Allen to call for a "variant perspective model" that would "underscore the diversity but also the normalcy of all types of families, including the African American family" (Prater, 2005, p. 384-385).

CHALLENGES FACING THE
AFRICAN AMERICAN FAMILY

Despite all the strengths and the adaptability of the African American family emphasized by the majority of black people and scholars of other racial and cultural backgrounds, no one can deny that the black family institution in the United States is facing almost insurmountable social, political, economic, and health challenges that need to be addressed carefuly, lest it finds itself losing some of its relevance to a society that is undergoing rapid and unpredictable change. Social scientists have attempted to explain why the black community, only 13 percent of the US population, is plagued with so many problems. The most common explanation has been that the American government has not fulfilled its social contract with black people. Beyond the vestiges of slavery, racism, and discrimination by individuals and institutions (banks, insurance companies and other businesses, big and small, universities, the housing industry, the armed forces, the legal system, and even federal and state agencies), white America has not lived up to fair practices and continues to pay only lip service to the enforcement of the laws and statutes designed to uplift the living standards of all Americans so that a true melting pot might emerge. Indeed, one can accurately say that, socially, economically, and politically, America has not lived up to its motto of "ex pluribus unum." As a result, many African Americans live unemployed, and, if they land employment, they are underpaid and do not make enough to sustain a family. The legal system, on its part, through profiling and other means, targets African Americans, especially young males, as the criminal element, and enforces a system that has been proven to be partial, favoring white criminals. Furthermore, the educational system in the various States, especially in the South, neglects the education of African American children, punishing them disproportionately when compared to white children committing the same crime, as happened in now infamous Jena town, Louisiana, in 2007. School disparities have resulted in an appalling number of drop-outs about which one hears daily but without the proper accountability of school officials. Schools in black communities, especially in the inner city where black people tend to congregate, are usually old and dilapidated and lack the educational resources and facilities that white suburban schools have for their children, often due to state and county unfair tax formulas.

On the so-often mentioned cultural decadence related to the black youth, irate Star Parker, after enumerating the problems of the black community, especially regarding uncontrollable sexual activity that has resulted in babies born out of wedlock, and indicting the nefarious impact of rap music and its lyrics, writes that "certainly, the traditional American family is under siege, with the challenges for young parents never greater." She goes on to say: "Our permissiveness [which, according to her research, is supported by 63 percent of the Democrats and 51 percent of the Republicans] has brought upon us not the wrath of God, but the consequences of our actions" (Parker, 2006, p.40).

The result is a state of despair that provides no incentive for black youngsters to pursue dreams and careers that uplift their status in society. These conditions force them to "hit the streets" and try to survive at all means at their disposal, legal or illegal, and to live on the fringes of society, giving little room to parental supervision. What about the new welfare laws? The welfare system "as we knew it," altered radically by Congress in 1996, is said to have contributed to a higher level of poverty among black people, as it has not lived up to its aim of training welfare recipients and finding employment that would enable them to meet the needs of their families and care for their children. The elimination of the welfare system, for example, increased to 500,000 the number of children in foster care. Most of the jobs promised by the Personal Responsibility and Work Opportunities Reconciliation Act (PRWORA), which provided states six-year-block grants through the so-called Temporary Assistance for Needy Families (TANF) program, provide only the minimum wage. As McAdoo notes on the new system, "…many children experienced higher rates of poverty after their families left welfare…In addition, more children in families that left welfare were reported for child neglect, a neglect that resulted from the increased economic deprivation of their families" (2007, p. 335). Whereas before 1997, almost all poor, or 94 percent of them, received food stamps and 100 percent were on Medicaid, the number of poor families receiving stamp benefits was reduced to 33 percent, and only 42 percent are currently enrolled in Medicaid (McAdoo 2007, p.333-334). McAdoo concludes by pointing out that many studies have found that "despite government efforts, welfare reform has not been effective in encouraging welfare recipients, especially black couples, to marry," as the reform intended. Furthermore, under the present welfare reform system, 4.7 million or 22 percent of children, especially black, not only are not covered under Medicaid but also do not have health insurance under TANF, notwithstanding the fact that the number of food stamp recipients dropped from 28 million in 1996 to 19 million in 2000.

Some analysts (labeled as "liberals') place the blame for these ills not on the victim but on the victimizer, namely, society and its physical environment. Say Bill Lawson and Sanders-Lawson: "Even middle-class parents in affluent suburbs feel ambivalent about citizenship in a country that has so far failed to fulfill the social contract. Mistrust is even greater in urban areas. Unless opportunities are made available to inner city youth, the cycle of violence will continue" (McAdoo, 2000, p.217). The two scholars add, conceding a point both conservatives and liberals agree on:

> Black parents face a dilemma. They must teach their children to believe in their own abilities but at the same time must acknowledge that, in the United States, ability is often not enough. This is a challenge for middle-class blacks as well as inner city residents. Meanwhile, significant decreases in violent crime and an increase in positive feelings about being full members of society are very unlikely for blacks (Lawson and Renee, 2000, p. 218).

Lawson agrees with McCord who wrote in 1977 that "High rates of societal violence seem partially explicable as reflecting an emphasis on presumed equality in the face of a reality that is exclusionary, coupled with concern for status differentiation and a learned tolerance for the use of violence," common to inner city neglected neighborhoods, result in part from our socio-political structure and policies (Lawson, 2002, p. 210).

Conservative politicians and scholars tend to place the blame on African Americans themselves, especially parents, for not inculcating in youngsters the values, the discipline, and the skills they need to survive in a very competitive and rapidly changing world as American society is today. The conservatives stress that "the negative cultural values" of the urban residents are the culprit and are based on bad parenting by young single mothers, divorced couples, and absent fathers. Conservative columnist William Raspberry, quoting and agreeing with the conclusion of a gathering of Pentecostal ministers and the Seymour Institute for Advanced Christian Studies, wrote (July 25, 2005) that "There is a crisis of unprecedented magnitude in the black community, one that goes to the very heart of its survival. The black family is failing." He compares it to "the sociological equivalent of global warming." The culprit, he and ministers claim, is the decline of marriage, vividly reflected in the absence of the husband:

> Father absence is the bane of the black community, predisposing its children (boys especially, but increasingly girls as well) to school failure, criminal behavior and economic hardship, and an intergenerational repetition of the grim cycle (Raspberry, July 2005, Washingtonpost.com: p. 19).

To those who claim that too many black men are in jail, which precludes the opportunities of a black woman to find suitable mates, the conservatives, including William Raspberry, reply that "…black men aren't born incarcerated, crime-prone dropouts. What principally renders them vulnerable to such a plight is the absence of fathers and their stabilizing influence" (Raspberry, 2005, p. 19).

The controversy over parents' responsibility was fueled in 2007 by Bill Cosby's remarks, which blamed under-class parents for instilling the most distorted values as their tendency to purchase for children fancy shoes and clothes, while neglecting their school needs. Cosby's comments provoked a furor among some members of the African American community. Between those who blame the victim and those who place the blame on the victimizers, a group of scholars indict both the system, which perpetuates poverty, and the lack of adequate supervision of children by parents who, as a result, do not deserve to bring children to the world. John Niemonen remarks that: "…concentrated poverty results from the net in migration of low-income housing in a racially discriminatory housing market, as well as the rapid deterioration of life-circumstances, including employment opportunities, brought about by the structural transformation of the US economy" (2002, p. 183).

The inner city violent and frightful conditions, along with destructive behaviors, apparently have also spread to black middle class neighborhoods, which have forced parents to instill not just mainstream values to their children but also to make them "street" wise, thus enabling them to survive the surrounding social environment as they mingle with other children. Say Lawson and Lawson, "the code of the street" can't be overcome by parents who want to pass their own decency to children," forcing them to educate them to be "street smart" because "it would be imprudent if they did not." In addition, like Niemonen, the two scholars note, inner city parents must instill so-called mainstream values but at the same time teach their children how to survive in violent neighborhoods" (2002, p. 211, 217).

On drug use, which, proportionally, has affected black families the most, even those who are staunch defenders of the African American family acknowledge that drug trafficking and consumption is ruining the fabric of the black community. African Americans account for 14 percent of the drug users, and 35 percent of those arrested for drug use. Also, several reliable sources reveal that one out of five African Americans, especially males, have been or are in jail, serving a jail sentence averaging 39 months, while that of whites averages 33 months. McAdoo acknowledges that "… regardless, the sum of experience of the current urban generation of black youth has been more negative than positive" (2007, p. xv). Sudarkasa is quick to point out that:

The dependence on the underground economy, which is of course not unique to African Americans, is for us one of the patterns that must be broken if we are to rescue black families who are long-term victims, even if they think themselves as short-term beneficiaries, of the illegal drug traffic and the many destructive patterns it breeds (Sudarkasa, 2007, p. 179).

The heated debate over the plight of the black family in the United States cannot overlook the disproportionate disparities that exist between the life and living standards of black and white families in the nation. Invariably, blacks remain at the bottom of the ladder. In employment, whereas the nation's unemployment rate is 4.4 percent, the rate of black unemployment is more than twice as high, 10 percent (10.8 percent in 2005), and this number does not include those unemployed blacks who have given up looking for a job or the underemployed who do not make enough to feed their families. In some cities, as is the case in New York, the rate of unemployment among blacks between the ages of 16 and 64 is as high as 48.2 percent. In Illinois, 30 percent of back people live in poverty, compared to only 8 percent of white people. The Pew Hispanic Trust reports that, from 1996 to 2002, "The median networth of blacks dropped by 16 percent, to a "paltry $5,998 per household, while that of whites grew by 17 percent in the same period, to $88,651." During the last recession (2002), black families are said to have lost 25 percent of their wealth in "their job recovery" effort. This means, says Thomas Shapiro, Professor of Law and Social Policy at Brandeis University, that "…more black people [were] struggling in 2006 with such basic conditions as securing employment, paying rent and mortgage, paying utilities and insurance, obtaining affordable health coverage, and buyingfood"(http://blackstarproject.org/home/template/def></indepx.phip?option=com_content&fash=view&id=22&Itemd'39).

In addition, the Children's Defense Fund reports that, currently, one million black children live in poverty because members of the extended family network are unable to care for them. In fact, 65 to 75 percent of the black population in the United States lives below the poverty level; and 75 percent drop out of school. Likewise, less than one-half of black Americans own homes, compared to three-fourths of whites.

Health wise, although only 42.2 percent of the population (40.2 million in 2002), African Americans account for 44 percent (18,121) of the estimated 37,331 new HIV/AIDS cases in the United States (in the 33 States that keep such statistics), 64 percent being women. (The black population grew only at 1.3 percent in 2005-2006). Revealing is the fact that "of all black men living with HIV/AIDS, the primary transmission category [is] sexual contact with other men, followed by injection drug use and high-risk heterosexual contact." Furthermore, of every 141 infants prenatally infected with HIV in the United States in 2006, 91 or 65 percent were black. African Americans' life expectancy at birth is 72 years, while that for whites is 78 years. The state of the health of married black people in general is 76 percent that of married whites; one-third of black diabetes-related deaths among adult African Americans was 135 per 100,000 in 1999, and have continued to rise since then. Long-term home care services were unavailable to 17.3 percent in 2001, and the overweight and obese adults' rate was 45 percent in 2002 among African Americans.

The Equality Index reveals that "despite societal progress, the overall status of black America is just 73 percent compared to that of their white counterparts," and has remained only marginally unchanged from 2004 results"(http://fundarticles.com/p/articles/min_m1355/is_18_107/ai_n15694037).

These conditions may in part explain why only 48 percent of African Americans live as married couples, and 43 percent of the households are headed by females. The African American male has the hardest time maintaining his presence at home. He often suffers from a lack of appropriate education, adequate employment skills, and has the highest potential of ending up in jail, enlisting in the armed forces, and fighting in such deadly wars as Iraq. Statistics also show that "about four out of 10 African American women have never been married, the highest proportion in every category" (State of Black America, 2007, National Urban League). Again, to quote the Pew Charitable Trust,

> About half of the African Americans born to middle-class during the late 1980s fell into or near poverty as adults and 45 percent of black children whose parents were solidly middle class in 1968—a stratum with a median income of $55,000 in inflation-adjusted dollars—grew up to be the lowest fifth of the nation's earners, with a median income of $23,000. Only 16 percent of whites experienced similar mobility. At the same time, 48 percent of black children whose parents were in an economic bracket with a median family income of $41,700 sank into the lowest income group" (http://www.pewtrusts.org/news_room_ektid31288.aspx).

When the 2000, 2003, and 2005 black and white family incomes are compared, the following picture emerges (U.S. Census, May 17, 2007: 1, http://www.census.gov/Press-Release/www/releases/archives/population/010048.html, retrieved 1/14/2008):

Years	Black	White	Total Differential
2000	$33,676	$53,029	2000 and 2005
2003	$34,369	$55,768	Black: $1,788
2005	$35,464	$59,317	White: $6,288

In 2005, in similar jobs, blacks earned only 65 percent of white wage earners, a decline of 85 percent from 1975.

Other figures are also disconcerting. For example, even though births to unwed mothers among the two races have risen since the 1950s, the rate among blacks remains three times higher than that of whites, which presents a dilemma on how to sustain them. Teen-age pregnancy is high in the black community, even though, in absolute numbers, white teen-agers bear more out-of-wedlock children. In 2002, the rate of births among unmarried Hispanics was 87.9 per 1,000 births, whereas, in the black community, it was the second highest in the nation, at 66.2 per 1,000; abortion rates were 22 per 1,000 and 29 per 1,000 among Hispanics and African Americans, respectively. Interestingly, reflecting society's views, 54 percent of Americans see no problem with out-of-wedlock births, while 43 percent disapprove it. Similarly, in 2005, reportedly, 63 percent of Democrats and 51 percent of Republicans had no problem with the idea of sex outside marriage (Parker, 2006: 5-6). It is likewise important to remember that, since the 1980s, the incidence of "common-law marriages" and what has been known as "serial polygamy" have increased in both the black and the white communities, especially among the poor and members of the lower socio-economic class (Boamah-Wiafe, 2001, p. 124).

Out of all these gloomy characterizations of the current black family, one needs to distinguish between nostalgia and the new global reality. Invariably, one hears older people lauding the past and indicting the present, without realizing that the world is not static and that, whoever resists change, will eventually pay a price. Criticism is also directed to the culture of the black youth, reflected in the popularity of hip hop, rap music, and its lyrics, which, according to many, has done further damage to the black family: Disrespect for the black female, glorification of crime, and repudiation of the traditional role assigned to the family. Todd Boyd, however, does not condemn this trend among the youth. He blames this negative attitude on the culture of the civil rights movement, which, in his view, has disposed the black community to accept only one definition of common and collective good. Instead, he sees the rap phenomenon as a new type of civil rights struggle, which allows the disenfranchised to express their suffering and aspirations through unique music styles and provoking lyrics. Hip hop, he says, has allowed black youngsters to throw the "shackles" placed around their bodies and free their minds. Writes Boyd:

> The other lingering remnant of civil rights lies in the way that we now assume that this era define Blackness for the ages, that in order to be truly black, one had to have been attacked by dogs and doused with water-hoses, that one had to be forced to get up from a segregated lunch counter in order to claim to be truly black. In all this, Blackness was cloaked in suffering and defined by the degree which one had to be abused (Boyd, 2002, p. 150).

Boyd adds: "Civil rights had its day. Now it is time to move out of the way civil rights was a struggle, and it remains an ongoing struggle for all disenfranchised people of color to pursue their civil rights" (Boyd, 2002, p. 152).

CONCLUSION

The debate over the black family in the United States will not relent in the years ahead, and, as more and more accurate statistics become available to researchers, the arguments in favor and against will continue. However, if one focuses only on the negatives, forecasting the doom of the African American family becomes a self-fulfilling prophecy. To understand the strength and resilience of the African American family, one needs to realize the historical obstacles and trials it has experienced and overcome over the centuries, both during and after slavery, and the continuing environment of racism and discrimination, as well as the assault on affirmative action and the welfare system (the latter designed to eliminate, as President Ronald Reagan used to say, "the welfare queens"). The concerted effort on the part of the black educational institutions to assist in the uplift of black youngsters and the work of black leaders, who have assumed unprecedented positions in Congress and in the executive branch must also be acknowledged. Out of all these developments, a major conclusion ought to be that the institution is strong and will continue to be so for the foreseeable future. Its ability to adapt is commendable. Researchers should spend more of their time carefully examining this aspect of the black family.

As McAdoo, Billingsley, John Hope Franklin, and Robert Hill point out, the positives seem to outweigh the negatives, as long as African Americans have equal access which offers "…flexible responsive services in which differing needs are identified and accommodated so that each person, regardless of 'race, color, creed, national origin, gender, marital status, class, disability or sexuality,' benefits equally" (Judith Scott and Alix Henley, 1996, p. 48). The positivist scholars further note that the extended family structure is becoming stronger and not weaker: 85 percent of the children, they point out, in single parent female households live with grandparents; 87 percent of black children born to single teenage mothers live with grandparents; 41 percent of married women and 83 percent of black mothers who never married "use relatives for day care services" and these instill values in them (Boamah-Wiafe, 2007, p. 137). More black mothers are off of welfare, and, while most fathers are not "deadbeat dads," 40 percent of young unmarried mothers live with the fathers of their children, and 82 percent remain romantically involved" (McAdoo, 2007, p. 331).

In education, not all statistics are gloomy for black families and communities. In fact, in 2006, 20 percent (5,211) of the U.S. citizens awarded doctorates from American universities were ethnic minorities, the largest percentage ever recorded for minority recipients. The percentage drops to 11 percent when international student awardees are included. Among minorities, however, blacks earned the most doctorates at 1,659. It is of interest to note that the 5 percent increase in doctorates in 2006 over 2005 was fueled by increases in certain fields of study with the largest increase found in engineering and the physical sciences, while education dropped by 2 percent. At the same time, African Americans received 55 percent of education doctoral degrees (Healy, 2007, p. 9). Of note is the fact that the first doctoral degree choice, based on degrees conferred, among students of color remains education for Blacks, Hispanics, and American Indians; whereas Asian Americans or non-U.S. citizens prefer the STEM disciplines (science, technology, engineering, and mathematics). The percentage of STEM doctoral degrees conferred in 1994-1995 was only 1.3 percent and a decade later is only 1.9 percent of degrees awarded (Border and Brown, 2006, p. 35). Likewise, among the first professional degrees pursued that require a license, among them law, health, and divinity, blacks and other U.S. students of color select law first, except Asian Americans who choose health. (Border and Brown, 2006, p. 24-25). Related to these career choices, although Blacks, Hispanics, and American Indians make up slightly more than a quarter of the population in the U.S., they only constitute 6 percent of the practicing physicians, less than 5 percent of dentists, and less than 7.5 percent of nurses (Scott, 2006, p.33). What then are the proposed solutions to the problems of the black family?

Black scholars and activists alike have criticized the black community for being less community-oriented and more individualistic now than was the case during the pre-civil rights era. Lois Benjamin, using the "sugar bin" metaphor, says that the half-empty "sugar bin" syndrome has prevented African Americans from sharing the remaining little amount of "sugar," particularly among the generation that has not attended undergraduate

African American institutions, which, in his view, are more successful in instilling in their black students a "greater sense of community, culture, and racial consciousness." In his view, the "I" generation has completely replaced the "we" generation. Parents need to emulate what black colleges and universities have succeeded in doing when many families have been unable to accomplish the same. Lois Benjamin writes: "With the eroding economic, political, and civil rights at the end of the twentieth century, we need a collective strength to defend against this new nadir in the twenty-first century" (Benjamin, 2000, p. 187). The author also laments the great gap that seems to exist between middle-class families and the under-class, which has made parenting more difficult, as the cultures of the two divides do not coincide (Benjamin, 2005, p. 282). Classicism and self-interest have set in among the educated and highly-achieved blacks living in white neighborhoods, a situation that does not help the black family to fulfill its obligations to the household and the community-at-large.

For Sudarkasa, one of the solutions to the problems of the black family is to re-instate the extended family structure and function, which, in her view, promotes "reciprocity" and "support." Apart from government fair policies and programs, Robert Hill has advocated adopting the following five general strategies, which black families must instill in their children if they wish to guarantee the survival, stability, and advancement of the institution: 1) strong work orientation; 2) flexibility of family roles; 3) strong achievement orientation; 4) extended family networks; 5) and strong religious orientation. Summing up, there is no doubt that the African American community must focus its energies on addressing and eliminating, to the extent possible, the following challenges: Single-head parenthood; adolescent pregnancy; doubtful child support services; detrimental foster care policies; family and black—on—black violence; drug and alcohol abuse; shortage of marriageable males; school drop-out rates; the accelerating number of high HIV/AIDS infections within the black community; and a sense of complacency in view of the struggles won in the past (Prater, 2005, p. 395).

In the face of these challenges, it is wise that young and adult African Americans remain vigilant new occupants of the White House. They must always be scrutinized, lest their often insensitive and discriminatory policies dilute or efface the milestones so-hardly achieved by blacks before, during, and following the civil rights era. There is no doubt that, during the past few years, the balance has been slowly tilting toward the loss of previous civil rights gains that have helped the black family to adapt and survive.

References

Allen, W.R.(1978). The Search for Applicable Theories of Black Family Life. *Journal of Marriage and the Family*, 40, 117-1129.

Atwood, Joan D. & Fran Genovese. (1993). *Counseling Single Parents*. Alexandria, VA: American Counseling Association.

Azevedo, M. (Ed.) (2005). *Africana Studies: A Survey of Africa and the African Diaspora*. Durham, NC: Carolina Academic Press.

Benjamin, L. (2005). *The Black Elite: Still Facing the Color Line*. New York: Row and Littlefield Publishers,

_____(2000). *Three Generations at the Crossroads: Community, Culture, and Consciousness*. Chicago: Burham, Inc., Publishers.

Billingsley, A. (1968). *Black Families in White America*. Englewood Cliffs, NJ: Prentice Hall.

Blassingame, J. (1972). *The Slave Community*. London: Oxford University Press.

Boamah-Wiafe, D. (2001). *The Black Experience in Contemporary America*. Omaha, NE: Wisdom Publications.

Border, V. M.H. & P. C. Brown. (2006). The Top 100: Interpreting the Data, *Diverse Issues in Higher Education*.23, (11), 35.

Du Bois, W.E.B. (1962). *Black Reconstruction in America 1860-1880*. New York: Athenaeum.

Byrd, T. (2000). *The New H.N.I.C. (Head Niggers in Charge). The Death of the Civil Rights Movement and the Reign of Hip Hop*. New York: New York University Press.

Dodson, J. E. (2007). Conceptualizations and Research of African Family Life in the United States. In H. P. McAdoo (Ed.) *Black Families*. pp. 51-66.Thousand Oaks, CA: Sage.

Franklin, J. H. (1974). *From Slavery to Freedom*. New York: Alfred Knopf.

Frazier, E. F. (1939). *The Negro Family in America*. Chicago: University of Chicago Press.

Herskovits, M. (1941). *The Myth of the Negro Past*. New York: Harper and Row.

Gutman, H. (1976). *The Black Family in Slavery and Freedom*, 1750-1925. New York: Pantheon.

Healy, J. 2007). Diverse *Issues in Higher Education*, 24(23), p. 9.

Hill, R. B. (2007). The Impact of Welfare Reform on Black Families. In H. P. McAdoo (Ed.) *Black Families*. (pp. 328-336) Thousand Oaks, CA: Sage.

http://www.cde.gov/hiv/to_pics/aa/resources/factsheets/aa.htm.

http://www.pewtrusts.org/pews_room_ektid31288.aspx.

http://blackstarproject.org/home/template/def><index.php?option=com=content &fash=view&id=&Itemd=39

http://fundarticles.com/p/articles/mi_m1355/is_18_107/ai_n15694037'

_____(1989). Critical Issues for Black Families by the Year 2000. *The State of Black America*. New York: National Urban League,

Lawson, B & R. Sanders-Lawson. (2002). Violent Crime, Race and Black Children. In H. P. McAdoo (Ed.) *Black Children: Social, Educational and Parental Environment*. Thousand oaks, CA: Sage.

McAdoo, H. P. (Ed.) (2007). *Black Familes* Thousand Oaks, CA: Sage,

McAdoo, H. P. (2002). *Black Children: Social, Educational and Parental Environments*. Thousand Oaks, CA: Sage,

Moynihan, D. P. (1965). *The Negro Family: The Case for National Action*. Washington, DC: Government Printing Office.

Niemonen, J.(2002). *Race, Class, and the State of Contemporary Sociology*. Boulder, CO: Lynne Rienner Publishers.

Parker, S. (2006). *White Ghetto: How Middle Class America Reflects Inner City Decay*. NY: Nelson Current, Special Markets.

Prater, G. S. (2005). The African American Family. In M. Azevedo (Ed.) *Africana Studies: A Survey of Africa and the African Diaspora*. (pp. 383-398). Durham, NC: Carolina Academic Press.

_____(2000). Child Welfare and African American Families. In N. A Cohen (Ed.) *Child Welfare: A Multicultural Focus*. Boston: Allyn and Bacon.

Rainwater, L. (1966). Crucible of Identity: The Negro Lower Class Family. *Daedalus*, 95, 171-215.

Raspberry, W. (2005). Why our Black Families are Failing." *Washington Post*, Monday, p. 19.

Scott, M. (2006). Serving the Underserved. *Diverse Issues of Higher Education*, 23(3), 33

Scott, J & A. Henley. (1996). *Culture, Religion, and Chidlbearing in a Multiracial Society*. Oxford: Linacre House.

Sudarkasa, N. (2007). African American Female-Headed Households. In H. P. McAdoo, (Ed.) *Black Families*. (pp. 173-183) Thousand Oaks, CA: Sage.

U.S. Department of Health and Human Services. (2005). *Administration for Children and Families: Preventing Child Abuse and Neglect Reporting 2004*. Washington, D.C.: Government Printing Office.

Wilson, W. J. (1978). *The Declining Significance of Race: Blacks and Changing American Institutions*. Chicago: University of Chicago Press.

www.census.gov/PressRelease/www/releases/archives/population/010048.html

CHAPTER *9*

AUTOETHNOGRAPHIC ANALYSIS OF AFRICAN AMERICAN EXTENDED FAMILY COMMUNICATION EXPERIENCES: PASSING ON HARMONY, UNITY, AND UNDERSTANDING

Rhunette C. Diggs

INTRODUCTION

> "In my mother's house there is still God." (*A Raisin in the Sun,*
> Act 1, Scene 1, Topic Tracking: Family 4, pg. 37)

The epigraph is from the 1959 stage play /1961 film *A Raisin in the Sun* written by Lorraine Hansberry. The words are spoken by a passionate mother to remind her willful adult daughter of the overarching value that governs the home. Besides the extraordinary performances of the 1961 actors, the play/film represents the values, conditions, hopes, determination, and complaints of a traditional extended Black family. The story exudes communication content that reflects the struggle and conflict over money, relationships, identity, values, and a vision of the future. *Keepin' It Real* (1998) by Kevin Powell is another creative book project that speaks to a model of an extended Black family. Powell, described as a writer, poet and cultural critic, offered glimpses of extended family life that was tumultuous and frustrating as two sisters with their young children lived together for survival. The book is characterized as follows: "letters and reflections take us on the dizzying tight-rope walk between two worlds. From the poverty and misery of his New Jersey childhood to the excesses and successes" (Powell, 1998, African American Book Club book description).

My own family story has its merits and frustrations too, as I reflect on the five decades of living in a Black family that has strong ties to family unity and its survival. I will reference the experiences of living in close proximity to biological kin from childhood to young adulthood and my middle age experience of living in East Africa for 16 months as the basis for my analysis of African American extended family. The experiences, memories, conversations, and reflections from these contexts are utilized to further develop an expanded understanding of extended family and to identify communication patterns that reflect traditional and innovative African American extended family models. What are the purposes of this communication that occurs in the traditional and innovative African American extended family models? What kinds of communication enable extended families to achieve harmony or unity and understanding?

The perspectives and facts that guide this study are as follows: (a) African and Christian perspectives emphasize harmonious aspirations of family relationships; (b) the realities of extended families are not altogether idyllic; (c) extended family models exhibit a variety of functions and manifestations; and (d) communication functions enhance and create unique extended families; (e) communication within African American families is understudied, yet communication characteristics are emphasized in Afrocentric concepts to stimulate growth and development (e.g., Asante, 1981, p. 408, "confront"; Diggs & Socha, 2004, p. 255, "culture as opportunity"; Hilliard, 1995, p. 69, "listening").

The chapter is organized by first addressing literature that recognizes African and African American (or Black) extended families as distinctive social groups, followed by a description of the autoethnography methodology that grounds the study, the analysis of the author's experiences within Black extended families, and concludes with summary and recommendations for future research.

THE AFRICAN AMERICAN EXTENDED FAMILY MODELS

Billingsley (1992), a leading sociology scholar of the African-American experience, characterized the African-American family as a sense of belonging with persons of African descent by blood, marriage, formal adoption, informal adoption or by appropriation that is sustained by a common history in America and "deeply embedded in a network of social structures both internal to and external to itself.... Numerous interlocking elements" (p. 28). Thus, the Black family is conceptualized as a system of interacting (or interlocking) elements. Systems theory has guided the bulk of family research. Assumptions of interdependence, wholeness, patterns (process and structure), change/adjustment, openness, and complexity are hallmarks of this theory (e.g., see Hess & Handel, 1967; Pinderhughes, 2002; Rogers, 2001). This conceptualization makes it possible for verbal and nonverbal messages within the family as well as messages and social institutions outside to impact upon the family relationships and outcomes.

Structural

Extended family topics are most often approached from the structural perspective of who is in the family. Consider Martin and Martin's (1978) definition of extended family:

> When we speak of a Black extended family we mean a multi-generational, intergenerational kinship system which is welded together by a sense of obligation to relatives, is organized around a "family base" household, is generally guided by a "dominant family figure," extends across generational boundaries to connect family units to an extended family network and has a built-in mutual aid system for the welfare of its members and the maintenance of the family as a whole (p. 1).

White (as cited in Boyd-Franklin, 2003) explained that family members, adults and children, make up a kind of extended family to help raise the Black child. These individuals carry out duties and responsibilities based on needs rather than rigid male and female social roles. Dilworth-Anderson and Goodwin (2005) addressed the extended Black context for seniors or the elderly. They contend that obligation, necessity, consanguinity or blood, principle of reciprocity or giving guide the support for the elderly family member. They also note rather than focusing on a single or primary caregiver, a focus on multiple caregivers is more realistic and reflects research findings that reveal the primary caregiver has the highest level of responsibility and tasks; secondary caregivers provide high levels of care but do not carry the overall caregiving responsibility as do primary caregivers. Their research reported an additional type of caregiver, the tertiary caregiver "who had little or no responsibility for making decisions about the care recipient and mostly performed specialized tasks" (p. 212). This research yielded different extended family structural types: PST, primary, secondary, and tertiary; PS primary and secondary; PT primary and tertiary; and PO primary only.

In addition, an emphasis on extended families in Black societies warrants some indication of the connections of peoples in the African diaspora. In addressing African and African American family structure, Sudarkasa (1996) explained that African family structure implies generalization regarding indigenous Africans and also explanations about "features of African family organization that have had relative permanence or persistence over time, so that they represent aspects of kinship that are legitimately termed a part of the African heritage" (p. 90).

Harmonious, Spiritual, & Creative Aspirations

African and Christian perspectives emphasize harmonious aspirations of family relationships. The Afrocentric (or Africentric) perspective points to understanding self, having a sense of self-worth and racial pride as important aspects of the African ethos. This perspective emphasizes an examination of the historical context of being. Understanding the concepts of slavery, institutional racism, and power in society while envisioning and attaining the goals of liberation and harmony are critical to an Afrocentric examination of phenomena. An Afrocentric framework emphasizes the pragmatic value of our theorizing and behaviors in the pursuit of liberation and well-being, harmonious relationships, and centering of African values (e.g., spirituality, respect, belonging) (Asante, 1988; Hilliard, 1995; Karenga, 2001, 2002; Myers, 1993). Peters and Haney (2006) noted that "Africentricism is a manifestation of culture while the message of Christ is salvific" (p. 53). The position of this researcher and others is that Spirit may be encountered without a particular religious perspective; "however, those who recognize this Spirit are often aware of something or someone typically referred to as God; they are operating with a God consciousness" (Clark & Diggs, 2002).

Hill (1993) emphasizes a complementary holistic approach to the study and problems of Black families. He views families as the "preeminent mechanism for socialization and for pooling resources for upward mobility among blacks and whites" (p. 6). The holistic framework offers five areas of foci to guide research and policy: diversity (what is learned from different families), dynamism (change versus static), balance (weaknesses and strengths), solutions (answers to questions), and empiricism (scientific inquiry using quantitative and qualitative methods).

Historically, an emphasis on understanding self, having a sense of self-worth, and racial pride are important to African American's respect for humanity. The value of acceptance and caring for others is related to this assumption. African Americans are bi-cultural and diverse people of African descent who share a sense of belonging. Such people can vary in social status but typically share a sense of "peoplehood" which Gordon (as cited in Billingsley, 1968) describes as a sense of historical identification. The concepts of slavery and institutional racism are oppressive in nature; those who are oppressed are made to forget "**who** they are and **whose** they are" (Kunjufu, 1989, p. 62). It is assumed that in remembering who they are, African Americans can embrace the Nia (purpose) of their journey and engage in communication that is reflective of that purpose.[1] Optimal communicative environment creates understanding (which can be challenging) and motivates the interactants to continue in contact—to desire contact.

The extended family from this perspective provides an environment for potential nurturing, relationship building, growth, and understanding. This perspective might include going back to reclaim the family we were disconnected from—to better understand the family we are with—and those families we can form in the future by choice. The potential lies in evolving, creating, and extending backward to generate empowering meanings of family. For example, an African proverb that says, *Family is like a forest, when you are outside it is dense, when you are inside you see that each tree has its place* is an insightful reminder of the uniqueness and importance of each member.

Family characteristics of love and harmony are created by and require communication to perpetuate and to deal with the everydayness, problems, and issues that arise there. One can create family through language and interaction (e.g., Alexander, 2001; Diggs & Socha, 2004; Segrin & Flora, 2005, p. 8). Family ideals of harmony, stability and love are maintained, assaulted, tested, contested, and nurtured through communication. As families live, there are varied ranges of efforts to communicate members' needs, goals, concerns and problems. An ideal traditional aspect of the Black family such as belongingness is evident in this quote: "Throughout Ethiopia, neighbours feel responsible for the behaviour of each others' children; they commonly take care of them and may even informally adopt them. Ethiopian children are expected to respect their parents and adults, and obey their decisions" (Family Life in Ethiopia, 2004). Yet, this characteristic of assumed or automatic respect is changing in Ethiopia as are traditional values throughout all world cultures. For example, according to BBC journalist correspondent Nita Bhalla (2002, para. 4), the respect historically reserved for elders "is now changing and people over the age of 60 are one of the most marginalised and poorest groups in the continent."

Spirit (or *Spiritual*) is the term used to refer to individual and interpersonal experience of being motivated, prompted and supported in daily life by an immaterial but tangible reality or presence (Diggs & Clark, 2002). Other scholars who articulate understandings about knowledge based on the immaterial, yet tangible, include Afrocentric psychologists Nobles (1998) who explains Spirit (or Malian term "wayne bibi") at the physical level as "an urge and desire for what is excellent, good and right" (p. 195); and Myers (1993) who talks about a "permeating essence we come to know in an extrasensory fashion (i.e., via energy or consciousness or God)" and asserts that, "the truth of one's being had to be manifest" (p. 12-13).

Keepin' It Real

A brief interaction with a parent (usually the mother) with children will soon reveal that caring for a family requires stamina or strength. Imagine dropping off your child at a peer's home for a study session. Mom greets you and in your brief exchange she tells you how one challenging event after the other has transpired (e.g., son hyper-extended his knee—in emergency room last night and again today; toe was fractured when cans from the pantry fell on her foot, etc.). As a fellow parent you nod and agree, offering some hope (through her faith in God) that this period of disasters will soon be over. However, as a researcher writing an analysis of extended families you wonder how the parent's own self-reminders of comfort and belief made a difference. The context for the ideal balance of that strength depends upon the context. Some families deal with more physical stressors in the form of sicknesses or disease, others, emotional (temper tantrums, mental health issues). Still others experience a preponderance of the lack of resources and income. Some researchers address families as functional and dysfunctional, suggesting that there is a way that functional families function that is ideal. Boyd-Franklin (2003) addresses the characteristics of functional and dysfunctional extended families. The dysfunctional families "are sometimes over-involved, more disengaged and some are cut off entirely from extended family contacts. Whereas, the functional extended families have clearer and flexible boundaries and are emotionally balanced in meeting the needs of the family members" (p. 61-62). These challenges of living with extended familes are all to be found in the real world.

To emphasize *real* for some scholars is to de-emphasize or dismiss the subjective (rather, all is objective, the world as given; the interpretation is obvious in manifest content). And to emphasize *real* for some scholars is to de-emphasize or dismiss the existence of anything that is strictly observable (rather, all is subjective and constructed, the world is what we as human actors make it). However, in this research *real* often implies beyond the visible as when we say, "I want to engage in real communication." Real suggests *more than meets the eye*. Real reflects a reciprocity, struggle, complementarity, disjunction, and intersection between and among *what is* (objective), and *what we make of it* (subjective). Real is the actual and the imagined. Real reflects the functional (operative) and constitutive (essential, meanings) perspectives to communication.

Communication Ties that Bind Families

Along with the general acceptance of the commonality of extended families is the acceptance that with all of their imperfections, extended families bring qualities of strength, sustenance, discipline, and role models (e.g., Crouch, 1994). This strength is often implicated in the management of everyday life. Everyday, families deal with a range of public and private experiences reflective of a range of mundane to serious events and topics: household chores, finances, childcare, health, relationships, and conflicts. Efforts to maintain family unity and stability in the midst of this everydayness should not be taken for granted and it is not bound by location. As the opening epigraph indicates ("In my mother's house there is still God."), there are explicit messages that are spoken to remind the home dwellers that a vision or image of the home exists and that vision or image directs certain kinds of communication or messages.

Communication is defined as a symbolic, transactional process (actual and manipulated, simultaneous multidirectional) or the process of creating and sharing meanings" (Galvin & Brommel, 1996, p. 20). Communication is the "process of humans creating, sending, receiving, and interpreting signals—the perception, interpretation, and response of people to signals produced by other people" (Brilhart, Galanes, & Adams, 2001, p. 46); "the process of meaning-making" (Turner & West, 1998, p. 13). Galvin and Brommel (1996) offer a definition of family as a "system constituted and managed through its communication" (p. 44). Conceptualizations of family and culture have profound impact on the communication that occurs and that is permitted as acceptable, challenging or unacceptable. Finally, communication "is the most important means by which to achieve social order, for within communication lies the power to create and to control the images that legitimize authority" (Smith, 1998, p. 107). Within the family itself communication is expressed and often sought to restore intergenerational misunderstanding and differences. The challenges may become even more noticeable or intense when significant change occurs in the family.

A symbolic interaction perspective, which focuses on meanings and interpretations of self and society, is also at the heart of the extended family communication environment. A basic assumption of the symbolic interaction framework is that humans are actors as well as reactors within the social environment. Therefore, individuals use information from interactions to assist with future interactions and individuals can be influenced, become who they are, by interactions. Specifically, emphasis on knowing oneself and others via interactions is primary. This aspect of self-knowledge allows the self-ascribed or co-creation of families outside of biological boundaries. Individuals who interact and exchange messages may begin to identify themselves as "family" because of the needs, behaviors, and feelings that they experience (e.g., Alexander, 2001).

Finally, a systems perspective attempts to include all the components that bear on the observed family interactional behavior (e.g., Billingsley, 1992). Black extended families exist beyond the physical structure. Long after people exit the physical setting of the extended family they continue to occupy a mental space. Extended families exist physically/materially and mentally/psychologically. The traditional Black extended family is very near and dear because when Blacks didn't have identifiable blood families they still had names for family representativse: *big poppa, big mama* (e.g., Boyd-Franklin, 2003, chap. 3). These names or images were a creation of the Black extended family.

METHODOLOGY

Autoethnographic Approach

The autoethnographic approach is a qualitative method that allows me as a Black female extended family member and communication scholar to center my life experiences and observations toward addressing the extended family issues of a Black family. Autoethnography is a type of ethnographic practice which "involves highly personalized accounts where authors draw on their own experiences to extend understanding of a particular discipline or culture" (Holt, 2003, p. 2). The emphasis on the telling of one's life is both liberating and controversial. The liberating aspect is that the author is not bound by strict rules of anonymity, distancing, and structural reporting that are evident in traditional social science. Controversy lies in the ongoing conversations about *how* one should *do* autoethnography. Anderson (2006) advocates analytic autoethnography that reaches beyond the self or obtains data from informants, and Atkinson (2006) insists that we "guard against any implicit assumption that self-transformation is the main outcome of such research processes (p. 403). However, Ellis and Bochner (2006) in their research conversation remind readers that the whole project of autoethnography is to do research differently than the realist and analytic ethnographer. "Our goal is to open up conversations about how people live, rather than close down with a definitive description and analytic statements about the world as it *truly* exits outside the contingencies of language and culture....evocation is a goal" (p. 435).

With these autoethnographic conversations in mind, I recalled that I completed a dissertation in 1994 in the quantitative tradition, but I always had yearnings for the qualitative. During that period, I audited a qualitative course and felt connected to the worldview and approach. In subsequent years, I settled for triangulation as a way to assuage my methodological angst. In the present study, autoethnography, philosophical and theoretical perspectives (of Afrocentricity, Symbolic Interaction, and Systems), and the nature of the study itself allow me to reveal my challenges with treading the terrain of self revelation while still holding on to "other" data. The African centered perspective complements autoethnography by emphasizing ideals of creativity and self-knowledge. Symbolic interaction points to the knowledge, experiences, and perceptions of the individual while the family systems theory emphasizes the influence and roles of all members on the family experiences (e.g., see Segrin & Flora, 2005, 2). Therefore, the procedures are grounded in centering the researcher and participants' histories, the culture of the participants under investigation, and the communication meanings and resultant problems and solutions of the research participants. In essence, I embrace a diunital approach of both/and rather than either/or. The voices of the author and participants are not in opposition, rather they create a holistic view of the family and family communication: "The African worldview finds it difficult to make a distinction between the self, or the "I," and one's people, or the "we." In identifying oneself, we can make choices about who we are and who we are becoming while simultaneously maintaining a sense of self that is "extended in time to include all of the ancestors... and the entire community" (Myers, 1998, p. 7).

My extended family stories are about three different family contexts; each represents a functional family that is striving for wholeness in body, mind, and spirit (i.e., they are concerned about their internal spirit; internal/external health and wellness; their family; their work; society and world) to different degrees (see Boyd-Franklin, 2003, discussion of functional and dysfunctional families). *Everyday* family communication is the medium to achieve these objectives.

Crawford, utilizing the autoethnographic method, agrees that "falling in love with the people about who one is curious may avoid misuses and perhaps lead to a deeper form of knowing" (1996, p. 167). The concept of *loved one* is applicable because in effective research we must exhibit conscious effort to care for those who we target as objects of research and for those who conduct research. Such caring in this respect is found in examining our own pre-conceived notions and assertions. *Loved one* is a symbolic concept that is a free choice. I choose to use the term to identify who I am and what I am in relationship to those family members interviewed in my research. My roles as an educator, family communication researcher, a member in several Black family kin-networks, and a coordinator of biennial family reunions since 1996 have provided ample experiences and opportunities to participate and observe extended families. I interviewed each family member to gain a more diverse perspective on the extended family experiences.

Before describing the process of collecting the stories, terms and their explanations are first offered.

TERMS AND EXPLANATIONS

Family merger: coming together of one or more individuals or family members into an existing family unit or home space.

Entering family member: The individual or family members who move into an existing family unit or home space.

Established family members: The individual or family members already occupying the home space.

Fictive kin: Individuals connected by goals and needs rather than biological.

Home space: Physical family dwelling.

Lead: the female or male who occupies the traditional "head of household" role.

Three African American biological and fictive kin relatives (*loved ones*), two females and one male in the age range of 52-56, were interviewed by telephone. The following questions were emphasized: (1) Who and/or what situation initiated the family merger? (2) What was the nature of the family merger (you/child came to live with parent, entire family, etc)? (3) Which family or members seemed most instrumental in maintaining the family merger? (4) What actions/behaviors maintained or sustained the family merger (5) Length of time in family merger; (6) What was your/other's experience like from your perspective?

The interviewees are labeled by sex, race/ethnicity, and the state or place where the extended family experiences occurred and/or current residence: FAAGa, FAAEthi (e.g., female African American Georgia, female African American Ethiopia), and MAAOh (male African American Ohio). All have participated in family mergers as an "entering family member" and one of the three interviewees provided home space for biological and non-biological family members or fictive kin. The stories are presented in the first person voice. A brief commentary which connects my voice to the extended kin's voice follows each story.

Two Southern African-American Extended Family Experiences: *Pass it On*

I grew up in a southwest Georgia town (population of 12,000 in 2007), living with and near a set of first cousins (we share two of the same grandparents). My mother's father lived within our household and his care was shared by my mother and this set of first cousin relatives (in particular, one of my mother's sisters). Also, my mother and this sister (both born in the early-late 1920s) reared their children alongside each other, geographically. I grew up living between the worlds of these two families, my biological parents and this aunt and her family (husband and children). There was a fluidity that was not questioned, being in each other's *business* (affairs) was an ordinary way of life. The context of these extended family histories might be summed up in an anecdote about my grandfather Marcus that I collected over my years of participating in family reunions.

My grandfather Marcus and his sister Millie were raised by their maternal aunts Polly and Alice after the death of their mother Lucinda. Millie was grown with eight children when she met her father again. Her father saw her in a grocery store one day and said that she favored his "Millie." He reunited with his daughter and lived with her until her death. He spent his remaining years with her children.

I observed and learned that the mother or a female relative has largely assumed the role of caring for the children (e.g., Boyd-Franklin, 2003; Segrin & Flora, 2005, p. 8). My older sister FAAGa was married with one child and another on the way in 1977 when I came face-to-face with this reality. Her story leads out the three stories; FAAGa uses the terms "mother, mom, and mama" interchangeably.

FAAGa's Story

> I moved in with mom in 1977 due to marital problems. Our mother had been separated from our dad for many years with no expectation of reuniting. Our youngest sister was still living at home; she was about 10 years old. I had a toddler and I was pregnant with a second child. During the time when the relationship between my husband and I dissolved, there were some drugs—and just—relationship had more or less ended—and that and distrust. And I think also a financial situation had something to do with it—a combination of things.

237

Mom welcomed me back into the home. I viewed the relationship with mom as friendly and comfortable. Mom didn't just say go back. I helped out financially with mom; mama was helpful in keeping the children when I went back to work and well at the time I knew I needed a place. I didn't have a place on my own, not a steady job, just trying to get at job wherever I could. It was helpful to have some place to stay. When I began to work again, I felt a need to help as much as I could. Mama was there to help with the children; I didn't have to look for a baby-sitter and I was willing to help take on some of the bills. My children got attached to their grandmother and that bond.

The communication with mom was good until I was trying to move out. Mom didn't want me to go back to my husband because she didn't want anything to happen to me. Sometimes my husband had threatened physical violence but never followed through. Well, at that time I didn't believe the marriage would work; I didn't desire to go back; he didn't have a job to take care of us.

I stayed with mom for 10 years. Living in the house with mom was fine. There were times when I didn't like what the children were eating, grandma thing, feeding them what grandma wanted them to have. There was always displeasure when I began to speak about wanting to move. Our aunt (mom's sister) would make certain remarks—about momma did more for the children than I did. Even though I wanted the children to be with me, I believed that mama needed them more; she wanted them with her…I didn't like what was going down, but I didn't want to give them (the children) more stress, regardless of what anybody said…health wise she (mama) needed them to help her…and they wanted to stay.

Looking back, I don't think it was a good decision; I should have been more aggressive, assertive. I wasn't in my own place—topsy-turvy. I went through the pain of decisions I had made, but when I moved in my own place with a new husband, the children didn't like him and I didn't try to push them. When I look back on that, due to the situation and my children's feelings, it was a good decision to leave them with my mother.

Even though FAAGa was welcomed by the Lead, her mother, into the home place, our small hometown where she continues to live, the source of the friction was the possibility of FAAGa returning to the marriage that sent her packing in the first place. I remember those struggles even though I was away from home attending college. This disharmony was seldom addressed in a win-win manner. As a sibling concerned about my sister, I often sided with my mother, thinking that FAAGa was not making the best decision for herself and her children if she chose to return to the spouse. These bouts of disharmony (fussing and fighting, win-lose) were very loud at times or very quiet and hurtful. Even though every person inside the extended family system (FAAGa, mother, sibling, children, including aunt) seemed to have their expressions, all involved were left with unresolved thoughts and feelings 20 years later. FAAGa's older child (a daughter) who harbored much resentment about her mother's choices of marital partners since the divorce from her father, came to live with me at 18 years old. She literally left home without her mother's "blessing."

FAAGa (in 2008, during the interview) expressed ambivalence about the decision to leave her children behind. How can a good mother justify that, morally? I wanted to assure her that she needed to look at the present. Her son adores her and I have used my skills in listening and positive relationship with FAAGa's older daughter to promote reconciliation. FAAGa's daughter while living with me for four years found her voice and began to express to her mother her resentments. It has taken several years for understanding to emerge between them.

I felt FAAGa's pain as she continued to question her decision to leave her children with our mother. I'm her sister and I felt (and knew spiritually) that she needed to let go of the guilt! "Black spirituality is a dynamic, cosmic process, the creative and translative propensities of the spirit of God have strong implications for African-American spirituality. The great gift of African-American spirituality is its capacity ritually to translate harsh and brutal realities into idioms, rituals, and hermeneutics that create their own survival mechanisms for human existence" (Stewart, 1999, p. 16). I asked her to look at her children today and consider if her choice was so bad. She has divorced two men (one on drugs who physically abused her and the other in prison for sexual assault) since she gave in to leaving the children with her mother. The beauty of this analysis is that the voices and the present lives of this extended family validate my urging to FAAGa to look at the end of the story. FAAGa concluded, *When I look back on that, due to the situation and my children's feelings, it was a good decision to leave them with my mother.* Her children who are now adults were grateful to be left with the grandmother for another decade, even though they struggled with their mother's decision to marry men that they perceived (with our mother's confirmation) did not have their mother's best interest. Thirty-one years ago, FAAGa sought support in her mother's home and found it (a traditional extended family situation); she can now find comfort in knowing how the story ended and pass it on.

MAAOh's Story

I was 17 months old when my mother died. My baby sister and I went to live with our mother's parents. My dad was a migrant worker. A host of cousins, nieces, nephews lived on an extended basis in our grandparent's home for educational, relational, and economic reasons. Since our grandparents' family home was close to the only Black school most came to obtain an education, for summer months, and always to improve their situation. Over the years, the list has been long.

Both grandparents were involved with us. Since I've been married with my own children, my wife and I have also opened our home to family members, biological and non-biological members. Our support in education has been the primary reasons for family mergers. We look back and consider our ancestors; we want to pass on the value of family support to our children. And they seem to get it because our children who are financially stable have assisted others and those who are not presently, look forward to their time to contribute and to help others.

I believe that the life-long stability offered by my extended family has made me who I am today. I truly benefitted. The "big house" (akin to a hotel, large rooms with multiple beds left to his grandparents by his maternal great grandparents) brought different families in for various reasons. I have come to realize that this passing on of support is in my value system and it is an established cultural tradition that began with my great grandparents who were slaves and during reconstruction brought in different families for various reasons. For example, when I went off to college in the 1970s, I created a different family structure based on survival for educational purposes. I am now passing on the importance of family support through the extended family model in an interesting manner. My wife and I have told our children that they must be independent; they can't return when they leave the nest. This might appear to be a contradiction, but it is really an incentive to move their children forward to create more power in opportunities for them to give back to others. Their independence will allow them to be inviting to others.

MAAOh's early childhood occurred in rural southern Georgia; he currently lives in a large metropolitan city with a population of over 700,000. The inviting atmosphere that MAAOh experienced with his grandparents is an aspect of what he wants to leave as a legacy. I have been aware of this valuing in MAAOh's household for the last 23 years as we have raised children in close geographical proximity, and I have witnessed the efforts in this household through the process of family meetings and outings (e.g., family reunion trip, birth celebrations, recognitions) that demonstrate these values in action. *Passing on* the value of supporting the next and future generations is an enduring aspect of African American culture (e.g., Billingsley, 1992; Boyd-Franklin, 2003; Dilworth-Anderson & Goodwin, 2005).

New family constructions are being passed on in that a different physical arrangement and different individuals are coming together. Typically this has been the merger of biological entities or non-biological connecting with established family members in an existing home space, but we see with MAAOh something traditional and something different (i.e., a co-creation, self ascribed). MAAOh introduces a new family construction called the African American College Club: *look outside of family into community to build-create a much larger family.* MAAOh spoke of mothers and grandmothers who expressed interest *to extend knowledge through education, and to make a stronger family unit-through regular meetings and visits/ trips around the country.*

Finally, MAAOh and his wife also passed on a paradoxical statement to the children: *don't come back when you get out the nest.* The children didn't feel unwanted nor did they believe that they couldn't return home if necessary. The lesson, buried in the statement, had been taught from years of living in the household. The lesson was *an incentive to move their children forward to create more power in opportunities for them to give back to others. Their independence will allow them to be inviting to others.* My knowledge of this family supports the truth of this paradoxical statement. Every biological child of this family has attained high achievements by completing college and pursuing careers in medicine, banking, and theatre. They often return home to visit, while showing others in need the way to a family merger. MAAOh promotes *passing on the importance of family support through the extended family model.* This family's legacies of creating family mergers with biological family members and beyond (the African American College Club) point to an emphasis on belonging and a shared sense of peoplehood (Billingsley, 1968, 1992).

ETHIOPIAN EXTENDED FAMILY EXPERIENCES: *GURSHA* PROCESS

In 2003, eighteen hours and 7,441 miles (11,973 km) from my U.S.A. home, my 10 year-old-daughter, husband, and I were in Addis Ababa, Ethiopia, immersed in an Ethiopian culture (2007 population, over 3 million). I had accepted a position as a volunteer teacher with an NGO (non-governmental organization). This change in our living space created certain opportunities; we met a dozen or more ethnically diverse teachers in our group who were dispatched to different cities and regions in Ethiopia. Three of the African American female teachers developed into fictive or extended family members out of necessity and circumstance. They made regular visits, exhibited caring, and a willingness to participate in the family rules and interactions. My large family early upbringing, Spiritual background, and this new Ethiopian cultural experience provided insights into the characteristics and meanings of extended family in Black societies. The interview below with FAAEth represents one of the females who visited most frequently and continues to be a close extended family member.

FAAEth's Story

> In 2005 I became part of a new family that was established for support because we were in a strange land. I came to the family home almost every weekend. I would travel by bus, risking life and limb. The support at the home was more like family: There was a couple with a child, an older woman in a grandmother role, and two younger women, one who was like a teen sister or aunt and the other like an older sister, aunt or cousin
>
> You (Rhunette), as the wife, were very helpful to maintaining the family merger. I think that was because of your "mother space" more so than that of wife and your personality/identity as a woman of God or extension. I saw you support and encourage your child. Perhaps with your younger child, the support was an extension of who you are, to care for others. You helped me in a crisis during my accident and my close proximity played a role in getting me to the family home (130 km or 81 miles). I got to see crises, family interactions, deal with problems.
>
> I was with in the family merger for 18 months. This family merger was helpful, enlightening, and kept me going. I think the only problem that I experienced was not understanding the rules that were assumed but were not verbalized. I could see that the established family members had a way of relating and the rules were unfamiliar to me.

FAAEthio (fictive *aunt*) viewed me (the wife, Rhunette) as the most instrumental in maintaining the family unity. She believed that my "mother space" offered support, help, and encouragement. Her perspective was that the Ethiopian family experience was a learning experience: *I got to see crises, family interactions, deal with problems. It was helpful, enlightening, and kept me going.* Of particular note was her concern that my husband, our daughter, and I were a *real* family, with particular rules and norms of behavior.

To some degree I assumed that the entering family member (fictive kin) already understood by observing alone certain pragmatic (or practical) rules from her own family background and having experienced the dusty city streets. For example, the notion of washing feet before getting into bed was a rule I made (female lead of the household) having experienced the dusty roads of our new Ethiopian community and the absence of a washing machine in the home; feet-washing by all members would clean our feet before bed and sustain the sheets. One of the fictive kin members found the rule *nit picky* (parochial—overly concerned about an unimportant item). It became a problem if the rule was not followed and ultimately I had to articulate the importance and value of a rule that was not really valued by the fictive kin.

Within the extended family context I developed a novel approach to address a perceived stress felt by a fictive family member. I learned that FAAEth felt that I assumed that everyone understood (i.e., accepted without explanation) the family rule of feet-washing before bed. At first, I didn't want to deal with it; I was at times angry about the intrusion into our space, but something deep within my soul pushed me to think beyond myself. I believed the Holy Spirit prompted this thinking. The Holy Spirit provides power and direction to believers. I use the term to reflect a God consciousness that can guide and provide assurance and fulfills desires. In addition, being knowledgeable of interpersonal and family communication, I took notice of the extended family participants' behaviors, I recognized my feelings of frustration, and I took action on what I realized in this extended family—an opportunity afforded by being in the Horn of Africa. As I reflected on the non-compliant behaviors of extended family members and the spiritual prompting, I thought about other Ethiopian culture traditions that I had reservations in performing initially (e.g., using my fingers to eat food with others from the same plate or participating in coffee ceremonies), but I eventually saw the behaviors as acts of love and community. The cultural tradition that came to mind and seemed appropriate to help with the extended family issues was the concept of *gursha*. It was settled in my spirit/soul: *try this new thing*. *Gursha* in Ethiopian culture is a friendly, communal gesture of sharing food by feeding the other with your hands. "If someone asks you to join them for a meal, accept their offer or take a little food to thank them for the gesture....simply refusing is considered rude. When your hosts raise handfuls of food to your mouth, this is a sign of respect and friendship known as *gursha* and you should accept the favour, being careful not to bite their fingers in the process" (Tilahun & Snow, 1996, p. 36-37).

I saw the fictive kin as a co-created and innovative community who accepted my invitation to participate in an event in which they could partake and offer advice (i.e., morsels of food) into the heart and mind of those present (i.e., around the table). All present were willing to *eat* (i.e., talk, discuss) even if occasionally there was a *bite* (some information that was stinging or challenging). Routine family meetings or *gursha* became a strategy to share concerns. The Appendix provides the sequence or steps of the *gursha* model. Each round represents each family member speaking about the person or the situation.

In the gursha model, we routinely brought issues and discussion topics to the small adult group (3-4 family members). A journal entry on February 2, 2004 stated:

> through weekly interactions in the home, we formed the ability to talk about crucial subjects that mattered—lifted facade— darkness and came to light. In this instance only two of the three teachers were present. Both women (older sister and aunt) were typically verbal and seemed to value our family context and the feedback we shared about a range of topics. Our personalities were generally extroverted and the communication behaviors seemed to range from low talkers to very high. With my husband being the only male, he would be perceived as more quiet (yet spontaneous); he seemed to enjoy our extended kin and their request for his input from time to time.

FAAEth's story and my commentary serve to get inside the manifestation of extended family values of harmony, unity and understanding through communication. It was necessary to enact some process if we were going to be successful in our family space. There is work to do, and it is largely communicative responses to the complexity of individuals, events, and behaviors that coalesce into family.

CONCLUSION

Utilizing the analytical perspective of autoethnography, the author's African American extended family heritage and immersion in an Ethiopian culture were explored to provide insights into the characteristics and meanings of extended family and resultant communication in Black societies. I organized the three stories under two major themes as reflected in the interviewees' stories and the author's commentary. The conclusion explicitly answers questions raised in the study and offers insight into future research.

First, the stories support what we already know about extended Black families. Extended Black families function to provide support, materially, emotionally, and relationally (e.g., Boyd-Franklin, 2003; Hill, 1993; Martin & Martin, 1978). In addition, this research shows that the extended family offers actual and/or perceived *moreness*: more people; more risks; more good and/or bad experiences. The experiences with *moreness* translate into the subjects' continuum of good, indifferent, to bad evaluations within extended families (e.g., Powell, 1998). For example, all of the families showed risk-taking: FAAGa's merger with her mother during a failing marriage; MAAOh's African American College Club (*look inside and outside of family-into community to build-create a much larger family*); and FAA-Eth's challenge to the assumptions of the household. The extended family stories reveal an unconscious to conscious valuing of the extended family. It should not be automatically assumed that family members themselves value the extended family experiences. Future research is recommended to identify the proportion of risks and negative and positive experiences that yield the assessments of harmony or unity. The challenge for researchers is to illuminate the holistic reality of Black extended families (Hill, 1993).

Next, the Black extended families demonstrate that the communication purposes or goals are varied. Communication that sought help, expressed emotions, offered reassurance, problem-solved, confronted, educated are all represented in the stories. For example, in the self-ascribed, co-constructed or innovative African American extended family models as reflected in MAAGa's and FAAEh's stories, the communication purposes were to understand the need to educate and organize for desired outcomes and to problem-solve. As an adopted family member of his grandparents, MAAGa is passing on (explaining and enacting) the cultural values of the extended family for this purpose. MAAOh's African American College Club is designed to teach and mentor minority youth who have been isolated (from educational opportunities and supportive agents) to desire and work to achieve educational and economic goals. The required planning, organization, and purpose of such a model reminds me of the African concept of hometown associations. Abbott's (2006) analysis of the origin and purposes of Nigerian hometown associations within Africa and North America point to economic, affiliative, and cultural needs as primary reasons for their development. Even though the appearance or structure harkened to the traditional African system of sharing and support (e.g., "age grade associations, work bees, kinship networks/corporate lineage, traditional councils, and other patterns of associational life," p. 147), the organized manifestations ("written constitution, roster of elected officials," p. 146) developed in response to the prejudiced and colonial environments.

Abbot offers five crucial elements of the Nigerian context. The one closely resembling the extended family focus is element number four: "urban migrants relied on kin networks, hometown associations, and co-ethnics for mutual aid—strangers-quarter (*sabon gari*) system promoted residential segregation and isolation" (p. 148). The communicative *gursha* model proposes that all members come to the environment to share in the topic and offer their ideas and insights on the topic with the direction of the Home Lead present and instrumental in providing guidance. Future research might address which members are instrumental in creating the ascribed, co-constructed or innovative (i.e., non-biological) extended family and how is that instrumentality manifested?

Finally, all of the extended family stories reflected beliefs and ideas that value harmony, unity and understanding: FAAGa weighed the happiness of her children against her own and decided to leave her children with her mother for the next 10 years; MAAOh told their children to not return home once they leave, with the understanding that they could come back whenever a real need arose; and FAAEth's complaint and the communication knowledge and spiritual insight of the female household Lead created *gursha* conversation rounds that maintained the fictive kin network. An exciting prospect for future research is the diversity of communication methods that everyday families can create to problem-solve family issues. What are the family issues that can benefit from this type of model?

The value of *passing on* is perhaps the overarching and most stable or enduring aspect of Black or African extended families, while the people come and go. *Passing on* care, struggle over disintegration, problem-solving (i.e., support, harmony, unity, and understanding), education, parental and ancestral involvement were evident in the extended family stories. The diverse voices that pass on these goals and values might be tentative, philosophical, confrontative, or passionate. Living with and interviewing these diverse voices helped me to be more caring and to be more committed to *passing on*.

Note

Nia is one of the seven Nguzo Saba social and spiritual principles which was conceived and developed by Dr. Maulana Ron Karenga. "The Nguzo Saba responds to current needs which can be the method used by Blacks to solve the problems on every level which confronts us as a people. Thus, the Nguzo Saba are social and spiritual principles, dealing with ways for us to relate to each other and rebuild our lives in our own images" (Karenga, 1977).

References

A Raisin in the Sun. BookRags. BookRags Book Notes. [World Wide Web]. Retrieved February 27, 2008, from the http://www.bookrags.com/notes/rai/

Abbott, C. W. (2006). Nigerians in North America: New Frontiers, Old Associations? In Konadu-Agyemang, B. K. Takyi, & J. Arthur (Eds.) *The New African Diaspora in North America: Trends, Community Building, and Adaptation* (pp.141-165). Lanham, MD: Lexington Books.

Alexander, A. L. (2001). Regulars at the Hole in the Wall: An Ethnographic Study of a Self-Defined Family at a Local bar. Paper Presented at the National Communication Association Conference, Atlanta, GA.

Atkinson, P. (2006). Rescuing Autoethnography. *Journal of Contemporary Ethnography, 35*(4), 400-404.

Anderson, L. (2006). Analytic Autoethnography. *Journal of Contemporary Ethnography, 35*(4), 373-395.

Asante, M.K. (1981). Intercultural Communication: An Inquiry into Research Directions. In D. Nimmo (Ed.) *Communication Yearbook 4* (pp. 401-410). New Brunswick, NJ: Transaction Books.

Asante, M.K. (1988). *Afrocentricity* (Rev. ed.). Trenton, NJ: Africa World Press.

Bhalla, N. (2002, September 5). Ethiopia's elderly on the streets [Electronic version]. Retrieved September 14, 2004, from http://news.bbc.co.uk/2/low/africa/2236683.stm

Billingsley, A. (1968). *Black Families in White America.* New York: Touchstone Book.

Billingsley, A. (1992). *Climbing Jacob's Ladder: the Enduring Legacy of African-American Families.* New York: Simon & Schuster.

Boyd-Franklin, N. (2003). *Black Families in Therapy: Understanding the African-American Experience.* New York: The Guilford Press.

Brilhart, J. K., G. Galanes, & K. Adams, K. (2001). *Effective Group Discussion.* Boston, MA: McGraw Hill.

Clark, K. & R. C. Diggs (2002). Connected or Separated?: Towards a Dialectical View of Interethnic Relationships. In T. A. McDonald, M. Orbe & T. Ford-Ahmed (Eds.) *Building Diverse Communities: Applications of Communication Research.* Creskill, NJ: Hampton Press.

Crawford, L. (1996). Personal Ethnography. *Communication Monographs, 63,* 158-170.

Crouch, J. (1994). "Traditional" or not, real families are under attack from right and left. Retrieved 10 June 2005 from the World Wide Web. http://patriot.net/~crouch/artj/family.html.

Diggs, R. C., & K. D. Clark. (2002). It's a Struggle but Worth it: Identifying and Managing Identities in an Interracial Friendship. *Communication Quarterly,* 50(3/4, Summer/Fall), 368-390

Diggs, R. C., & T. J. Socha. (2004). Communication, Families, and Exploring the Boundaries of Diversity. In A. Vangelisti (Ed.) *Handbook of Family Communication*. Mahwah, NJ: Lawrence Erlbaum.

Dilworth-Anderson, P., & P. Y. Goodwin. (2005). A Model of Extended Family Support: Care of the Elderly in African American Families. In V. C. McLoyd, N. E. Hill, & K. E. Dodge (Eds.) *African American Family life: Ecological and Cultural Diversity* (pp. 211-223). Guilford Press: NY.

Ellis, C. S., & A. P. Bochner. (2006). Analyzing Autoethnography: An Autopsy. *Journal* of Contemporary Ethnography, 35(4), 429-449.

Family life in Ethiopia (2004). [Electronic version]. Retrieved September 14, 2004, from http://www.settlement.org/cp/english/ethiopia/.

Galvin, K. M., & B. J. Brommel. (1996). *Family Communication: Cohesion and Change* (4th ed.). New York: HarperCollins.

Hess, R. D., & G. Handel, (1967). The Family as a Psychosocial Organization. In G. Handel (Ed.) *The psychosocial interior of the family* (pp. 10-24). Chicago: Aldine.

Hill, R. B. (1993). *Research on the African American Family: A Holistic Perspective*. Westport, CT: Greenwood Publishing Group

Hilliard, A.G. (1995). *The Maroon Within Us: Selected Essays on African American Community Socialization*. Baltimore, MD: Black Classic Press.

Holt, N. L. (2003). Representation, Legitimation, and Autoethnography: An Autoethnographic Writing Story. [Electronic Version]. *International Journal of Qualitative Methods*, 2(1). Article 2. Retrieved March 30, 2004, from http://www.ualberta.ca/~iiqm/backissues/ 2_1final/html/holt.html

Karenga, M. (1977). Nguzo Saba. Retrieved March 3, 2001, from http://melanet.com/kwanza/principles.html

Karenga, M. (2001, October). Featured Speaker. Presented at the 13th Annual Cheikh Anta Diop International Conference, Philadelphia, PA.

Karenga, M. (2002, October). Khun-Anpu's *Maat* and Plato's *Dikaiosynê* Concepts of Justice in Ancient Egypt and Greece. Presented at the 14th Annual Cheikh Anta Diop International Conference, Philadelphia, PA.

Kunjufu, J. (1989). *Critical Issues in Educating Black Youth*. Chicago: African American Images.

Martin, E. P. & J. M. Martin (1978). *The Black Extended Family*. Chicago: University of Chicago Press.

Myers, L. J. (1993). *Understanding an Afrocentric Worldview: Introduction to an Optimal Psychology* (2nd ed.). Dubuque, IA: Kendall/Hunt.

Myers, L. J. (1998). The Deep Structure of Culture: Relevance of Traditional African Culture in Contemporary life. In J. D. Hamlet (Ed.) *Afrocentric Visions: Studies in Culture and Communication* (pp. 3-25). Thousand Oaks, CA: Sage.

Nobles, W. W. (1998). To Be African or Not to Be: The Question of Identity or Authenticity—Some Preliminary Thoughts. In R. L. Jones (Ed.) *African American Identity Development* (pp. 185-206). Hampton, VA: Cobb & Henry.

Peters, R. E., & M. S. Haney (Eds.) (2006). *Africentric Approaches to Christian Ministry: Strengthening Urban Congregations in African American Communities.* Lanham, MD: University Press of America, Inc.

Pinderhughes, E. B. (2002). African American Marriage in the 20th Century. Family Process, 41(2) 269-282.

Powell, K. (1998). *Keepin It Real: Post-MTV Reflections on Race, Sex, and Politics.* New York: Ballantine Books. Retrieved January 8, 2008, from African American Literature Book Club, http://aalbc.com/authors/kevin.htm

Rogers, L. E. (2001). Relational Communication in the Context of Family. *Journal of Family Communication, 1*, 25-36.

Segrin, C., & Flora, J. (2005). *Family Communication.* Mahwah, NJ: Lawrence Erlbaum.

Smith, J. W. (1998). Culture, Communication, and Afrocentrism: Some Rhetorical Implications of a New World Order. In J. D. Hamlet (Ed.) *Afrocentric Visions: Studies in Culture and Communication* (pp. 107-117). Thousand Oaks, CA: Sage.

Stewart, C. F., III. (1999). *Black Spirituality and Black Consciousness.* Trenton, NJ : Africa World Press, 1999.

Sudarkasa, N. (1996). *The Strength of Our Mothers, African and African American Women and Families: Essays and Speeches.* Trenton, NJ: Africa World Press.

Tilahun, K. G. & , C. Snow (1996). *Ethiopian Amharic Phrasebook.* Lonely Planet: Oakland, CA.

Turner, L. H., & R. West, (1998). *Perspectives on Family Communication.* Mountain View, CA: Mayfield.

Appendix: Conceptualized in Addis Ababa, Ethiopia, January 25, 2004 Gursha Model of Small Group Family Communication

1. Round One: Say the most positive and negative comments about the other/situation.
   Rationale: Balance/harmony/Self-esteem/Sensitivity-Caring

2. Round Two: Offer each person the opportunity to give a self-evaluation of their most positive and negative (if relevant).
   Rationale: Voice/Empowerment; Self Esteem

3. Round Three: Offer information that could minimize the negative.
   Rationale: Balance/harmony; Self Esteem

4. Round Four: Offer a challenge to what was said about you/situation.
   Rationale: Voice/Empowerment/Self-Esteem

5. Close

CHAPTER *10*

WOMEN, PATRILATERAL KINSHIP, AND THE FAMILY COMPOUND AMONG THE RURAL GULLAH

Bamidele Agbasegbe Demerson

INTRODUCTION

In societies across Africa and in many communities throughout the African disapora, *the family* is often a multigenerational group of close kinspersons living together in a cluster or set of adjacent households called the compound. Consanguineal relationships constitute "the ties that bind" the members of such a family together. That is to say, the family compound is built around a core of "blood" related persons. The land on which the set of households is established, moreover, is frequently owned collectively by an even larger body of "blood" relatives, many (if not most) of whom do not reside in the family compound setting.

An intriguing ethnographic case study of an African American population is that of the people who live in rural communities on the chain of low-lying Sea Islands that fringe the coastal plain of South Carolina, Georgia, and northeast Florida (Demerson, 1973; Demerson, 1991).[1] Known by the African derived ethnic designations Gullah and Geechee (Turner, 1949, p. 194), their families also co-reside in compounds. What social and economic factors led to the development of these compounds in the Sea Islands? Moreover, is there a recognizable African cultural heritage in Gullah family life? This latter query is difficult to ignore given that numerous scholars have documented a vibrant African heritage in both material and non-material aspects of Gullah culture (Jackson, Slaughter, & Blake, 1974; Pollitzer, 1999; Twining & Baird, 1991a).

This modest contribution toward understanding social organization in the Sea Islands offers a four-part focus. The first entails a review of pertinent notes on the history and socioeconomic character of the ethnographic setting. The second, based on observations from Wadmalaw Island and other isles in Charleston County, South Carolina, includes a description of family compounds rooted in: patrilateral kinship (i.e. ties traced through the father), a post-nuptial residence pattern that is virilocal (i.e. with the family of the husband), and the joint ownership of land by consanguines. The third provides an examination of women in their roles as wives and mothers in one family compound, and daughters and sisters in yet another. And the fourth outlines some of the implications of the ethnographic data for explaining the African cultural heritage in Gullah family life. This is followed by some concluding questions on families as agents of economic growth and development in Sea Island communities.

A BRIEF SOCIOECONOMIC HISTORY OF THE SEA ISLANDS

One hundred or more Sea Islands buffer the coastline of southeastern United States from the force of the Atlantic Ocean. Readily described as a picturesque subtropical region, the landscape features lush verdant flora dominated by moss draped trees, winding waterways, boggy marshes, and abundant wildlife. On the Atlantic front of the isles, sandy beaches stretch as far as the eye can see. But the scenic environment harbors a saga that is more compelling than its apparent beauty. In centuries past, many captive Africans who endured the horrific voyages across the ocean in the dank dark holds of ships, found themselves enslaved on these islands. Without bridges and ferry services to the mainland, the region, also feared for its malaria, remained remote. And due to its physical geographic isolation, as late as 1858—three years before the beginning of the Civil War—a cargo of fettered humans were surreptitiously offloaded here (Calonius, 2006). This occurred despite the 1808 congressional ban on the importation of captives to the United States directly from the continent of Africa. Thus it should hardly be surprising that scholars would discern distinctive Gullah cultural practices grounded in ancient traditions of peoples from the continent of Africa. Certainly nineteenth century arrivals would have enriched an African-derived folklife that had already begun the process of creolization.

Before the Civil War, enslaved men and women developed the reputation of the Sea Islands as a major agricultural area for the growth of livestock and especially selected crops. The rice grown in the region, for example, achieved distinction as a staple. Sea Island cotton enriched the coffers of planters whose numerous bales supplied the textile mills of Europe. And manufactures prized the locally produced indigo for its blue dye. The cultivation of these and other plants, well known in Africa, were expertly grown by Gullah men and women who gained their knowledge from their forebears. Following the demise of slavery, many Sea Islanders tilled the soil primarily as subsistence cultivators, with some of their crops marketed to support their domestic groups. The same may be said for their descendants, who during and since the late twentieth century continue the use of preindustrial cultivation techniques to plant, grow, and harvest peanuts, tomatoes, cucumbers, snap beans, corn, potatoes, and other truck crops. While some small scale farmers market their agricultural yield, many more gardeners grow vegetables and fruits for domestic consumption. In an effort to increase their bounty, on some islands, Gullah landowners form cooperatives to acquire access to expensive tractors and other equipment like that used by large scale mechanized commercial farms owned by European Americans.

Besides subsistence cultivation and animal husbandry, many Sea Islanders support themselves and their families with fishing, shrimping, and harvesting oysters. Such efforts may be full-time or part-time pursuits. Others however, establish small businesses such as grocery stores, restaurants, service stations, and night clubs as places of employment for themselves and members of their families. Many Sea Island women are competent at sewing. In some localities elderly women form quilting cooperatives to create and market bedcovers locally, as well as by mail order. On those islands where military installations, hotels, and tourist attractions have made significant inroads, Gullah men and women procure employment in a range of related service industries. But Sea Islanders, sometimes seeing the limited employment opportunities in their communities, are increasingly pulled into the orbit of neighboring mainland urban centers. Some commute to work in the cities as professionals—e.g., as educators and nurses. However, far more commuters find employment as domestics and unskilled laborers. This fact is correlated with lower educational levels of the black population, and predictably, lower incomes to support families.

The constraining socioeconomic reality, since the early twentieth century, has served as an impetus for some to relocate to cities across the country to find employment (Kiser, 1932). Often parents must leave their young children in the care of grandparents, uncles, and aunts. And while the outmigration brings with it periodic remittances to the family compound, the situation is far from ideal. Some families even become unwitting participants in fierce competitions with land developers who use legal and extralegal means that continue to erode black property ownership in the Sea Islands (Agbasegbe, 1978; Demerson, 1991, p. 77; Moore & Washington, 1970; Thomas, 1977, 1978, 1980). Thus, against a backdrop of the natural beauty of the Sea Islands environment is the saga of a determined people struggling throughout history against formidable social and economic forces. Yet the people of the Sea Islands endure with a sense of pride, strength, and optimism. In part this is because their families—based in compounds—offer encouragement, as well as provide some measure of social and financial security. Indeed, Gullah family compounds function as bulwarks in a world that is all too often precarious.

PATRILATERAL KINSHIP AND THE FAMILY COMPOUND

On Wadmalaw and nearby islands, many neighborhoods bear the names of antebellum era plantations. Within the perimeters of these once thriving agricultural estates, one encounters footpaths and roads that lead to clusters of households, sometimes numbering as many as eight. Thus in this community, people are born and reared in family compounds that transcend the definition of *the family* as simply a unit comprised of a married pair and their children. This is not to say that households structured around a conjugal pair are not significant. Indeed, the union between a man and a woman, idealized as enduring until the death of one of the spouses, appears to be a reality for most couples. But among the Gullah, the conjugal bond is not the core of *the family*, a kin group that resides in a multi-household compound. Rather *the family*—i.e. the compound—is built around a core of adult household heads, usually male, who share bonds of patrilateral kinship. That is to say, members of this core generally trace a "blood" connection to each other through a line of fathers back to the original title holder of the land on which the compound is established. Of this patrilaterally related core group, the eldest male usually serves as the head of the family compound. (See: Figure 10.1, Table 10.1, and Table 10.2.) It should also be noted that Sea Islanders do recognize ties of bilateral kinship, and thereby embrace genealogical connectedness to the relatives of one's mother, as well as those of one's father. Yet they place greater emphasis on "blood" connections reckoned through the father's side. The development and persistence of the family compound is linked to three key factors: collective landownership, "blood" kinship, and post-nuptial residence norms.

Figure 10.1. The Smiths: Genealogy and Family Compound

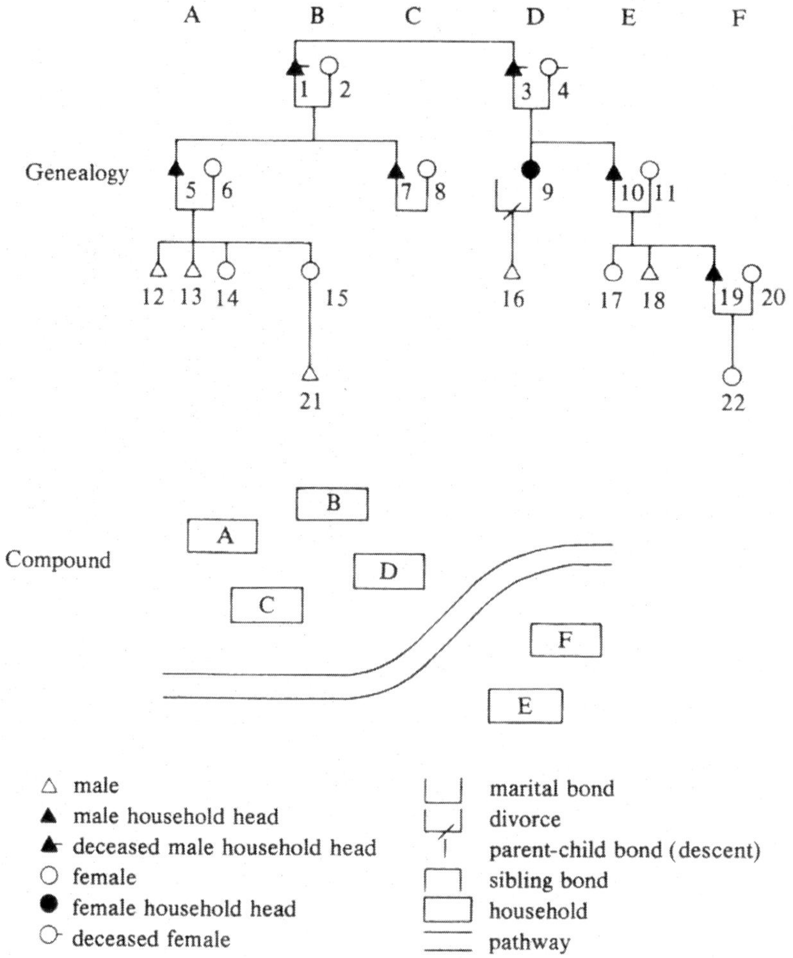

Genealogy

Compound

△ male
▲ male household head
◣ deceased male household head
○ female
● female household head
◐ deceased female

⊔ marital bond
⊿ divorce
⌐ parent-child bond (descent)
⊓ sibling bond
▭ household
═ pathway

The genealogy is a partial one in that only co-resident members are depicted. (Of course deceased persons, whose inclusion is necessary for a comprehension of the genealogical connections among co-resident members, are illustrated.) Thus those males and females who have migrated to other locales, and those females who have moved to the compounds of their husbands, are not represented here. It may be further noted that siblings are not always presented in order of seniority based on age.

Table 10.1. Household Compositions in the Smith Compound

Household	Head	Members (and relation to head of household)
A	5	6 (wife); 12, 13 (sons); 14 (daughter)
B	5	2 (mother); 15 (daughter); 21 (grandson)
C	7	8 (wife)
D	9	16 (son)
E	10	11 (wife); 17 (daughter); 18 (son)
F	19	20 (wife); 22 (daughter)

Table 10.2. Some Observations about the Smith Family Compound

Census	The Smith family compound—comprised of nineteen members who co-reside in a set of six households—spans four generations.
Consanguineal Core	The family compound is built around a paternally linked consanguineal core. This core includes: four males 5, 7, 10, and 19; and one female, a divorcee 9, who lives in household built by her parents (now deceased). Each member of this core is a head of household. (The shaded triangles and circle denote male and female heads of households.)
Generation #1 Household Heads	Two deceased brothers, 1 and 3, owned the land on which the Smith family compound is established. They constitute the consanguines in generation #1.
Generation #2 Household Heads	Brothers 5 and 7 are the adult offspring of 1. And sister and brother, 9 and 10 are the adult children of 3. The two sets of siblings, paternal first cousins, belong to generation #2.
Generation #3 Household Head	In generation #3 is 19, a young married adult and head of household. His father and paternal grandfather are respectively 10 and 3.
In-marrying Wives	The in-marrying wives of the family compound include: 2 and 4 (deceased) in generation #1; 6, 8, and 11 in generation #2; and 20 in generation #3. Their post-nuptial residence may be characterized as virilocal.

Non-paternally Related Males	Adult male heads of household are usually "recruited" as core members of the family compound *via* paternal kin linkages. There are exceptions to this pattern. The son born to an unwed mother is one case in point. When 21 becomes a married adult, he too may establish a household in the natal compound of his mother, 15. It is also possible that the continued residential affiliation with the Smiths will accrue to 16 when a married adult, by way of his mother, 9, who rejoined her natal compound following her divorce.
Dual Household Headship	Sometimes, a person might simultaneously function as the head of more than one household. The head of household A, 5, has also assumed most of the duties of headship for household B. For a while household B was occupied by an elderly widow. The movement of 15, a teenage mother, and her son, 21, from household A to household B served a two-fold function. First, it relieved the overcrowding of household A. Second, it provided someone who could monitor and assist the eldest resident in the Smith family compound.

The landholding histories of Gullah "blood" related kin groups has yet to be fully researched. But remarkably for some, landownership dates back to the period of the Civil War when federal occupation of a number of Sea Islands resulted in the liberation of those held in bonded servitude. Some ex-bondsmen—whether as individuals or as an association (presumably composed of "blood" relations and close friends)—started purchasing land, or perhaps more precisely, parcels of estates abandoned by planters fleeing the conflict. This redistribution of land *via* the Freedmen's Bureau, Direct Tax Act of 1861, and the South Carolina Land Commission was a bold experiment. The objective was to ascertain the extent to which the formerly enslaved population had the capacity to become landowners and develop a stable community and family life that apparently mirrored norms of the dominant sector of society. Thus in the months preceding the Reconstruction Era, some Gullah men were free proud landholders. (See: Abbott, 1967; Agbasegbe, 1977; Bleser, 1969; Hoffman, 1956; Pease & Pease, 1963; Rose, 1964; Verney, 1983.) During the latter part of the nineteenth century, others not so fortunate had tenant farming as their only option (Blackman, 1880; Lander, 1960). Over the ensuing decades, well into the twentieth century, African American Sea Islanders attempting to remove themselves from the constraints of tenant farming would save to buy property once worked by their enslaved ancestors. And hardly surprising, kinspersons frequently purchased parcels of land near, if not adjacent to each other.

When present day Sea Islanders from Wadmalaw speak of earlier generations, they note that their forbears worked tirelessly to purchase land, particularly with the intention of passing it on to their descendants. The original titleholder of a parcel of land would build a house for himself, his wife, and their children. As his children became adults, they married. However, newlyweds generally did not establish neolocal or independent households. The married sons would build homes on their father's land in close proximity to his house. Repeated over the course of a few decades, a patrikin based compound might grow to include as many as four generations living together in several households. Of course whenever daughters married, they left their natal compound and moved to live with their husbands in houses built in the family compounds of their affines, i.e. in-laws. Hence a virilocal post-nuptial residence is a normative pattern in Gullah communities.

In some cases, a couple lives among the paternally related kinsfolk of the wife. When this occurs, the husband is "off island"—a Gullah term for residents and visitors not from the region. As such, the husband has no family relations nearby. But even when the husband is from a Gullah neighborhood, at times social and economic circumstances may dictate that a couple occupies a vacant house within the natal compound of the wife's paternal kin. This residence is usually a temporary one until the couple builds a house on the grounds of the husband's patrilateral kin based compound. Of course, sometimes a couple has saved money for several years in order to establish a household apart from the natal compounds of either spouse. Depending on the size of the plot(s) of land owned by this couple, predictably their residence over a period of time would become a multigenerational compound comprised of several households grounded in patrilateral kinship and a pattern of virilocal post-nuptial residence.

The death of the original titleholder of a plot of land would not necessarily entail subdivision of the estate. Indeed in Gullah communities, men and women rarely make wills to stipulate the disposition of their moveable and immoveable properties. This means that land more frequently than not, passes from one generation to the next by intestacy. And the tract(s) on which a family compound is established, thereby becomes heirs' property that could presumably pass to all descendants of the original title holder. However, not all descendants will come forward to press their claims to landownership, especially since that means assuming responsibility for the payment of property taxes. A married woman's children, for example, may feel a greater sense of responsibility regarding the patrimony of their father and his partrikin. And the task of paying such taxes is usually narrowed to the patrilateral core group occupying a compound.

Such *de facto* land tenure practices, part of Gullah folk traditions, have apparently worked well for many generations. However, contemporary Sea Island families face challenges regarding their property because time honored folk traditions do not carry the weight of law. In the clash between *de facto* and *de jure* perspectives, developers and their attorneys have succeeded all too frequently in forcing sales of tracts designated as heirs' property. And while organizations offering legal assistance have attempted to impress upon Sea Islanders the importance of writing wills, their triumphs have been limited. Of course, some Sea Islanders lack the financial resources to pay the stipulated property taxes. In other cases, a family member or group of kinspersons decides that selling land, or some portion thereof, will ease impoverishment. Not surprisingly, the expropriation of black family owned land in the Sea Islands continues. (Agbasegbe, 1978; Demerson, 1991, p. 77; Thomas 1977, 1978, 1980).

Whatever the social, economic, and legal hardships the Gullah face, no one confronts challenges alone. Thus while their households have varying degrees of financial self sufficiency, these units, as part of a compound, function interdependently to fulfill the functions of *the family*, including among others: sharing and management of financial resources, procurement and distribution of food, care of the infirm and elderly, and socialization of the young. Reciprocity is valued and cultivated every day through the exchange of goods, services, and monetary gifts. Many households within the compound include a married pair and their offspring. But this is not a rigid pattern, especially because the composition of a household will shift over time due to marriage, infirmity, death, divorce, outmigration, and the informal fosterage of minors. Therefore the occupancy of a household includes numerous modal configurations: sometimes one person who may be widowed or divorced; commonly a married couple and their children; recurrently a married couple, their children, and other relatives; and repeatedly consanguines of different generations (for example an aging parent with an adult child as primary caregiver, or a widowed grandparent with grandchildren, or an uncle and nephew).

Without question, the men, women, and children who live together in a family compound have rights, roles, and relationships beyond the individual households in which they sleep. These rights, roles, and relationships are shaped by many variables, including for example: "blood" kinship, household headship, age, longevity of marriage to a member of the consanguineal core, level of education, financial standing, and position of responsibility within a spiritual or faith-based community. Residents of the compound are involved in a constant face-to-face interaction with each other. For example, a man may sleep in one household with his wife and children, take evening meals regularly in a unit occupied by his elderly parents, and contribute financially to the home of a sibling who has difficulty in procuring steady employment. Moreover, this man—in accordance with Gullah expectations of behavior—instructs, advises, praises, and disciplines not only his children, but all minors in the constituent households of the family compound. Suffice it to say, he plays some role in the developmental histories of these households. But whatever the developmental histories of such households, it must be remembered that these units exist within a compound that has evolved in relation to folk land tenure practices, patrilateral kinship, and a pattern of virilocal post-nuptial residence. All this has distinctive dynamics for males and females.

WIVES, MOTHERS, DAUGHTERS, AND SISTERS

The family in the Sea Islands is in effect a multigenerational compound comprising several households. This co-residing group, moreover, fosters, strengthens, and reflects the solidarity of consanguines, especially adult males, but also males and females of the same generation. It is within the compound that a man first seeks: assistance in activities such as farming or gardening, or perhaps repairing a house or car; advice regarding domestic problems; information about new employment prospects, a business venture, or current events; a small scale loan; or partners for recreational activities. The right to build a house or use land to farm is extended to males and females born into the family compound. But by virtue of their co-residence, adult male household heads have activated their rights to establish and maintain households on land belonging to their patrilateral kin group. Furthermore, their rights to land use are particularly visible in cases where men support their households *via* the farming and marketing of truck crops. Thus in Gullah traditions, a male appears to be intensely involved in the affairs of his patrikin based compound throughout his life cycle. But a female will be significantly involved in two: the natal compound of her father's kinsfolk and that of her husband (Agbasegbe, 1976b).

Wedding vows among Sea Islanders—whether exchanged at home, in church, or in a civil setting—are undertaken with the idea of marital permanency. This is also true of those older couples who created "common law" unions. Wherever and however contracted, what is important is the acceptance of these marriages by the kinsfolk of the spouses, and recognition of these matrimonial bonds by the community. In a closely knit Sea Island community such as Wadmalaw, a bride is likely to know her in-laws very well, long before the exchange of nuptial vows. Understandably, she is expected to quickly establish a rapport with the members of her husband's compound, especially his parents. This rapport also includes according respect to the elders in her new domestic setting as she would in her natal compound. As a bride, she certainly focuses her early activities on setting up a comfortable household among her in-laws. And a few months following the wedding, family, friends, and the wider community eagerly anticipate that the newlyweds will announce their expectant parenthood.

Men often express that it is their duty to provide shelter, food, and clothing for their wives and children. In reality, most Sea Island women work for remuneration and thereby substantially contribute to the maintenance and improvement of their domiciles. They use their monies moreover, to care for their offspring and themselves. This is part of being a "good" (i.e. industrious and resourceful) wife and mother. Wives strategize with their husbands on how best to share in meeting the financial needs of their households. Even as this financial collaboration is a reality, women and men also maintain separate "purses" and "wallets" for their personal needs. Equally significant, one spouse is expected not to encumber a small business venture that belongs to the other. Hence "separate ownership" of such commercial undertakings is also a "characteristic" phenomenon among some couples (Moerman, 1974, p. 97-99).

While a wife is well aware that marriage is certainly a commitment to her spouse, she also understands that virilocal residence entails obligations to the members of the family compound of her husband. Indeed, a woman's contributions to the social and economic well being of her in-laws includes cooperatively assisting (and at times taking the lead) in caring for children, i.e. babysitting while a sister-in-law is at work outside the home, counseling youth on expected behavior, and fostering minor relatives whose parents have migrated, divorced, or died. A daughter-in-law may prepare meals or serve as one of the care givers for the sick and aged parents of her husband. With other adult women—those born, as well as married into the compound—a wife plays her role in preparing for, and if necessary, contributing to the expenses of rituals such as wedding celebrations, graduation fetes, school and church programs, family reunions, and funerals. And as an in-law, a woman may also be expected to work in, or lend assistance to the operation of a small business operated by members of her husband's kin. Marriage and residence in the compound of her husband does not extinguish a woman's responsibilities to her natal patrikin group. Thus the services and financial support she gives her affines is also expected to be provided to her natal compound when needed.

The normative behavior exhibited by the wife in Gullah communities is observed and learned at an early age. That is to say a young girl reared in a patrilateral kin based family compound witnesses the conduct of her mother, as well as that of the wives of her paternal uncles, older brothers, and cousins who married into her natal residence. As a fully socialized adult, the new wife emulates what she has learned over the course of her childhood and youth. She has learned that respect and cooperation must govern interpersonal relations between family members, inclusive of in-laws. Although at times disagreements arise, the overall interaction between women who belong to the same compound—whether by birth or by marriage—appears to be warm and embracing. They after all, depend on each other for the social well being of the compound in which they reside together. Suffice it to say, the acrimonious mother-in-law/daughter-in-law relationship, often projected as an expected syndrome in some sectors of American society, appears minimal in Gullah communities.

Monogamy, the marriage of one man to one woman, is the socially accepted practice in the Sea Islands. Yet some men fulfill facets of the husband/father role configuration in more than one household simultaneously. While tolerated, not everyone in Gullah communities expresses approval of either plural mating or plural marital-like arrangements that approximate in some very basic manner the tradition of polygyny (i.e. one man with two or more wives). In some cases the women sharing one man occupy the same domicile such that "one wife and her offspring live on one floor of the house, and another wife on the other. In other cases there might be a wall, with no door through, separating one wife's section of the dwelling from another's" (Twining & Baird, 1991b, p. 5). On Wadmalaw and other islands, a man may very well maintain plural domestic group affiliations with the women and their children residing in different family compounds. His officially recognized wife and children may live in a household established among his patrikin. However, the woman and children not resident with him may live in a house that she heads in her natal compound. Separated by their location in different family compounds, the women sharing one man appear not to have an apparent ongoing relationship as co-wives. But their children recognize that they are siblings. And dependent on their father's efforts, sons and daughters by different mothers may develop close bonds with each other.[2]

A monogamously married Gullah husband and wife expect their union to last until the death of one spouse or the other. This expectation is not realized by all. Divorces do occur and are also correlated with the presence of female headed households. In one case, a recently divorced woman remained with her two children in the domicile built by her ex-husband who migrated to New York. Although the principal wage earner for her household, she receives periodic remittances from her former spouse and some assistance from one of his kinsmen. In decision making for the household and socializing the children, the divorced mother also relies on her affines (Demerson, 1974, p. 1019-20). More often, a divorced mother relocates. It should not be forgotten that in Gullah communities, a woman—as a daughter and sister—has the right to establish a household in her natal compound and cultivate some portion of the land on which it is established. Not surprising is the case of a divorcee, who with her young son, returned to her patrikin group to live in a household once occupied by her deceased parents. In this setting they receive emotional, social, and monetary support, even though the household is financially self-reliant. The son continues to see his father and interacts with his paternal kin group. At the same time, he becomes more fully integrated into the kin group of his mother (Demerson, 1991, p. 73). As a sister, this mother can count on her brothers to also model the behavior of her son. And just as a divorced woman may return to her natal compound with her children, so too a young widow with offspring may do the same. In each case, disruption of the conjugal bond, whether by death or divorce, is cushioned by the presence of strong patrikin based family compounds whose households are profoundly interdependent.

Men, women, and children of Wadmalaw offer a demonstrable show of respect for, and deference to the elderly. This is especially the case with aged widows who—as mothers, grandmothers, and great-grandmothers— are the focus of constant attention and care. When a widow of advanced years can no longer adequately attend to the needs of herself and her home, her adult children meet to determine an effective, but least disruptive approach to guardianship. In some cases, they decide that one of her adult children or adult grandchildren must move in with her. And at other times, they reach a decision that it is best to move her into the house of one of her adult sons, who with his wife function as primary care givers.

Gullah communities, of course, are not monolithic in their ideas regarding the residential status of widows. In one locale south of Wadmalaw, women who had lived with their husbands for as long as thirty to fifty years, upon the deaths of their spouses, returned to the patrimonies they left as brides. (Moerman, 1974, p. 83). Although such widows had no rights to property in the compounds of their late husbands, not even *via* the filial relationship to their children, they could activate their access to land *via* their roles as daughters and sisters in their patrikin groups. Of course widows are not strangers to their natal families because they have been involved in the affairs of these compounds, even when their husbands were alive. And as they seek the social comfort and economic security of their patrikin groups, revelations that widows continue to draw support from their sons and daughters, and close affines should come as no surprise.

Whether widowed, divorced, or married, Gullah women conduct their lives within the contexts of two patrikin based family compounds: as wives and mothers in the affinal setting, and as daughters and sisters in the natal one. But Gullah men, although connected to their in-laws, nevertheless enact their roles as husbands, fathers, sons, and brothers primarily in the compounds of their birth. In rural Sea Island communities, *the family* is a multigenerational, multi-household compound shaped by patrilateral kinship, virilocal residence, and the joint ownership of land by consanguines. Such an ethnographic portrait significantly contrasts with that for urban European Americans who idealize *the family* as a husband/father, wife/mother, and their children living in a neolocal household apart (but not necessarily isolated) from other kinsfolk. Equally significant, the observation may be made that Gullah families, while possessing their own cultural distinctiveness, also present remarkable similarities to families in Africa and the African diaspora. However, the underlying reasons for this observation have yet to be fully explored.

THE AFRICAN CULTURAL HERITAGE

The Gullah people of the Sea Islands are the inheritors, bearers, and transformers of cultural traditions that have been shaped to a great extent by formidable social and economic forces. There is the legacy of the institution of slavery that lasted into the mid-1860s. In its aftermath, from the Reconstruction Era through the early decades of the 1900s, the "peculiar institution" revived itself as tenant farming. During the later twentieth century, Sea Islanders also saw a decline in farming for a livelihood. They witnessed limited employment opportunities on the islands and the correlated phenomenon of outmigration. And since the late 1950s, Gullah joint landholders have been engaged in a battle with developers intent on using legal and extralegal means to expropriate heirs' property in the region. With such a history of struggle against difficult circumstances, it would be all too easy to explain the development, structure, and functioning of Gullah family compounds as either coping mechanisms that emerge as reactions to a depressed environment, or socioeconomic adaptations that serve as responses to long-term impoverishment. While such explanations have to be examined, research investigations should not stop there. Given the ethnographic data from the Sea Islands (e.g. Demerson, 1991) and comparative studies of kinship and domestic groups in global black societies (see especially Sudarkasa, 1980, 1981, 1996; also Agbasegbe, 1976a; Herskovits, 1941, p. 167-206; Okediji, 1975; Shimkin, Shimkin,

& Frate, 1978; Shimkin & Uchendu, 1978), the researcher may very well hypothesize that multigenerational and multi-household Gullah family compounds reflect a resilient cultural heritage rooted in peoples of the African continent.

The phenomenon of residential clusters comprised of close "blood" kin, their in-marrying spouses, and their offspring forming multigenerational families has been documented for the peoples of Africa and the African diaspora over vast periods of time and across geographic locales. In precolonial and present day Africa, family compounds can be found in societies that trace kinship both patrilineally, i.e. through a line of fathers, and matrilineally, i.e. through a line of mothers (e.g. Fadipe, 1970; Fortes, 1950; Marshall, 1968). For the period of enslavement in North America, there is documentation of the presence of multi-household family groups within the confines of a single plantation, as well as kinship networks that stretched across the estates of several planters (see e.g. Gutman, 1976; Kilikoff, 1977; Webber, 1978, p. 111-17 & 157-79). And in twentieth century rural, urban, northern, and southern United States, residential propinquity—even in the absence of collective land ownership—is a verifiable characteristic of African American multigenerational families (see e.g. Aschenbrenner, 1975; Frazier, 1939; Martin & Martin, 1978; Shimkin, Shimkin, & Frate, 1978; Stack, 1974). Moreover, groupings of multiple domiciles functioning as one family has been described for peoples of African ancestry in Central America, South America, and the Caribbean (see e.g. Gonzalez, 1969; Kobben, 1973; Laguerre, 1978; Mintz & Price, 1977). The families in these societies and communities are hardly monolithic. These families in part reflect the unique sociopolitical history, set of economic opportunities and constraints, and other variables distinctive to each locale. Yet, there are notable similarities.

When captive Africans forcibly crossed the Atlantic Ocean in holds of ships, they were bound for enslavement in the Americas. Not recorded on the manifests of the seafaring vessels were the tremendous amounts of "cultural baggage" they brought with them. The memories of their parent societies packed in that baggage included among other things: ideas about kinship, family, and marriage; complex sets of rights and responsibilities attached to age, sex, marital status, and other markers of social differentiation; codes of behavior governing intra-familial relations; a profound respect for the elderly; an appreciation for land and its symbolic tie to the ancestors; values and world view; and other facets of life. Some of these memories of social life would become forgotten over time, others remembered very well, yet others recast in creolized forms.

Anthropologists familiar with ethnological reports as well as the research of historians offer useful insights and approaches to interpreting African cultural memories and their transformation throughout the Americas. In a survey of the studies on family life by historians of slavery in the United States, an Africanist anthropologist remarks that their scholarly writings "reveal the presence of African patterns in Afro-American consanguineal kin groupings ('kin networks'), husband-wife relations, sibling bonds, socialization practices, patterns of exogamy, marriage rules and rituals, naming practices, relationships between alternate generations (grandparents and grandchildren), patterns of respect and deference, and the extension of kinship terminology to elders throughout the community" (Sudarkasa, 1980, p. 54). Furthermore, a comparative examination of the anthropological and sociological literature on African and African American family structures and their principles of organization support the interpretation that "*after slavery*, when Black American extended family organization was not encumbered by ... restraints we find the reemergence of kinship groupings that exhibited many of their African antecedents" (Sudarkasa, 1980, p. 56). We need more Africanists to provide periodic reviews of both the growing literature on the history of slavery in the Sea Islands and the present day sociological scholarship on this region. From their reviews and assessments of such writings we should gain greater insights on the ways creolized values and traditions of the Asante, Yoruba, Bamileke, Kongo, Ovimbundu, and other peoples reveal an African presence in past and present day Gullah social organization.

Slavery would have rendered inoperative the direct transfer of many features of African social organization such as lineages—corporate descent groups through which one gained access to the use and inheritance of land, as well as succeeded to political and religious offices owned by or allocated to such entities. Even so, the assessment of the anthropologist familiar with the data on African and African American kinship and domestic groups imparts the view that "after slavery, some of the corporate functions of African lineages reemerged in some extended families which became property-owning collectives" (Sudarkasa, 1981, p. 48). This would certainly stand as a cogent assessment for the Gullah for whom real estate, over the course of generations, carries the designation of heirs' property.

Caribbeanist anthropologists studying societies whose black ancestors were once enslaved, have also emphasized that "one might well be surprised by the extent to which people may keep alive, even under conditions of extreme repression ... fundamental ideas about kinship ... widespread in West Africa" (Mintz & Price, 1977, p. 39). Thus in some areas of post-emancipation Jamaica: "Once individuals had gained access to land ownership, large kinship groups ... may have been built in at least some ways upon African models" (Mintz & Price, 1977, p. 39). These non-unilineal land-based groups had a resemblance to those of the Para region of Suriname, South America, where former captives linked through ties of kinship, communally purchased the plantations on which they were formerly enslaved (Mintz & Price, 1977, p. 36 & 39). During the period of slavery in Haiti, family compound-like settlements were also created by the captives (Laguerre, 1978, p. 440). And following the acquisition of land by the former captives during the early nineteenth century, in the evaluation of one anthropologist, "they developed—perhaps reinstituted—a kind of familial settlement similar to existing patterns in [the West African Fon communities of] Dahomey" (Laguerre, 1978, p. 441). Such family settlements exist in present day Haiti. Thus the phenomenon of property ownership by kin groups among post-emancipation peoples in South America and the Caribbean also parallels in some ways that observed in the Sea Islands among the Gullah.

The examination of Gullah family compounds with cross-cultural references to Africa, and as well communities in the African diaspora during slavery, in post-emancipation contexts, and in the present day, facilitates recognition of some of the similarities extant in the social organization of black societies. The comparisons within the global African world also serve to highlight apparent contrasts between the Gullah family compound built around a consanguineal core of paternally related adult males and the idealized European American family household based on a conjugal pair. Indeed, researchers must be aware that: "The implications of the operation of the principle of consanguinity in relation to that of conjugality must be fully explored before the dynamics of Afro-American families can be appreciated and their similarities to African families and differences from Euro-American families fully understood" (Sudarkasa, 1980, p. 54). Of course the structure and functioning of the Gullah family compound, a refuge during insecure times, does indeed represent an adaptation to the social and economic forces that have shaped it over time. But equally significant, the researcher must also collect ethnographic data, advance conceptual frameworks, and test theories regarding the ways a resilient African cultural heritage is part of Gullah domestic groups today. The value that Africans place on consanguinity as an organizing principle in family life is also reflected among the Gullah. This value on consanguinity moreover, would impact the development of the compound and post-nuptial residence observable in African American Sea Island communities.

Some Questions on Families and Development

The natural beauty of the Sea Islands contrasts with its hideous past defined by slavery. And even as the region continues to cast an alluring spell on the outsider, for many who live there, the difficulties of privation linger. Yet some island communities are undergoing urbanization, following the pathways of land developers, and participating in an ever burgeoning tourist industry. Such initiatives for the most part, are not conceived by, nor necessarily formulated in the best interests of African American Sea Islanders. These initiatives, presumed indicators of progress, may very well leave negative impacts on Gullah family life.

Black Sea Islanders must find ways that they—indeed their families—may become agents in planning for the economic growth and development of their communities. What roles might the Gullah family compound play in spurring entrepreneurial success stories in mechanized agricultural and fishing pursuits? What collaborative organizations, institutions, and governmental agencies may support such family efforts? Is there a place for Gullah families—the very repositories of Sea Island life and lore—in heritage tourism? What models of collective land ownership, compatible with Gullah values, can help to eliminate contemporary problems attendant with heirs' property? These questions and so many others need answers. As in years past, Sea Islanders still possess a "can do" spirit. And it is with self-determination and fortitude that Gullah families will not merely survive, but flourish in the future. Concerted planning is required. The future of families and communities must not be left to chance.

Notes

1.   The ethnographic portrait of Sea Island social organization presented here is based on anthropological fieldwork conducted during the spring and summer of 1971while resident on Wadmalaw Island in Charleston County, South Carolina. Visits to neighboring isles and those in other counties provided additional data. Dr. Niara Sudarkasa, under the auspices of the Center for Afro-American and African Studies at The University of Michigan, directed the research efforts. Her insights on African and African American social organization (Sudarkasa, 1975, 1980, 1981, 1996) have significantly informed the perspectives of the author on Gullah kinship and family compounds.

     This discussion summarizes and updates information on Sea Island family life presented in the author's published and unpublished reports (Agbasegbe [Demerson], 1975, 1976a, 1976b, 1977, 1978, 1980; Demerson, 1973, 1974, 1982, 1991). Figure 10.1 and Table 10.1 have appeared previously in Demerson (1982). The author also consulted other observers of twentieth century family life (Cooley, 1926; Derby, 1980; Guthrie, 1977, 2001; Kiser,

1932; Moerman, 1974; Pollitzer 1999, p. 130-34; Reid, 1956; Smith, 1973; Woofter, 1930).

2. The study of plural mating and/or plural marital-like arrangements among African Americans has not been without social controversy. A "polygynous family-farm system" has been documented for rural Alabama around the middle of the twentieth century (King, 1947) and "polygamous family formation" noted for an urban setting during the 1970s (Scott, 1980). However, there is not agreement that these arrangements are best characterized as polygamy (the marriage of one person to two or more spouses), or more specifically polygyny (see e.g. Scott, 1980; Allen & Agbasegbe, 1980). Nevertheless these plural mating and/or marital-like arrangements deserve further study.

References

Abbott, M. (1967). *The Freedmen's Bureau in South Carolina: 1865-1872.* Chapel Hill: The University of North Carolina Press.

Agbasegbe [Demerson], B. (1980). *Males and the Patrifocal Complex in the South Carolina Sea Island Family.* Paper presented at the Sixty-fifth Annual of the Association for the Study of Afro-American Life and History, New Orleans, Louisiana.

_____ (1978). *The Acquisition and Alienation of Land in the South Carolina and Georgia Sea Islands.* Paper presented at the Eighty-second Annual Meeting of the Michigan Academy of Science, Arts and Letters, Eastern Michigan University, Ypsilanti, Michigan.

_____ (1977). *Contemporary Rural Black Family Life.* Paper presented at the Ninth Annual Conference of the African Heritage Studies Association, Wayne State University, Detroit, Michigan.

_____ (1976a). Social Change and Extended Family in the Black World: A Report on Research in Progress. *Michigan Discussions in Anthropology 2,* 46-54.

_____ (1976b). The Role of Wife in the Black Extended Family: Perspectives from a Rural Community in Southern United States. In D. G. McGuigan (Ed.), *New Research on Women and Sex Roles* (pp. 124-38). Ann Arbor: The University of Michigan Center for Continuing Education of Women.

_____ (1975). *Ethnographic Notes on the Domestic Structures in a Gullah Sea Island Community, with Comparisons from Haiti and Yorubaland.* Paper presented at the Seventh Annual Conference of the African Heritage Studies Association, Washington, D.C.

Allen, W.R. and B.A. Agbasegbe [Demerson]. (1980). A Comment on Scott's Black Polygamous Family Formation. *Alternative Lifestyles, 3,* 375-81.

Aschenbrenner, J. (1975). *Lifelines: Black Families in Chicago.* New York: Holt, Rinehart and Winston.

Blackman, J.K. (1880, April 22). The Sea Islands. *News and Courier* (Charleston, SC), pp. 354-61.

Blesser, C. & K. Rotroch. (1969). *The Promised Land: The History of the South Carolina Land Commission, 1869-1890.* Columbia, SC: The University of South Carolina Press for the South Carolina Tricentennial Commission.

Calonius, E. (2006). *The Wanderer: The Last American Slave Ship and the Conspiracy that Set Its Sails.* New York: St. Martin's Press.

Cooley, R. B. (1926). *Homes of the Freed.* New York: New Republic.

Demerson, B. A. (1991). Family life on Wadmalaw Island. In M. A. Twining & K. Baird (Eds.) *Sea Island Roots: African Presence in the Carolinas and Georgia* (pp. 57-87). Trenton, NJ: Africa World Press.

_____ (1982). Some Aspects of Contemporary Rural Afro-American Family Life in the Sea Islands of Southeastern United States. *The Western Journal of Black Studies,* 6, 60-65.

Demerson, W., III [Demerson, B.A.]. (1974). Household and Compound: Domestic Structures in a Rural New World African Sea Island Community. In J. S. Williams & W. G. West (Eds.) *Sociological Research Symposium IV* (pp. 1012-24). Richmond: Virginia Commonwealth University Department of Sociology.

_____ (1973). *Household, Compound, and Family in the Sea Islands: A Study of Domestic Organization in a Rural Afro-American Community.* (Undergraduate honors thesis in anthropology, The University of Michigan, 1973).

Derby, D. A. (1980). *Black Women Basket Makers: A Study of Domestic Economy in Charleston County, South Carolina.* (Doctoral dissertation, University of Illinois, 1980). *Dissertation Abstracts International, 41*(6A), 2668-2669. Abstract.

Fadipe, N.A. (1970). *The Sociology of the Yoruba.* F. O. Okediji & O. Okediji (Eds.) Ibadan, Nigeria: Ibadan University Press.

Fortes, M. (1950). Kinship and Marriage Among the Ashanti. In A.R. Radcliffe-Brown & D. Forde (Eds.) *African Systems of Kinship and Marriage* (pp. 252-83). London: Oxford University Press.

Frazier, E. F. (1939). *The Negro Family in the United States.* Chicago: University of Chicago Press.

Gonzalez, N. L. S. (1969). *Black Carib Household Structure: A Study in Migration and Modernization.* Seattle: University of Washington Press.

Guthrie, P. (2001). "Catching Sense" and the Meaning of Belonging on a South Carolina Sea Island. In S. Walker (Ed.) *African Roots/American Cultures: Africa in the Creation of the Americas* (pp. 275-83). Lanham, MD: Rowman & Littlefield Publishers, Inc.

Guthrie, P. (1977). *Catching Sense: The Meaning of Plantation Membership among Blacks on St. Helena Island, South Carolina.* (Doctoral dissertation, The University of Rochester, 1977). *Dissertation Abstracts International, 39*(3A), 1967. Abstract.

Gutman, H. (1976). *The Black Family in Slavery and Freedom: 1750-1925.* New York: Pantheon.

Herskovits, M. J. (1941). *The Myth of the Negro Past.* Boston: Beacon Press.

Hoffman, E. (1956). From Slavery to Self-Reliance: The Record of Achievement of the Freedom of the Sea Island region. *Journal of Negro History,* 41, 8-42.

Jackson, J., S. Slaughter & J. H. Blake. (1974). The Sea Islands as a Cultural Resource. *The Black Scholar*, 5, 32-39.

King, C.E. (1947). A Polygynous Family-Farm System in Bullock County, Alabama. *Rural Sociology*, 12 , 174-76.

Kiser, C. V. (1932). *Sea Island to City*. New York: Columbia University Press.

Kobben, A.J.F. (1973). Unity and Disunity: Cottica Djuka Society as a Kinship System. In R. Price (Ed.) *Maroon Societies: Rebel Slave Communities in the Americas* (pp. 320-69). New York: Anchor Press/Doubleday.

Kulikoff, A. (1977). The Beginnings of the Afro-American Family in Maryland. In A. C. Land, L. G. Carr & E. C. Papenfuse (Eds.) *Law, Society, and Politics in Early Maryland: Proceedings of the First Conference on Maryland History, June 14-15, 1974* (pp. 171-96). Baltimore: The Johns Hopkins University Press.

Laguerre, M. (1978). Ticouloute and His Kinsfolk: The Study of a Haitian Extended Family. In D. Shimkin, E. M. Shimkin & D. A. Frate (Eds.) *The Extended Family in Black Societies* (pp. 407-45). The Hague: Mouton Publishers.

Lander, E. M. (1960). *A History of South Carolina, 1865-1960*. Chapel Hill: University of North Carolina Press.

Marshall, G. A. [Sudarkasa, N.]. (1968). Marriage: Comparative Analysis. In *International Encyclopedia of the Social Science* (Vol. 10, 8-19). New York: The Macmillan Company and The Free Press.

Mintz, S. W. & R. Price. (1977). *An Anthropological Approach to the Afro-American Past: A Caribbean perspective. ISHI Occasional Papers in Social Change, No. 2.* Philadelphia: Institute for the Study of Human Issues (ISHI). Republished: (1992). *The Birth of African-American Culture*. Boston: Beacon Press.

Martin, E. P. & J. M. Martin. (1978). *The Black Extended Family*. Chicago: University of Chicago Press.

Moerman, D. E. (1974). *Extended Family and Popular Medicine on St. Helena Island, S.C.: Adaptations to Marginality*. (Doctoral dissertation in anthropology, The University of Michigan, 1974).

Moore, C. & R. Washington. (1970). *The Island Colonies: A Profile of Rural Poverty*. Prepared for the United Methodist Church. n.p.

Okediji, P. A. (1975). Developing a Measure of Extended Family and Kinship System. *Nigerian Journal of Sociology and Anthropology* 2, 75-79.

Pease, W. & J. H. Pease (1963). *Black Utopia: Negro Communal Experiments in America*. Madison: The State Historical Society of Wisconsin.

Pollitzer, W. S. (1999). *The Gullah People and their African Heritage*. Athens: University of Georgia Press.

Reid, J. D. (1956). *The People of St. Simon: A Social Psychological Study of a Contemporary American Subculture*. (Doctoral dissertation in sociology, The University of Chicago, 1956).

Rose, W. L. (1964). *Rehearsal for Reconstruction: The Port Royal Experiment*. New York: Bobbs-Merril Company.

Scott, J.W. (1980). Black Polygamous Family Formation: Case Studies of Legal and Consensual "Wives." *Alternative Lifestyles*, 3, 41-64.

Shimkin, D. B., E. M. Shimkin & D. A. Frate. (1978). *The Extended Family in Black Societies*. The Hague: Mouton Publishers.

Shimkin D. & V. Uchendu. (1978). Persistence, Borrowing, and Adaptive Changes in Black Kinship Systems: Some Issues and their Significance. In D. B. Shimkin, E. M. Shimkin & D. A. Frate (Eds.) *The Extended Family in Black Societies* (pp. 391-406). The Hague: Mouton Publishers.

Smith, F. O. (1973). *A Cross Generational Study of Parental Discipline Practices and Beliefs of Gullah Blacks on the Carolina Sea Islands*. (Doctoral dissertation in education, The University of Massachusetts, 1973).

Stack, C. B. (1974). *All Our Kin: Strategies for Survival in a Black Community*. New York: Harper & Row.

Sudarkasa, N. (1996). *The Strength of Our Mothers: African and African American Women and Families*. Trenton: Africa World Press.

_____ (1981). Interpreting the African Heritage in Afro-American Family Organization. In H. P. McAdoo (Ed.) *Black Families* (pp. 37-53). Beverly Hills: Sage Publications, Inc.

_____ (1980). African and Afro-American Family Structure: A Comparison. *The Black Scholar*, 11, 37-60.

_____ (1975). An Exposition on the Value Premises Underlying Black Family Structure. *Journal of the National Medical Association*, 67, 235-39.

Thomas, J.M. (1980). The Impact of Corporate Tourism on Gullah Blacks: Notes on Issues of Employment. *Phylon* 41, 1-11.

_____ (1978). Effects of Land Development on Black Land Ownership in the Sea Islands of South Carolina. *The Review of Black Political Economy*, 8, 266-76.

_____ (1977). *Blacks on the South Carolina Sea Islands: Planning for Tourist and Land Development*. (Doctoral dissertation in urban and regional planning, The University of Michigan, 1977).

Turner, L. D. (1949). *Africanisms in the Gullah Dialect*. Chicago: University of Chicago Press.

Twining, M. A. & K. E. Baird. (Eds.) (1991a). *Sea Island Roots: African Presence in the Carolinas and Georgia*. Trenton: Africa World Press.

_____ (1991b). Sea Island Culture: Matrix of the African American Family. In M. A. Twining & K. E. Baird (Eds.) *Sea Island Roots: African Presence in the Carolinas and Georgia* (pp. 1-18). Trenton: Africa World Press.

Verney, K. J. (1983). Trespassers in the Land of their Birth: Blacks and Land Ownership in South Carolina and Mississippi during the Civil War and Reconstruction, 1861-1977. *Slavery & Abolition* 4, 64-78.

Webber, T. L. (1978). *Deep Like the Rivers: Education in the Slave Quarter Community, 1831-1865*. New York: W.W. Norton & Company, Inc.

Woofter, T. J. (1930). *Black Yeomanry: Life on St. Helena Island*. New York: Holt and Company.

CHAPTER *11*

"MY AUNT TALKS ABOUT BLACK PEOPLE ALL THE TIME": THE SIGNIFICANCE OF EXTENDED FAMILY NETWORKS IN THE RACIAL SOCIALIZATION OF AFRICAN AMERICAN ADOLESCENTS.[1]

Erin N. Winkler

INTRODUCTION

Much of the scholarly literature on African American families published in the last forty years acknowledges the central role of extended family in African American family function and form (Billingsley, 1968; Billingsley, 1992; Gutman, 1976; Hill, 1993; McAdoo, 1981, 1988, 1997, & 2006; Staples, 1998). Recently, research on African American families has confirmed that extended families are critical in fulfilling both instrumental and expressive roles (Jarrett & Burton, 1999). According to Stack and Burton (1994), these familial functions are part of extended families' "kin-work," or "the collective labor expected of family-centered networks across households and within them" (p. 34). In this chapter, I will posit that the racial socialization of children is one aspect of "kin-work" that is shared collectively amongst extended African American family networks.

Socialization is defined as the process through which individuals acquire an understanding of their own identity, role, and position in society, as well as the roles and positions of others (Boykin & Toms, 1985; Bron-

fenbrenner 1979; Damon, 1988; Thornton et al., 1990). Racial socialization, then, is the process through which children come to understand their
own and others' identities, roles, and positions vis-à-vis race in various contexts, and how race will function in their lives. African American children
receive racial socialization messages from several sources. Most commonly
cited are family, school, media, and peers (Boykin & Ellison, 1995; Murray
& Mandara, 2002), although neighborhoods (Bennett, 2006; Caughy et
al., 2006; Stevenson et al., 2005), community and religious organizations,
and people such as police officers, health care workers, retail store clerks,
and others also play a role. Each of these sources can send young people
vastly different messages about what it means to be African American.
Societal institutions, such as mainstream media, schools, policy-making
bodies, and the legal system, often explicitly and implicitly suggest that
being black is negative in a number of areas, such as beauty, intelligence,
culture, heritage, productive citizenship, and life chances (Boykin &
Ellison, 1995; Murray & Mandara, 2002). African American families
counter negative societal messages and teach children how to function in
a racially hostile and inequitable society through *responsive* familial racial
socialization, and teach their children about the inherent value of African
and African American culture and heritage through *procultural* familial
racial socialization (Winkler, 2008).[2] Research has shown that familial
racial socialization, both responsive and procultural, can impact outcomes
such as racial identity (Anglin & Whaley, 2006; Demo & Hughes, 1990;
McHale et al., 2006; Stevenson, 1995; Thomas et al., 2003; Thomas &
Speight ,1999), self-esteem (Constantine & Blackmon, 2002; Goodstein
& Ponterotto, 1997; Walker et al., 1995), mental health (Constantine et
al., 2006; Scott, 2003; Thomas et al., 2003), and academic achievement
(Chavous et al., 2003; Grantham & Ford, 2003; Marshall, 1995; Neblett et
al., 2006; Oyserman et al., 2003; Robinson & Biran, 2006).

Although there is some disagreement in the literature about whether
family or society holds the most influence in the racial socialization process,
family is most frequently cited as the primary agent of racial socialization
(Boykin and Ellison 1995; Brown et al., 2007; Demo & Hughes, 1990;
Hughes, 2003; McHale et al., 2006; Thomas et al., 2003; Thornton et
al., 1990; Townsend & Lanphier, 2007; Tyler at al., 2005; Wakefield &
Hudley, 2007). While extended family networks are commonly noted as
part of the family ecologies of African American children (Harrison et
al., 1990), the role of extended family members in the racial socialization
of African American children is largely unexplored in the racial socialization literature (Johnson et al., 2003; Lesane-Brown, 2006). In this chapter,
I use data collected through 47 open-ended, qualitative interviews con-

ducted with 19 African American mothers and their 28 middle school-aged children in Detroit, Michigan to illustrate the role of extended family in the racial socialization of children. All of the mothers participating in this study, regardless of income, education, employment, martial status, or other demographic factors, revealed that they chose to live in Detroit because they had extended family networks there, and all of the children in this study interacted with extended family on a regular basis. Although the interviewed children were not asked any questions regarding extended family, more than one-third cited the role of extended family members in teaching them about racial identity and racism. The data reveal that extended family members actively engage in the racial socialization of children through both verbal messages and modeled behaviors.

METHOD: RESEARCHING RACIAL SOCIALIZATION IN DETROIT

Methodology

Most racial socialization studies employ quantitative methodologies, using close-ended interviews, questionnaires, and surveys as their primary data collection tools. Quantitative studies are extremely useful to understanding racial socialization in that they allow for surveys of larger, more representative samples, which permits broader generalization of the findings. However, quantitative studies can be restricted by their adherence to a predetermined set of questions and responses, which disallows participants to raise issues not covered by these questions or responses, and by their limited ability to give voice, complexity, and nuance to the experiences of their participants. Qualitative, open-ended interviewing is an effective research method in that it allows for direct access to the voices of African American children and families regarding experiences with racial socialization. Collins (1991) asserts, "Experience as a criterion of meaning with practical images as its symbolic vehicles is a fundamental epistemelogical tenet in African-American thought systems" (p. 209). Thus, as Stack and Burton (1994) argue, instead of imposing "conceptual frameworks... derived from explorations involving white, middle-class families," it is critical that we develop theoretical models from the self-articulated experiences of African American families (p. 34). Open-ended interviewing, more so than positivistic or close-ended methodologies, allows us to do so. Through this method, the interviewees can identify what they see as key areas of discussion and address issues not covered by a pre-established set of questions and responses (Silverman, 1993). This kind of interaction

275

between interviewee and interviewer "...implies talk between two subjects, not the speech of subject and object. It is a humanizing speech, one that challenges and resists domination" (hooks 1989, p. 131, as cited in Collins, 1990, p. 212). Although open-ended interviewing as a method of understanding racial socialization is imperfect, in many ways it allows for a more nuanced understanding of racial socialization.

The current study puts into practice the theoretical assumption that children are active participants in their own racial socialization (Hughes & Johnson, 2001; Stevenson et al, 2005; Thornton et al., 1990). Until recently, most racial socialization studies examined the process of racial socialization from an adult perspective, either that of parents currently engaging in racial socialization practices or that of adults remembering back on their own racial socialization experiences as youngsters. Indeed, Zwiers and Morrissette (1999) note that in social science research in general, "Few researchers have made a consistent effort to include the thoughts, feelings, experiences, and specific statements of children in their empirical investigations" (p. 127). Recently, an increasing number of racial socialization studies involve the collection of primary data from children and adolescents, but this data collection most often takes the form of closed-ended questionnaires or surveys, and very few involve open-ended interviews with children (Hughes at al., 2006). The current study utilizes open-ended interviews with middle school-aged African American children and a parent or primary caregiver in an attempt to gain a more complete understanding of racial socialization that gives equal weight to the experiences and perspectives of both children and adults.

Sample and Procedures

The families whose experiences are presented in this chapter were part of a larger study that sought to examine how children learn to negotiate all of the various and conflicting messages they receive about race. Data collection involved forty-seven open-ended, qualitative interviews conducted in Detroit, Michigan from August 2003 to January 2004. These interviews were conducted with a purposive sample of nineteen African American mothers[3] and their twenty-eight middle-school-aged children. Of the twenty-eight children interviewed, eighteen were girls and ten were boys. The average age of interviewed children was 12.37 years, and their mean grade level was seventh. The interviews focused on the racial socialization of children in this early adolescent age group because child development literature indicates that children in this age group are coming to understand complex, abstract constructions like race and racial identity (Stevenson, 1995).

The interviewees were recruited through computer literacy programs, neighborhood associations, fliers, and word of mouth. The purposive sampling allowed for comparison of racial socialization methods, content, experiences, and outcomes across socioeconomic groups, while controlling for racial demographics of neighborhood. The participating families represented a wide range of incomes, educational backgrounds, and household structures. Five of the families in this study reported household incomes that were below the city median of $29,526 (U.S. Census Bureau, 2000), six families had household incomes roughly equal to the city median, and eight families reported household incomes above the city median. When asked to describe the highest level of formal education they had completed, two mothers reported some high school, nine a high school diploma, two an associate's degree, four a bachelor's degree, and two a graduate degree. Of the nineteen families involved in this study, ten were single parented and nine were dual parented. At least three of the families interviewed had extended family living in the household, including grandparents, nieces and nephews of the interviewed children. All of the interviewed children had extended family in Detroit with whom they had regular contact.

The nineteen families interviewed for this study all lived within Detroit city limits at the time of their interviews, and were drawn from seven different zip codes. All of the families lived in neighborhoods that were predominantly African American, and most lived in zip codes that were at least ninety-five percent African American. Of the twenty-eight children interviewed in this study, only four attended schools that had less than ninety-five percent African American enrollment (National Center for Education Statistics). These neighborhood and school demographics reflected the demographics of the entire city. In the year 2000, among U.S. cities with populations of at least 105,000 people, Detroit had the highest percentage black population, with eighty-three percent of its 951,270 residents reporting as black or African American (U.S. Census Bureau, 2001).

THE ROLE OF EXTENDED FAMILY: RACIAL SOCIALIZATION AS "KIN-WORK"

Stack and Burton (1994) argue that kin-work is "the work that families need to accomplish to endure over time" (p. 34). This includes both instrumental functions, such as wage labor and economic support, and expressive functions, such as reproduction and care for dependents. Part of kin-work is "reinforc[ing] shared values" and meeting "family obligations defined by economic, social, physical, and psychological family needs" (Stack & Burton, 1994, p. 35). Scholars in the field of racial socialization agree that such needs in African American families include imparting to children a set of values based in African and African American culture and a set of critical tools for negotiating a racially hostile and inequitable society (Hughes et al., 2006). These needs, in fact, are so essential that one of the mothers in this study argues, "How to deal with racism as a black person is a *major* question, and it's even a determining question, in terms of how you raise your kids and how you are." The families in this study are deeply invested in helping their children sort through the conflicting messages they receive from various sources about race, and consider racial socialization to be an imperative aspect of good childrearing. The interviewees, both mothers and children, make clear that this aspect of childrearing is not the jurisdiction of parents alone, but is shared in many ways by the extended family.

The interviews in this study bespeak the broad influence that extended family members hold on the racial socialization of children. The young people and their mothers raised examples of extended family members—especially grandparents, but also aunts, uncles, cousins, great-aunts, great-uncles, and other relatives—affecting racial socialization. As we will see in this chapter, the data suggest that this kin-work can sometimes cause confusion and contradiction when various family members impart conflicting messages to children. Nevertheless, the data also show that the sharing of this kin-work is often beneficial, with extended family members supporting parents or even taking a primary role in racial socialization.

"My grandma and granddad tell me": Racial Socialization from Extended Family

Scholars in the field of racial socialization acknowledge that racial socialization takes a variety of forms, including both intentional and unintentional verbal and nonverbal messages (Hughes & Chen, 1999, p. 470). Murray and Mandara (2002) argue that, "When children overhear parents talking about race, observe their reactions to people of other races, or receive direct instructions from them regarding other races, their racial awareness and identity are being developed" (p. 84). The responses of participants in this study substantiate this idea, but suggest that extended family members may be as important as parents in directly socializing children about race. These interviews evidence extended family members verbally and nonverbally communicating several messages to children, including messages about African American strength, pride, and achievement in the face of oppression, the rejection of racist ideas, and attitudes towards people of other races.

"Just be proud of who you are": Strength, Pride, and Achievement in the Face of Oppression

The children in this study were asked a variety of questions, including but not limited to questions about their daily routines, their friends, their families, their teachers, their self-perceived strengths and weaknesses, their likes and dislikes, their understandings of beauty and attractiveness, and their favorite books, magazines, television shows, and musical artists. They were also asked about what, if anything their parent(s) or primary caregiver(s) tell them about being African American; what, if anything their parent(s) or primary caregiver(s) tell them about racism; and what they think is the most important out of all of the messages they receive regarding being African American. Although the young interviewees in this study were not asked any questions about whether or not their extended family members talk to them about racial identity or racism, more than one-third of them raised the issue on their own. Several of these children pointed to their extended families' emphasis on maintaining strength, pride, and achievement despite historical and contemporary racism.

One such youngster, Travis[4], is a thirteen-year-old boy who lives with his mother and father on the west side of Detroit, just a few minutes' drive from his maternal grandmother and a number of other relatives. His grandmother runs a free after-school program out of her home for neighborhood children two afternoons each week. When asked about what his parents have taught him about being African American, Travis responds that his parents have not talked to him about this at all. However, he says, "My grandma [did] in our after-school classes… she told us mostly about how most of the black inventors made most of the things that we use today." According to Travis' report, it is his grandmother, rather than his parents, who is taking a primary role in talking to him about being African American, by discussing the accomplishments and contributions made by African Americans, even in the face of great oppression. Similarly, when asked the same question, another young interviewee, Brianna, reports that her grandparents send direct messages regarding strength, pride, and achievement despite racism. Brianna is one of only five children in this study who lives in a household that permanently includes extended family members. A fourteen-year-old girl living with her mother and maternal grandparents, Brianna says "My grandma and my granddad…they do [talk to me about being African American]. They talk about different people, like the first black person that did this. They generally like the pictures." In Brianna's home, her grandparents take on some of the responsibility of racial socialization, displaying portraits of famous African Americans and talking with her about their pioneering accomplishments.

Other young interviewees also report their relatives talking with them about strength and pride despite racism, but say that their extended family members impart these messages by sharing their own life stories. Both Ruth, a quiet fifteen-year-old who lives with her mother, step-father, and grandmother, and Shani, a twelve-year-old who lives with her mother and sister, say that older relatives talk to them about their own struggles with racism. Ruth says that her grandmother teaches her about black history by sharing her experiences with racism, saying, "my grandmother basically talks about the stuff she did in the south." Shani says that her great-grandmother also discusses her own struggles with racism, especially the circumstances she faced as a domestic worker for whites. "My great-grandmother," Shani says, "she tell me stuff about how important it was when she used to be working at other people houses, white people houses." Shani says she listens closely to these lessons and takes them to heart, adding, "I write it all down in my journal." In their interviews, both Ruth and Shani only discuss the racial socialization messages that their extended family members share with them. Both girls describe their extended, rather than immediate, family members as primary in their racial socialization.

Toussaint is an eleven-year-old boy growing up in a household that his mother describes as African-centered. Indeed, Toussaint reports that, unlike Ruth's and Shani's experiences, his parents and teachers "always" talk to him about being African American. Nevertheless, Toussaint reports that some of the most important things he learns about being African American come from his extended family, "because," he says, "a lot of people in our family are really strong." When asked to share an example, Toussaint shares a story of his grandmother's strength in confronting racism.

> My grandma...she got ran over by some racist police...and her foot almost got cut off. But my dad, and other people—my dad and his brothers and sisters—took her down to the beach everyday and bathed it in some salt water, and her foot got to stay on. And I think going through the pain made her strong.

When asked whether he has had to deal with racism, Toussaint responds, "I haven't been in the situation before." However, as a result of the examples set by his family, Toussaint says if he does find himself in such a situation, he will "stay strong."

Thirteen-year-old Cara says that she, too, has learned a lesson about standing up to racism from relatives who directly confronted racism when they recently integrated a white neighborhood.

> My cousin, he live in Tennessee. And he looks like he's white, but he's not. [...] He looks like he's white, but he's actually black. So, he moved to Tennessee, and it was white neighbors on each side. So they was all welcoming him. And so then, when he brought his wife and kids, they was black. So they [the neighbors] thought he was white, and was like [*Stares intently and looks confused, imitating the neighbors*], "Oh no!" They shut they door, turned around. All that. It's was like—he told us about it. I was like [*exhales loudly*]—whew!

Cara conveys that her cousin's first-hand description of his experience had a profound effect on her. Although her cousin had these experiences in Tennessee, Cara says, "I think that could happen here, too." She says that her cousin's experience taught her that the most important thing about being African American is "sticking with it and staying. Don't try to betray your culture. And don't try to not want to be what you are. Just be proud of who you are or what your culture is." Like Travis, Brianna, Ruth, Shani, and Toussaint, Cara says that her extended family teaches her important lessons about being African American by maintaining strength and pride in the face of racism, and advancing despite such racism.

"YOU DON'T HAVE TO BUY INTO THAT": CRITIQUING RACISM

The mothers and children in this study revealed that extended kin networks play a role in helping children critique racism and resist the absorption of racist ideas they encounter in the broader society. Sarah is the mother of two middle school-aged children, fourteen-year-old Trisha and twelve-year-old Elijah. Sarah is clearly invested in the racial socialization of her children, and articulates this process as a delicate balancing act. "I don't want them to feel inferior, because I sincerely believe that I'm raising just some dynamic people," Sarah says, "At the same time, I don't want them to use their blackness as an excuse of why they can't be all that they can be. So I'm constantly looking for that balance and I'm constantly talking about values." From their separate interviews, it seems that both children listen closely to their mother's racial socialization messages—each displays a positive black identity and a strong sense of self, and both often begin their answers to interview questions with the phrase "My mom says...." In addition to their mother, the children also independently cite the influence of a number of family members, including grandmothers, aunts, uncles, and cousins, on their own racial identity development. For example, Trisha points out that her aunt urges her to respond to current racial inequities by supporting African American businesses. Trisha says, "My aunt talks about black people all the time. She says, 'Black people need to own more businesses.' Because she's a business owner. So she's always talking about black people and businesses." When asked if she thinks her aunt influences her own developing identity as a young black woman, Trisha replies, "I think so. Because I think I want to be an entrepreneur of some kind of business."

In her interview, Sarah, Trisha's mother, discusses the ways in which she relies upon such extended kin networks to engage in the collective kin-work of racial socialization. For example, Sarah says she relies upon the men in her children's extended family to counter stereotypes about black men and to show her son Elijah that he does not have to buy into such stereotypes in order to be "authentic." She starts by explaining the "boxes" into which she believes African American men are expected to fit:

> Well, with Elijah, because he is a male, I try to— see, I can honestly say, that whole male thing and man thing in the African American community, I don't totally get it. I'm serious, I don't get it. It seems like, either the guys are—they're extreme—either they're gang bangers or they're nerds. And, it's not a middle ground. Now, that's my understanding, I could be off. But I'm thinking, OK, my son is neither. But because he's not a gang banger, or has that whole look of toughness, he gets labeled as that other thing, the nerd. And it seem like, whatever's predominant in the hood, that's what rules. And so because it's more of a gang banger type—and half of them are not even that, they just have the look—he's the other extreme. But he's not! [...] He's more into his computer and his Game Boy and his X-Box and being a silly boy, farting and laughing at silly jokes.

Sarah is concerned that her son will face pressure to fit into one of these two extremes, or face the consequence of being ostracized. She talks about it with him, and is pleased that he does not yet appear to feel too pressured by his peers.

> And so I tell [Elijah], I said, "Well, that whole gang thing don't appeal to you?" And he looked at me like this, he said, "No!" And I said, "Well, you know you're going to get labeled as a sissy or a punk, don't you?" So he said, "Yeah. I don't care." I said, "Does that bother you?" He said, "No, not really, because I'm big, too." I'm like, "Yup, that does help!" So we'll laugh about that.

Still, Sarah wonders whether peer pressure might mount as twelve-year-old Elijah gets older. She is also concerned that Elijah might feel pressure from his own father, who lives nearby and spends time with Elijah on a regular basis.

> And, you know, I talked to his father about it, and his father has a tendency to want Elijah to be tough, to get along with the norm. And so he doesn't know quite how to deal with Elijah. And so, for his whole male socialization, I take him around my brother and some folks at work that I really like. [...] I just tell him, "You don't have to buy into that. Elijah, that's a lie." And I tell him, "Well, look at our pastor." I'm like, "Look at Uncle Philip. Look at Ronald. Look at your dad. They're not like that, so you don't have to be like that in order to be, you know." And I think he's OK, but because I don't totally get it, I'm not sure where he totally is with that.

As an African American woman, Sarah states that she is not sure that she entirely understands what her son is going through in terms of racialized notions of masculine identity, or what she calls "that whole male thing and man thing in the African American community." She therefore relies on trusted men in her network, including adult male family members, to share the kin-work of racial socialization. She depends on her extended family network to help Elijah critique racialized stereotypes of what a black man can or is supposed to be.

Two of the child interviewees also raise examples of relatives sending them racial socialization messages that critique racism in society. In this case, both girls say that their grandmothers critique racialized images of African Americans on television. Ten-year-old Lanáe lives with her mother and her thirteen-year-old sister, but says that it is her grandmother who helps her understand the racism inherent in the local television newscasts. "When we watch the news," Lanáe says, "my grandma used to say that they make it seem like all of us are ghetto." She adds that her grandmother wanted to be sure that she and her sister "didn't think that," and resisted buying into such racist notions. Similarly, fourteen-year-old Cara, who lives with her mother, maternal grandmother, twin brother, and three younger siblings, indicates that her grandmother is careful to help Cara critically examine portrayals of African Americans on television. Cara indicates that her grandmother takes an active role in her upbringing, including selecting the schools that Cara and her siblings attend, and talking to them about racial identity. When asked about her favorite leisure activities, Cara states that she is not particularly interested in watching television because television does not accurately portray the real life experiences of African Americans. Cara says:

> [W]atching television is not really realistic. I'd rather read a book that's based on fact of something that's more interesting than TV. I was watching a TV show the other day, and it's just like…what are you all doing? And then my grandma was like, "It's Hollywood. Of course they going to act." I was like, [*sarcastically*] "Great."

Here, Cara's grandmother reinforces Cara's questioning of the images on television and encourages her to see them as unrealistic. Cara's grandmother, like Lanáe's, engages in racial socialization by teaching her to recognize and reject racist images in the media.

Some extended family members encourage children to critique racism in ways that are not necessarily in line with their parents' approaches. In these cases, children have to negotiate not only the conflicting messages they receive from schools, media, peers, and family, but also the varying messages they receive from within their own family. Annette and her husband are raising their thirteen-year-old son, Matthew, and eighteen-year-old daughter, Tanya, to be aware of racism and the ways it may affect their lives, but not to allow it to impact their own values and goals. In her interview, Annette says she is teaching her son that, "No, life isn't fair. No, they probably shouldn't have done that [racist thing] to you. But I don't expect you to do that back to them." Annette notes that her husband's father often talks to Matthew about critiquing both historical and contemporary racism. Matthew's grandfather favors governmental reparations as a means of redressing the societal inequities racism has caused. Annette says:

> My father-in-law…his nickname is Reparations Roger. He is very active in terms of reparations for African Americans. Because he's from the South, he's eighty-some years old. He has that Southern mentality. And when he begins to preach and get on his soap-box, his comments are addressed to my husband, my son. And so I have to, I have to explain to Matthew where his grandfather is at and what he's experienced in life, which doesn't make him a bad man. But we know that he has some concerns, and he voices them with anger—any means necessary to get the reparations. So. Basically, that's how I've discussed it with my children.

In this case, Matthew's grandfather is sending him a strong message critiquing racism and encouraging a particular form of action as a means of redressing the effects of racism. At the same time, Matthew's mother makes clear in this quotation that she does not agree with her father-in-law's approach to racial socialization. As such, she attempts to mitigate the impact of his words upon her son by discussing with Matthew her own interpretation of his grandfather's stance. Although Matthew's parents and his grandfather both believe in socializing Matthew to critique racism, the approaches they take in doing so vary to some degree.

"Just like us"?: Attitudes Towards Others

According to the children and mothers in this study, extended family members also send messages to children about the attitudes they should adopt towards people of other races, especially whites. These messages run the gamut, from skepticism and mistrust of whites, to selective trust and coexistence, to individualism, and even to the message that whiteness is more desirable than blackness. In some cases, parents embrace the messages being sent to their children by relatives, and are grateful for the active role extended family members are taking in the kin-work of racial socialization. In other cases, the messages sent by certain extended family members are viewed by parents and children as negative or confusing. When the latter occurs, the entire extended kin network often works together to counteract negative messages.

The mothers in this study struggle with when and how to talk to their children about racism (Winkler, 2008). On the one hand, they assert that it is critical to prepare their children for inevitable encounters with racism. On the other hand, they worry about how to do so without overwhelming their children or making them feel victimized. Some of the mothers report that their relatives, through verbal or modeled messages, clearly tell their children that they should adopt skepticism or mistrust of people of other races, particularly whites. Hughes et al, (2006) note that several studies reveal racial socialization messages regarding "promotion of mistrust" which "emphasize the need for wariness and distrust in interracial interactions" (p. 757). "Promotion of mistrust" is viewed as a protective practice in which families attempt to shield children from racist encounters.

Lena is the mother of thirteen-year-old Tanika and ten-year-old Lanáe. Lena was not raised in Detroit, but her husband, Michael, was, and the couple decided to move to Detroit to be near Michael's extended family. Lena describes herself as "a military brat" and says that, because of this, she can live anywhere. However, she finds Detroit to be "a very strange city in regards to race." Having spent most of her childhood in areas where African Americans comprised a small minority of the population, Lena appreciates the sense of community Detroit provides for her children. However, she worries that "everything is so separate" racially, and wishes that "there was more of a mix." She expresses concern that her daughters might pick up what she sees as Detroit's "close-minded" approach to race, in which "people tend to stay to themselves and look at other things as being foreign." Lena says that her mother-in-law embodies this position, and models it for Lena's daughters, Tanika and Lanáe.

> My mother-in-law, in fact, won't eat Mexican food. She'll go to Taco Bell, but she won't eat Mexican food. It's a trust thing or whatever. And I don't know if that's a carry-over or a take-off of the southern mentality, where, you know, you need to be friendly, but, you know, you can't trust white folks too much. Or you can't trust—you don't know anything about them, so you need to stay away from them, type of mentality.

Lena also comments on what she sees as the lack of trust between the large African American and Middle Eastern populations in the metropolitan Detroit area. "So here we are," she says, "we have the Middle East in our back yard, but I bet you 80% of the African American population has never eaten Middle Eastern food." Lena views her mother-in-law's refusal to patronize Detroit's ethnic restaurants as a modeled message to her children that they need to be cautious of people of different races. On the one hand, Lena is frustrated by this, and considers this approach to be "close-minded." On the other hand, Lena admits that she, too, is socializing her daughters to understand that "life is so contradictory, it's not fair, [but] you still do have to be cautious" of others and stay on the lookout for racism.

Conversely, Demo and Hughes (1990) found that "individualistic and/ or universalistic" messages are also common racial socialization messages in African American families. Several recent studies corroborate this point (Hughes et al., 2006), as do many of the adult and youth participants in this study. Twelve-year-old Elijah says that, although his family is open with him about racism and the negative impact it has on American society, they also encourage him to see others as individuals.

> [B]ack when I was little, I used to always have a little grudge against Caucasians, white people. And then [my grandmother] had taught me, she had said, "As long as they don't do anything to me, I don't have a problem with them. They're just like us, they're just light-skinned." And then from there on out...I've been hanging around more and more white people.

Throughout his interview, Elijah is clear that he has already experienced quite a bit of racism, and that he knows that "being a black male is pretty hard because of racism." He is aware that "because of racism and slavery back in the day, people still, they still hold their grudge against you," but he credits his grandmother with teaching him not to "have a little grudge" in return. His grandmother also told him that, "[he is] not inferior," and that people of other races are "just like us." Elijah says his grandmother taught him to reject notions of white superiority, as well as broad generalizations about any racial group.

Several of the mothers in this study argue that their extended families teach their children open attitudes towards people of other races by modeling harmony and coexistence within the extended family itself. Anita is the mother of twelve-year-old Shani. When asked if she talks with her daughter about race or racism, Anita replies:

> I've never really thought about it. I guess because we have white people in our family too, so. My uncle, he has a white wife. My brother, all his women are white. All of them! [*Laughs.*] So, it's never really been too much of an issue.

While Anita jokes about Shani's uncle having numerous girlfriends, she indicates that she believes these relationships, as well as other interracial relationships in Shani's extended family, send Shani clear messages about the potential for positive relationships with people of other races. Another interviewed mother, Cora, makes a similar argument, stating that her daughters see interracial relationships modeled by their extended families on both their mother's and father's sides. Cora points out that her daughters' maternal and paternal grandparents were involved in interracial relationships, and that each had a "mixed" or biracial child.

> Growing up my mom basically felt like I do [now with my children], because my mom didn't raise us to be prejudiced. My older brother is mixed. And my husband is mixed. So. [*Laughs.*] So, I mean—because my oldest brother, his father was white. And my mom never grew us up with prejudice in our household. That was something that she totally was against.

Cora contends that her daughters' extended family thus models the message that, "[some] people will judge you by your color…[but] really we're all the same. The color of our blood is the same. So I mean, should it matter because the color of our skin? No." Both Anita and Cora feel that their extended families take on part of the kin-work of racial socialization by modeling individualistic or universalistic messages through their own interpersonal relationships.

Yolanda makes a similar argument, although she says that the messages from her boys' extended family are sometimes mixed, and she worries that this will confuse her boys. On the one hand, Yolanda says that the multiracial composition of their extended family demonstrates universalism and equality.

> We have a lot of white people back in our family; we have a lot of Hispanic people in our family. So we go places and I be like, "Well, that's your cousin," or "That's your aunt." Then [my sons] are like, "Well, she's white!" [And I respond], "OK. She's white." You know? And so I explain to them…it's just a big racial mix.

On the other hand, Yolanda says some of her relatives favor whites, and she worries this might send her boys the false message that white people are better than, or preferable to, black people.

> [M]y grandmother, her best friend was a [white] lady, a rich lady that [my family] all worked for, that they all cleaned her house, that they all raised their [the white family's] kids. So, we grew up like with the nanny and the housekeeper, and then it progressed, you know, and they had generations in our family worked for generations of that family. You know? So, and it's just like, we tease my grandmother about it, "You love them damn white people!" You know what I'm saying? She just love them to death! You know what I'm saying? And she'll pick them sometimes over some of her relatives. [*Pause.*] But that's just her personal choice. Yup. It is. Yup. The whiter the skin, it seems like the more that they [some family members] like them.

While this troubles Yolanda, she says that she simply tells her sons, "It's just that certain people just think that they're superior, and they're not. They're no better than [you]." Her sons, she says, have avoided internalizing their great-grandmother's partiality towards whites, and have instead embraced the broader message from their extended family to "take each person for each person, because it could be another person from another race that could be exposed to you as a sister or brother."

Still, thirteen-year-old Cara confirms that racial socialization messages from family can sometimes be confusing. On the one hand, Cara has overheard her grandmother telling some light-skinned children in the family that they should attempt to pass as white if they are able. On the other hand, Cara says that her grandmother tells her she "should be proud to be black." When asked whether or not anyone in her household talks to her about racial identity, Cara says:

> In a way, they do. Because my grandma had adopted some foster kids, and they was white, but they wanted to be black, and my grandma was telling them how if you want to be a black man, then some black mens don't get everything that a white man gets. I mean, they actually looked like they was white, but I think they was mixed. But my grandma said if you have a chance to pick if you was white or black, to go white because white people have special, just...[*pause*] access to stuff. [...] But I really didn't understand what she was saying. But I do. I do, but I don't. [Because to me], she will say stuff like..."You should be proud to be black." [...] So I'm like, "Okay...."

Cara feels that she is receiving conflicting racial socialization messages about black pride. She gives examples of her maternal grandmother, who lives in the home with her, sending messages encouraging both the rejection of, and pride in, a black identity. Cara expresses her confusion, saying that she does not really understand what her grandmother is trying to communicate to her: "I do, but I don't." Her broader extended family, she says, helps to clear up her confusion, explaining racism to her and telling her, "Don't let that get to you." As we heard earlier, Cara cites the experiences of her cousin and his family in Tennessee as one example of how her extended family teaches her to "just be proud of who [she is] or what [her] culture is."

Thirteen-year-old Nina says that her grandmother likes "white people better than black people," but that her parents and other extended family members do not allow Nina to take these messages to heart.

> My grandmother—well since she was raised on a plantation, she'll talk about how...they never really knew their mother and their father, but they were raised by ... a white family. And the plantation owner. And so she really, like, she like white people better than black people. And she'll, she'll ... sometimes she'll think she white. I don't know, she's kind of crazy. But she'll be like, "Yeah, my mother is white and my dad is black." And so we'd be like, "Okay." But yeah, she had me believe that, too, until my dad was like, "No." [...] My auntie will be like [*placating*], "Okay, ma, okay. [...] Yeah, you were, okay. You were, though. You were raised by them. Okay."

Although Nina's grandmother sends the message that it is preferable to be white, the stronger message comes from Nina's broader network of kin, who humor her grandmother while still rejecting her ideas. When asked what effect her grandmother's ideas have on her, Nina responds, "I don't want to be affected by her sayings." Thus, although some children receive conflicting racial socialization messages, their extended family members collectively help them decide which to filter out and which to embrace.

CONCLUSION

The children and mothers interviewed in this study reveal that the extended family plays a critical role in the racial socialization of African American children. In fact, as we have seen, some of the youth argue that their extended family members play a more primary role in this process than their parents or primary caregivers. Interviewed mothers and children say that their relatives teach children about race and racism through both verbal messages and modeled behaviors. The messages these relatives send are not always consistent, and as with racial socialization in general, children have to sort through and decipher these messages, making conscious and unconscious decisions about which to internalize and with to reject. However, the young people in this study state that, even when one relative communicates a racial socialization message that reinforces racism, it is often other extended family members who work together to counteract the negative influence of that message. As such, racial socialization for these families is truly part of the collective family labor Stack and Burton (1994) describe as "kin-work."

It is particularly telling that, even though the children and mothers were not directly asked about the role of the extended family in the racial socialization of children, more than one-half of the mothers and one-third of the children raised the issue on their own. Further studies examining the extent to which extended family members influence children's developing understandings of race and racism are necessary. Although this issue has remained largely unexplored in the racial socialization literature to-date, the current study supports the argument that racial socialization is indeed collective "kin-work" in which entire extended kin networks actively participate.

Notes

1. This research was made possible through the generous support of the Berkeley Center for Working Families, The American Association of University Women, the Berkeley Center for the Development of Peace and Well-being, and the Northwestern University Postdoctoral Fellowship in African American Studies. The writing of this draft was funded in part by a grant from the University of Wisconsin-Milwaukee.

2. Please see Winkler (2008) for further discussion of "responsive" and "proactive" familial racial socialization. The broad categories of familial racial

socialization I call "responsive" and "proactive" overlap in many ways with Stevenson's (1995) discussion of "creative" and "reactive" racial socialization, Boykin and Ellison's (1995) discussion of "tricultural socialization," and Hughes' (2003) discussion of "Cultural Socialization" and "Preparation for Bias." As Hughes et al. (2006) note, scholars in the field of racial socialization have yet to agree upon common terminology for discussing types of familial racial socialization messages (749).

3. Although the recruitment information for this study made a non-gender-specific request for middle school-aged children and their parents or primary caregivers, all of the adults who agreed to be interviewed were mothers of the interviewed children.

4. "Travis," like the names of all study participants cited in this chapter, is a pseudonym.

References

Anglin, D. M. & A. L. Whaley. (2006). Racial/Ethnic Self-Labeling in Relation to Group Socialization and Identity in African-Descended Individuals. *Journal of Language and Social Psychology*, 25(4), 450-463.

Bennet, M. D. J. (2006). Culture and Context: A Study of Neighborhood Effects on Racial Socialization and Ethnic Identity Content in a Sample of African American Adolescents. *Journal of Black Psychology*, 32(4), 479-500.

Billingsley, A. (1992). *Climbing Jacob's Ladder*. New York: Simon and Schuster.

_____ (1968). *Black Families in White America*. Englewood Cliffs, N.J., Prentice-Hall

Boykin, A. W. & C. M. Ellison. (1995). The Multiple Ecologies of Black Youth Socialization: An Afrographic Analysis. In R. L. Taylor (Ed.) *African-American Youth: Their Social and Economic Status in the United States*, (pp. 93-128). Westport, Connecticut: Praeger.

Boykin, A.W. & F. Toms. (1985). Black Child Socialization: A Conceptual Framework. In H. P. McAdoo & J. L. McAdoo (Ed.) *Black Children: Social, Educational, and Parental Environments*, (pp. 33-51). Beverly Hills, California: Sage Publications.

Bronfenbrenner, U. (1979). *The Ecology of Human Development: Experiments by Nature and Design*. Cambridge, Massachusetts: Harvard University Press.

Brown, T. N., E. E. Tanner-Smith, C. L. Lesane-Brown, & M. E. Ezell. (2007). Child, Parent, and Situational Correlates of Familial Ethnic/Race Socialization. *Journal of Marriage and Family*, 69(1), 14-25.

Caughy, M. O., S. M. Nettles, P. J. O'Campo & K. F. Lohrfink. (2006). Neighborhood Matters: Racial Socialization of African American Children. *Child Development*, 77, 1220-1236.

Chavous, T. M., D. H. Bernat, K. Schmeelk-Cone, C. H. Caldwell, L. Kohn-Wood, & M. A. Zimmerman. (2003). Racial Identity and Academic Attainment Among African-American Adolescents. *Child Development,* 74(4), 1076-1090.

Collins, P. H. (1991). *Black Feminist Thought: Knowledge, Consciousness, and the Politics of Empowerment.* New York: Routledge.

Constantine, M. G., V. L. Alleyne, B. C. Wallace & D. C. Franklin-Jackson. (2006). Africentric Cultural Values: Their Relation to Positive Mental Health in African American adolescent Girls. *Journal of Black Psychology,* 32(2),141-154.

Constantine, M. G. & S. M. Blackmon. (2002). Black Adolescents' Racial Socialization Experiences: Their Relations to Home, School, and Peer Self-Esteem. *Journal of Black Studies,* 32(3), 322-335.

Damon, W. (1988). Socialization and Individuation. In G. Handle (Ed.) *Childhood Socialization,* (pp. 3-10). New York: Aldine De Gruyter.

Demo, D. H.& M. Hughes. (1990). Socialization and Racial Identity Among Black Americans. *Social Psychology Quarterly,* 53, 364-74.

Goodstein, R. & J. G. Ponterotto. (1997). Racial and Ethnic Identity: Their Relationship and Their Contribution to Self-Esteem. *Journal of Black Psychology,* 23(3), 275-293.

Grantham, T. C. & D. Y. Ford. (2003). Beyond Self-Concept and Self-Esteem: Racial Identity and Gifted African American Students. *The High School Journal,* 87(1), 18-29.

Gutman, H. G. (1976). *The Black Family in Slavery and Freedom, 1750-1925.* New York: Vintage Books.

Harrison, A. O., M. N. Wilson, C. J. Pine, S. Q. Chan & R. Buriel. (1990). Family Ecologies of Ethnic Minority Children. *Child Development,* 61, 347-62.

Hill, R. B. (1993). *Research on the African-American Family: A Holistic Perspective.* Westport, Connecticut: Auburn House.

Hughes, D. (2003). Correlates of African American and Latino Parents' Messages to Children about Ethnicity and Race: A Comparative Study of Racial Socialization. *American Journal of Community Psychology,* 31(1-2), 15-33.

Hughes, D. & L. Chen. (1999). The Nature of Parents' Race-Related Communications to Children: A Developmental Perspective. In L. Batter & C. S. Tamis-LeMonda (Eds.) *Child Psychology: A handbook of Contemporary Issues.* eds.,pp. 467-490. Philadelphia: Psychology Press.

Hughes, D. & D. Johnson. (2001). Correlates in Children's Experiences of Parents' Racial Socialization Behaviors. *Journal of Marriage and Family,* 63, 981-995.

Hughes, D., J. Rodriguez, E. P. Smith, D. Johnson, H. C. Stevenson & P. Spicer. (2006). Parents' Ethnic-Racial Socialization Practices: A Review Of Research and Directions for Future Study. *Developmental Psychology,* 42(5), 747-770.

Jarrett, R. L. & L. M. Burton. (1999). Dynamic Dimensions of Family Structure in Low-Income African American Families: Emergent Themes in Qualitative Research. *Journal of Comparative Family Studies,* 30(2), 177-188.

Johnson, D. J., E. Jaeger, S. M Randolph, A. M. Cauce & J. Ward. (2003). Studying the Effects of Early Child Care Experiences on the Development of Children Of Color in the United States: Toward a More Inclusive Research Agenda. *Child Development,* 74(5), 1227–1244.

Lesane-Brown, C. L. (2006). A Review of Race Socialization Within Black Families.*Developmental Review,* 26, 400-426.

Marshall, S. (1995). Ethnic Socialization of African American Children: Implications for Parenting, Identity Development, and Academic Achievement. *Journal of Youth and Adolescence,* 24(4), 377-396.

McAdoo, H. P. (Ed.) (2006). *Black Families, 4ᵗʰ ed.* Thousand Oaks, CA: Sage Publications

_____ (1997). *Black Families, 3ʳᵈ ed.* Thousand Oaks, CA: Sage Publications.

_____ (1988). *Black Families, 2ⁿᵈ ed.* Newbury Park, CA: Sage Publications.

_____ (1981). *Black Families.* Beverly Hills, CA: Sage Publications.

McHale, S. M., A. C. Crouter, J.Y. Kim, L. M. Burton, K. D. Davis, A. M. Dotterer, & D P. Swanson. (2006). Mothers' and Fathers' Racial Socialization in African American Families: Implications for Youth. *Child Development,* 77(5), 1387-1402.

Murray, C. B. & J. Mandara. (2002). Racial Identity Development in African American Children. In H. P. McAdoo (Ed.) *Black Children: Social, Educational, and Parental Environments* (pp.73-96). Thousand Oaks, CA: Sage Publications.

National Center for Education Statistics. Detroit, Michigan Public Schools. http://nces.ed.gov/globallocator/index.asp?search=1&State=MI&city=Detroit&zipcode=&miles=&itemname=&sortby=name&School=1&CS=CD559B3C

Neblett, E. W., C. L. Philip, C. D. Cogburn & R. M. Sellers. (2006). African American Adolescents' Discrimination Experiences and Academic Achievement: Racial Socialization as a Cultural Compensatory and Protective Factor. *Journal of Black Psychology,* 32(2), 199-218.

Oyserman, D., M. Kemmelmeier, S. Fryberg, H. Broshi & T. Hart-Johnson. (2003). Racial-Ethnic Self-Schemas. *Social Psychology Quarterly,* 66(4), 333-347.

Robinson, J. & M. Biran. (2006). Discovering Self: Relationships Between African Identity and Academic Achievement. *Journal of Black Studies,* 37: 46-68.

Scott, L. D. Jr. (2003). The Relation of Racial Identity and Racial Socialization to Coping with Discrimination Among African American Adolescents. *Journal of Black Studies,* 33(4), 520-538.

Silverman, D. (1993). Interpreting Qualitative Data: Methods for Analyzing Talk, Text, and Interaction. London: Sage Publications.

Stack, C. B. & L. M. Burton. (1994). Kinscripts: Reflections on Family, Generation, and Culture. In E. N. Glenn, G. Chang & L. R. Farcey (Eds.) *Mothering: Ideology, Experience, And Agency* (pp. 33-44) New York: Routledge.

293

Staples, R. (1998). *The Black Family: Essays and Studies*. Belmont, CA: Wadsworth Publishing.

Stevenson, H. C., Jr. (1995). Relationship of Adolescent Perceptions of Racial Socialization to Racial Identity. *Journal of Black Psychology*, 21, 49-70.

Stevenson, H. C., J. D. McNeil, T. Herrero-Taylor & G. Y. Davis. (2005). Influence of Perceived Neighborhood Diversity and Racism Experience on the Racial Socialization of Black Youth. *Journal of Black Psychology*, 31(3), 273-290.

Thomas, A. J. & S. L. Speight. (1999). Racial Identity and Racial Socialization Attitudes of African American Parents. *Journal of Black Psychology*, 25(2), 152-170.

Thomas, D. E., T. G. Townsend, F. Z. Belgrave. (2003). The Influence of Cultural and Racial Identification on the Psychosocial Adjustment of Inner-City African American Children in School. *American Journal of Community Psychology*, 32, 217-228.

Thornton, M. C., L. M. Chatters, R. J. Taylor & W. R. Allen. (1990). Sociodemographic and Environmental Correlates of Racial Socialization By Black Parents. *Child Development*, 61, 401-409.

Townsend, T & E. Lanphier. (2007). Family Influences on Racial Identity Among African American Youth. *Journal of Black Psychology*, 33(3), 278-298.

Tyler, K. M., A. W. Boykin, C. M. Boelter & M. L. Dillihunt. (2005). Examining Mainstream and Afro-Cultural Value Socialization in African American Households. *Journal of Black Psychology*, 31(3), 291-311.

U.S. Census Bureau. (2000). Fact sheet: Detroit City, Michigan, Census 2000 Demographic Profile Highlights. http://factfinder.census.gov/servlet/SAFFFacts?_event=&geo_id=16000US2622000&_geoContext=01000US%7C04000US26%7C16000US2622000&_street=&_county=Detroit&_cityTown=Detroit&_state=04000US26&_zip=&_lang=en&_sse=on&ActiveGeoDiv=&_useEV=&pctxt=fph&pgsl=160&_submenuId=factsheet_1&ds_name=ACS_2005_SAFF&_ci_nbr=null&qr_name=null&reg=null%3Anull&_keyword=&_industry=.

U.S. Census Bureau. (2001). Majority of African Americans Live in 10 States; New York City and Chicago are Cities with Largest Black Populations. Press Release, August 13, 2001. http://www.census.gov/Press-Release/www/2001/cb01cn176.html.

Walker, K., E. Taylor, A. McElroy, D. A. Phillip & M. N. Wilson. (1995). Familial and Ecological Correlates of Self-Esteem in African American Children. In M. N. Wilson (Ed.) *African American Family Life: Its Structural and Ecological Aspects* (pp. 23-34). San Francisco: Jossey-Bass.

Wakefield, W. D. & C. Hudley. (2007). Ethnic and Racial Identity and Adolescent Well-Being. *Theory Into Practice*, 46(2), 147-154.

Winkler, E. N. (2008). "It's Like Arming Them" : African American Mothers' Views on Racial Socialization. In E. Rudd & L. Descartes (Eds.) *The Chang-*

294

ing Landscape of Work and Family in the American Middle Class: Reports from the Field. (pp. 211-241). Lanham, MD: Lexington Books (Rowan & Littlefield).

Zwiers, M. L. & P. J. Morrissette. (1999). *Effective Interviewing of Children: A Comprehensive Guide for Counselors and Human Service Workers*. Philadelphia: Accelerated Development.

Part III

THE CARIBBEAN

CHAPTER *12*

INSIGHTS TO THE CARIBBEAN FAMILY: LEGACY, TRADITION, AND CULTURE

Michele Sogren

INTRODUCTION

Consistent with the universal conceptualization of the family, in the Caribbean, the family is perceived as being instrumental in meeting the needs of its members and according to Goldenberg and Goldenberg (2004) in fashioning and instilling fundamental and powerful assumptions about the world and the society in which it exists. There is also a strong belief in Caribbean societies that ideally, the family provides the critical base from which its members develop their roles and functions in maintaining social order and influencing societal advancement. However, there is a growing body of evidence that highlights the impact of global technological and environmental changes and developments on the family's ability to respond to its mandates in the customary fashions. This chapter attempts to capture the reality of the Caribbean family, examine the tenets that underlie the traditional family organizations and showcase contemporary transformations and challenges to family functioning. The perceptions of Caribbean scholars are blended with the narratives of the people of Trinidad and Tobago who participated in a qualitative study conducted by the Ministry of Social Development. Further, it is intended that this interrogation would inform the curriculum content of related educational and training courses and the intervention approaches with Caribbean families.

The Caribbean (Its Geography and History in a Nutshell)

Barrow (1996, p. xi) provided a vivid capsule of the history and geography of the Caribbean region and in a way, an explanation for the trajectory of the development of the families of the Caribbean.

> The Caribbean, an arc of island states stretching from Belize in Central America southward through the Caribbean Sea to Guyana on the South American coast, is home to approximately 50 million people. Geographically separated, these countries nevertheless share the common history and contemporary imprint of discovery, plantation slavery and colonialism.

The Caribbean family was therefore nurtured in a complex environment of major transformations (economic, political and social) and a "pot pourri" of cultures and ethnicities. So it is not at all surprising that the construction of all-encompassing definitions or descriptors of the Caribbean family continues to be elusive.

The Literature

The review of literature presented here is not a comprehensive review of the literature available on Caribbean family life but rather is a summary of the key themes identified from specific texts. While the literature selected reflects the work of some of the major social commentators and writers on the subject in the Caribbean, there are a number of gaps. For instance much of the literature reviewed is written with specific reference to families of African Caribbean origin and there are relatively few texts included which address ethnic diversity and the specific circumstances of families of Indian Caribbean origin. This limitation aside, the literature discussed raises issues that are important across the spectrum of Trinidadian society.

Historical Context and Contemporary Developments

The family, viewed in most societies as the primary social institution, has been for decades, the focus of attention for researchers, academics, professionals and policy makers and there exists a large body of research and literature on Caribbean families, the origins, structures, functioning and roles. Of note, are the shifts in emphases and focus that characterized Caribbean family studies from the mid 1940s to the early 1970s. Barrow (2001) has charted the development of research on Caribbean families from the mid 1940s and identifies the ways that these studies:

...attempted a revised explanation of Caribbean family and pre-sented varying images of masculinity and femininity (p. 418).

Though the focus of contemporary studies of Caribbean families bears some similarity to those of earlier studies, it is evident that the stereotypical perceptions and biased assumptions of Caribbean family and family relationships which dominated that era of writings have been upstaged by the reports generated from the empowering, post-modernistic approach to the interrogation of Caribbean family life. Barrow (2001) noted that the previously labelled dysfunctional patterns of black lower-class families were reframed as culturally appropriate solutions to the problems of daily living experienced by these families.

The signature characteristic of the more current studies of Caribbean family life has been the use made of the narratives of the men and women of the Caribbean, the insights these have provided for the researchers and the expanded vision and range of the studies undertaken. The current literature has demonstrated and generated interest in a range of topics, in particular: the gendered roles and responsibilities in families; the popular beliefs and the realities about family forms; the ethnic and cultural variations with regard to child-rearing and child-caring practices (see for example, Durant-Gonzalez, 1982) and employment and education. Further, contemporary research has explored the impact of specific social phenomena on family life in Trinidad and Tobago such as domestic violence (Holder Dolly & Sogren, 2004) and parental migration (Jones, Sharpe & Sogren, 2004). The key themes to emerge from the study on the family to which this review of literature relates are: gendered roles, family structure, parenting practices, challenges and support systems. In the section that follows, these themes are discussed in relation to the wider literature on the topics.

Gendered Roles

The discourse on gendered roles and male/female dominance in family life is prolific and spans decades of writings from Herskovits (1940s) to Jones et al (2004). While there exists some variations among Caribbean countries, especially within the Hispanic Caribbean, the literature has demonstrated with relative consistency that females bear major responsibility for 'producing, providing, controlling or managing those resources essential to meeting daily needs within families (Durant-Gonzalez, 1982, p.3). Durant-Gonzalez further contended that this feature was not limited to single parent families but was common among women in other family types as well (Durant-Gonzalez, 1982).

The responsibility for the well being of families has been viewed and accepted, in the main, as an expectation of women in most Caribbean countries. Role expectation and role fulfilment are in part, sanctioned by cultural and ethnic traditions across races and classes. This matrifocal centeredness on familial responsibility does not however necessarily extend to decision-making and conceptualisations of 'headship'. Safa (1986) cautions that a distinction must be made between the symbolism of head of the household and the actual decision-making and notes that

> ...nominal deference to men as head of the household may also
> be how women try to make men comply with their responsibilities as economic providers (1986, p. 11).

There is consensus in the literature that men are assigned or assume the title of 'head' whether or not in actuality they perform major roles in managing and maintaining their families. Safa (1986) refers to this practice as 'adherence to the middle-class norm of respectability' (p.11). Interestingly, St. Bernard (1997) in his study of 'Kinship and Family Dynamics in Laventille' notes that the Afro-Trinidadian male persists in adhering to the perception of the male as head of household despite the acknowledgment of the major role that women play. St. Bernard points out that:

> [the men keep] traditional orientations regarding household decision-making...despite their recognition of the phenomenal contributions that women have made to their families' well being. (p. 291)

In spite of the wealth of evidence that women bear the primary responsibility for the family, it appears that there has been no equivalent shift in the way women are perceived or in their status. This indicates that the ideology of male dominance in the conceptualisation and formation of gender roles within the family has not been dented. (Moses, 2001; Durant-Gonzalez, 1982).

Importantly the literature highlights the multiple and interconnected ways in which the responsibility for the family is borne by women. It is noted that there are increased numbers of female headed households (Massiah, 1982), increased numbers of women participating in the labour force (McKenzie, 1979) and increased numbers of women migrating for employment (Jones, Sharpe & Sogren, 2004). These developments suggest that women increasingly have a primary or major financial role as the family 'breadwinner'. Furthermore women continue to bear the greater part of familial responsibility as has been discussed above (Durant-Gonzalez, 1982). These trends must impact the family and the quality of family life.

Family Structure

There is a long-standing debate among researchers and scholars about the definition of 'family' in the Caribbean context and the literature is replete with descriptions, perceptions and postulations about the variety of family arrangements that exist in Caribbean countries. According to Hodge (2002), the traditional Caribbean family referred to a network of people that was not necessarily organized around a mating couple, yet the nuclear family continues to enjoy a prestigious status in Caribbean societies. Le Franc, Bailey and Branche (1998) argue that while the ideal of the legal monogamous unit is still widely held, in reality there is more likely to be multiple partnering and involvement in various types of unions.

The notions of 'fluid household boundaries' (Le Franc et al, 1998, p. 8) and 'rational alternatives' (St. Bernard, 1997, p. 289) provide the context (economic and social survival) for the proliferation of varying family organizations and offer positive reframe for the existing realities. In contrast the more 'established' family forms, such as, the nuclear, (legal or common-law) visiting, single female or male and the extended family have been linked to a number of social factors, for example, economics, history and culture, ethnicity and social class. In particular, the impact of the history and culture of Afro and Indo Caribbeans on the past and contemporary family structure is noted as being significant. Russell and Brown et al (1997) and Massiah (1982) remarked on the unchanged characteristics of Afro-Caribbean family forms in the 150 years since emancipation and Reddock (1994, p. 41) refers to the 'submerged consciousness' as the pivotal point at which the 'caste ideology' (Barrow, 1996 p. 340) has survived to influence contemporary East Indian family patterns.

The concepts of survival, change and acculturation have been debated and argued among researchers such as Klass (1961), Nevadomsky (1980) and Rauf (1974). Barrow (1996) contends that a fundamental issue in this debate is the notion of continuity being linked to cultural survival and

> change being attributed to the process of creolisation as a result of the impact of Caribbean conditions... p. 340.

The literature suggests that within the Caribbean context of cultural persistence, change and revival (Barrow, 1996), the contemporary family patterns among East Indians reflect relaxed patriarchal gender relations, changes to conjugal arrangements and changes to household composition.

Parenting Practices

There is universal agreement that the quality of family life and indeed the survival of this critical social institution have depended, in large measure, on healthy developmental parenting practices nurtured and supported, literally, by the 'entire village.' This concept of 'collective parenting' a notion implied within some of the literature, is based on studies of kinship networks and family histories of parenting. Contemporary studies however point to the changing nature of kinship networks and the increasing challenges that families face and in this context, some writers suggest that opportunities for the acquisition of positive parenting skills are limited.

The observation is made that there exists a tendency to rely on inherited parenting practices (Thomas, 2004) with relatively limited reference to a knowledge and skills base. This seems to be the case even where families are fractured or where poor parenting practices have been inherited. In this context, Mahabir-Wyatt (2004) advocates parenting training for all before attainment of adulthood and suggests the 12-14 year age group as being the ideal starting point. The practice of providing educational and training programmes on effective parenting and parenting behaviours is not new to the Caribbean and there is a growing body of research on parent education approaches and methodologies which accommodate the culturally determined child-rearing and child-caring practices of the Caribbean (Wint & Brown, 2001). Given the severe strains and challenges that many families experience which in turn impact the provision of adequate parenting, it is argued that education initiatives such as these should be a prerequisite of parenting. Le Franc et al (1998) refer to the challenges faced by many families as the 'environmental incivilities' (p. 22) that mould and influence parenting practices. Le Franc's work is based on a study of inner-city families in Jamaica and Barbados in which parenting practices are described as being characterised by chronic and unrelenting stresses. There is evidence in the literature to suggest that the consequences of these 'incivilities' and related social phenomena are dire and long-term, with pervasive and frequently deleterious effects on the children, families and by extension the wider communities.

Holder Dolly and Sogren (2004) in a study of the impact of domestic violence on children note:

> children were under siege psychologically, emotionally and socially... Their family situations are complex and dysfunctional... Some of the predominant psychological issues experienced by these children included, depression, anxiety, aggression and a series of serious behavioural and educational difficulties (p. 22).

Further, research by Jones et al (2004) on children's experiences of parental migration revealed the high emotional and social costs to family life and the emotional health and well-being of children, notwithstanding the financial benefits and improved material conditions. In summary, the literature points to the need for the transmission and acquisition of adequate parenting skills and the formalising of family support systems and services (Le Franc et al, 1998; Holder Dolly & Sogren, 2004). Of significance, is the pivotal role identified for Governments of the region in rationalizing, collaborating and instituting the requisite support to ensure that the rights of the families of the Caribbean are visibly acknowledged so that they can continue to survive and flourish.

THE FOCUS GROUPS

Juxtaposed against these scholarly perceptions, interpretations and inferences, are the voices and realities of these families, represented by members of two focus groups (employers/employees and counsellors/service providers) conducted in Trinidad and Tobago. Contextually, these focus groups were part of a series held with critical stakeholders in a qualitative study conducted in 2004 by the Ministry of Social Development which examined the status of the family in Trinidad and Tobago. These two focus groups were selected because they provided unique perspectives about family life as clinicians, programme planners, resource managers, members of the work force and as well, of family units themselves. The participants for the focus group series were selected by purposive non-probability sampling procedures and they represented the various ethnic, social and economic groupings that exist in Trinidad and Tobago and included, to a large extent, equal numbers of males and females and a wide age range.

LOCATING TRINIDAD AND TOBAGO

The Republic of Trinidad and Tobago is a twin-island state located at the southernmost end of the Lesser Antilles. Its history is characterised by colonisation by the Spanish, French and British, long periods of slavery and indentureship and an influx of immigrants from China, the Middle East and Portugal spanning several decades. The population of approximately 1.26 million comprises several ethnicities, with individuals of African descent accounting for 37.5% of the population, of East Indian descent, 40% and those of mixed ethnicity 20.5% (Central Statistical Office, 2000).

ANALYSIS

The focus group series sought to obtain the current views and perspectives of key stakeholders on the status of the family and the central themes that guided the discussions were:

- functions of the family
- gender relations and gender roles
- challenges to family life
- parenting practices
- historical factors
- solutions and recommendations

FUNCTIONS OF THE FAMILY

Two main streams of thought emerged concerning the critical functions of the family:

- that the family held primary responsibility for the holistic development of children (physical, cognitive, spiritual, social, emotional, moral development) and the mastery of skills
- the notion of the family creating an environment characterized by love, respect, concern; sharing and reciprocity; an environment which accommodates the "positives and negatives" of interpersonal relationships and rewards and disciplines appropriately.

There was general agreement that within such an environment, the "ideal family" could be germinated, since according to the participants,

> a family like a pillow and is there for one another in good times and bad times; the family supports and looks after one another's interests; being one another's keeper.

GENDER RELATIONS/GENDER ROLES

This issue pervaded the discussions in both groups and was flagged as being a central element of family functioning. In general the views expressed seemed to suggest that the socialization and parenting experiences of males and females, the differences in the relational practices of males and females, the ways in which gendered roles are configured and acted out, largely influenced and determined the gender issues within the family context. The points of divergence between the two groups occurred in the areas of ideological perspectives and assumptions, frames of reference and focus. In one group in which there were twenty-five (25) responses on this issue, the dominant male respondent expounded on the traditional roles of males and females in the family, the practice of socializing male and female offspring along these traditional gendered lines and the notion of leadership being the sole domain of males.

- Father is the head of the house, he is the man that has to go and exchange his labour for money to bring to the family.
- The man is in charge and you have to go out there and get the money.

The other respondents also cited the socialization practices as being largely influential on the gender relations in the family both between parents and among male and female offspring. Interestingly, two female respondents expressed their desires to be "stay at home mothers" but with the expectation of "respect" from her partner, according to one respondent. The discussion in the other group though more analytical and introspective, was flavoured with emotional overtones of mutuality, empathy and insight. There was overwhelming agreement that the "business" of being male in Trinidad & Tobago was underestimated, unattended and undirected and the male functions, to a large extent, on "auto-pilot" as described by one male respondent. There were frequent references to society's neglect of the needs of males, termed "psychological negligence" by one male respondent. The extensive discussion identified some of the peculiar, but often "hidden" experiences of male socialization which directly affected the parenting styles and even the ability to accept paternal responsibilities. The issues of emotional deprivation, emotional stunting, emotional immaturity, experiences deplete of positive male role models, of being parented by emotionally distant and abusive mothers brought sharp focus on the challenges imposed on male parenting and by extension on the roles and functions that evolve within the family. While there was some agreement that it was desirable and beneficial to have male presence in the family, there were compelling arguments by the four respondents who challenged this position and introduced to the discussion examples of long term emotional scarring, dysfunctional relationship patterns and psychological resistance to parenting responsibility. These were described as being the direct consequence of unhealthy male parenting, either in instances of abuse, emotional unavailability or pathological passivity. Of significance, one female respondent, who held the position that "a man is a necessary role model," argued strongly that in cases where extreme trauma existed (e.g. child sexual abuse) the absence of a male in the family would yield a far healthier and safer environment for a functional family experience. This view was supported by another female respondent who proposed that "the ideal family could have grandparents and aunts and didn't necessarily have to have a father."

Essentially, the participants in both groups presented convictions that the gendered roles and relational styles, were either learnt (by modelling) acquired or "created." Of note, however, was the skewed slant on "maleness" in one group, the unbalanced focus, in both groups on the role of females in family functioning and limited discussion of the positive influences and elements of gender on the family.

CHALLENGES TO FAMILY LIFE

That there exist serious challenges to contemporary family life in Trinidad & Tobago was established at the outset in both groups and throughout the discussion, repeated references were made to the challenging issues experienced by many families and to the evidence of the impact and consequences of these on the families, communities, institutions and society in general. In general, from the discussion the challenges seem to merge naturally into the following categories:

- economical
- psychological
- environmental / situational

Economical

The central theme was the direct relationship between the wage earning capacities of parents and the quality of their family life. There was consensus that low wage earners logically experienced low spending and providing capacity and that these parents were often compelled to either work overtime or take on more that one job. The consequences of these options were viewed as being detrimental to the health of families, in that children were often unsupervised for long periods, there was inadequate time for meaningful family interactions and the risks for exploitation of the children's vulnerability increased significantly.

Psychological

The respondents in one group viewed the psychological make-up and experiences of parents and children as imposing considerable limitations to effective family functioning and to the creation of the "ideal" family. Specifically, they highlighted the "plight" of the males who too frequently experienced "entrapped fatherhood," emotional isolation, unpreparedness for parenting and family responsibilities and diminished capacity for relationship building and negotiating emotional contracts. Children were considered to be the bearers of these psychological "burdens," especially in the "less than ideal" families where oftentimes the children literally had no one on whom they could depend. The respondents described the young users of their services as being typically angry, volatile, mistrustful and depressed. This emotional context is further compounded for parentified children, the children in sibling families and children whose parent/s has/have migrated.

Environment / Situational

The environmental and situational circumstances and experiences were targeted as having major influence on the families. Some of the effects of these challenges on family life were previously presented, however the specific sources of these constraints were located as follows:

- the changes in community and societal values
- the unsupportive and "unfriendly" work environment
- the displacement of family time and interpersonal communication by "technological and electronic" activities
- part-time and long-distance parenting typical of migrant parents, parents who work long hours, parents separated from their families for other reasons e.g. divorce
- the unprecedented and myriad stresses related to the logistics of commuting to work and to school
- the perennial "tiredness syndrome."

PARENTING PRACTICES

The discussion of this issue was absorbed into the discussion of challenges to family life in general as such, the concerns and positions expressed apply in most instances to these related issues. A noteworthy peculiarity in the positions of one group was the emphatic view that gendered roles and responsibilities, socialization experiences and practices were significantly influential on parenting styles and skills and that they were characterized by inherent challenges. Interestingly the female respondents in this group, though in general agreement with that view, also identified as a challenge, the reality of the family being a private domain and so obscured in a sense from public scrutiny and monitoring. The other challenges specific to parenting centred around the management of the crises and tasks of the developmental ages and stages of children, managing and understanding the differences in experiences in growing up as a male and female and the implied requirement for varying parenting styles and practices.

The insights of the respondents are captured in the following excerpts:

- Men and women have different psychological needs..... it reflects on how we raise our boy children, and girl children, we don't nurture their differences and psychological needs.
- It's about trying to engage children in activities which they are naturally disposed to.
- Sometimes we tend to be narrow-minded in terms of what we want for our children.
- If you had impaired relationships with your parents, that will impact how you parent.
- We must know how to socialize our boys.
- You have to be firmer with a boy; I did not want femininize boy children.
- A boy without a father believes he has to be the man of the house.
- If the ideal family is ever to come on board, mother and father relationships must be upheld and strengthened.

HISTORICAL FACTORS

The changes and adjustments to community and societal values and cultural practices were suggested as having significant influence on contemporary family life and parenting. References were made to the current migratory patterns, establishment of transient communities within traditional village communities and the mushrooming of up-scale communities adjacent to "home" communities. The discussion suggested that these changes to the established order of these villages and communities resulted in alterations to the interactional patterns, to the reciprocal learning, sharing and caring historically typical of those communities and logically to the genre of family life. In the discussion of ethnic differences in family practices, two female respondents in one group commented on the changing roles of the East Indian female from being homemaker and supporter to her husband to being independently and separately employed and they noted the resultant changes to family practices e.g. children being unsupervised. This in their view marked a dramatic divergence from the traditional way of life in the East Indian family.

The typical perceptions included:

- People in these new communities don't talk to one another.
- We used to have a village life.... Now people coming and going.
- We used to have parks where children used to play.
- The families just going through the motions, not with a deep sense of spiritual bonding.
- Time is changing, in Indian families, the young ladies are moving away from the mother-in-law syndrome and they have their own homes.
- Long ago the Indian woman would get married and stay at home and take care of the family... now women are not at home.
- In days gone by the man and woman (in East Indian families) would work together in the fields or the shop. Now both are working in different places and a domestic worker taking care of the children.

SOLUTIONS AND RECOMMENDATIONS

There was universal agreement that the State should take the lead in developing new family specific legislation with multi-pronged scope and jurisdiction to:

- manage, enforce and support parental responsibility
- institute legally constructed accountancy and evaluating systems for State, private sector, and NGO agencies and services
- establish funding systems for families.

The other suggestions focused on the expansion and development of clinical, programmatic and care services such as:

- educational workshops and seminars on parenting, male/female relationships, family relationships, anger management, accessing services
- men's groups
- work based and other accessible day care centres
- institutionalized support for males
- crisis centres
- community based interventions
- pre and post marital counselling

The discussions also highlighted the need to review the education system in general with a view to developing a more child-friendly and child-centred curriculum which would facilitate the holistic development of the nation's children. In that regard, it was further recommended that of necessity, the needs and requirements of teachers and school administrators should be considered and accommodated. Overwhelmingly, there was the caution that these services, programmes and legal systems should be family centred, accessible and user-friendly.

CONCLUSION

The synergy that emerged between the existing literature and the current research findings suggests that notwithstanding the grave challenges that threaten the stability and capacity capital of many families singularly, as an institutional unit, the family still possessed significant strengths, remarkable resilience, sensitivity and commitment to the wider society. Within this context, there was wide recognition of the need for tangible and overt support for families in order to maximize their potential for optimum functioning. In that regard, it will be necessary to acknowledge the significance and impact on family life of such social constructs as gendered role expectations and demands, fluid family forms and care-giving arrangements and as well contemporary social phenomena like violence in families and parental migration. It is evident that the relationships that exist among these are profound and pervasive and offer indisputable insights which ought not to be ignored. The post-modernistic strengths-based approach adopted by contemporary scholars provides a valid and valuable framework for understanding the ways in which Caribbean families are configured and for distinguishing the myths from the lived experiences and realities. This discourse highlighted the almost inextricable link among race, ethnicity, religion, culture, language, tradition, parenting practices and the status of family life in the Caribbean. Further, it is important to understand and accept that the needs of Caribbean families are not homogenous and may require specific and localized interventions in order to support families in general and vulnerable families in particular as they negotiate relationships with their environment. The current debate about family life in the Caribbean is advanced as being neither pathological, deviant nor defensive but rather as a re-configured construct that embraces a rights-based and strengths-based philosophy. This perspective could infuse new confidence and self-efficacy into the families of the Caribbean, validate the positive parenting practices that exist and offer hope, motivation and support to the families as they strive to maintain their viability and status as critical pillars in society.

ACKNOWLEDGEMENTS

I wish to congratulate the Ministry of Social Development for initiating this vital study of family life in Trinidad and Tobago. I wish also to express my gratitude to the participants of the focus groups, Prof. Adele Jones and Ms. Rachel D'Arceuil for their generous input and assistance.

References

Barrow, C. (1996). *Family in the Caribbean: Themes and Perspectives.* Jamaica: Ian Randle Publishers.

Barrow, C. (2001). Men, Women and Family in the Caribbean. In C. Barrow, and R. Reddock (Eds.) *Caribbean Sociology: Introductory Readings.* Jamaica: Ian Randle Publishers.

Durant-Gonzalez, V. (1982). The Realm of Female Familial Responsibility. In J. Massiah (Ed.) *Women in the Caribbean Project. Vol. 2. Women and the Family,* Cave Hill, Barbados. Institute of Social and Economic Research.

Goldenberg, I & H. Goldenberg (2004). *Family Therapy: An Overview.* 6th Edition, U.S.A. Thomson Brooks/Cole.

Holder Dolly, J. & M. Sogren (2004). The Impact of Domestic Violence of Children in Trinidad and Tobago. *Caribbean Journal of Social Work.* Vol 3, 7-23.

Hodge, M. (2002) We Kind of Family, In P. Mohammed (Ed.) *Gendered Realities: Essays in Caribbean Feminist Thought.* Jamaica: The University of the West Indies Press and Centre for Gender and Development Studies.

Jones, A. J. Sharpe, & M. Sogren, (2004) Children's Experiences of Separation from Parents as a Consequence of Migration. *Caribbean Journal of Social Work.* Vol 3: 89-109.

Klass, M. (1961). East Indians in Trinidad. In C. Barrow (Ed.) *Family in the Caribbean: Themes and Perspectives,* Jamaica: Ian Randle Publishers

Le Franc, E W. Baily, & C. Branche (1998). The Family Unit: An Illusive Dream? In Ryan, & R. McCree, (Eds.) Caribbean Dialogue: *A Journal of Contemporary Caribbean Policy Issues.* 4(1), Trinidad: Institute of Social and Economic Research.

Le Franc, E., W. Baily, & C. Branche (1998). Parenting and Socialisation in Caribbean Family Systems. In S. Ryan and R. McCree (Eds.) *Caribbean Dialogue: A Journal of Contemporary Caribbean Policy Issues.* 4(1) Trinidad: Institute of Social and Economic Research.

Massiah, J. (1982). Women Who Head Households. In J. Massiah (Ed.) *Women in the Caribbean Project. Vol. 2. Women and the Family.* The University of the West Indies. Cave Hill, Barbados: Institute of Social and Economic Research.

Mahabir-Wyatt, D. (2004) Express Woman. *Express Newspaper.* Trinidad.

Mc Kenzie, H. (1979). The Individual, the Family and Society in the Caribbean. In J. Massiah (Ed.) *Women in the Caribbean Project, Vol. 2. Women and the Family.* The University of the West Indies. Cave Hill, Barbados: Institute of Social and Economic Research.

Moses, Y. (2001). Female Status, the Family and Male Dominance in the West Indian Community. In C. Barrow & R. Reddock (Eds.) *Caribbean Sociology: Introductory Readings.* Jamaica: Ian Randle Publishers.

Nevadomsky, J. (1980). Changes in Hindu Institutions in an Alien Environment. In C. Barrow (Ed.) *Family in the Caribbean: Themes and Perspectives.* Jamaica: Ian Randle Publishers.

Reddock, R. (1994). Women, Labour and Politics in Trinidad and Tobago: A History. In C. Barrow (Ed.) *Family in the Caribbean: Themes and Perspectives.* Jamaica: Ian Randle Publishers.

Russell-Brown, P. Norville, B., and Griffith, C. (1997). Child-Shifting: A Survival Strategy for Teenage Mothers. In J. Roopnarine and J. Brown (Eds.) *Caribbean Families: Diversity among Ethnic Groups.* Advances in Applied Developmental Psychology: Ablex Publishing Corporation.

Rauf, M. (1974) Indian Village in Trinidad: A Study of Cultural Change and Ethnic Identity. In C. Barrow (Ed.) *Family in the Caribbean: Themes and Perspectives.* Jamaica: Ian Randle Publishers

Safa, H. (1986). Economic Autonomy and Sexual Equality in Caribbean Society. In J. Massiah (Ed.) *Woman in the Caribbean* (Part 2) Cave Hill, The University of the West Indies, Barbados: Institute of Social and Economic research.

St. Bernard, G. (1997). Kinship and Family Dynamics in Laventille. In S. Ryan and R. McCree (Eds.) *Behind the Bridge.* St. Augustine, The University of the West Indies, Trinidad: Institute of Social and Economic Research.

Thomas, RM. (2004) Express Woman. *Express Newspaper.* Trinidad.

Wint, E. & J. Brown, (2001) The Knowledge and Practice of Effective Parenting. In C. Barrow and R. Reddock (Eds.) *Caribbean Sociology: Introductory Readings.* Jamaica: Ian Randle Publishers.

CHAPTER *13*

EXTENDED FAMILY RHETORIC: REVIEWING CHILDHOOD AND FAMILY IN BARBADOS AND THE CARIBBEAN

Christine Barrow

INTRODUCTION

Historically, Afro-Caribbean families have been a popular target for criticism and blame interspersed with only occasional words of praise. Public opinion is overwhelmingly negative, while academic interpretations are mixed. In Barbados, views expressed by politicians, educators, magistrates, the clergy and the general public repeatedly highlight family dysfunction and breakdown. Favorite fodder for the press, radio call-in programs and public discussion is an alarmist tirade of families *in crisis* and parents who neglect their responsibilities. All manner of social ills are assumed to have their source in family failure—from *unmannerly* children, to early sexual debut, teenage pregnancy and HIV infection, to delinquent youth, to neglected or abandoned elderly. In the process, fingers are pointed at parents, mothers in particular, and extended families. Little if any reference is made to any shortcomings in State social policy and provisions.

A mix of images frames this public outcry. There are *irresponsible* fathers, that is men in visiting unions with multiple partners and *outside* children, single mothers who are unable to care for or who neglect or abandon their children, and grandmothers who are less involved in child care than they were in the past. Family *breakdown* is thus measured against an ideal that combines nuclear and extended family forms, with parents, grandparents and other members of a wide kinship network performing their assigned roles of care and support. The tirade centers children and occasionally the elderly as the principal victims, let down by the very persons who should be devoted to their well-being. Children in single parent, female-headed families need fathers, and those in nuclear families need grannies, aunties and cousins.

The public debate calls for family restructuring with moral and cultural renewal, the two yoked in tandem. The longstanding message, dating back to post-emancipation campaigns is for moral regeneration to solve the problems of family life, *"promiscuity"* and *"illegitimacy"* in particular ((Barrow, 1995; Great Britain, 1945). Perpetuating this rhetoric, the Barbados Strategic Plan, 2006-2025 lists among its objectives: *"Develop programs that promote a strong and healthy family life and adherence to traditional moral and ethical values"* (Government of Barbados, 2007, p. 110). And in May 2008, with the support of the Barbados government ministry responsible for family, an event entitled *Jesus Week* was launched with the message that *"no matter how broken a family is, once you put Jesus at the helm, you would get through any problem ... If you can transform families, then you can transform a nation"* (The Barbados Advocate, 2008, p. 5). The debate thus extends family matters into ethical and social concerns, fueled by an imported moral fundamentalism sweeping through the country and the region. Secularization and the exposure of youth in particular, to the disruptive foreign influences of music, dance and dress have, the argument goes, promoted a modern era of social normlessness in which *anything goes*. Even the law, that pillar of the establishment, is seen to have undermined family life, traditional values and social order. By legalizing abortion, abolishing the distinction between legitimate and illegitimate children, according succession rights to women in common law unions, and facilitating divorce by removing at-fault clauses,[1] law reform furthers moral and social decline.

In sharp contrast to the public prophecies of doom and decay, academic scholarship has, since the early 1970s, made a U-turn by highlighting the *strengths* and *resilience* of Caribbean families. From this position, researchers contested the deficit models of their predecessors for whom the nuclear group, based on marriage and co-residence, was the norm against which Caribbean families were viewed, judged and found wanting. Labels such as *loose, casual* and *promiscuous* for conjugal unions and *denuded, incomplete* and *disorganized* for family structures proliferated in their writings. Rejecting this litany of family failure, the new generation adopted the extended family as its frame of reference—a kinship network anchored by women as mothers and grandmothers, breadwinners and household heads. The concept of *adaptive response* was the frame through which they rewrote matrifocality, conjugality, child-shifting and transnational families as flexible, resilient kinship forms appropriate and viable within the circumstances of unemployment, poverty and marginality. No longer a social and moral problem, family patterns were recast as *survival strategies* and solutions in response to economic conditions. But economic reductionism with family as the dependent variable persisted in this paradigm. It was not until some time later that family and conjugality in the Caribbean were viewed through the lens of ideology, culture and history.[2]

With these images and constructs in mind forming a backdrop, the body of this chapter reviews the realities of Caribbean childhood and family life. A critical measure of family life the world over lies in the care and support of those most vulnerable, children in particular, and it is from this perspective that we challenge the rhetoric and myths surrounding Afro-Caribbean families. After a brief historical and cultural overview and a discussion of social policy for children in Barbados, we review the findings of research that centers the role of the extended family in child care. This takes us to children who are without families and the alternative arrangements made for them, whether by legal adoption and fostering or State provided care in Children's Homes. We conclude the discussion by addressing some implications for research and social policy.

THE HISTORY AND CULTURE
OF CARIBBEAN CHILDHOOD

Deeply embedded in Caribbean culture is the positive value of children. In general, they are wanted, protected and cared for. Writing of village life in Barbados, Greenfield (1966, p.106) says: *"The desire for children is felt quite strongly by both man and wife and the failure to have any is a disappointment"*. Children are essential to family and community life, a home is empty without them and the daily domestic routine revolves around their care and socialization. But children are also valued for their work, inside and outside the home.

Although child labor is a thing of the past in Barbados (United Nations, 1997, p. 201-202), their contribution to domestic chores persists as a social norm. For both men and women also, the birth of a child symbolizes social and sexual identity (Barrow, 1998; Dann, 1987; Greenfield, 1966. See also for Jamaica, Brown, Newland, Anderson & Chevannes, 1997; Mohammed & Perkins, 1999). The notion of an *unwanted child* is alien to Caribbean

317

culture and peoples of the region are somewhat mystified by reports from elsewhere that women and men actually decide to remain childless.

But child-centeredness was not always this evident in Caribbean society and there have been enormous changes in the ideology and reality of childhood. It is generally acknowledged that the appearance of childhood as a distinct phase in the life cycle is a relatively recent phenomenon worldwide, more so perhaps in Barbados and the wider Caribbean region. Under slavery, family life and childhood were virtually non-existent. It was considered more cost-effective to buy than to breed slaves. Children were thus, a burden to the system and infant and child mortality rates were appallingly high. Those children that did manage to survive were earning their keep in agricultural and domestic work from the age of five and graduated to full plantation labor by the time they were ten years old (Beckles ,1989; Brown & Inniss, 2005, p. 260).

After Emancipation in 1834 and gradually over the latter half of the century, children as children became more visible. Within homes and communities, it is possible that little changed in practice. The information we have paints a paradoxical picture of deplorable domestic conditions, combined with the positive value of children within their families where they were loved and the centre of attention. At a national level, however, the spread of primary education from the elite to the wider population meant that children were gradually relocated from work to school, although child labor persisted for sometime after it was abolished by law. Right up to the mid 1950s, it was normal for children to be kept from school to perform a wide range of tasks in and outside the home. They assisted with cooking, cleaning, washing dishes and shopping, collecting water from communal standpipes, weeding and tending livestock, carrying food to their fathers at work, and caring for their younger siblings (Greenfield, 1966, p. 84-6, 107).

Over the last generation or so, public education expanded to secondary and tertiary levels. In addition, official birth control policies and practices were successfully introduced in the mid-1950s. The overall result was that employment, pregnancy and parenting were delayed to later in life. In effect, adulthood was postponed and childhood extended to include the period socially recognized as adolescence.

Along with these social changes, the local cultural construct of the child was transformed from mini-adult to minor defined as vulnerable and in need of special care and support. The State assumed greater responsibility for children in law and in social policy, and special provisions were made for their health, education and protection. Children as children were withdrawn from the world of work and adult responsibility and given special protective places in the home, at school and in the community.

SOCIAL POLICY FOR CHILDREN

Barbados has been singled out for commendation by UNICEF as one of ten *"high achiever"* countries across the globe, with social indicators for children *"far higher than might be expected, given their national wealth"* and *"comparable to those found in the industrial world"* (Mehrotra, 2000, p. 1). Good governance and social policy with consistent investment in health and education, have enhanced social development for the population in general and for children and other vulnerable groups especially. Basic social indicators for children are in most instances above the average for CARICOM member States[3] (See Table 13.1).

Table 13.1: Select Indicators for Child Health and Education in Barbados and CARICOM Member States

	Barbados	All CARICOM Member States*
Health		
Infant Mortality Rate (under 1) (2005):	11	18
Child Mortality Rate (under 5) (2005):	12	22
Immunisation coverage (%) (2005)**:	94	93
Skilled attendant at delivery (%) (1997/2005):	100	96
Infants with low birth weight (%) (1996/2005):	11	11
Education		
Enrolment Ratio: pre-school*** (%) (2004):	89	77
Enrolment Ratio: primary school (2000/2005):	100	92
Enrolment Ratio: secondary school (2000/2005)		
Male:	93	75
Female:	98	80

Notes: * for which data are available
** 1 year old children immunized against TB, DPT, Polio and Measles
*** for children aged 3-5 years.
Sources: UNICEF, 2007; UNESCO, 2007; Government of Barbados, 2007.

Table 13.2: Child Abuse in Barbados, 1982-2007

Year	Sexual Abuse	Physical Abuse	Neglect	Emotional Abuse*	Abandonment	Total
1982-85**	49	147	315	–	36	547
1985-90	121	215	375	–	30	740
1990-95	139	263	497	17	6	922
1995- 2000	198	271	499	55	3	1026
2000-05	211	271	602	97	8	1189
2005-07	242	251	490	107	1	1091

Source: Child Care Board, Barbados
Notes: * Figures on Emotional Abuse were first collected in 1993/4.
             ** Mid-year figures

The picture is less encouraging in relation to the protection of children from abuse and neglect (See Table 13.2). Although official records of child abuse and neglect are notoriously inaccurate, we note very little evidence of decline in any forms of abuse, apart from abandonment. Among the children affected there is little distinction between the number of boys and girls in cases of emotional abuse, neglect or even physical abuse where, in 2004-05, 45.8 percent were girls. However, girls constitute the overwhelming proportion of victims of sexual abuse, 94.2 percent in 2004-05.[4]

The persistence and pervasiveness of child abuse throughout the Caribbean has recently been attributed to persistent cultural beliefs and attitudes. Despite the principles enshrined in the Convention on the Rights of the Child (CRC) which Barbados and all other CARICOM countries signed and ratified by 1993, local practices of child discipline continue to favour *beating, lashing* and *flogging* that still form *"part of the 'tradition' of schools, the judicial system and the home"* (UNICEF, 2006, p. 2). Although there is some evidence that parents and adults are selecting non-abusive forms of discipline, child rights advocates of the region point to the authoritarian nature of the adult-child relationship, the silencing of children, the emphasis in child socialization on obedience and *good manners*, and a *property mentality* among parents that allows them to deal with their children as they see fit (Barrow; 2003; Le Franc, 2001; Rock, 2001). Most disturbing are the continuously high rates of sexual abuse and the reports of a cultural normalcy relating to these practices (Le Franc, 2002, p. 293-295).

Despite the enlarged scope of State responsibility for health and educational provisions and for the care, support and development of children and other vulnerable persons, families still play a major role. The household continues to a large degree to be culturally and officially defined as private space. The reporting of abuse is not yet mandatory[5] and neighbours are reluctant to *interfere*, as they put it. Only when things go really wrong and incidents of abuse and violence become publicly known, will the State intervene. Based on an unspoken official assumption that they have the capacity and resources to do so, families continue to be given responsibility for the protection of their own.

FAMILY DYNAMICS

There is virtually no research to support, indeed to contest, the public perception of extended family breakdown. What concrete evidence we have is a series of Census reports on household composition that reveal a decline in the proportion of large households. Defined somewhat arbitrarily as households with 6 plus persons, these have declined 20 percent in 1980 to 9.5 percent by 2000 (Barbados, 1980; Barbados, 2000). But these figures say nothing about the quality of family relationships both within and across households and communities, or beyond national boundaries within what have become known as Caribbean *transnational families*.

Nevertheless, there are clear indications of other changes in family patterns that impact on the lives of children. On the positive side, among the most significant is the concept and practice of fatherhood. In the past, the role of father was narrowly defined as the provision of financial support and occasional heavy-handed discipline. As they reflect on their childhoods, many Barbadian adults would identify with the young boy in George Lamming's classic novel who spoke of: *"My father who had only fathered the idea of me and left me the sole liability of my mother who really fathered me"* [Lamming, 1970 (1953), p. 11]. Today's men are re-imaging fatherhood to embrace child-care and socialization. Contrasting their roles with what they now perceive as the marginality of their own fathers, they claim to be emotionally and practically involved in the care, nurture and socialization of their children, as one Barbadian man put it, *"to be there"* for their children (Barrow, 1998, p. 350. See also Brown, Newland, Anderson & Chevannes, 1997).

Working against the entry of men as fathers into the home and family is the brittleness of conjugal unions and the frequent separation between parents. This shows up officially in divorce rates. Climbing steadily, divorces rose from an average of 192 per year during the 1980s to 507 in 2004. In that year, a total of 352 children were affected by the divorce of their parents.[6] Although the law gives priority to the interests of children as *"the first and paramount concern"* during divorce proceedings, concerns have been raised.

> The major reactions among children of divorce in Barbados vary with age and level of maturity. They run the full range from guilt to anxiety, fear of abandonment, sleeping problems, eating disorders, hyperactivity, withdrawal and physical development regression. These problems are exacerbated by the fact that children are often used as pawns in the divorce proceedings such as when parents take opposite sides in relation to them and refuse to compromise in their interest"(Carter, 1994, p. 36).

The children of separated or divorced parents invariably remain with their mothers, even more so perhaps in the Caribbean where families are matrifocal. They become *outside children* to their fathers, many of who move on to form new conjugal unions and co-residential families with children *inside*, as it were.

CHILDREN, ADOPTION AND EXTENDED FAMILIES

Anthropological literature from throughout the Caribbean region shows that many children, both girls and boys, are raised by care-givers other than their biological parents for at least some period of their childhoods.[7] This is quite normal and culturally accepted. In Barbados, the practice is commonly referred to as *adoption*, though there is no legal procedure involved and parents, culturally and legally, retain custodial rights and ultimate responsibility for their children. The practice has become generally known in Caribbean social research as *"child-shifting"*, though is also referred to as *"serial parenting"* (Jones et al, 2004) and *"child-lending"* (Sanford, 1974), or the *"borrowing"* (Pulsipher, 1993; Senior, 1991) and *"passing on"* (Brodber, 1974) of children.

Sharing childcare among female kin and the *adoption* or informal fostering of children is characteristic of African kinship patterns (Goody, 1982; Le Vine, 2003) and widespread throughout the Diaspora among populations of Afro-Caribbean origin (Collins, 1992; Reynolds 2005; Stack, 1974). While it might be possible to trace historical antecedents to African roots, this feature of family life reflects the pattern of childcare common during slavery, though the line of connection must be drawn with caution. The plantation system assigned mothering to elderly women who raised all children as a communal group, while their mothers labored for long hours in the fields and planter households. Shaped by this legacy, mothering continues to demand the income-generating work of women and to separate them on a daily basis from their children. Well-established also in contemporary Caribbean culture is the pivotal role of the grand-mother as care-giver for children, the enduring bonds formed between her and those she has raised, her position at the center of an extended family network and the community status and respect accorded to her. Reported for the slave period are grandmothers who emerged as matriarchal figures on estates, *"empowered with immense moral and social authority in the slave communities"* (Beckles ,1989, p. 123). Mentioned also is *"commuting family culture"* of slaves who traveled across the country to maintain family rela-tionships (Beckles, 1989, p. 120). Slave children who were orphaned or separated from parents who were sold and relocated, were absorbed into their own or other families within the wider slave community, the pattern persisting after Emancipation as a survival strategy (Brown & Inniss 2005, p. 262). By that time, however, destitute children were also housed in infir-maries, that is multi-purpose public centers for the sick, elderly, homeless and orphaned, their institutionalization clear evidence of the incapacity of families to secure resources to care for their own.

Emancipation opened the door for the mass exodus of Barbadians. With extreme poverty their daily lived reality, and freedom and resistance to the plantation system high on their agenda for life, they migrated—ini-tially to Trinidad and Guyana (Roberts, 1955, p. 247) and later *en masse* to Panama as labor for canal construction. Between 1904 and 1914, an estimated 60,000 Barbadians left for Panama, equivalent in number to one third of the total population (Newton, 1987, p. 105). As new opportunities arose, Barbadians navigated their way to ever-distant shores—to Cuba and the United States early in the 1900s, to the UK during the 1950s and early 1960s, and subsequently back to the US and on to Canada. The exodus of one generation had a *"demonstration effect"* on the next (Thomas-Hope, 1992, p. 8), migration became culturally and socially embedded as a fact of life and a diasporic world view emerged in the Barbadian psyche. But migration is not so much about an individual leaving home and family as it is about extending families to become globalised networks. Geographi-cal distance and national immigration restrictions are mere barriers to be overcome as these transnational webs of kin facilitate the active and con-tinuous circulation of people, material goods and remittances.

Family migration is patterned as a phased process, one or other parent paving the way leaving children behind in the care of grandmoth-ers or other female kin. It has been estimated that, by 1960, a total of 250,000 children in the Anglophone Caribbean had one or both parents in Britain (Lowenthal, 1972, p. 220). Women as well as men migrated in large numbers. Between 1950 to 1970, male and female migration from

Barbados was close to equal (Ebanks et al, 1979, p. 435) and since then, feminisation has continued in response to the global demand for teachers, nurses, domestic servants and sex workers (UNFPA, 2006, p. 23). When compared with their male counterparts, women migrants are reported as more likely to keep in regular contact and to remit *a higher proportion of their earnings—regularly and consistently*" (UNFPA, 2006, p. 28). At the same time, the inevitable consequence is large numbers of children living without their mothers. It is expected that these children will join their parents abroad, but in practice the migration process does not always unfold as predicted. Reunification may be delayed for many years or may never happen. If and when it does, it may be emotionally problematic for both mother and child, an issue to which we return below.

Contemporary Caribbean studies of shared childcare have emerged throughout the region, mainly from Jamaica [Brodber, 1975; Clarke, 1970 (1957), Crawford-Brown & Rattray 2001; Roberts & Sinclair, 1978; Senior, 1991] though also from Barbados (Barrow forthcoming, Dann 1987, Russell-Brown et al, 1997). Roberts and Sinclair (1978, p. 162) estimate that about 15 percent of Jamaican children are cared for by relatives and friends and Dann (1987, p. 8) reports that the same percentage of the men in his Barbados sample were raised, not by their parents, but *by a relative, such as an aunt, or grandmother, and occasionally by just a friend of the family.*" Matrifocality in Caribbean families privileges motherhood and it is surrogate mothers, rather than fathers, that are featured: *Foster-mothers, unlike foster-fathers, are plentiful in Caribbean cultures*" (Senior, 1991, p. 11). Studies agree that adoptive mothers are found principally within the extended family, more often on the mother's side, again reflecting matrifocality. Most important are maternal grandmothers, though paternal grandmothers acting on behalf of their sons also *adopt* children (Roberts & Sinclair, 1978, p. 64-5).

A special domestic variant reflecting the Caribbean culture of shared child care and socialization is the *yard* or *houseyard*. In her work in Montserrat, Lydia Pulsipher (1993) presents a detailed ethnographic mapping of these traditional matrilocal spaces. She describes household groups of maternal kin who share domestic, childcare and social activities, under the authority of a female elder.[8] One of her informants, Joycelyn Cabey had four young children, whose three fathers supported only occasionally and who were cared for *in shifts by Joycelyn, her mother and sisters, all of whom held jobs in town, but spent most of their time in the yard*" (Pulsipher, 1993, p. 59). Her plans to migrate include childcare arrangements during her absence: *An uncle plans to take one child, the other three will stay in her mother's houseyard looked after, as they have always been, by her female kin"* (Pulsipher, 1993, p. 59).

Interpretations of extended family child care range from economic functionalism and adaptive family responses in the context of poverty to those more culturally nuanced.[9] The former are grounded in the family *strengths* and *resilience* approach, mentioned earlier, according to which *child-shifting* is an *adaptive strategy* in response to matrifocality and the poor economic circumstances of mothers. Acknowledging his explanation as *"functional rather than historical"*, Hyman Rodman claims that, in Trinidad, a woman who parents single-handedly *"cannot both care and mind her children and so she turns their care over to a female relative while she takes on the job of minding them financially"* (Rodman, 1971, p. 183-186). Roberts and Sinclair (1978, p. 165-6) also identify maternal economic constraints as paramount. In their study of women and family in Jamaica, mothers report that *"their having to go to work necessitates sending the child away to be maintained by relatives or others"*. Similarly, for adolescent mothers in Barbados, who have been *"prematurely thrust into the parenting role"*, child-shifting is a survival strategy to assist them to *"navigate socioeconomic and domestic hardships"* (Russell-Brown et al, 1997, p. 228, 240). Also given as reasons for the relocation of children are the migration of one or both parents, the incarceration, ill health or incapacity of a mother, father, grandmother or other care-giver, and domestic conflict and violence.

Harder to find in the literature are references to alternative mothering and living arrangements considered to be culturally appropriate and historically rooted. But some scholars have noted a pattern whereby children live simultaneously in several homes and move seamlessly from one caregiver to another. As Olive Senior (1991, p. 13) explains: *"A childless woman might wish to mother a child and 'borrows' one from someone else. Children are sent off to be 'company' to ageing grandparents. A lonely older woman requires a companion and takes a child from a large family. Children in need—motherless or homeless—will be taken by relatives or others"*.

In this culture where a home is considered empty without children, they will also be taken in or *adopted* to fill a gap in the family. Mention is made, for example, of grandmothers *"wanting the child"* (Roberts & Sinclair, 1978, p. 166). There are children who *stay over* elsewhere: *"she always like her grandmother. One day she sleep over at her grandmother and she stay over ever since"* (Russell-Brown et al, 1997, p. 232). Others just happen to move gradually from one care-giver and family to another as in the case of neighbourhood handiboy who became a member of the family: *"So it just happened like this. He comes and he gets his little dollar and his food and I can't even tell you where it began, where we got so attached, but coming and coming and coming, he gets his food. Now and then I'll buy him a little shirt. And it's just a cycle. He moved in and moved in and he's living here altogether"* (Senior, 1991, p. 14).

REALITIES OF CHILD-SHIFTING

Caribbean scholars have attempted to assess the benefits and costs of *child-shifting* for the well-being and quality of life of children. They are divided in their conclusions. Some have been persuaded by the model of Caribbean extended family resilience, adaptability and extensiveness to present positive images, hardly surprisingly. For Hyman Rodman (1971, p. 176-178) family organization and *child-shifting* are adaptive responses to a man's inability to fulfill his role as economic provider.

> In present-day Trinidad the child-shifting pattern ... permits the redistribution of children into households where they can be taken care of, and it makes it possible for the mother of the child to work and to contribute financially to her child's support (Rodman, 1971, p. 183).

Sally Gordon's interpretation carries a similar message. For her, *child shifting* in Antigua is a *"household economic strategy"* that shares the costs and benefits of child rearing between different households—*"manipulating household composition in order to manage dependency relative to resources, or 'equalize' this relationship among households within the community"* (Gordon, 1987, p. 438). There is general agreement among researchers that the separation of mother and child is intended to be temporary, a *"necessary breathing space"* for the mother (Russell-Brown et al, 1997, p. 228), and that mothers continue to be emotionally involved in their children's lives. They are said to be *"worried about their children, meaning that they had 'longings' to see or be with the child"* (Russell-Brown et al., 1997, p. 235).

Other researchers challenge these images of extended family functionality by implying an erosion of family social capital for the *adoption* and longer-term care of children. A study of child vulnerability in Barbados, St. Lucia and St. Vincent and the Grenadines, identified grandmothers as the most significant caregivers after parents, mothers in particular, but added that for large numbers of children there was no secondary caregiver (UNICEF, 2006, p. 3-4). Others report that grandmothers no longer assume child care responsibilities as they did in the past. Interrogating life-story interviews over three generations of Caribbean nationals resident in Britain and the Caribbean, Dwayne Plaza contends that the role of grandmother in Caribbean migrant families to Britain has been transformed by settlement patterns and physical distances, acculturation and the *"pressures of a 'modern' lifestyle"*. No longer is she *"the lynch pin who keeps everyone and everything together"* and grandmothers *"are no longer relied upon to take over the long-term responsibilities of child care for their grandchildren"*. In Britain, the role traditionally filled by a grandmother has been assumed by the state social safety net, and she plays a *"transnational emissary role"* moving between family located in England, Europe and the Caribbean, providing short-term care and support for specific periods of time (Plaza, 2000). Others also refer to the diminishing role of grandmothers. From Trinidad and Tobago, Carol Logie (1997, p. 14) reports that: *"Children can no longer be dropped off at grandmothers, aunts and uncles as in the past without advanced warning and preparation"*.[10] And from Jamaica, Crawford-Brown and Rattray (2001, p. 114) claim that *"as grandparents become busier, other caretaking options are increasingly used"*, including friends, strangers and institutions, notably Children's Homes. The extreme situation is abandonment. As Brodber's findings show, virtually all the mothers of abandoned children in Jamaica were socially isolated from all sources of support including the extended family: *"To perform the act so successfully that the irritated public can give the police no leads must mean such acute isolation from social interaction ..."* (Brodber, 1974, p. 48).

The insights we have into the lives of adopted children reveal a wide range of experiences, from one extreme where they are treated no differently from other children of the family, to the other where they are neglected, abused or exploited as unpaid labor in adoptive families (Senior, 1991, p.17; Green, 1998, p. 11). Caribbean social workers tend to highlight the downside of *child-shifting*. From Jamaica, Claudette Crawford-Brown (1999, p. 53) describes children as *"victims of the migration experience"* and as *"barrel children ... waiting to rejoin parents, who receive material gifts in barrels from parents who reside in the metropolitan capitals, but receive little emotional nurturing from these parents"*.[11] Children separated from their mothers are at risk of sexual abuse and institutionalization (Crawford-Brown & Rattray, 2001, p. 114-115). In Trinidad and Tobago, research on children separated from parents who migrate exposes severe psychological problems:

> In these situations, that one might call 'serial parenting' the children are sad, at risk of depression, may succumb to aggressive impulses and have low self-esteem. ... Children moved from one care-giver to another are at great risk of impaired mental health (Jones et al, 2004, p. 93).

In a three-country Caribbean study, young people raised the issue of ill treatment, including sexual abuse, among children sent to live with other families (UNICEF, 2006, p. 7). For Jamaican social historian and novelist, Erna Brodber, the transfer of childcare responsibilities shades into abandonment. She identifies a widespread cultural practice of *"passing on"* children to grandmothers, fathers, other kin and non-kin assumed to be better able to take care of them and ensure their educational and social development. In her view, abandonment is *"only the most total and extreme form of 'passing on'"* whereby children are left in *"a borrowed toilet, at a busy street corner, in someone's car"* or passed on *"to the elements"* (Brodber, 1974, p. 49).

Also articulated was the authority of biological parents to determine alternative childcare arrangements and, ultimately, to reclaim their children. But this can contradict and undermine extended family child-care arrangements. Things may go wrong, for example, when mothers activate their rights and *come back for the child* after many years of separation. Sidney Greenfield's research in Barbados points to the problems that may occur on these occasions.

> The informality of adoptions can at times cause trouble, especially if the mother claims her child at a later date. Many violent arguments are the result of a woman's coming to claim her son from its father's kinsman at the time he starts to work. The mother may have never so much as inquired as to his well-being, but now, desperate for financial assistance, she wants him back. The foster parents, who have supported the child all along, are deprived of the child's services just as they are becoming valuable. Legally, the mother can claim the child, but court action to enforce the right is rarely resorted to. It is not necessary; the child is returned to his mother, often against his wishes (Greenfield, 1966, p. 122).

Leaving aside the economics of the situation, this episode sheds a different light by exposing potential conflict between extended family child sharing and individual parental rights. Reading between the lines suggests that the claim on the part of the mother, while socially and legally privileged, also violates the cultural principles of child-sharing within the extended family.

In mentioning the wishes of the child, this scenario also hints at problems of reunification between parents and children after a period of absence (Arnold, 1997; Crawford-Brown & Rattray, 2001, p. 117-121). In reclaiming children, parents may disrupt primary emotional attachments children have formed with grandmothers and other adoptive parents. Children *"mourn the loss of the close emotional ties they had developed to grandparents and to other relatives and caregivers in the Caribbean during periods of separation from parents"* and, when reunited with their parents, *"were unable to form close emotional ties with their mothers and fathers because of the long separation"* (Arnold, 1997, p. 251, 254). *Child-shifting* then, may turn out to be traumatic for all concerned. As the most vulnerable with little say in these matters, children often pay the highest price.

One or two studies also refer to motherhood in the context of child sharing, pointing out that it may be a mixed blessing for them. In their research in Barbados, St. Lucia and Dominica, Patricia Mohammed and Althea Perkins (1999, p. 115) find *"stresses for women"* in situations where they resided with and depended on their in-laws or parents. Here they were *"less free to bring up their children as they wanted and felt both imposed upon as well as imposing on another relatives' needs"*. At the other extreme, as Brodber's research in Jamaica points out, mothers who are without such help and who abandon their children are reviled and go to great extremes to hide their identities (Brodber, 1974, p. 48). Most of her informants were unforgiving and attributed abandonment to a mother's *"irresponsibility and selfishness"* (Brodber, 1974, p. 22).

CHILDREN IN CARE

It seems obvious to say that quality of family care for dependent children is reflected in the numbers and conditions of those who live without their families either on the street or in institutional care. Barbados claims to have none of the former and incidents of abandonment have been much reduced (See Table 13.2). So we turn here to the latter. A total of 105 children are resident in eight government operated Children's Homes and 3 so-called Transitional Colleges for adolescents who have finished school and are making the transition to independent living.[12] Nearly 50 percent of the children are aged 12 years and over and boys outnumber girls by a ratio of 3 to 2.

The basic principles underpinning the Barbados policy of child-care are institutionalization as a last resort and the reunification of children with their families or placement in foster homes at the earliest opportunity. Children's visits to their family homes for short periods are arranged and encouraged and, at the time of writing, 11 children had been returned to their own homes for a test period. The integration policy also involves attending neighboring schools and participating in local clubs and sporting activities.

There has been marked improvement in the circumstances of children in care over the last generation or so. In the late 1960s, there were only three publicly run children's homes[13] with a roll of 159 children. Insufficient accommodation in these homes meant that a further 107 children continued to be housed, as they had in the past, in multipurpose infirmaries that also catered to the elderly, sick and destitute. A total of 88 children lived in the largest Home. At the time, staff shortages made it impossible to implement a family unit system (Edmunds, 1973, p. 240-241), but today the same Home has been divided into small *"cottages"* of 6 or more children of mixed age, under the care of a houseparent or *"auntie"*.

Many of the children have been resident in these Homes for long periods of their childhoods. Among those aged 10 years and over, 47 percent have been there for 10 years or more. There is little distinction between boys and girls in this regard. However, a total of 62 percent of resident children are visited by family members. Mothers appear most frequently as visitors, and siblings, aunts and grandmothers are also on the list. Fathers are mentioned, though less frequently.

Only 23 children are in foster care and adoption is rare. In 2007, only 3 children were legally adopted compared with the situation in the 1960s when the relevant government department was handling between 50 and 150 cases each year (Edmunds, 1973, p. 242). Resident in Children's Homes at present are 7 children whose mothers put them up for adoption at birth. All are males, boys being more difficult to place for adoption than girls, according to Child Care officials. There are also 5 cases of children readmitted to Children's Homes because a foster care arrangement was unsuccessful.

In the majority of cases, *"mother unable to care"* was mentioned as the reason for a child's placement in one of the Children's Homes. This, in turn, was attributable to various social problems relating to the situation of these mothers, as well as fathers and other family members and also to the children themselves. Poverty related to the loss of a job, the lack of accommodation and fathers' drug addiction were highlighted. Frequently mentioned also were a child's severe mental or physical disability, and for adolescents, delinquency and referral by the courts. In some cases mothers were hospitalized, injured or deceased and the family reported as *"unable to care."* These cases are contrasted with others that mentioned *"neglect"* and occasionally *"gross neglect"* as the reason for placement in care. But neglect was given as a reason less than half as often as inability to care. Sexual abuse was also mentioned, but only in 8 cases[14] and abandonment in only one case.

CONCLUSION: EXTENDED FAMILIES AND CHILD CARE

The adoption of children and their care as a communal female activity within extended families is a norm of Caribbean childhood. Undoubtedly, *child shifting* is built into the economic survival strategies of mothers who migrate or who are too poor or too young as teenage mothers to cope single-handedly. The practice also redistributes and balances household resources in response to poverty and the absence of a male breadwinner. But child sharing is also rooted in the historical development of Caribbean family culture and childhood. Child-sharing and adoption is about children being wanted and homes being empty without them; about women's identity centered in motherhood and mothering perceived as *natural* to all women whether or not they bear children; about teenagers who are too immature for motherhood; about conjugal fragility and frequent separations between parents; about families that do not fit neatly into households; and about an inter-generational cycle of family life in which everyone raises children and, in turn, earns the right to be cared for during old age. Most of all, it is about mothering as a shared role within the extended female kin network and beyond, a reflection of the days when children as a social group were the collective responsibility of the community and before that the plantation, and when the village raised the child.

But things do not always work out as they should and children may be put at risk. Separation between mother and child is intended to be temporary but life's contingencies intervene, grandmothers no longer hold families together or assume full-time, long-term child care responsibilities, and the cultural principles of shared child care within the extended family may conflict with the legally prescribed custodial rights of a parent. All this says much about family relationships across the generations, but cannot support either the sweeping generalizations of family *breakdown* or the comforting image of extensive supportive networks of kin. To challenge the rhetoric and debunk these myths we need more research, qualitative research that privileges children's voices and experiences of family life and, importantly, their daily realities in the absence of family protection and support.

There are also clear implications for the design of supportive social policy for children and their families. But this appears to be low down on the agenda for development. The recent Barbados Strategic Plan, quoted at the beginning of this chapter, mentions the family only in passing with objectives vaguely defined as the *"empowerment of families"* (along with communities and vulnerable groups) and *"programs to promote greater parenting skills"* (Government of Barbados 2007, p. 194, 196). It is clear that there are parents and families in Barbados under strain and unable to cope with the care of children. It is more than time to abandon the litany of assumed ills—and evils—of family dysfunction and the call for a return to *traditional values*, and to direct efforts to the design and implementation of concrete and targeted social policy to support children and their families. The place to begin might be to highlight poverty, abuse and disability, major reasons for the institutionalization of children, and to unpack and challenge the cultural, social and economic drivers of these problems that undermine family care and put children at risk.

Notes

1. The relevant legislation includes The Succession Act, 1975; The Status of Children (Reform) Act, 1979; The Barbados Family Law Act, 1981; The Medical Termination of Pregnancy Act, 1983),

2. These perspectives are discussed in more detail elsewhere (Barrow, 1996).

3. The Caribbean Community and Common Market (CARICOM) was established in 1973 to promote regional unity and to coordinate economic and foreign policy among 13 Caribbean member nations.

4. Most recent figures available.

5. Barbados is presently developing a Management Protocol on mandatory reporting of child abuse (Newman and Barrow, 2008).

6. These figures say nothing about the frequency of separation between parents who are in common law and visiting unions. These outnumber marital unions.

7. See for example, Clarke 1957 (1970) for Jamaica, Greenfield (1966) for Barbados, Midgett (1977) for St. Lucia, Otterbein (1966) for the Bahamas, Philpott (1973) for Montserrat, Rodman (1971) for Trinidad, M.G. Smith for Carriacou (1962), and R.T. Smith (1956) for British Guiana, now Guyana.

8. See also Brodber, 1975.

9. These have been explored in more detail elsewhere (Barrow, forthcoming).

10. See also Mohammed and Perkins, 1999, p. 114-5.

11. The unfortunate epithet *'barrel children'* is also commonly used in Trinidad and Tobago (Jones et. al. 2004), but is not familiar in Barbados.

12. Gratitude is expressed to Joan Crawford, Director, Barbados Child Care Board and her colleague Vivian Simpson who provided this information.

13. One small home with a maximum of 7 children was run by a voluntary organization.

14. This seems somewhat anomalous when compared with the figures in Table 13.2, and can be interpreted in several ways. It could be that few child victims are removed to protective custody, or that the extended family steps in to rehouse children.

References

Arnold, E. (1997). Issues of Reunification of Migrant West Indian Children in the United Kingdom.. In J. Roopnarine & J. Brown (Eds.) *Caribbean Families: Diversity among Ethnic Groups.* (pp. 243-258). Connecticut: Ablex Publishing Corporation, Advances in Applied Development Psychology,

Barbados. (1980). *1980/1 Population Census of the Commonwealth Caribbean.* Barbados:Volume 1.

Barbados. (2000). *Population and Housing Census.* Government of Barbados: Barbados Statistical Service.

Barbados (Various years). *Report on the Registration Department.* Government of Barbados: The Registration Department of Barbados.

Barrow, C. (1995). Living in Sin: Church and Common Law in Barbados. *The Journal of Caribbean History, 29* (2), 47-70.

Barrow, C. (1996). *Family in the Caribbean: Themes and Perspectives.* Jamaica: Ian Randle Publishers.

Barrow, C. (1998). Masculinity and Family: Revisiting 'Marginality' and 'Reputation.' In C. Barrow (Ed.) *Caribbean Portraits: Essays on Gender Ideologies and Identities.* (pp. 339-359). Jamaica: Ian Randle Publishers.

Barrow, C. (2003). Children and Social Policy in Barbados: The Unfinished Agenda of Child Abuse. *The Caribbean Journal of Social Work, 2,* 36-53.

Barrow. C. (Forthcoming). *Childhood and Family Culture in the Caribbean: Growing up Outside, Shifted* or *Left Behind?* Jamaica, Ian Randle Publishers.

Beckles, H. (1989). *Natural Rebels: A Social History of Enslaved Black Women in Barbados.* London: Zed Books Ltd.

Brodber, E. (1974). *The Abandonment of Children in Jamaica.* Jamaica: University of the West Indies, Institute of Social and Economic Research.

Brodber, E. (1975). *A Study of Yards in the City of Kingston.* Jamaica: University of the West Indies, Institute of Social and Economic Research Working Papers, No. 9.

Brown, J., P. Newland, A. Anderson & B. Chevannes (1997). Caribbean Fatherhood: Underresearched, Misunderstood. In J. Roopnarine & J. Brown (Eds.) *Caribbean Families: Diversity Among Ethnic Groups.* (pp.85-113).Connecticut: Ablex Publishing Corporation, Advances in Applied Development Psychology,

Brown, L. & T. Inniss (2005). The Slave Family in the Transition to Freedom: Barbados 1834-1841. *Slavery and Abolition, 26*(2), 257-269.

Chevannes, B. (2001). *Learning to be a Man: Culture, Socialisation and Gender Identity in Five Caribbean Communities.* Jamaica: University of the West Indies Press.

Clarke, E. 1970 (1957). *My Mother Who Fathered Me.* London: George Allen and Unwin Ltd.

Collins, P. (1992). Black Women and Motherhood. In B. Thorne & M. Yalom (Eds.) *Rethinking the Family: Some Feminist Questions.* (pp.85-113.) Boston: North Eastern University Press.

Crawford-Brown, C. (1999). *Who Will Save Our Children? The Plight of the Jamaican Child in the 1990s.* Jamaica: University of the West Indies, Canoe Press.

Crawford-Brown, C.& M. Rattray. (2001). Parent-Child Relationships in Caribbean Families. In N. B. Webb (Ed.) *Culturally Diverse Parent-Child and Family Relationships: A Guide for Social Workers and other Practitioners* (pp. 107-130) New York: Columbia University Press,

Dann, G. (1987). *The Barbadian Male: Sexual Attitudes and Practices.* London: Macmillan Publishers.

Ebanks, G., P George & C. Nobbe (1979). Emigration from Barbados, 1951-1970. *Social and Economic Studies,* 28(2), 431-449.

Edmunds, J. (1973). Child Care and Family Services in Barbados. *Social and Economic Studies,* 22 (2), 229-248.

Evans, H. & R. Davies. (1997). Overview Issues in Childhood Socialisation in the Caribbean. In J. Roopnarine & J. Brown (Eds.) *Caribbean Families: Diversity Among Ethnic Groups (*pp.1-24). Connecticut: Ablex Publishing Corporation, Advances in Applied Development Psychology,

Goody, E. (1982). *Parenting and Social Reproduction: Fostering and Occupational Roles in West Africa.* Cambridge: Cambridge University Press.

Gordon, S. (1987). I go to 'Tanties': The Economic Significance of Child-Shifting in Antigua, West Indies. *Journal of Comparative Family Studies,* 18(3), 427-433.

Government of Barbados. (2007). *The National Strategic Plan of Barbados, 2006-2025. Global Excellence: Barbadian Traditions.* Barbados: Ministry of Economic Affairs and Development, Economic Affairs Division, Research and Planning Unit.

Great Britain. (1945). *West India Royal (Moyne) Commission Report, 1938-1939.* London: H.M.S.O.

Green, D. (1998). *Hidden Lives: Voices of Children in Latin America and the Caribbean.* London and Washington: Cassell.

Greenfield, S. M. (1966). *English Rustics in Black Skin: A Study of Modern Family Forms in a Pre-Industrialized Society.* New Haven, Conn: College and University Press.

Jones, A., J. Sharpe & M. Sogren. (2004). Children's Experience of Separation from Parents as a Result of Migration. *The Caribbean Journal of Social Work,* 3, 89-109.

Lamming, G. (1970). *In the Castle of My Skin.* Trinidad and Jamaica: Longman Caribbean. (First published by Michael Joseph in 1953).

Le Franc, E. (2001). Child Abuse in the Eastern Caribbean: Addressing the Rights of the Child. In C. Barrow (Ed.) *Children's Rights: Caribbean Realities.* (pp.285-304). Jamaica: Ian Randle Publishers.

Le Vine, R. (Ed.) (2003). *Childhood Socialisation: Comparative Studies of Parenting, Learning and Educational Change.* Hong Kong: The University of Hong Kong.

Logie, C. (1997). *The Status of ECCE Provision in Trinidad and Tobago.* Barbados:UNICEF/Caribbean Area Office, Working Paper No. 7.

Lowenthal, D. (1972). *West Indian Societies.* New York, London and Toronto, Oxford University Press.

Mehrotra, S. (2000.) *Integrating Economic and Social Policy: Good Practices from High-Achieving Countries.* Florence: UNICEF, Innocenti Working Papers, No. 80.

Midgett, D. (1977). *West Indian Migration and Adaptation in St. Lucia and London.* D.Phil Thesis, University of Illinois at Urbana-Champaign.

Mohammed, P. & A. Perkins. (1999). *Caribbean Women at the Crossroads: the Paradox of Motherhood among Women of Barbados, St. Lucia and Dominica.* Jamaica: University of the West Indies, Canoe Press.

Newman, D. & C. Barrow. (2008). The Reality of Child Abuse and Neglect in Barbados: Towards a National Child Abuse Reporting and Management Protocol. *Journal of Eastern Caribbean Studies,* 33(1), 86-101.

Newton, V. (1987). The Panama Question: Barbadian Emigration to Panama, 1880-1914. In W. Marshall (Ed.) *Emancipation II: Aspects of the Post-Slavery Experience in Barbados,* (pp. 102-130) Barbados: National Cultural Foundation and University of the West Indies, Department of History.

Otterbein, K. (1966). *The Andros Islanders: A Study of Family Organization in the Bahamas:* Lawrence, Kansas.

Philpott, S. (973). *West Indian Migration: The Montserrat Case.* London, University of London: The Athlone Press and New York: Humanities Press Inc.

Plaza, D.(2000). Transnational Grannies: The Changing Family Responsibilities of Elderly African Caribbean-born Women Resident in Britain. *Social Indicators Research,* 51(1)

Pulsipher, L. (1993). Changing Roles in the Life Cycles of Women in Traditional West Indian Houseyards. In J. Momsen (Ed.) *Women and Change in the Caribbean: A Pan-Caribbean Perspective* (pp.50-64). Jamaica: Ian Randle Publishers; London: James Currey Ltd.; Bloomington: Indiana University Press.

Reynolds, T. (2005). *Caribbean Mothers: Identity and Experience in the U.K.* London: The Tufnell Press.

Roberts, G. (1955). Emigration from the Island of Barbados. *Social and Economic Studies,* 4(3), 245-288.

Roberts, G. & S. Sinclair. (1978). *Women in Jamaica: Patterns of Reproduction and Family.* New York, Millwood: KTO Press.

Rock, L. (2001). Child Abuse in Barbados. In C. Barrow (Ed.) *Children's Rights: Caribbean Realities* (pp.305-329). Jamaica: Ian Randle Publishers.

Rodman, H. (1971). *Lower Class Families: The Culture of Poverty in Negro Trinidad.* London: Oxford University Press.

Russell-Brown, P., B. Norville & C. Griffith. (1997). Child Shifting: A Survival Strategy for Teenage Mothers. In J. Roopnarine and J. Brown (Eds.) *Caribbean Families: Diversity among Ethnic Groups*, (pp. 223-242). Connecticut: Ablex Publishing Corporation, Advances in Applied Development Psychology.

Sanford, M. (1974). A Socialisation in Ambiguity: Child-Lending in a British West Indian Society. *Ethnology*, 13(4), 393-400.

Senior, O. (1991). *Working Miracles: Women's Lives in the English–Speaking Caribbean.* London: James Currey; Bloomington: Indiana, Indiana University Press.

Smith, M.G. (1962). *Kinship and Community in Carriacou.* New Haven and London: Yale University Press.

Smith, R.T. (1956). *The Negro Family in British Guiana: Family Structure and Social Status in the Villages.* London: Routledge and Kegan Paul.

Stack, C. (1974). *All Our Kin: Strategies for Survival in a Black Community.* New York: Harper and Row.

Thomas-Hope, E. (1992). *Explanation in Caribbean Migration: Perception and the Image—Jamaica, Barbados and St. Vincent.* London: Macmillan.

UNESCO. (2007). *ECCE, Regional Overview: Latin America and the Caribbean.*

UNFPA. (2006). *State of the World Population, 2006.* A Passage to Hope: Women and International Migration. UNFPA.

UNICEF. (2006)). *A Study of Child Vulnerability in Barbados, St. Lucia and St. Vincent and the Grenadines.* Barbados: UNICEF, Office for Barbados and the Eastern Caribbean (in association with the Governments of Barbados, St. Lucia and St. Vincent and the Grenadines).

UNICEF. (2007). *State of the World's Children, 2007.* Women and Children: The Double Dividend of Gender Equality. New York: UNICEF.

United Nations. (1997). *Convention on the Rights of the Child (CRC)*, Initial Reports of States Parties: Barbados 11/02/97.

Newspaper

Barbados, The Barbados Advocate, April 24, 2008.

CHAPTER *14*

THE IMPACT OF FAMILY STRUCTURE ON CHILD DEVELOPMENT IN JAMAICA

Stacey N. A. Brodie Walker & Kai A. D. Morgan

INTRODUCTION

It is suggested that the breakdown in society is a result of the breakdown of the family unit. Recently on a popular Jamaican radio station, the hosts were discussing the new delinquent phenomenon being perpetrated by many of the "high schoolers" in the country. Apparently, there is a videophone text being circulated of two adolescents, approximately 13 and 14 years old, displaying what is described as very graphic sexual behavior while another adolescent is video taping and boosting them on. What is even more disturbing is that this act was being carried out on school premises. The hosts speculated on the reasons for such behaviors with the male host stating adamantly that the family, and more specifically, the parents were to be blamed, while the female host declared that some children are just "bad" and it does not matter what their parents do or what type of family structure they come from. She further stated that friends are quite influential and have a stronger impact on identity and behavior than do parents/family.

This argument is not a new one as researchers have been trying to identify the determining factors of youth behavior that influence both resilience and delinquency. Many reasons have been cited such as education, poverty, personality, family relationships and family structure. It is the intent of the authors to continue the search by examining the various family structures present in Jamaica and their impact on youth behavior, inclusive of delinquency, aggression, sexuality, attachment and identity.

History of Family Structure in Jamaica

"Nothing in the literature on Jamaica and the West Indies in general is more confused than discussions about the family" (Davenport, 1961). Although this quote was engendered some 40 years ago, and there has been a multitude of literature on the Caribbean family from prolific writers such as Boyd-Franklin (1989), Brice-Baker (1996), Chevannes (2006) and Gopaul-McNicol (1993), the rhetoric continues and the Jamaican family remains a continuously evolving dynamic, impacted by the historical antecedents of slavery, the emerging face of multiculturalism, and the influx of American ideals.

One cannot speak of the Jamaican family without mentioning the impact of slavery. The familial separation that was one of the hallmarks of slave traders has left a legacy of divisiveness in Jamaican families that is still apparent today. Braithwaite (1971) speaks of slaves on the plantations being dislocated from their families, for example fathers being uprooted from their wives and children and left to form new relationships or serving as "breeders" on other plantations. This engendered a sense of disconnect and disjointedness that is still evidenced in Black families today and partially explains the advent of the single parent and the blended family in Jamaica. It is also the African family tradition that states "it takes a village to raise a child" that has shaped the foundations of the extended family structure also visible and prevalent in Jamaica today while the European influence has promoted the nuclear family structure. It is important to note that the nuclear family does exist in Jamaica and is comprised of two biological parents (legal or common-law union) and their children. It is estimated that about 60% of children in Jamaica grow up in two-parent homes. However it is not clear whether these households also include other family members (thereby making them extended families) as the literature does not separate these very clearly ("Caribbean-Families-Extended-Family").

Single-Parent Households

In Jamaica, 40% of children live in single-parent headed households (UNICEF, 2005), making the single parent family structure, the second largest that exists today behind the "two-parent" home. According to Holness (2006) "it is [therefore] quite likely that the child will never grow up in a family structure with both parents, or with a male presence."

The single parent household has been cited as a problematic occurrence and has been identified by many researchers as one of the contributing factors to various problems exhibited by today's youths. Kotchick, Dorsey, Miller & Forehand (1999) have cited that ethnic minority adolescents from single parent homes (particularly African-American and Hispanic) engage in sexual activities at an earlier age and at a higher rate than their counterparts from two biological parent households.

Family structure has also been linked to the quality of attachment between parents and their children. Single parents are less likely to have the requisite time with their children because frequently, they are the sole breadwinners and nurturers which hinders their ability to adequately supervise their children. Further to this, the Jamaica Survey of Living Conditions (2002) reports that female headed households have the largest number of children. The attentiveness/attachment of the mother towards these children will be diminished by virtue of the number of children and time constraints. Poor supervision by and lack of attachment with the mother is more likely in delinquents than non-delinquents (Glueck & Glueck, 1962) and is more likely to influence aggression and conduct problems (Meeks Gardner, Powell, & Grantham-McGregor, 2000). Shelden (2005) has concluded from a meta-analysis of fifty studies that delinquency in broken homes is about 10-15% higher than in intact homes. Demuth & Brown (2004) also found that adolescents in single parent families are significantly more delinquent than their counterparts with two biological married parents.

Lonczak, Fernandez, Austin, Marlatt & Donovan (2007) have also reported greater levels of alcohol, tobacco and marijuana usage among American Indians in single-parent families when compared to extended and nuclear households.

On the other hand, it is believed that strong parent-child attachment is a positive contributing factor in developing one's identity and self-esteem. According to Mead (1934) and Cooley (1956) the self arises through the individual's interaction with and reaction to other members of society, i.e. his peers, teachers and most importantly his parents. Additionally, Kotchick et. al. (1999) found that adolescents who had open communication with their single mothers, suggesting better parent-child attachment, were less likely to engage in sexual risk-taking and other delinquent behaviors. Therefore, what is important is the relationship between parent and child regardless of family structure.

BLENDED FAMILIES

In Jamaica, the single parent family almost follows a trajectory into what is called the blended or stepfamily. This is so because the single parent may partner with a significant other (visiting or residing in the home) thus forming this new structure, which may or may not include children from previous unions. With the divorce rates being as high as 54% (4.1 per 1000) in the United States, the blended family becomes much more likely than even the single parent family. Although Jamaica's divorce rates are estimated at only 0.55 per 1000, common-law marriages are much more prevalent here (approximately 20% rate) (Roopnarine, 2002) and thus these figures do not reflect the termination of such relationships, which again almost always end up as blended families.

The issues of identity, attachment, sexuality and delinquency are also prevalent within the blended family structure. The period of adolescence is when children start to form their identity which includes detachment from parents and attachment to peers. Bray and Harvey (1995) report that in order for individuation to occur, in which the adolescent defines self and asserts independence in a non-destructive way, the detachment from parents has to be healthy. They go on to say that the key components to healthy individuation are maintaining active interaction with parents as well as a reorganization of the relationship between parent and child. Now that adolescents are distancing themselves from parents and moving towards their peers they begin to give up the values and beliefs of their parents in favor of their own. They begin to ask questions, disagree and argue against the established rules. They become more independent, talking less to their parents and choosing to share intimate details of their lives with friends. Parents don't understand this change in behavior and make the mistake of responding to their child using the same techniques/discipline and communication styles that were once effective instead of adapting and reorganizing the relationship based on these changes. These developmental issues are further enhanced in blended families as individuation may be hindered by power issues (Bray & Harvey, 1995) regarding the roles of each parent.

Attachment is another developmental issue that impacts identity formation and is affected by the blended family structure. Strong parent-child attachment is necessary for healthy adolescent individuation/separation from the parents. As long as the adolescent maintains intimacy with his or her family, he or she is better equipped to attain a sense of belonging in the extrafamilial world (Bray & Harvey, 1996). Formation of appropriate levels of intimacy among family members can be impeded by the triangulation (child—nonresidential parent—stepparent) which can occur in stepfamilies. Triangulated relationships can occur because of conflicted loyalties among family members, that is, the child who is caught between mother and stepfather's guidance or the adolescent who is torn between a well-loved stepfather and his biological father.

Sexuality, an impending issue of adolescent, is often overlooked in stepfamilies although it is a central and important one. Children in step-families have a higher risk of being abused. Further to this, girls are more likely to be sexually abused by a step-father than a biological father; as well, sexual abuse is more likely to occur by step-relatives (e.g. uncles, grand-parents, stepsiblings) since there is the diminished taboo of incest (Bray & Harvey, 1996). The Jamaica Surveillance System (Ministry of Health) indicated that in 2002 and 2003, 86% of the reported sexual assault cases were committed by a relative, friend, acquaintance or intimate partner. In 2006, the Centre for the Investigation of Sexual Offences and Child Abuse (CISOCA), documented a total of 1,389 sexual offences. Approximately 82 per cent of these offences were committed against women (707 rape cases, 11 attempted rape cases and 433 cases of carnal abuse). Additionally, 33 cases of incest were reported in 2004 (UNICEF, 2005).

Another aspect of developing one's identity is being able to identify one's sexual role and separate sexuality from sex or intimacy. Having a healthy parent-child relationship in which there is open discussion and emotional closeness helps the adolescent in doing this. However, this is difficult in step families as intimacy and emotional closeness may be confused with sexuality or sexual advances (Bray & Harvey, 1996). Therefore, stepfathers in particu-lar, may become sensitive to this issue and may appear detached and become less involved. Likewise, stepdaughters may become apprehensive with the presence of a non-biological male in the home and refrain from having contact, be it physical (hugs, embraces) or emotional (open discussion).

Although several studies (Bray & Harvey, 1996; Finkelhor & Asdigian, 1996) have found that adolescents in stepfamilies are at a higher risk of victimization, others (Hetherington, 1993; Hetherington & Clingempeel, 1992; Vuchinich, Hetherington, Vuchinich & Clingempeel, 1991) have found that adolescents in blended families are also at a high risk of becoming perpetrators/delinquent. Forming a new family structure to include step-parents and stepsiblings during early adolescence is difficult and adolescents may respond with increased levels of externalizing problems (e.g. acting out, conduct, behavioral). Researchers (Hetherington, 1993; Hetherington & Clingempeel, 1992; Vuchinich et al., 1991) believe that the behavioral problems exhibited by the adolescent stems from unresolved issues concern-ing parental separation; as well, externalizing problems are the results of the difficulty the adolescent (and his/her family) are experiencing in negotiating the developmental tasks of adolescence. As was stated earlier, establishing individuation through intimate relationships and mutually validating con-nections with parents and peers is key in the successful resolution of the developmental issues of adolescence in blended families.

EXTENDED FAMILIES

Although there appears to be no available data regarding the estimated number of extended families in Jamaica, anecdotally speaking this family structure is quite common. The lack of data regarding extended families is partially due to the complication associated with defining the extended family. In Jamaica the extended family can include parents along with other members of the family such as grandparents, cousins, aunts, uncles; grandparents, aunts but no parents; family friends; neighbors; or members of the community, all of whom are usually integrally involved in how the household functions and in child-rearing. The most common reason for the formation of extended families in Jamaica is economic. High unemployment rates or the inability of family members to work, due to age or injury, may force members of a family to pool their resources by living together. Another consequence of the economic situation in Jamaica is migration which also impacts the extended family structure. Parents from low socioeconomic classes in Jamaica, and the Caribbean as a whole, go overseas to work for short periods (6 months) or several years leaving their children in the care of extended family members, or board them with family friends or persons unknown to the child (Pottinger, 2005). Growing up in an extended family, with or without the presence of parents, is likely to affect the development of the child. In situations where parents are absent, children may experience emotional and behavioral difficulties over dealing with separation/attachment. Bhugra, Mallett & Leff (1999) postulated that prolonged separation from parents may play a role in the development of schizophrenia among Afro-Caribbeans in the United Kingdom. It appears that separation/attachment is more affected if the child feels marginalized in their new home or if they are being shifted from one caregiver to another. According to Bowlby (1982) although children may experience distress and detachment from their parents this is tempered by their familiarity with the adult in whose care they are left. Bowlby (1973) noted that most children who are separated from their parents recover and go on to develop normally. He credits this to the type of care the child received during the mother's absence as well as the level of attachment between parent-child prior to migration. In a study conducted by Suarez-Orozco, Todorova & Louie (2002), of 385 adolescents who had immigrated to the United States from various countries, 85% experienced separation from at least one parent during migration but the study found no correlation between separation and psychological symptoms. Thus the loss of the primary attachment figure may not be as traumatic or lead to psychological difficulties as was reflected in early attachment studies. Suarez-Orozco et al. (2002) suggest that the availability of extended family members may help to alleviate the potential problems of separation/attachment.

FAMILY STRUCTURE AND CHILD DEVELOPMENT IN JAMAICA

Brodie Walker and Morgan (2009) conducted a study examining various factors and their impact on the commission of delinquent behaviors among Jamaican adolescents. Although not part of the original study, the authors re-examined the adata in order to compare self-esteem/identity, aggression, delinquency and parent-child attachment across traditional/ nuclear, single parent, blended and extended families. Results showed a significant difference on self-esteem/identity between adolescents in single parent families and those in extended families. The adolescents in extended families reported higher levels of self-esteem (M = 91.89) than those in single parent homes (M = 82.41) as measured by the HARE Self-Esteem Scale (Hare, 1996). Although the differences were not significant, adolescents in extended families also reported higher levels of self-esteem than those who came from traditional/nuclear families (M = 87.9). All the adolescents from the extended family structure reported that they were living with relatives, either with or without their parents. This further suggests that they may have been more familiar, adapted better and felt less rejected by their biological parents, thus leaving room for a healthier sense of self and stable identity. This corroborates the earlier discussion (Suarez-Orozco et al., 2002) which emphasized the importance of the relationship between the adolescent and the caregivers in the extended family as a significant determining factor in their psychological well-being.

As was indicated earlier, an important part of healthy self-esteem/ identity is dealing with issues relating to sex and sexuality through open and intimate communication with parents (indicating good parent-child attachment). Although the adolescents reported average levels of self-esteem, the data indicated that most adolescents did not speak to their parents about issues related to sex, regardless of family structure. Forty-eight percent of adolescents living at home with both parents, 65% of adolescents in single parent homes and 69% living in extended families responded that they "never" spoke to their parents about sex. Even though adolescents in extended families registered the largest percentage, the majority of adolescents (68%) reported that they had never or almost never spoken to their parents about sex. This does not come as a surprise as it is fairly common for Jamaican families to avoid the topic of sex altogether, leaving adolescents to learn via other media (e.g. friends, television, books). When sex does enter the discussion, it is usually in an authoritarian manner in which the parent sternly warns the adolescent of the adverse consequences of having sex (e.g. pregnancy, STD), and there is very little interactive and exploratory communication between both parties.

How then do we explain the below-average levels of parent-child attachment reported by these adolescents who all have average levels of self-esteem? Parent-child attachment was measured using the Family Relationship Scale (Cernkovich & Giordano, 1987) which asks specifically about the relationship between the adolescent and their parents. Therefore, they responded to the questions based on the biological parents from whom they had been separated and not based on the extended family members with whom they had been placed. Attachment, according to Cernkovich & Giordano (1987) is comprised of (1) Control and Supervision which refers to the extent to which parents monitor the behavior of their children, (2) Identity Support refers to uncertainties and self-doubts, (3) Caring and Trust is the degree of intimacy of a relationship, (4) Intimate Communication refers to sharing private thoughts and feelings related to sex and other sensitive topics, (5) Instrumental Communication is defined as the content of the communication, specifically discussion about future plans, (6) Parental Disapproval of Peers refers to the parent's opinion of the child's friends, and (7) Conflict, the extent to which parents and adolescents have arguments or disagreements with one another. If parents are not the primary caregivers, then these factors, which encompass parent-child attachment, would be largely absent (only 2 participants indicated that their parents were a part of their extended family). Further to this, Meeks Gardner, Powell, & Grantham-McGregor (2001) reported that if parent-child attachment is lacking/absent, children are more likely to demonstrate aggression.

Adolescents, regardless of family structure expressed high levels of external aggression. In comparing further those adolescents who had actually been convicted of a criminal offense (25%) with those who had not (75%), descriptive statistics showed that approximately 50% of both groups were from single parent homes, while 37% of convicted group and 18% of non-convicted belonged to extended families. This is supported by Meeks Gardner et. al. (2001), who reported that there were no differences found in family structure (i.e. single-parents and both parents) between aggressive and pro-social children. Contrary to findings from developed countries, single parent households in Jamaica are not a significant predictor of aggressive behavior.

The aggressive behavior expressed by the adolescents regardless of family structure is further explained by examining the learning history of youths in Jamaica. The learning history is one in which the rewards of crime and violence are obvious. For example, most inner-city communities are led by "Dons" who regulate the daily functions of the residents within these communities through both legitimate and illegitimate means. These Dons have acquired power, wealth, prestige and respect mainly through criminal behaviors such as drug trafficking and murder (personal communication, K.A.D. Morgan & S.N.A. Brodie-Walker, 2006), and are recognized as extended family members providing financial assistance to families in these communities. Youths who live in these communities often perceive these Dons as role models/father figures and aspire to be like them.

Within families in Jamaica, corporal punishment is the dominant form of discipline (Smith & Mosby, 2003) with physical assault (i.e. spanking, beating, pinching, tying of hands and shaking) being the most widely used method at 46.6%.; secondly, psychological methods, which include stern looks, spiting, scolding, shouting, threatening to hit came at 24.4%; and lastly, non-violent methods (authoritative parenting style) such as talking, explaining, time-out and removal of privileges were used by 28% of parents (UNICEF, 2005). Aggressive children, when compared to prosocial children, were significantly more exposed to domestic conflict/family discord, and violence in general. They also received more physical punishment both at home and at school (Meeks Gardner et al., 2001).

THERAPEUTIC MODEL

Working with families in Jamaica poses some level of difficulty for several reasons. Firstly, the models that have been posited by the giants in family therapy (e.g. Minuchin, Bowen, Haley, Madanes etc.) have largely based their philosophies on the European culture, therefore cross-cultural differences and applications are rarely explored. The challenges that the Jamaican families present for the therapist are different and the approaches should be adapted accordingly. Secondly, the Jamaican mentality regarding therapy is largely one of closed-mindedness as individuals generally believe that problems must be solved within the family system and there is much resistance to accessing the services of an "outsider." Lastly, one individual is often identified as the problem, thus enabling the other family members to maintain their denial of the breakdown in the family system, while "scapegoating" this individual.

These challenges can be exemplified in the case of 15 year old Kacey Brogan, who was attending therapeutic sessions with one of the authors and was later referred to the other author for a psychological assessment. Kacey was the middle child being raised in an extended family consisting of both her parents, maternal grandmother, her 2 sisters, nephew and several cousins. Kacey was initially brought to therapy by her mother, Mrs. Brogan, as the identified patient. The presenting complaints included poor

345

academic performance, sexual promiscuity, low self-esteem, and conflictual relationships with both parents, especially her mother. Kacey attended the initial session with her mother. During this session, Mrs. Brogan dominated the conversation stating a host of problems with Kacey who she indicated would not listen to her, would invite boys into the home at nights to have sex, and was recently expelled from school for fighting, truancy and overall defiance.

Mrs. Brogan, 40 years old, was an attractive, vibrant woman who looked and dressed 15 years younger than her age. She lengthily described her own personality as outgoing and friendly and alluded to serious problems between herself and her husband, a close, possibly enmeshed relationship, with her eldest daughter, 20 years old, and an equally intimate relationship with her youngest daughter, 9 years old. Interestingly, these 2 children were light-skinned, while Kacey was of a darker complexion and it seemed that the family made much ado about this reality. Mrs. Brogan admitted to spending much of her time outside of the home after work, either at the bar with her friends or sometimes partying with her eldest daughter.

Mr. Brogan, 42 years old, was a quiet and firm gentleman who also spent much of his time either working or carousing with his friends. It was noted in the following sessions that he opted to take a more passive role despite many verbal attacks by Mrs. Brogan. Although Mr. Brogan was the primary breadwinner it was apparent that Mrs. Brogan was the head of the household and the disciplinarian. Mr. Brogan had a good relationship with all his daughters, but was said to favor Kacey, possibly as a means of countering the negative relationship between her and her mother.

In treating Kacey, the therapists had to be cognizant of several cultural, familial and therapeutic issues that were relevant to the case. According to Sue (1981), what is important is the therapist's knowledge about the client's culture in order to provide culturally responsive forms of treatment. Considering the role of culture and culturally relevant techniques in therapy is a very difficult challenge which continues to face the profession. When therapists over-generalize based on what they've learned, this causes major problems as treatment must fit the client's cultural lifestyles or experiences so as to avoid early termination and under-utilization of services and ultimately to result in positive outcomes (Sue & Zane, 1987).

In Jamaica, "shadism", a cultural phenomenon, which is defined as discrimination on the basis of one's skin tone, is very prevalent. The "whiter" one is, the more favored one is in the work environment, at home and amongst peers. This has resulted in the advent of bleaching one's skin to appear more appealing to members of the opposite sex and other environs. The issue of skin tone was very evident in the Brogan family as Kacey, who is the darkest of the three children, was made to feel less than equal to the other members of the family. It was obvious that Kacey's acting out behavior was her way of gaining attention and repairing her ruptured ego. As an adolescent dealing with the developmental issues of identity, self-esteem and sexuality, Kacey needed to have a healthy relationship with her parents. However, because Mr. and Mrs. Brogan were dealing with their own marital dilemmas and because Kacey was the least favored child, especially with her mother, she did not have the necessary emotional or physical attachment with her parents. Therefore, she looked outside her home for the approval and acceptance she so desperately needed in her efforts at formulating her identity/self-esteem and sexuality. As was reported earlier, Kacey exhibited sexual, promiscuous and other defiant behaviors.

The challenges of "resistance" and "scapegoating" were also obvious in the Brogan family. Although the problems being displayed by Kacey were clearly related to the dysfunction of the family, she was brought to therapy as the identified patient. In doing this the family was able to take the focus off of the unit while continuing to resist any suggested therapeutic intervention. Gopaul-McNicol (1993) talks about the reasons why many West Indian families will remain resistant despite the therapist's attempts to foster a therapeutic alliance. She equates this to the cultural belief of most West Indian families that what happens in the family should remain in the family or what she terms "family secrets". Every child is told at an early age that family business remains in the home. Therefore, discussing personal and more specific family issues with a stranger is difficult and at times forbidden. Further to this, the Jamaican family and the West Indian family as a whole will deny family problems because they believe there is nothing that they cannot solve themselves within the family (Gopaul-McNicol, 1993). This was apparent in the deep-seated issues in the Brogan family that largely remained hidden but, eventually revealed themselves to the therapists. Both Mr. and Mrs. Brogan were emotionally distanced from each other, spending most of their time outside the home with their friends and very little time in the home with the family. Although Kacey alluded to these issues in the initial sessions, the family was unwilling to address them, and became highly resistant when an attempt was made to deal directly with these issues. Gopaul-McNicol (1993) talks about the danger of pushing the family to tell the "family secrets" too early in therapy. She warns that this may provoke mistrust and resistance and jeopardize the therapist's position. After three sessions in which the first therapist tried to get to the root of the problem by insisting that the whole family, and not just Kacey, attend therapy, the family soon terminated and began seeing the second therapist.

Once again, after approximately five sessions, the family terminated, citing an impending divorce and disruption in the family as the reason.

Subsequently, this experience highlighted the need for flexibility when working with West Indian families as Gopaul-McNicol (1993) states that the therapist must be willing to adapt various therapeutic modalities and draw from the work of the differing cross-cultural theorists. Therefore, recommended treatment would be one that encompasses a multimodal, multisystems, multicultural and didactic approach. With multimodal therapy the family will realize that the problems being displayed by Kacey are more than the misbehaviors of a developing adolescent, but may also be the consequence of the interaction between behavior, affect, sensations, images, cognitions, interpersonal and biological modalities (Lazarus, 1976). "The multimodal approach focuses on the behaviors that get in the way of one's happiness and how one behaves when one feels (affect) a certain way, as well as what the sensations (e.g., aches and pains) are and what bearings these sensations have on behavior and feelings. Additionally, the approach examines how one perceives one's body and self-image, how one's cognitions affect one's emotions, and what one's intellectual interests are. It also explores who are the most important people in one's life (interpersonal) and what they are doing and how this impacts the client. Biological modality includes medical interventions such as nutrition, exercise, medications and hygiene" (Lazarus, 1976). In the case of Kacey it is imperative that she realizes that the behaviors that she was displaying were negatively impacting her affect as she experienced episodes of depression. Therefore, she would act out (e.g. defiance, sexual promiscuity) as a means of elevating her mood by accessing pleasurable sensations, even temporarily. Kacey's self-image is a complex issue and defined by her parents' introjects. Although she projected an image of great confidence, the realization of how she thinks about herself, how her parents think about her, and how her sexual partners perceive her, integrally define how she treats and views her own body and self. These thoughts/cognitions again impact her behaviors, and her affect as she seeks to find equilibrium in a chaotic environment. As a result of this, her interpersonal relationships are unstable as her mother, father, and grandmother no longer trust or respect her, her sisters feel torn between their loyalty to her and to their parents while her peers view her as a leader and there is great affinity between herself and her nephew. Lastly, Kacey was not eating regularly or healthily, but maintained good hygiene. The interaction between all these factors should have been explored in depth with Kacey in order to obtain a more holistic approach to treatment.

From a multisystems approach treatment would include working with Kacey, the family, the extended family, the community and the school

(Boyd-Franklin, 1989) which will help to provide flexible guidelines for intervention. In treating Kacey the therapist would invite the members of her extended family, as this would give the therapist an opportunity to understand the dynamics of the family (e.g. boundaries, enmeshment and power). The therapist will then be in a better position to challenge the family structure and help the family renegotiate these issues. The therapist would also work closely with the community and most importantly the school. Since there were reports of truancy, fighting at school and poor academic performance it is necessary that the therapist established rapport with Kacey's teachers, guidance counselors and all other key personnel.

Multiculturally, the therapist needs to be aware of the different cultural environs that the family members came from and how this impacted the family unit. In doing this, it is suggested that a detailed exploration of the background of each member is undertaken which helps to understand the cultural dynamics in the family. For example, Mrs. Brogan came from humble beginnings and can be described as a "browning" in Jamaican parlance. Mr. Brogan, on the other hand, came from a middle class background and is described as having a "near-white complexion". Marrying Mr. Brogan represented an upward shift in status for Mrs. Brogan who readily embraced this new status and consequently attempted to shun her darkest child, Kacey, who represented her past.

It is also highly recommended that a didactic approach in which the family is taught the different approaches (multimodal, multisystem and multicultural) is adapted. This will help the family to understand the relationship between the individual (identified patient), the system (family, extended family, community and school) and the culture and how the functioning of the family is impacted by all.

The Brogan family eventually endured a tumultuous separation. Kacey stayed with her father while her two sisters left the family home with their mother. The family moved through the three types of family structures explored in this chapter. They began as an extended family, became two separate single-parent families and as mother and father re-negotiate new relationships, the blended family is inevitable. Currently, as part of a single-parent family, with a father whom she respects, loves and who now trusts her, Kacey's acting-out behaviors are expected to be completely dissolved. Her psychological issues largely surrounded the conflicted relationship between her parents and with herself and her mother. Additionally, the estrangement between her and her sisters is a source of great distress for her. As she maneuvers this new paradigm, she will need different coping skills. This case serves to highlight what has been emphasized earlier: it is the nature of the relationship between the child and the parents/caregivers and not necessarily the family structure that is most influential in the child's psychological health.

References

Bhugra, D, R. Mallett, R. & J.Leff, (1999). Schizophrenia and African-Caribbeans: A Conceptual Model of Aetiology. *International Review of Psychiatry,* 11, 145-152.

Boyd-Franklin, N. (1989). *Black Families in Therapy.* New York, NY: Guilford Press.

Bowlby, J. (1973). *Attachment and Loss: Vol. 2. Separation: Anxiety and Anger.* New York: Basic Books.

Bowlby, J. (1982). *Attachment and Loss: Vol. 1. Attachment* (2nd ed). New York: Basic Books.

Brathwaite, K. (1971). *Development of Creole Society in Jamaica 1770-1820.* Ian Randle Publishers.

Bray, J. H. & D. M. Harvey, (1995). Adolescents in Stepfamilies: Developmental Family Interventions. *Psychotherapy, 32,* 122-130.

Brice-Baker, J.(1996). Jamaican Families. In M. McGoldrick, Giordano & J.K. Pearce (Eds.) *Ethnicity and Family Therapy* (2nd Ed.). New York, NY: Guilford Press.

Brodie Walker, S. and Morgan, K. (2009). Predicting Delinquency: Are Exposure to Violence, Self-Esteem and Parent-Child Attachment Predictors of Juvenile Delinquency? *Journal of Children's Issues Coalition,* 4, 19-34.

Caribbean families—Extended Family (n.d.). Retrieved March 14, 2008 from http://family.jrank.org/pages/204/Caribbean-Families-Extended-Family. html">Caribbean Families—Extended Family.

Cernkovich, S.A., & P.C. Giordano, (1987). Family Relationships and Delinquency. *Criminology, 25,* 295-319.

Chevannes, B. (2006). *Betwixt and Between: Explorations in an African-Caribbean Mindscape.* Kingston, Jamaica: Ian Randle Publishers.

Cooley C.H. (1956). *Human Nature and the Social Order.* Glencoe, III: Free Press.

Davenport, W.H. (1961). *The Family Syysystem in Jamaica. Social and Economic Studies,* 10, 420-454.

Demuth, S. & S. Brown (2004). Family Structure, Family Processes, and Adolescent Delinquency: The Significance of Parental Absence versus Parental Gender. *Journal of Research in Crime and Delinquency,* 4(1), 58-81.

Finkelhor, D. & N.L. Asidigian (1996). Risk Factors for Youth Victimization: Beyond a Lifestyles Theoretical Approach. *Violence & Victims, 11,* 3-20.

Glueck, S. & E. Glueck (1962). *Family Environment and Delinquency.* London:Routledge & Kegan Paul.

Gopaul-McNicol, S. (1993). *Working with West Indian Families.* New York, NY: Guilford Press.

Gosselin, J. (2007) What Affects the Quality of the Stepparent Relationship in Adolescence. *The Family Psychologist, 23* (1).

Hare, B.R. (1996). The HARE General and Area-Specific (school, peer and home) Self-Esteem Scale. In R.L. Jones (Ed.) *Handbook of test and measurements for black populations* (pp.199-205). Hampton, VA: Cobb & Henry Publishers.

Hetherington, E.M. (1993). An Overview of the Virginia Longitudinal Study on Divorce and Remarriage. *Journal of Family Psychology, 7,* 39-56.

Hetherington, E.M. & W.G. Clingempeel (1992). Coping with Marital Transitions; A Family System Perspective. *Monographs of the Society for Research in Child Development, 1-2,* 54.

Holness, A. (2006). *Our families are failing, let's rescue them!* Retrieved October 2, 2006 from http://www.jamaicaobserver.com/columns/html.

Jamaican Survey of Living Conditions (2002). *Summary findings.*

Kotchick, B. A. S. Dorsey, K. S Miller & R. Forehand (1999). Adolescent Sexual Risk-taking Behavior in Single Parent Ethnic Minority. *Journal of Family Psychology, 13*(1) 93-102.

Lazarus, A.A. (1976). *Multimodal Behavior Therapy.* New York: Springer.

Lonczak, H.S. A. Fernandez, L. Austin, G.A Marlatt & D. M. Donovan. (2007). Family Structure and Substance Abuse Among American Indian Youth: A Preliminary Study. *Families, Systems and Health, 25* (1), 10-22.

Mead, G.H. (1934). *Mind, Self and Society: Part III.* Chicago: University of Chicago Press.

Meeks G. J. C. Powell, & S. Grantham-McGregor (2000). *A case Control Study of Family and School Determinants of Aggression in Jamaican Children.* Kingston: Planning Institute of Jamaica.

Meeks G. J.M. C. Powell & S. Grantham-McGregor (2001). A Case-Control Study of Aggression Among Jamaican Children. Kingston: Planning Institute of Jamaica.

Pottinger, A.M. (2005). Children's Experience of Loss by Parental Migration in Inner-City Jamaica. *American Journal of Orthopsychiatry, 4,* 485-496.

Roopnarine, J. (2002). Father Involvement in English-Speaking Caribbean Families. In N. Cabrera & C. S. Tamis-LeMonda (Eds.) *Handbook of Father Involvement: Multidisciplinary perspectives.* New York, NY: Lawrence Erlbaum

Shelden, (2005). Juvenile Justice in American Society. USA: Waveland Press Inc. http://family.jrank.org/pages/204/Caribbean-Families-Extended-Family. html">Caribbean Families—Extended Family.

Smith, D.E., & G. Mosby (2003). Jamaican Child-Rearing Practices: the Role of Corporal Punishment. *Adolescence, 38* (150), 369-381.

Suarez-Orozco, C. I.L., Todorova & J. Louie, (2002). Making up for lost time: The Experience of Separation and Reunification Among Immigrant Families. *Family Process, 41,* 625-643.

Sue, S. (1981). *Counseling the Culturally Different.* New York, NY: Wiley.

Sue, S. & N. Zane, (1987). The role of Culture and Cultural Techniques in Psychotherapy. *American Psychologist, 55,* 37-45.

UNICEF. (2005). *Situational Analysis of Jamaican Cchildren.* Retrieved January 10, 2006 from http://www.unicef.org/jamaica.

Vuchinich, S. E.M. Hetherington, R.A. Vuchinich, & W.G. Clingempeel (1991). Parent-Child Interactions and Agender differences in early Adolescents' Adaptation to Stepfamilies. *Developmental Psychology, 27,* 618-626.

Part IV

CONCLUSION

CHAPTER *15*

EXTENDED FAMILIES IN AFRICA AND THE AFRICAN DIASPORA: COMMONALITIES, CHALLENGES, AND PROSPECTS

Osei-Mensah Aborampah

INTRODUCTION

This concluding chapter summarizes the major features associated with extended families in Africa and the African Diaspora, examines trends in various regions of the African world, and suggests a model for cross-national analysis of their extended families. In reviewing perspectives on the family in Africa and the African Diaspora, Mario Azevedo (chapter one), Gwedolyn Prater (chapter eight), and Michele Sogren (chapter twelve) argue that until recently there has been an overemphasis on the negative features of the family, especially the diasporan family. In the case of Africa, the approach took the form of colonial and missionary policies to undermine the traditional African extended family and impose nuclear family norms, as Azevedo points out. In the United States, the focus was on the so-called Black family instability, with several underlying features labeled as 'a tangle of pathology.' For the African Caribbean family, the focus was on a number of 'dysfunctional' patterns, including single-parent households, multiple shifting and father absence.

Nonetheless, and as the authors caution, there is no single family into which all families can fit. Thus the perception of the nuclear family as a universal family structure is a false one. Consequently, families may be defined separately as nuclear, extended, matrifocal, and so forth. Alternatively, a consideration may be given to the structure, function, historical origins, or the cultural environment, as is done in this volume.

Contributors recognize that the extended family in black societies exhibit a variety of features, some of which are common across the three culture clusters and others, unique to each area. What follows is a summary of the key features associated with each area. In a later section, features that are common across all three culture clusters will be presented and a model for further comparative studies suggested.

AFRICA

1. Patriliny and matriliny remain crucial kinship structures in Africa in the sense that both determine the rules of inheritance and succession, that is, the transmission of property and accession to traditional public office.

2. Extended family solidarity continues to be expressed in a variety of ways, including marriage and funeral ceremonies, even as social changes are taking place.

3. Related to family solidarity is the idea of collective responsibility that has been called out in a number of chapters. This notion of collective responsibility comes into play during moments of crisis, such as the ravages of HIV/AIDS. Such crisis moments tend to subject community cooperation to its greatest strains. However, and as is reported in the chapters, such situations demonstrate also the central value of collective responsibility.

4. African familial organization continues to be characterized by many traditional practices. For example, gendered spaces and the sex division of labor affect the manner in which children learn about sex roles. Gender differences also affect the manner in which lineages transmit or allocate land and other property, as well as financial and labor assistance.

5. Prevalent largely in rural areas of Africa are the customary practices of polygyny, bridewealth payment, widow inheritance, and levirate. The persistence of these practices derive partly from the reverence that continue to be accorded motherhood, as explained in chapter two. Womanhood is defined largely in terms of the capacity to produce children and motherhood serves as a source of personal identity for many African women.

6. Procreation serves as a means for the perpetuity of a lineage. Flowing from this imperative is a high value placed on having

children. Puberty and marriage rituals ensure that procreation occur within prescribed rules of conduct. However, many of the customary practices are being abandoned, as the social changes described in chapter five appear to suggest.

7. Informal adoption is a common practice. Children may be fostered to relatives in African cities and other urban areas.

8. Collective parenting continues to characterize African extended family networks, especially in rural areas. The new housing structures, more specifically single family homes, that are being built in the cities and towns have the potential to undermine the traditional collective socialization of children. These structures tend to be more accommodative of nuclear family units, rather than extended family households. These trends come across in the discussion of Ghanaian extended family networks (chapter three).

AFRICAN AMERICA

1. Kinship networks are significant in African American communities. Thus, earlier assumptions that posited an American cultural homogeneity and family norms to which every group was expected to conform are questionable. African American families exhibit some characteristics that are simply different from the 'normal' family.

2. African American families are characterized by single-parent households. A baby is valued and welcomed into a household regardless of its birth status.

3. Many out-of-wedlock babies live in three-generational households. Residential proximity is a strong feature that allows for face-to-face contact. Within these households, reciprocity in mutual aid is very strong.

4. Extended families continue to provide vital child care support to African American families. This is achieved largely through informal adoption and informal foster care. Blood relatives and fictive kin members provide these types of care. Support also is given by and to elders.

5. Both low and middle-income families are involved in their extended family networks.

6. African American extended family functions are of a varied sort, including not only economic functions, but non-economic functions such as display of love and affection, participation in social activities, and role modeling for the young.

AFRICAN CARIBBEAN

1. Kinship ties are significant in Caribbean societies. However, expression of these ties are influenced by a variety of factors, including race, class, color, gender, and ethnicity.

2. Throughout the Caribbean, individuals, including those of African descent, participate in multiple-partnering or in what Smith (1996) calls the 'dual marriage' system. Developmentally, many African Caribbean marriages progress from visiting to common-law unions, and ultimately to legal marriage. In the process, many change partners and this creates an environment for the operation of multiple-spouse marriage, real or imagined.

3. Children are seen as desirable and are highly valued not only by Caribbean people of African descent, but also by people of other ethnicities. To this end, many of the chapters in section three address socialization and issues of child development. For example, Brodie Walker and Morgan (chapter fourteen) report that low-income families employ punitive and restrictive approaches to child-rearing and discipline. There seems to be an underlying cultural belief which informs parents about 'sparing the rod to spoil the child.'

4. Child shifting is a prominent feature in Caribbean societies. Many children tend to grow up with relatives or neighbors rather than with their parents. This is typical among low income families.

5. Internal and external migration, along with other forces, continues to alter the operation of the extended family network. In the past, especially in the rural areas, children were collectively socialized. As in Africa, older members of a household were available to children of that household. In those circumstances, growing children experienced the influence of a range of elders. Now, as more and more members move elsewhere, the task has fallen on the grandmother, who tends to be over-burdened and burnt out over time.

6. Segregated gender roles and gendered spaces appear to characterize African Caribbean families of low-income status. While young girls tend to be confined to the domestic arena, boys are socialized to engage in 'outside' work. At the same time, boys tend to be treated more harshly than girls in terms of discipline.

COMMON FEATURES

A few broad categories of common features are called out here for further cross-national analysis. These categories include kinship ideology, marital unions, family types, sex role differentiation, child shifting/informal adoption, and single parenthood.

Kinship Ideology

In all clusters, kinship is expressed to a greater or lesser extent, depending on a number of factors including colonialism, race, class, color, gender, age, and ethnicity. In the African past, the system of kinship that emerged prescribed the kin group to which members of the elementary family belonged. This system of kinship recognized genealogical links that connected individuals to common ancestors in ways described earlier as either patrilineal—descent through male lines, or matrilineal—descent through female lines. Although a handful of bilateral systems could be identified, anthropological evidence suggests that the unilineal systems of the patri and matri forms were the most predominant. In either of the latter two systems, the living adults of a lineage formed the core of blood relatives around whom extended families were built. This unit was the organizing principle for family stability. As pointed out in chapter three, the lineage included venerated ancestors who acted in the minds of surviving lineage members as overseers or guardian angels. In most African societies offertory to ancestors took the form of libation and specially prepared dishes. African ancestral beliefs served to bind lineages together. Although factors of modernization have interacted to weaken kinship bonds, its principal role of social transmission of property and status is still recognized.

The kinship patterns which enslaved Africans established may be viewed as a complex process involving a shift from the unilineal principle to a bilateral one in light of European influence and control over the African. The pattern of European-African concubinage and the relative impermanence of their sexual relationships contributed to the emergence of the distinctly local forms of kinships alluded to earlier. Writing about Jamaica specifically and the Caribbean in general, Douglass (1992, p. 15) offers the following observations about kinship: "Kinship links all Jamaicans together but in a hierarchical way consistent with the larger social order. Each class is integrated into the Jamaican kinship system, yet they participate in that system in ways appropriate to their class." She adds that "who is included in a family's genealogical memory is determined by subjective selection that is informed by the local meanings attached to notions of gender, color and class" (p. 111). Despite the gender, color and class underpinnings, Jamaican genealogical reckoning is bilateral. Much of this descriptive analysis is applicable to other Caribbean societies in which many of the families are of African descent.

For African-American families, the boundaries of the kinship structure may be more or less fluid, but delimited by a genealogical connection to a universe of kin from which a circle of intimate kin may be drawn for daily contact. Within these kinship structures, there is a strong orientation toward the maternal kin very much like the matrilineal Akan of Ghana. In all the culture clusters, however, the stability of the extended family, for example, appears not to depend on the stability of conjugal unions. This structural characteristic would seem to arise from economic needs and the pooling of resources in all areas, even though the nature of the resources may be different. In Africa, property tends to be jointly or corporately held. By virtue of their membership, kin members have access to family lands, as well as goods and services. In Jamaica and other Caribbean societies, the pooling of resources could be a function of socio-economic circumstances (see the section on extended family in the preceding chapter by Brodie Walker and Morgan), in which reciprocal assistance in the form of child shifting and minding are frequent occurrences.

Generally, while the extended family is viewed positively for the additional social, economic, and emotional support provided to its members, there can also be a down side to it. For example, some middle class Africans tend to view the network as exerting a limiting impact on their upward mobility. In African Caribbean societies, the grandmother role is perceived as overburdened. The argument is that the grandmother's 'mothering' role could result in her own 'arrested' development as she suffers greater risk of parenting overload and burnout. Additionally, her role could lead to weakened 'parental' or 'disengaged' family systems. Further research is needed to determine the extent to which grandmothers in such environments may be 'damaged' themselves or 'damaging' to the children around them.

Marital Unions

Concerning marital unions and family/household types, conjugal or nuclear units, concubinage, visiting unions, common-law unions, polygyny or serial polygyny, matrifocality or female-headed households, and child-shifting or informal adoption are all common features, although the meaning attached to each may be different from one area to another. African mating patterns were developmentally polygynous. The practice of acquiring two or more spouses (multiple-spouse marriage) was reflected in the institution of polygamy with its two variants: polygyny and polyandry. The former described the marriage of one man to two or more women while the latter described the opposite situation. The latter was very rare in Africa. Explanations for the continued practice of the former include childlessness, labor force requirements for agricultural production, postpartum sexual abstinence and widow inheritance. The institution of polygyny entailed rules and obligations for the spouses involved. There were rules regarding sleeping and cooking rotations. Rules governed the determination of seniority. Polygynous husbands had obligations of impartiality. Custom required that co-wives in polygynous unions be treated equally and fairly. These and other practices, often enforced by mystical threats, produced the net effect of either widening individual's sentimental attachments to others or creating conflicts among the relevant spouses. Accusations of witchcraft provide ample testimony to tensions inherent in multiple-spouse marriages.

Raymond T. Smith (1988) insists that all forms of mating are practiced by West Indians of all classes. The important point, he suggests, is that marriage type tends to be inversely related to socio-economic status (Smith, 1988, p. 112). In practical terms, there is a greater incidence of multiple-partnering in the lower class. The contemporary mating patterns involve the practice of multiple-partnering (A lot of marrying). Although monogamous Christian marriage appears to be the norm for the middle class, some maintain a legal wife (with/without children), as well as households of concubines (with/without children). Writing about childhood socialization in the Caribbean, Evans and Davies (1997, p. 4) identify four types of family structures, each of which may be associated with socio-economic and lifestyle variables. Interestingly, all of the four types: marital union, common-law union (parents live together), visiting union (mother resides in parents' home), and single-parent households, are prevalent in most West African societies.

In the case of African America, as in Africa and African Caribbean societies, there is the tendency for conjugal units to be weak, as indicated in the introductory chapter. In many of the African world societies, the marital bond and joint activities tend to be less intense, especially among the lower class and in the rural areas. Among African Americans as among other peoples of African descent, consensual unions/common-law marriages are prevalent even though legal marriage is viewed as the ideal form. Adults, for example, may raise objections to children having children, particularly outside of marriage, and yet they ultimately come around to welcome the new additions to their extended families, just as one observes among continental Africans.

Family Types

While patriarchy, in its broad sense of structural domination of women by men, is a major characteristic of the three regions, matriarchy in its narrow sense of female domination of the household or domestic unit appears to carry a different import in the three areas. Thus one of the issues frequently raised in the Diaspora is the impact of matriarchy on the masculine development of male children. As pointed out in the chapters focused on North America, much of the past research on African American families blamed matriarchy for the so-called ills of the African American community. In the Caribbean, the culprit is matrifocality, which is interpreted to mean female-dominated households in which low priority is placed on conjugal relations. In the rural areas of Africa, female-headed households may not be perceived to be isolated from the purview of their extended families.

In all three areas, the extended family network seems to provide a buffer for the so-called negative impact of female-household headship. Moreover, and as has been suggested by Brodie Walker and Morgan in chapter fourteen of this volume, it is not the family structure per se that helps or hurts a growing child. Rather, it is the quality of interaction and communication between a child and her/his parents or surrogate parents that are crucial for the child's expected 'normal' development. For the African world, collective parenting is the most common practice. This traditional method of child raising is underscored by the popular African adage, "It takes a village." Given that Africans and their descent place so much intrinsic value on having children, it should surprise no one that the responsibility of child-raising is a shared one. The inability of a couple to produce children is viewed as a calamity. The importance attached to children is viewed as an African legacy. Reluctance on the part of African American women to have abortion underscores the intrinsic value placed in having children.

Illegitimacy has very little negative social consequences for children in the African world. Writing about Caribbean women, Bolles and Perry (2005, p. 472) inform us that "... since the late 1970s, starting with Jamaica, most commonwealth Caribbean governments have enacted a 'status of child' law which states that a person cannot be held responsible for the consequences of his/her birth." To a large extent, childbirth continues to define mother-hood and fatherhood in Africa and the African Diaspora. The intrinsic value placed in children was fostered directly and indirectly through socialization and naming practices, as well as patterns of respect and deference for elders. For continental Africans, the need for the continuation of the lineage was paramount as well. Thus, irrespective of the underlying factor, extended family members in all three culture clusters maintain vested interests in a member's transition to the status of a mother or father.

Sex Role Differentiation

African systems of sex-role differentiation were characterized by seg-regated or gendered spaces within diffused but parallel public and domestic domains. In general, African women were extensively involved in farming and trading that entailed working outside the home and occupied parallel religious and chieftaincy roles that involved them in the public as well as domestic arenas. However, special customs and taboos governing relations between spouses, men and women, boys and girls, aged and young, royal and commoner, etc. produced gendered spaces and sex division of labor, among others. Right from infancy, boys and girls in many African societies had separate and differing initiations. Upon marriage, husbands and wives resided in separate living quarters. They had different roles in farm work and along with that, very distinct eating arrangements in which men tended to eat together and/or separately from their spouses. Today women with the slightest business acumen and drive invest their labor power in farming and/or petty trading around various commodities, including raw and prepared foods, imported goods and cloth. McFerson (2005, p. 445) observes that women have important productive role in subsistence and market agriculture, in addition to reproduction. She adds that gender-specific roles can be observed in all aspects of social, cultural, and politi-cal organization. The social transmission of property within various types of lineages largely occurred among men, not women. The principles of inheritance gave wives and women in general, little or no access to lineage-controlled resources. These limitations continue to be obstacles to African women's progress (Clark, 1994).

In the case of the Caribbean, sex role segregation is rooted in the cul-tural meanings of social life developed over several centuries. According to Barrow (1996, p. 174), the fundamental cultural principles of family and society in the Caribbean include male dominance, sharp differentia-tion of sex roles, the segregation of conjugal partners, and the ideology of civilized male behavior. She quotes Alexander (1977) as reporting that female gender roles are identified primarily with the domestic domain. The sphere of male activity and authority is the world of work and public affairs. Women are not supposed to assume dominance in their relation-ships even if they are engaged in income generating employment outside the home. These forms of sex role differentiation were institutionalized at all levels of society and no fundamental change has taken place since emancipation (Barrow 1996, p. 181).

However, a major change, according to Barrow (p. 181), is the rise to middle class status of colored and black women in the post-emancipation period. Nonetheless, these women were (and I must add, continue to be) faced with their own husbands, fathers and sons, firmly embedded in Caribbean culture, for whom peer group popularity, non-domestic activity, marital segregation, concubinage, and outside children had become a way of life. Barrow adds that young, contemporary, middle-class women are demanding marital fidelity, domestic togetherness, and joint social activity. However, for now, there has been little change in spite of 'economic development' or social, legal and religious pressure. Evans and Davies (1997, p. 9) observe that children learn about sex-typed norms and expectations through direct instruction and observation. Consequently, boys and girls perform different tasks. Girls help with domestic chores in the kitchen and the rest of the house, while boys are assigned such duties as chopping wood or trimming the hedge.

In the case of African Americans, sex role flexibility characterized domestic life during the period of slavery and this fundamental family principle has served as a source of strength over the years (Hill, 1971), although male dominance in the American social structure persists. Thus, in the United States and in the Caribbean as in Africa, men and women are expected to play different roles: men as providers and women as organizers/nurturers. This role learning conforms to the classic patriarchal gender role differentiation in which women are predominantly located in the domestic arena, and men in the public arena, even though African world women have historically played significant roles in the economic domain.

Child Shifting/Informal Adoption

African domestic systems did not confine relations within easily defined and bounded households. Given that the principles of consanguinity and affinity anchor African kinship, solidary relationships could be built among a wide or narrow range of kin depending on one's age, gender and status in society. Members of the extended family could reside together and perform such life-sustaining activities as sexually based relationships, childbearing and rearing, as well as social and economic production and partnerships. Members could relocate and live with other relatives on a temporary or permanent basis.

In the past, children in many African societies constantly dealt with relatives who stood to them as substitutes for parents, as brothers and sisters, or as individuals with special duties to them. Apparently, this practice continues today as is made clearly evident in chapter five by Kisubi. In such circumstances, children often grew up with many affectionate relatives to whom these children built up sentimental attachments. This was possible largely because of the children's involvement in their extended family networks. For example, if a child was orphaned, members of the extended family were most likely to take his or her parents' place, as Kyomugisha and Rutayuga have explained in chapter seven of this volume. The shifting of children and other lineage members, along with gifts of goods, services and the implied reciprocation, allowed for the creation of a security system of mutual benefits and obligations that could be expected to minimize potential risks to lineage, clan or village members. In addition, a large household size ensured local political strength and social importance in terms of participation in local ceremonies.

Among African Americans, informal adoption as an institutionalized practice is well documented (Stack, 1974; Martin & Martin ,1985). The size and composition of individual households expand or contract depending on the number of people, especially children that are shifted around. Child shifting, as is made abundantly clear in chapters twelve, thirteen, and fourteen, is a major component of kin networks in Caribbean societies. Evans and Davies (1997, p. 7) inform us that child shifting is strongly embedded in Caribbean history and is very common among low-income African Caribbean families. As in Africa, many parents migrate overseas and locally to urban areas to seek work. In such cases children are left with relatives or friends (Evans, 1989, p. 181-82). According to Russell-Brown et. al. (1997, p. 224), "child shifting connotes the informal 'adoption' of children that may be permanent or temporary." Children may be shifted to relatives, friends or neighbors. As Evans (1989, p. 189) observes, the low-income Jamaican woman often moves from one type of union to another. Some of her children will, in the early years, grow up with a relative, particularly the grandmother. The majority will experience the changes in family structure and may have to relate to different step-fathers. (Evans, 1989, p. 189).

Children may be raised by someone other than both parents. Because of child shifting, expansion and contraction of households have become a constant feature of African-Caribbean family organization, just as they have been and continue to be major characteristics of African and African American family organization. Today, the practice allows women to turn the care of children over to other female relatives or maids while the mothers mind their children financially. However, and as Evans and Davies (1997, p 7-8) caution, a child that is 'forced' on a caregiver is most likely to encounter problems of development, anxiety, feelings of insecurity, and stunted development of self-confidence and self-esteem. According to them, when child shifting occurs under less than optimal conditions, as when children are shifted frequently, children may be prevented from forming lasting relationships with the surrogate parents. On the other hand, children are more likely to develop prosocial behaviors when they have warm supportive relationships with parents or surrogate parents. Thus the quality of the relationships would seem to be more crucial than anything else.

Nonetheless, it needs to be stressed that African, African American and African Caribbean realities are such that 'the boundaries of a dwelling cannot be assumed to define a family and what it does' (Bolles & Perry, 2005, p. 472). As the authors make clear, eating, sleeping, financial support, and childrearing were (and still are) shared among a network of male and female relatives and neighbors who may not be located in any bounded household or area.

Single-Parenthood: Father Absence

Although father absence has been described as a major feature of diasporan societies, it occurs on the African continent as well, except that single-parenthood is embedded in the extended family. Moreover, lineage membership defines one's legal status and identity. As explained in chapter three, in the past, and even today, a new baby is welcome regardless of its birth-status identity. That is, a child born outside of a legal union and without a recognized biological father was welcome nonetheless. Such a new baby would be socialized to identify herself or himself as the daughter or son of a particular lineage.

Part of the explanation for the apparent problematic nature of father absence in the African Diaspora lies in the cultural history of the "New World." Whereas in Africa, female independence co-existed with male authority in the form of lineage elders, slavery made it impossible for African males in the Diaspora to exercise authority. On the other hand, young girls in the Diaspora assumed, and continue to assume, responsibilities early in their lives. Thus, girls were (and are) socialized to be more disciplined and responsible than boys. Some observers of the diasporan scene suggest that the effects of this type of socialization are felt in the relatively 'better' school performance of girls/women in terms of enrollments, retention, and graduation.

Summary of Factors in the Persistence of the Extended Family

Africans have toiled, labored, fought and endeavored to succeed with great effort. Why does one discern many similarities in the principles that govern family formation and functioning among Africans on the continent and in the Diaspora? Several institutional configurations and a variety of social, economic, and political forces come to mind. Among them are the legacies of slavery and colonialism. The fact is that over the course of the antebellum period, racial prejudice and slavery became institutionalized and both have produced, in their trail, devastating social, economic and other consequences on Diaspora and African family organization. From my point of view, then, both racial and economic arguments appear overwhelming.

European colonization of Africa exhibited features similar to American slavery in many respects. The former was a form of political domination, economic exploitation and cultural subjugation. Culturally, Africans were forced to abandon their traditions, including religious practices, naming practices and marital systems. Economic motives were the primary reasons for the partitioning of Africa in the late 1800s. Human and natural resources were exploited to European advantage just as the labor of enslaved Africans and their descendants was exploited to produce wealth for Euro-Americans. Colonialism drew Africans into the capitalist market as dependents with mono-crop agricultural systems. Political control required adjustment to invented traditions. In addition, it distorted the evolutionary and natural process of African political development. The impact of colonialism is still felt in the artificial boundaries, mono-crop systems, and the type of democracies prevailing throughout the continent.

Even though Africans worldwide have been influenced by very different environmental conditions and are separated by time and distance, the common experiences of oppression, exploitation and racial subjugation of slavery and colonialism appear to partially account for common patterns of behavior, in addition to common conceptions of the universe. Africans in general have had to learn to deal with the ceaseless prejudice and discrimination that emanate from the hideous belief in racism held by others. In spite of the debilitating effects of racism, new levels of consciousness and interconnections have emerged in recent times. This is in response to the imperatives of the legacy of slavery and colonialism which demand that Africans not only raise their levels of consciousness but also assert their humanness.

According to Bryce-Laporte (1990, p. xvii), the contemporary processes of consciousness raising among Africans everywhere include the Caribbeanzation of carnival and the calypso, the internationalization of Raggae,

Rasta, Rap, Afro hair styles and Soul music, the ghettoization of Santeria, Susu, Capoeira (breakdance) and Sasa. He further observes that, and this is a crucial point, the processes demonstrate how, through intense interpenetration and continuous cross-fertilization which have resulted principally from migration and mass media [and now, surfing in cyber space], black people from the Diaspora and the continent have acquired and began to share generalized and transcendental dimensions of their Africanness or Africanity.

Contemporary macro-level factors that may account for extended family networks in the African world include demographic, economic, and cultural ones. The most basic socio-demographic factors affecting extended family networks are age, family size, rural-urban residence, migration, gender, class, race, color, ethnicity, and so-called tribalism. An extended family will not emerge among people who do not have non-nuclear family members. Thus survival of the non-nuclear members is crucial in family extension. African world family sizes tend to be large, although rural-urban and other differentials can be observed. Concerning economic factors, agricultural production is one of the major contributory factors. The more an area is geared toward agricultural or family mode of production, the greater the proportion of extended families is likely to be. Farm families tend to be larger and with more children than non-farm families. Another economic (utilitarian) factor is that the extended family is perceived as an economic benefit in both early and post-industrial societies. According to Goode (1963), in industrial and commercial settings where the nuclear family is dominant, extended families persist only because the requirements of an industrial economy and society have not yet become fully operative. When there are no alternatives to elderly parental family living, for example, adult children may have to take care of their elderly parents. One more factor to consider is availability of housing space. Just as a couple cannot form an extended family without non-nuclear members or surviving members of previous generations, a physically interactive extended family cannot form if there is not enough space to accommodate non-nuclear members.

The normative factor is just as crucial. As Ruggles (1987) has suggested in the context of western European and American extended family formation, people may develop an acute sense of obligation to kin and willingness to support relatives at great economic and psychic cost. Families may continue to participate in an extended family network in accordance with a community's traditional family values, which underscores the cultural dimension of extended family networks in the African world. However, the reality is that African families everywhere, especially urban ones, are becoming more and more nucleated. Socialization of the child depends less upon the use of tradition-backed precepts. The older generation appears ruffled by the loss of grip on the younger generation, as pointed out in chapter three. Nonetheless, whether training and sponsorship take place within the nuclear family or outside, both involve constraint, discipline, direction and heavy capital outlays, all of which continue to be provided, to a large extent, by successful members of either the nuclear or the extended family. Communal responsibility and obligation for the well being of the family and community beyond an individual's personal preference remain vibrant. A point made earlier and worth repeating here is that individualism as a normative construct has its roots in the Western tradition, and was a later development in the African world as a result of slavery and colonialism.

Even though Africans worldwide have been influenced by very different environmental conditions and are separated by time and distance, slavery, colonialism, communalism as a normative construct, and contemporary demographic, economic, and cultural factors appear to partially account for common patterns of familial organization and behavior. If one accepts the proposition that the descendants of the African forebears in the New World are "African American or African Caribbean fruits with African roots" or that they are "African in nature and American or Creole in nurture", then there is nothing mysterious about the extent of similarities in the world views and familial organization held and practiced by Africans on the continent and in the Diaspora.

A Model for Comparative Studies

The attempt here is to suggest a definition capable of accommodating the major features of the myriad kin networks prevailing in the African world. To my mind, the definition that permits this sort of comparative analysis is the one offered by Martin and Martin in their work on the Black extended family (i.e., in the United States). Martin and Martin (1978, p. 2) offer the following definition:

> When we speak of a black extended family, we mean a multi-generational, interdependent kinship system which is welded together by a sense of obligation to relatives; is organized around a 'family base' household; is generally guided by a 'dominant family figure;' extends across geographical boundaries to connect family units to an extended family network; and has a built-in mutual aid system for the welfare of its members and the maintenance of the family as a whole.

The major defining characteristics may be summarized as follows: interdependent kinship system; multi-generation; dominant family figure; family base household; extension across geographical boundaries; and built-in mutual aid system. A number of these defining characteristics has been assessed empirically by Hatchett and Jackson (1999). They offered the following as part of their conclusion: "In sum, we have contributed to substantiating claims in both lore and literature about the general nature of black extended kin systems. Black Americans, on the whole, are very much involved in extended kin systems" (Hatchett and Jackson, 1999, p. 189).

I suggest that in order to fully understand families/households in the African world it is necessary to view them not only in terms of their structures, but also in terms of their functioning. The middle class families among African Americans, Africans and Caribbean families of African descent do indeed participate in their respective extended kin networks even though they may be dispersed in widely scattered geographical areas. Thus, it is the nature of the participation in the network that is becoming increasingly significant. The core features that best represent the African world kin network are the six characteristics identified above. Each of these characteristics is critically evaluated in the context of the three geographical areas.

Kinship System

For African extended family networks, the nucleus is the consanguineal group that includes the living, the dead and those yet to be born. This nucleus is reckoned unilineally for the most part. There is also the outer group (i.e., the affinal group or in-marrying members and their consanguines), as already explained. For the Caribbean, it is pointed out in this volume that distinctly local forms of kinship prevail and that kinship links Caribbean people in their respective societies together but in a hierarchical way consistent with the larger social order. This is certainly the case for Jamaicans (Douglass, 1992). According to Douglass, each class is integrated into the Jamaican kinship system, yet they participate in that system in ways appropriate to their class. For African Americans in the United States, kin may denote individuals who would appear on an objective genealogy based on the criteria of consanguineal and affinal relations. For example, "men are involved primarily as brothers, sons, uncles and nephews; as husbands and fathers, they play important but less defined roles that are subject to negotiation. If they fail in their roles, the family (i.e., extended), including uncles and brothers as well as mothers, sisters and aunts, remains as a continuing support" (Aschenbrenner, 1975, p.15). According to Aschenbrenner, a man looking for a wife will accept a woman capable of making a 'home' for the prospective husband. He would want her to allow him to maintain ties with his kin. However, her extended family often takes precedence over his in terms of utilization of resources.

The Dominant Family Figure

The dominant family figure occupies the leadership role. In many African societies, there are clearly defined rules for the selection of this figure. The dominant figure may be the guardian of an ancestral stool which is considered the soul of the lineage. The dominant figure is the custodian of all lineage property, and with the help of the lineage core, land and other lineage resources are allocated to members. As quoted from Clark (1994, p. 95), Asante lineage elders still allocate considerable property and financial assistance through decisions pertaining to inheritance, loans or gifts, residence and schooling, with women participating as elders and as recipients. Among African Americans, the dominant family figure is central to the continuing existence of the family network. The dominant figure is often the oldest man or woman in the household, or are family members that have grown into the leadership role. Most of the time, the dominant family figure is usually a woman because she often out lives her husband, and inherits his role. The dominant family figure is the most respected member of an African American extended family. The dominant family figure has proved time and time again his/her ability to lead the family. The dominant family figure makes personal sacrifices and maintains the continuity of the family through trials and tribulations. The dominant family figure usually directs and guides family members and reinforces the family's sense of belonging and self worth. He/She keeps family members in touch with each other. The dominant family figure does this by organizing family reunions and family meetings. This leader always makes sure the lines of communication are open. The dominant family figure constantly implores family members to remain close and to watch out for each other. The dominant family figure believes that the family members should always stand up for each other and believe that "blood is thicker than water."

In African Caribbean societies, the dominant family figure is well defined and a respected elderly person. "The dominant figure offers a strong sense of family and kin relationships, offers advice, guidance, moral support and closeness of love" (Beckwith, 1969). Concerning Jamaican extended family, Beckwith (1969, p. 52) suggests that the dominant figure is selected based on age relationship rather than a "blood" one. She adds that this figure has to provide for their family in many ways. He/She makes sure the family is fed, clothed, and is raised with a good education, if possible. According to Henriques (1953, p.10), the dominant figure helps the family to serve two basic functions. The first is leadership which gives the family a sense of security and wholeness from within, and second, helps to promote welfare for those family members in need of assistance.

In all three culture clusters, the leader expends much energy to keep the extended family together. The leader helps to develop a deep sense of family solidarity. The leader serves as the hub of the communication network for members and directs joint family activities (i.e., reunions, funerals, etc.)

The Extended Family Base Household

This home is the center of extended family activities. In Africa, the lineage head's home may serve this purpose. The residence of the dominant family figure also is usually the base household among diasporan Africans in the U.S. and the Caribbean. The base household is the most stable unit of the network where members may meet on a periodic basis for family and other reunions.

Multi Generation

In all three areas, the extended family consists of three or more generations of relatives whose recognition may be lineal or collateral or both. By definition, the depth of African lineages is indefinite. African lineages are conceived to include those yet to be born. Thus, the generational dimension of an African extended family is of a wide sort. The typical African American or Caribbean extended family consists of three or four generations of relatives, real and fictive.

Extension Across Geographical Boundaries

All members do not live in the family base household or even in the same geographical area, even though residential propinquity allows for face-to-face interaction. When kin or non-kin members relocate with or without their spouses, they may provide significant and continued aid. Alternatively, they may receive significant and continued aid from other members. Over time, a migrant may or may not develop a deep and sustained sense of obligation and commitment toward the base. When a migrant, and for that matter any family member, no longer feels a deep sense of obligation or commitment and emotional attachment to the base for whatever reason(s), then he/she may cut him/herself loose from the network.

Built-in Mutual Aid System

The mutual aid system may be regarded as the most important component of the extended family network. Mutual aid may be necessitated by economic or emotional need or by a powerful and enduring sense of obligation toward kin. Two types of mutual aid have been distinguished for African Americans in the United States: expressive aid and instrumental aid (Billingsley 1968). Expressive aid is the moral, emotional, and spiritual support members of the extended family share with one another. It could be as simple as calling family members to tell them hello and to share words of love. It can also take the form of an expression of appreciation for a favor received from a member. Expressive aid can also come in the form of self-esteem building, as pointed out earlier.

According to Billingsley (1968), instrumental aid is the giving of material goods and money within the mutual-aid system. Usually a family member gives money to the dominant family figure and he/she allocates the money to the family members who are most in need. According to Martin and Martin (1978), money or other resources can be contributed in three ways: First, it may be contributed on a regular basis by certain family members. Second, it may be contributed on a periodic basis. Third, it can be contributed on an emergency basis. As explained earlier, instrumental aid is very important because, for many, it is a vital survival mechanism. It provides members of the extended family with security. As pointed out earlier, the mutual aid system provides security to those who need it and builds family unity because those who do not need support display their sense of commitment by supporting those who do. The direction of flow of the mutual aid, in all three ways of giving, may be multilateral in which goods move from scattered families to the base household to be redirected to needy members, or bilateral in which the goods move from family to family or from one individual member to another.

Research along the lines outlined here will unearth more of the intricacies of micro-level functioning of a variety of extended families in a variety of settings in the African world. On a theoretical level, research of this sort can provide additional insights into the modernization perspective that predicts the demise of the extended family in the face of urbanization and/or industrialization.

Challenges and Prospects

The processes of social change will continue to challenge many features of the African and Diasporan families presented in the preceding pages. Migration (rural-urban, regional and international) continues to undermine traditional social control mechanisms, which makes it possible for African world youth to indulge in behaviors that would otherwise receive community disapproval. The issue of teen pregnancies will engage the attention of policy makers and family advocates across the African world. Sexually transmitted diseases and infections, especially HIV/AIDS, will continue to ravage African world communities if public health policy reforms are not massively undertaken to stem the tide. Globalization may accelerate the process of family nucleation in African and Caribbean societies. The emphasis on 'free' trade rather than 'fair' trade and the pressure on businesses to adopt western norms may force African and Caribbean governments to adopt policies that may undermine the operation of extended family networks in the respective regions.

The middle-class ideal of female equality conflicts with the general societal gender role socialization that consigns women to domestic chores and less prestigious jobs. According to Parkin & Nyamwaya, 1987, p. 15), lower-class women have not converted their income-earning opportunities into ideological criticism of current relations between men and women. On the other hand, educated women are developing a coherent ideological critique of gender relations, but significant change in practice is yet to occur.

In spite of the daunting challenges called out in a number of the chapters in this volume, it needs to be stressed that the authors portray also extended families that still possess significant strength, remarkable resilience, and adaptability enough to survive into the twenty-first century and beyond.

References

Alexander, J. (1977). The Role of the Male in the Middle Class The Caribbean Family: A Comparative Perspective. *Journal of Comparative Family Studies* 8(3), 369-389.

Aschenbrenner, J. (1975). *Lifelines: Black Families in Chicago.* Prospect Heights, IL: Waveland Press.

Barrow, C. (1999). *Family in the Caribbean: Themes and Perspectives.* Kingston: Ian Randle Publishers and Oxford: James Currey Publishers.

Beckwith, M. (1969). *Black Roadways: A Study of Jamaican Folk Life.* New York: Negro University Press.

Billingsley, A. (1968). *Black Families in White America.* Englewood Cliffs, NJ: Prentice Hall.

Bolles, L. A. & B. S. Perry. (2005). Women of the Caribbean. In M. Azevedo (Ed.) *Africana Studies: A Survey of Africa and the African Diaspora* (pp. 465-480) Durham, NC: Carolina Academic Press.

Bryce-Laporte, R. S. (1990). Foreword: On the Black Diaspora and its Study. W. Bonnett & G. L Watson (Eds.) *Emerging Perspectives on the Black Diaspora.* (pp. ix-xx.) Lanham, MD.: University Press of America.

Clark, G. (1984). *Onions Are My Husband.* Chicago: The University of Chicago Press.

Douglass, L. (1992). *The Power of Sentiment.* Boulder, CO: Westview Press.

Evans, H. & R. Davies. (1997). Overview of Issues in Childhood Socialization in the Caribbean. In J. L. Roopnarine & J. Brown (Eds.) *Caribbean Families: Diversity Among Ethnic Groups.* (pp. 1-24) Greenwich, CT: Ablex Publishing Corporation.

Goode, W. J. (1963). *World Revolution and Family Patterns.* New York: Free Press. p.432.

Hatchett, S J. & J S. Jackson. (1999). African American Extended Kin Systems: An Empirical Assessment in the National Survey of Black Americans. In H. P. McAdoo (Ed.) *Family Ethnicity: Strength in Diversity* (pp. 171-190). Thousand Oaks, CA: Sage Publications.

Henriques, F. (1953). *Family and Color in Jamaica.* London: MacGibbon and Kee.

Hill, R. (1971). *The Strength of Black Families.* New York: Emerson Hall Publishers.

Martin, E P. & J M. Martin. (1978). *The Black Extended Family.* Chicago: The University of Chicago Press.

Martin, J. M. & E P. Martin. (1985). *The Helping Tradition in the Black Family and Community.* Silver Spring, MD: National Association of Social Workers.

McFerson, H. M. (2005). African Women. In M. Azevedo (Ed.) *Africana Studies: Survey of Africa and the African Diaspora,*(pp. 443-464.) 3rd Edition. Durham, NC: Carolina Academic Press.

Ruggles, S. (1987). *Prolonged Connections: The Rise of Extended Family in Nineteenth Century England and America.* Madison: University of Wisconsin.

Russell-Brown, P. A., B. Norville & C Griffith. (1997). Child Shifting: A Survival Strategy for Teenage Mothers. In J. L. Roopnarine & J. Brown (Eds.) *Caribbean families: Diversity Among Ethnic Groups.*(pp. 223-242.) Greenwich, CT: Ablex Publishing Corporation.

Smith, R. T. (1988). *Kinship and Class in the West Indies: A Genealogical Study of the Caribbean and Guyana.* Cambridge: Cambridge University Press.

Smith, R. (1996). The Matrfocal Family: Power, Pluralism, and Politics. New York: Routledge.

Stack, C. B. (1974). *All Our Kin: Strategies for Survival in a Black Community.* New York: Harper & Row.

Sudarkasa, N. (1996). *The Strength of Our Mothers, African & African American Women & Families: Essays and Speeches.* Trenton, NJ: Africa World Press, Inc.

LIST OF CONTRIBUTORS

Aborampah, Osei-Mensah, Associate Professor
Department of Africology
University of Wisconsin-Milwaukee, Wisconsin
mensah@uwm.edu
Osei-Mensah Aborampah is an Associate Professor and former chair in the Department of Africology, University of Wisconsin-Milwaukee. He received his undergraduate education and earned his B.A.(Hons.) from the University of Ghana-Legon, his master's degree from the University of Guelph, Ontario, Canada, and Ph.D. from the University of Wisconsin-Madison. His academic interests and scholarly work range from traditional to modern cultures of Africa, Black America, and the Caribbean, with special focus on West African, African-American and African-Caribbean family patterns, as well as the general problems of women and development in African societies.

Mario J. Azevedo, Professor & Chair
Department of Epidemiology and Biostatistics
Jackson State University, Jackson, Mississippi
mario.azevedo@jsums.edu
Known internationally for his extensive scholarly work in African Studies and Public Health, Professor Mario J. Azevedo is Interim Dean of the College of Public Service at Jackson State University. He earned a Ph.D. in African History at Duke University, an MPH at the University of North Carolina at Chapel Hill, and an MA and a BA in History at American University and Catholic University, respectively.

Christine Barrow, Professor
Department of Government, Sociology and Social Work
University of the West Indies, Cave Hill, Barbados
christine.barrow@cavehill.uwi.edu

Christine Barrow, a professorial fellow and former Deputy Principal, has been a staff member of Sir Arthur Lewis Institute of Social and Economic Studies (SALISES), Cave Hill Campus, The University of the West Indies from August 2006. Professor Barrow holds a BA (Hons.) and a D.Phil. degree in Social Anthropology from the University of Sussex. Her numerous publications include *Family in the Caribbean: Themes and Perspectives* and *Gender: A Caribbean Multidisciplinary Perspective* (Co-editor).

Stacey N. A. Brodie Walker
Department of Sociology, Psychology and Social Work
University of the West Indies, Mona, Kingston, Jamaica
stacey.brodie@uwimona.edu.jm

Dr. Stacey Brodie Walker is a Counseling Psychologist with over 15 years of clinical experience. She currently lectures at the University of the West Indies, Mona and Cavehill campuses. Dr. Brodie Walker's areas of interest include juvenile delinquency and eating disorders; she has researched and published extensively within these areas.

Bamidele Agbasegbe Demerson, Executive Director
International Civil Rights Center & Museum
134 South Elm Street
Greensboro, NC 27401
bdemerson@stinmovement.org

Bamidele Agbasegbe Demerson is executive director of the International Civil Rights Center & Museum in Greensboro, North Carolina. His research and current exhibitions focus on social history, visual art, and human rights. Trained in cultural anthropology, Demerson, a graduate of The University of Michigan, has conducted fieldwork in Nigeria, Brazil, and southern United States on social organization.

Rhunette C. Diggs
Department of Communication, Columbus State Community College
Adjunct Instructor
dr.diggs@yahoo.com

Rhunette C. Diggs is a Communication Educator and teaches in the Department of Communication at Columbus State Community College. She received her Ph.D. from The Ohio State University. She is the co-editor of *Communication, Race, and Family: Exploring Communication in Black, White, and Biracial Families*. Her research interests include African American family, spiritual, and relational communication.

Alfred T. Kisubi, Distinguished Full Professor
College of Education and Human Services
University of Wisconsin-Oshkosh, Wisconsin
kisubi@uwosh.edu
Dr. Alfred T. Kisubi is a poet and writer of socially significant stories with several books to his credit. Alfred was born in Uganda and holds advanced degrees from Makerere University (Kampala) and the University of Missouri-Kansas City. He is a distinguished professor in the College of Education and Human Services at the University of Wisconsin-Oshkosh and a U.S. Human Services Board Certified practitioner.

Florence Kyomugisha, Associate Professor
Gender and Women's Studies
California State University, Northridge, California
florence.kyomugisha@csun.edu
Florence Kyomugisha is an Associate Professor in the Department of Gender and Women's Studies at California State University Northridge, California. Her research focuses on societal economic and cultural changes that are associated with health disparities in women, children and other marginalized populations; and the functioning and variations in the family organization of people of African descent

Kai A. D. Morgan, Lecturer
FMS-Community Health & Psychiatry, Faculty of Medical Sciences
University of the West Indies, Mona, Kingston, Jamaica
kai.morgan@uwimona.edu.jm
Dr. Kai A. D. Morgan is a lecturer in clinical psychology at the University of the West Indies, Mona, Jamaica. She has a Doctorate in Clinical Psychology and manages a private practice where she conducts therapy and assessments. Dr. Morgan's research interests include sexuality and couples dynamics/therapy, sport psychology, cross-cultural psychology and borderline personality disorder.

Zacharia N. Nchinda, Senior Lecturer
Department of Africology
University of Wisconsin-Milwaukee
znchinda@att.net
Zacharia N. Nchinda completed his BA in Yaoundé, and MA and PhD at UW-Milwaukee. His teaching and research interests include global poverty, immigration, and urbanization. He is presently working on a book that profiles recent African immigrant fathers in America.

Gwendolyn S. Prater, Founding Dean
College of Public Service
Jackson State University, Jackson, Mississippi
gwendolyn.s.prater@jsums.edu
Dr. Gwendolyn Spencer Prater is Professor of Social Work and Public Health and former Dean of the College of Public Service and the School of Social Work at Jackson State University. She holds a Ph.D. and a Master's degree in Social Work from the University of Southern California and The Ohio State University, respectively, and a B.A. in Sociology from Tougaloo College. She has published extensively on African-American and African issues.

John B. K. Rutayuga
UKIMWI Orphans Assistance, Inc.
Washington, DC
ukimwiorphans@yahoo.com
Dr. John B.K. Rutayuga is the Founding President of Ukimwi Orphans Assistance. His work centers on building the capacity of orphans and vulnerable children (OVC) in Africa to grow free of HIV/AIDS to full self-reliant maturity. He provides resources to families/caregivers to serve OVC under their care. He promotes and researches traditional African medicine and the environment. John is a senior linguist teaching KiSwahili at the ICLS in Washington, DC.

Michele Sogren, Lecturer
Department of Behavioral Sciences
University of the West Indies, St. Augustine, Trinidad & Tobago
michele.sogren@sta.uwi.edu
Michele Sogren is a lecturer in Social Work, Coordinator, Social Work Unit and Deputy Dean in the Faculty of Social Sciences at the Univer-

sity of the West Indies, St. Augustine, Trinidad and Tobago. Her research interests include Caribbean families, families in violent situations, children whose parents have migrated, children and HIV-AIDS as well as children in care. She serves on several university committees and national boards.

Niara Sudarkasa, Consulting Scholar
African American Research Library & Cultural Center of Broward County, Florida
nsudarkasa@gmail.com
Niara Sudarkasa spent most of her career as a Professor of Anthropology, African and African American Studies at the University of Michigan in Ann Arbor. She also served as Associate Vice President for Academic Affairs before leaving to become the first female President of Lincoln University in Pennsylvania (1987 to 1998). She received her bachelor's degree from Oberlin College, and M.A. and Ph.D. from Columbia University. Her various publications include *Where Women Work*, on Yoruba market women, and *The Strength of Our Mothers*: Essays on African and African American Women and Families.

Erin N. Winkler, Assistant Professor
Department of Africology
University of Wisconsin-Milwaukee, Wisconsin
winklere@uwm.edu
Erin N. Winkler is assistant professor of Africology at the University of Wisconsin-Milwaukee, where she teaches courses on racial identity development and the psychology of racism. Her research on racial learning among children has appeared in *Sociological Studies of Children and Youth, Practical Approaches for Continuing Education,* and the edited volume *The Changing Landscape of Work and Family in the American Middle Class.*

INDEX

110113-100-2-60W